# The Ultimate Water Garden Book

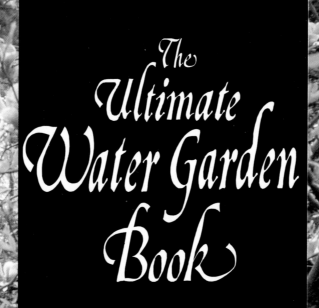

# The Ultimate Water Garden Book

JEAN-CLAUDE ARNOUX

The Taunton Press

# CONTENTS

*The author wishes to thank the garden designers whose talents and advice have contributed so largely to the preparation of this guide, and especially Jean Mus, Guy Lainé, Gilbert Galoché, Camille Muller and Jean-Marie Jurdant, who made the whole thing possible...*

*For their friendly assistance, the author thanks Colette Sainte Beuve and the Plantbessin Nurseries, Mme Baron, of the Etablissements François Huet, M. Quenette and Avia Diffusion, Job Knoester and the Job Knoester Nurseries, Jacques Gaillet and the Poisson d'Argent, Dominique Albert and the Alisma Nurseries, Richard Cayeux and the Etablissements Cayeux, Yves Crouzet and the Bambouseraie of Prafrance, Yves Hervé and the De la Foux Nurseries, together with Thierry Morlot and Bernard Vreicig for their very precious collaboration.*

*For their welcome and their help, the author thanks the Papiliorama in Marin, Madame Beausoleil and the Albert Kahn Foundation, Anne Laurence, of the Société Nationale de Protection de la Nature, Pierre Valck, Curator of the Nancy Botanical Gardens.*

*The publishers and the author express their thanks to the numerous people who allowed photographs to be taken in their private gardens to illustrate this book, and in particular M. and Mme Cristos, M. and Mme Denis, M. and Mme Michel, M. et Mme Roguenant.*

*Conception and execution : Jean-Claude Arnoux*
*Consultant for B.T. Batsford Ltd. : Barbara Davies*
*All the photographs and illustrations are by the author (except where otherwise stated, page 216).*
*General design, composition and layout :*
*Jean-Claude Arnoux*
*Photogravure : Euresys*
*English translation : Gillian Benson*

# INTRODUCTION

*In our day, water is becoming an indispensable element of the pleasure garden where we seek relief from the stresses of modern life. Its increasing popularity can be attributed, naturally enough, to the fact that it helps to create an atmosphere of cool well-being in summer, but also to the fact that it offers a multitude of uses in many forms : mirror effects or transparency, cascades and watercourses, jets and fountains. Its mere presence is enough to create an impression of space and add a new dimension to the most modest garden. It is not necessary to have an enormous pond or pool to obtain a spectacular effect. The modern conception of the garden, calm, alive, natural and in harmony with the environment, together with the ease of cultivation of aquatic plants, inspire in us a fuller appreciation of these areas of water which provide a calm and relaxed atmosphere with a minimum amount of maintenance.*

*The advice and ideas presented in this guide are based on the experience of specialist garden designers and enthusiastic amateurs, and reflect their capacity for admiration of the wonders of nature, while suggesting some means of recreating a fragment of "authentic" nature in one's own garden. Our aim has been to provide answers to the most important questions so that the best possible use can be made of the numerous ways in which water features can be incorporated in any garden.*

*Chapter 1 contains a brief historical and aesthetic consideration of the question, with a few examples chosen from among the vast number of ways of using water in a garden. Our main aim has been to try, with the help of the numerous colour photographs and illustrations, to define the specific characteristics of each style.*
*We hope that we have provided a key to the different types of garden, to assist you in designing and creating a garden that expresses your ideas and personality. Perhaps some of the examples given correspond to a certain extent with your own projects.*
*Examine them carefully : some ideas can be transposed to larger or smaller areas. In any case, they will need to be adapted to the special and unique conditions of your own garden.*

*Chapter 2 describes the natural wet zones, and examines the relationship which is established between water and its environment. Mention is made of the vital role that man must play in assuring the survival of these zones on which a large proportion of the fauna and flora of our planet depend. We show how the tradition of water gardens, heritage of a rich past, is more than ever a matter of great importance, for the preservation of the exceptional biological diversity of wetlands.*

*Chapter 3 details the different steps in garden design, from the rough preliminary drafts to the definitive plan. The various techniques of*

*waterproofing are described, and the practical and aesthetic considerations governing their choice. Construction techniques are described in detail, step by step, together with the different phases of building a pool or pond. Although these instructions may seem rather technical at times, they are addressed to a wide public, including those who entrust the building of their pool or garden to a professional. A degree of knowledge of the different techniques available will simplify contact with the professionals and give you a better appreciation of the choices which are open to you.*

*In chapter 4, you will find explanations for the use of plants and some suggestions for composing an aquatic décor. There is some discussion of the way to go about designing and drawing up a plan for planting, the basic principles for garden planting in general, the composition and positioning of groups of plants, together with the use of planting shelves and baskets. A comprehensive catalogue lists more than 500 species and varieties of aquatic and bog plants, with colour illustrations, methods of cultivation and suggestions for use.*

*Chapter 5 contains a few useful principles for making your garden pool a welcoming place for wild life. A number of wild or ornamental species living in or near water are described, together with their requirements as regards habitat, food, reproduction, etc.*

*Please note that, while every effort has been made to ensure that the information in this book is accurate, some of the projects are sufficiently ambitious that, in case of any doubts, professional advice should be sought.*

# Chapter
# 1

# Water
# in
# Every Garden

# A CHINESE GARDEN

From very early times, the Chinese sought to achieve harmony with the fundamental laws of the universe, an intimate relationship with the earth's elements, and particularly water and the mineral element. This extraordinary reverence towards stones and water became, and still is, the major theme in the art of Chinese gardens.

TO FOLLOWERS OF the Taoist philosophy and lovers of mountains and nature in its wild state, rocks and mountains were the earth's skeleton. They symbolized the enchanted world of the immortals in Chinese legends and mythology. Taoist philosophers also meditated on the nature of water, and considered that waterways were the earth's vital arteries.

## The universe in miniature

In Chinese, the expression for "landscape" is "Shan Shui", meaning "mountain and water". The Chinese garden represents the landscape, and it is also an attempt to reproduce in a confined space all the richness and variety of the universe. In a most imaginative way, mountains, streams, rivers and rocks were represented by a few carefully selected elements, and this is certainly the first example of an artificial landscape designed as a symbolic microcosm of the known universe.

Heavy, monochrome rocks of tortuous shapes had the same decorative value as sculptures in a European garden. In the composition of a garden, water became an essential element by means of which the artist expressed the notion of life. It is an element of calm, and inspires contemplation. The flat surface of a stretch of water is a mirror to the sky, and the sky is half the universe.

▼ By appropriating the mountains, lakes and waterfalls of the Chinese landscape, without transforming them, man undoubtedly wanted to make sure of his place in the universe.

▶ Paths are the third important component of a Chinese garden. They are decorative elements in their own right, often made of mosaic or using pebbles to create images in relief.

*Pinus densiflora*

*Yucca filamentosa*

*Pseudosasa japonica*

Prunus mume

Phormium tenax

Festuca glauca

Carex morrowii

Carex morrowii

Festuca glauca

▲ Calm and mirror-like, or tumbling
in a cascade from an artificial stream, water
becomes a source of life in the hands of
Chinese gardeners. The juxtaposition
of mountains and water is one
expression of Yin and Yang.

## PLANTS SUITABLE FOR A CHINESE GARDEN

*Although China has one of
the richest and most varied ranges
of flora in the world, the Chinese
were and still are relatively
indifferent to the cultivation of
garden flowers.
The choice of plants for a garden
is often made for their perfume,
and for symbolic powers they are
sometimes believed to have.
Among the most frequently used :*

*bamboos, camellias spp.,
flowering cherry, chrysanthemums,
giant clematis, hibiscus,
iris, lilac, lilies,
lotus, orchids,
osmanthus, tree-peonies,
pines, primula,
prunus, rhododendron,
roses, willows.*

# A JAPANESE GARDEN

From the most ancient times, the Japanese have always had a deep feeling for natural landscape. Their sensitivity to the beauties of nature gave rise to a true art form that has become a tradition, fifteen centuries old and in constant evolution, which still influences garden designers throughout the world.

ANCIENT TEXTS CONCERNING the art of gardens reveal the existence in Japan, in about the year 550 A.D., of the first "pond gardens", where people took pleasure in riding in boats while feeding the birds and fish. This tradition originated in China, and developed in Japan as a result of the numerous cultural and commercial exchanges which strengthened the ties between the two countries, from the year 607. In 612 the Empress Suiko-tennô transformed the garden of her palace by creating a pond crossed by a wooden bridge in the Chinese style with a red lacquered parapet. During this period of close contact with China, Japan was also influenced by Buddhism, whose concepts were to leave an indelible mark on the art of gardens.

## The garden as landscape

The instinctive respect which the ancient Japanese felt for nature, their admiration for the spectacle which the natural landscape offered them each day (so very

special in the Japanese archipelago), gave rise to a style of garden combining hills, rocks and streams together with lakes and islands. This three-dimensional representation in miniature of a real or imaginary landscape offers a small fragment of universal nature for the pleasure of the eye and for quiet contemplation. The materials which compose it have been taken from nature and are arranged according to the rules of nature. Water is the most important element. The garden is often constructed around a pond representing a lake or the sea, dotted with islands and fed by a winding, cascading stream. Even in a dry landscape, water plays a major part, being represented by a stretch of sand evoking a pond, or by stones placed side by side to evoke the tumultuous course of a river. Rocks, either isolated or in

▼ *However modestly, water is almost always the central element in a Japanese garden. Here, the well and the oki-gata lantern are framed by maples and clipped box.*

carefully constructed groups, play an important aesthetic role. Their position is selected with the greatest attention to detail, to create a steep mountain, a bridge, or a tumbling stream. When used to consolidate the banks of a pond, they will evoke a wild, rocky coast, with a few outlying islets. Artificial grass-covered hills are created, sometimes studded with rocks to give an impression of real mountains.

## Religious symbolism

Introduced into Japan about the year 550 A.D. by the Emperor Kimmei-Tennô, Buddhism further strengthened

the concept of the landscape garden. Its representation of paradise was an island in a garden pool, and Buddha was "enthroned on a terrace above a lotus pond". This association of the notion of paradise with that of a lotus pond gave added impetus to the development of gardens with pools, which gradually became the place where religious rituals were performed. It had considerable influence on the evolution of the Japanese garden, whose arrangement was an earthly representation of the "Pure Land of the West", as is evidenced by the description of the "highest mountain in the world" which, in the Buddhist universe, "towers above the spheres of earth, water and wind. On the slopes of the mountain live the four kings of the sky, and at its foot are nine mountains, and between them eight seas with islands at their extremities". Thus, the art of composition of a Japanese garden was enriched by the mythology and symbolism of the Buddhist vision of paradise as an aquatic garden.

## Creating a Japanese garden

From this short note on the historical origins of the Japanese garden it will be seen that it embodies a feeling for nature and universal harmony which is not far removed from our present-day preoccu-

▲ *In this magnificient modern garden on the outskirts of Paris, the landscape gardener Fumiako Takano used water to evoke the life of Albert Kahn. A spring rising from a cone of white pebbles symbolizes the birth of the great man, while the water disappearing into the depths of a wide, dark spiral represents the end of his life. This handsome homage is also a fine example of a successful blending of ancient and modern.* (Albert Kahn Museum, Boulogne).

pations. It is through our own sensitivity and feeling for nature, rather than by mere imitation or exact historical reconstruction, that we can best perceive what an authentic Japanese garden should be.

Acer palmatum

Fats

Sasa veitchii

Athyrium filix-femina

Soleirola soleirolii

## THE THREE FORMS OF LANDSCAPE GARDEN

• The **water garden** is a pleasure garden *(Kaiyùshiki teien)*, which is often large, and is constructed around a stretch of water. At each bend of the path and at each curve of the pool margin the visitor, whether on foot or on the water, discovers a new scene : waterfalls, streams, islands, etc.

• The **contemplative garden** is designed to be viewed from the porch of a house or temple. Like any work of art, it can inspire reflection of a spiritual or aesthetic nature. It is often very small, and the visitor does not enter it. Although it is sometimes built around a pond, this type of garden is generally a dry landscape *(karesansui)*.

• The **tea garden (roji)** is a garden in which the tea ceremony takes place. It is small and intimate, sometimes enclosed by walls or hedges, with vegetation resembling that of light woodland. It contains elements of the other two types of garden, and almost always has a spring or stream. There is a lantern, and a basin for washing the hand *(tsukubai)* before entering the tea-house.

▲ This little waterfall evokes the power of a turbulent mountain torrent. The height of the cascades and the flow must be carefully calculated to provide the desired effect.

▶ This tea garden no larger than 30 m² (36 sq yd) finds room for a small pond with a yukumi-gata lantern and a traditional tsukabai. The rocks forming the pond margin contrive to give an impression of an extensive landscape, allowing free play to our imagination.

▼ The curved Japanese bridges have an irresistible charm. They have several forms, and are often lacquered in bright red to contrast with the surrounding vegetation. Less brilliant colours can be used to create an effect of quiet harmony.

## LACQUERED WOODEN JAPANESE BRIDGES

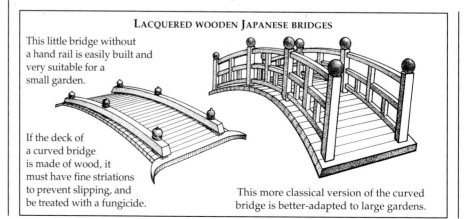

This little bridge without a hand rail is easily built and very suitable for a small garden.

If the deck of a curved bridge is made of wood, it must have fine striations to prevent slipping, and be treated with a fungicide.

This more classical version of the curved bridge is better-adapted to large gardens.

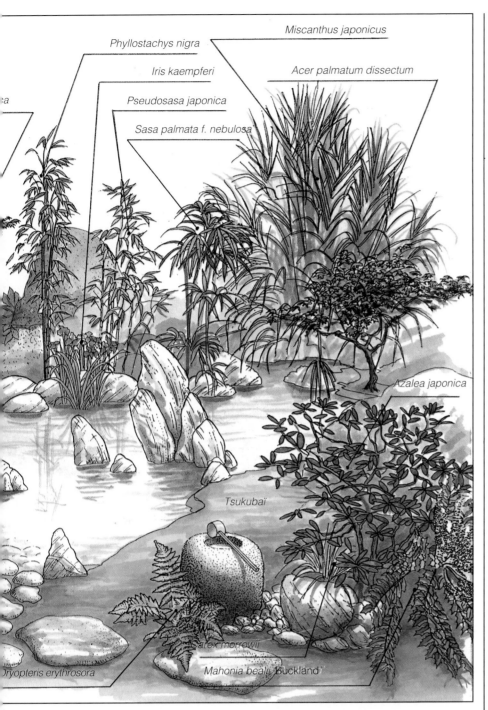

Miscanthus japonicus

Phyllostachys nigra

Acer palmatum dissectum

Iris kaempferi

Pseudosasa japonica

Sasa palmata f. nebulosa

Azalea japonica

Tsukubaï

Carex morrowii

Dryopteris erythrosora

Mahonia bealii Buckland

▲ *Top : this rustic bridge of simple wooden beams prolongs a path of stepping stones among the water irises.*

*Centre : at regular intervals, the sonorous clacking sound of this* shishi odoshi, *or "stag scarer" gives a reminder of the passing of time, while the water of the spring, symbolizing life, flows on to a bed of pebbles.*

*Bottom : Japanese koï carp are easily tamed, and extremely attractive with their wide range of colours and patterns.*

### PLANTS SUITABLE FOR A JAPANESE GARDEN

| | |
|---|---|
| Acer palmatum | Iris kaempferi |
| Arundinaria flexuosa | Mahonia japonica |
| Astilbe spp. | Matteuccia struthiopteris |
| Rhododendron japonicum | Miscanthus sinensis |
| Buxus microphylla | Phyllostachys aureosulcata |
| Camellia japonica | Phyllostachys nigra |
| Fatsia japonica | Phyllostachys nuda |
| Hemerocallis hybrids | Pieris japonica |
| Hosta fortunei | Sasa palmata |
| Hosta undulata | Sasa veitchii |
| Hydrangea macrophylla | |
| Ilex pedunculosa | |

# A MOORISH GARDEN

The origin of the Moorish garden harks back to the Persian Empire, where the fountains, canals and luxuriant vegetation of the gardens of Cyrus II the Great were an evocation of the paradise described by the Prophet. During the Middle Ages, this tradition was extended to the whole of the territory conquered by the Arabs in North Africa, in the India of the Moghuls, and in southern Spain.

THE ARABS, A NOMADIC people whose usual environment was one of arid desert, certainly took hope and comfort from the promise of an afterlife in a garden of paradise. This oriental vision of paradise as described in sacred texts inevitably influenced the art of the ornamental garden; its design represents the quest for purity and perfection which are absent from nature and from the human character, and which are best expressed by the use of abstract symbols and geometrical motifs.

### A geometrical design

Introduced into North Africa and Andalusia from the end of the 9th century, the Moorish garden enclosed within the house walls is a representation of a private universe in which one can enjoy the most sensual pleasures promised in the afterlife. The high walls which surround the garden provide the privacy which Arabs feel to be essential in a place dedicated to the pleasure of the senses and of the mind. They create the silence which is the background to the music of water. The courtyard garden is strictly geometric in design, divided into four squares representing the four quarters of the universe, separated by the four rivers of life. At their intersection, in the centre of the garden, is an ornamental fountain. The sensuality of the fountains and the luxuriant variety of plants and flowers are the result of highly refined irrigation techniques. They reveal just how far the knowledge and techniques of Eastern gardeners in the 12th to 14th centuries were in advance of those of their European counterparts, as evidenced by the Alhambra Gardens in Granada, which were built in the middle of the 13th century.

▼ *With its luxuriant vegetation and its four sections separated by a central canal, the Spanish garden of Baroness Ephrussi de Rothschild, completed in 1912, was inspired by the Moorish gardens of Aranjuez.*

Canna indica

Canna indica

Aloe arborescens

Chamaerops humilis

Yucca aloifolia

Yucca aloifolia

Aloe arborescens

Aloe arborescens

Cyperus papyrus

Cyperus papyrus

Aloe arborescens

Chamaerops humilis

Yucca aloifolia

▲ The use of water in pools and fountains accentuates the sensual character of Oriental gardens. Its constant presence is perhaps a reminder of the desert-dweller's age-old preoccupation with finding dependable supplies of water.

◄ The high walls around Mediterranean patios enclose a private realm protected from the pressures of the street and the outside world.

▼ Belief in a divine cosmic order superior to our world of agitation and confusion encouraged Islamic artists to express their faith by the use of geometrical patterns, in gardens, in carpets and in ceramic tiles. The square represents terrestrial order, the circle, divine perfection, and the octogon symbolizes man's earthly combat before attaining the heavenly spheres.

### TRADITIONAL MOTIFS IN HISPANO-MOORISH CERAMICS

### PLANTS SUITABLE FOR A MOORISH GARDEN

| | |
|---|---|
| Canna indica | Laurus |
| Chamaerops humilis | Lilium |
| Citrus limon | Myrtus |
| Citrus microcarpa | Nelumbo nucifera |
| Cyperus papyrus | Philodendron |
| Datura stramonium | Phœnix |
| Fatsia | Punica granatum |
| Gardenia | Rosa spp. |
| Jasminum spp. | Strelitzia |
| Kaki | Thalia dealbata |
| Kniphofia | Zantedeschia aethiopica |

# A CLASSICAL GARDEN

In the 15th century, Italian humanists rediscovered the ancient classical poets and philosophers and their vision of a universal order in which beauty and perfection could be attained only by reason and knowledge. The classical garden, an idealized landscape inhabited by the legendary gods of Olympus, formed the perfect setting for the pursuit of the arts and philosophy.

THE MOST EMINENT Renaissance architects understood intuitively that a formal and masterly use of water, that major element of the finest gardens in the world, together with a rational use of plants and earth, could but enhance the impression of absolute control over nature and the elements. The fountains and other water devices of the Italian gardens, part of a tradition dating back to imperial Rome, Islam and the Byzantine Empire, formed the dominant centre point around which the whole of the classical garden was designed. The exuberant use of water in all its forms called for much creative imagination, and required the installation of a complex hydraulic system. This made possible a whole range of special effects which enlivened these somewhat rigid, geometrically shaped gardens : the smooth surface of the pools, the fountains, cascades and streams, the rivulets and the play of light upon water are all an essential part of our heritage from the Italian Renaissance.

▶ *Created between 1905 and 1912 at Cap Ferrat on the French Riviera, the garden in the French style of the Ephrussi de Rothschild property illustrates the Roman Renaissance type of garden with its characteristic dominant central axis. French gardeners were strongly influenced by this concept, which persisted in England and in the rest of Europe until the end of the 17th century. Rising at the top of the hill, in a replica of the Temple of Love in the Petit Trianon at Versailles, the water then cascades down the steps of a stone staircase, ending its course in a long pool which is a mirror for the "Palazzino".*

▼ *In the magnificent gardens of Arceen, in Holland, this pool is an example of the Dutch interpretation of the classical tradition : the spontaneous appearance of the flowers relieves the monotony of the predictable geometrical perfection of the plots.*

### PLANTS SUITABLE FOR A CLASSICAL GARDEN

| | |
|---|---|
| *Antirrhinum* spp. | *Hyacinthus* spp. |
| *Anthemis* spp. | *Ligustrum* spp. |
| *Begonia* spp. | *Lilium* spp. |
| *Buxus* spp. | *Magnolia* spp. |
| *Carpinus betulus* | *Nymphaea* spp. |
| *Crataegus* spp. | *Pelargonium* spp. |
| *Dahlia* spp. | *Rosa* spp. |
| *Euonymus* spp. | *Salvia* spp. |
| *Fuchsia* spp. | *Schizanthus* spp. |
| *Hibiscus syriacus* | *Taxus* spp. |

◀ *Subjects from ancient mythology and history were used to accentuate the theatrical quality of classical gardens. Statues representing the gods of Olympus were placed in the four corners of the courtyard and at the centre of each of the enclosing walls, in painted and decorated recesses called* cappelette. *These were intended to arouse the interest of the visitor in the ancient myths and legends.*

# A SUBURBAN GARDEN

As we approach the end of the 20th century, the relationship which once existed between man and nature is under threat from ever-increasing urban sprawl. Modern man is more and more conscious of a need to concern himself with ecology and environmental conservation, as is evidenced by an increasing interest in natural-style gardens, where water plays a dominant role.

THE STRESSFUL NATURE of life in large, modern cities, polluted and over-crowded, has aroused in many people the desire for a "return to nature". The naturalistic garden concept, preceding the environmental preservation movement, led to the development of a new style of free, informal garden, an idealized representation of nature. This style is suitable even for small areas, and often has as its centre-piece a pool, which represents nature in an apparently untamed state. This corresponds to the image that modern man would like to present, of a desire to play a positive role in the environment. In this haven, sheltered from the pressures of the outside world, the individual finds contact with nature on a human scale, whose beauty and unchanging rules are a constant source of pleasure and enrichment.

▼ *The contemporary landscape gardener reflects the spontaneity of nature in informal gardens which often have a dreamlike quality. Since man has learned to use technology to harness nature, he no longer feels uncomfortable in its presence or threatened by it. (Designer : Guy Lainé).*

▶ *The informal, irregularly-shaped gardens of new suburban areas, are a marked contrast to the uniformity and rigid formalism of the past. The disappearance of garden walls and hedges opens up private spaces and may express a desire for greater contact between neighbourhood residents, or for a certain degree of continuity with the surrounding countryside. (Designer : Guy Lainé).*

▶ *The choice of plants and materials, textures and colours, reflected light and the sound of water are the language of the landscape gardener. (Designer : Guy Lainé).*

▶ ▶ *Poetic and accessible, Guy Lainé's gardens represent nature in an ideal state, pleasantly calm and restful. The absence of strict proportions and symmetry suggests that irregular shapes, without any easily identifiable planning or organization, can be even more beautiful and harmonious than a rigorous artificial composition.*

# A COURTYARD

It is not a simple matter to make a paradise out of a confined space hemmed in by tall expanses of glass and concrete. Landscape gardener Camille Muller took up the challenge and succeeded in creating this exotic haven, by an inspired choice of boldly-shaped plants carefully placed around a pool and a wooden walkway.

SITUATED IN THE HEART of Paris, this garden provides a green focal point for all the windows of the office blocks which surround it. The evergreen foliage of the giant bamboos (*Phyllostachys* spp.) masks the facades of the buildings and helps one forget that this is a cramped courtyard which receives only a few hours of sun in summer. On the thick concrete slab which forms the base of the courtyard, Camille Muller has created a pool 55 cm (22 in) deep, with an area of 200 m² (239 sq yd) bordered by large planting troughs and a wide walkway made of duckboards. The whole of the garden is designed to be viewed from above. The strong lines of wooden elements form a harmonious contrast with the foliage which has been chosen for its bold, exotic shapes. The enormous leaves of the paulownias (*Paulownia tomentos*) are easily recognizable even from the eighth floor. This enclosed courtyard, sheltered from wind and hard frost, creates a micro-climate perfectly suited to the fragile leaves of the paulownias, which stand up well to urban pollution. Their violet flowers, which appear in May before the leaves, are followed by the irises in June, bringing a note of colour to this garden which is green all the year round.

▼ *The entrance to the garden is lower than the pool, so that eyes of the visitor as he comes in are on a level with the surface of the water. The gaze is then drawn naturally towards three stones, framed by handsome clumps of* Iris pseudacorus, *from which spring three fountains symbolizing Beauty, Strength and Wisdom.*

▲ *The margins of the pool are masked by duckboards reminiscent of the deck of a boat. The warmth of the wood and the graphic foliage of the iris, the bamboos and the paulownias create an exotic atmosphere which is a constant source of pleasure for the people who work in this office block.*
*The part shown here faces the glass-fronted staff cafeteria.*

◀ A limited number of species of plants have been used, chosen for their silhouette and for the shape of their leaves : in several places, the large, heart-shaped leaves of the Paulownia tomentosa create an interesting contrast with the fine foliage of the Dutch poplars (Populus alba) and the elegant architectural vegetation of the giant bamboos (Phyllostachys aureosulcata, Phyllostachys nigra, Fargesia murieliae and Phyllostachys nigra 'Boryana').

# FOUNTAINS

Fountains and jets of water can be used to create a centre of interest even when means and space are limited. Water can be used to animate and draw attention to a part of the garden. Sometimes the fountain or jet will be the main feature of the garden, with all the other elements serving only to highlight it.

THE STYLE OF A FOUNTAIN or a simple jet of water, and its position, must be chosen with the greatest care, to harmonize with the style and the proportions of the pool, the garden and the architecture surrounding the site.

## Jets

A wide range of nozzles is available for jets of various forms. The height of the jet will depend on the size of the pool, and will be controlled by choosing the appropriately sized pump and then adjusting the pump output. To avoid having the water blow outside the limits of the pool, which is extremely wasteful, and

could run the pump dry, the height of the jet should not exceed 50% of the diameter of the pool. The growth of certain aquatic plants (especially water lilies) may be adversely affected if a nearby jet splashes and creates currents in the water.

## Fountains

Whether it is figurative or abstract in style, a fountain, like a work of art, must be set off to best advantage. Care must be taken in planning the surrounding area, so that it is pleasing throughout the year, whatever the angle from which one approaches it.

▶ *Even if it is the main feature of a composition, a fountain need not necessarily be at the exact centre. In this garden designed by Jean Mus, the off-centre position of the Provençal fountain counters the symmetrical organization of the garden "à la française" in the background.*

▼ *Statues are often used in association with fountains, and bring an additional dimension to a garden. Here, a creation of the sculptress Edith Brinkman representing water lilies.*

◄◄ *The bronze or terracotta spouts of wall fountains, like this typically Mediterranean lion's head, can often be used to introduce a note of imagination or humour into a garden. The continuous movement of water from fountains also helps to maintain the biological balance of the pool and to oxygenate the water, which is essential if there are many fish.*

◄ *This fountain, based on a very ancient model, is framed by two sandstone urns which make a balanced composition, further enhanced by the two bull's-eyes in the wall, and the design of the crazy paving. The frame of evergreen foliage makes this a pleasant place whatever the season. (Designer : Jean Mus).*

# A VERY SMALL GARDEN

Even if you have very little room, you can profitably use water in one form or another, since it gives an impression of space and transforms the general picture completely. Far from being merely a cheap alternative to a "proper" pool, a small aquatic arrangement will create a dynamic focal point.

IF AN AQUATIC TUB GARDEN OR A MINIPOND is desired, there are a large number of prefabricated units available, made of fibreglass-reinforced cement, PVC, plastic, or synthetic resins. These are relatively-light in weight, strong, and regular in shape, which makes them excellent for decorating terraces and balconies. You can also use other objects not originally intended for the purpose, such as barrels or reinforced concrete pipes. 20-40 cm (8-16 in) of water with 8-15 cm (3-6 in) of soil at the bottom are sufficient for planting. Choose two or three varieties of small growing aquatic plants, for a balanced composition.

## Birdbaths

At all times of the year birds require water for drinking and bathing. It is easy to instal a small birdbath in a quiet corner of the garden, but make sure that the surrounding area is open enough to discourage predators from attacking the birds. The sides of the pool must slope very gently, so that the smallest birds can bathe without risk of drowning. A few centimetres (or a few inches) of water are enough, but it must be possible to change it regularly to prevent fouling. The pool itself can be made of natural materials, or from flexible liners, con-

▼ *This very successful composition created by the designer Guy Lainé is to be found on a small terrace on the 7th floor of a block of flats in Paris. It is centred around an erect stone rising from a bed of pebbles. The geometrical lines of the terrace, the bold shapes of the evergreens (bamboos, rhododendrons, junipers) form an interesting contrast with the raw, natural appearance of the materials used (wood, rock, pebbles).*

Birdbaths can be made from a wide range of materials : carved or naturally hollowed stone, moulded polyester or reconstituted stone, etc.

*The water in birdbaths must be clean and changed frequently.*

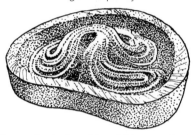

*The gently sloping sides of this attractively carved stone provide easy access for even the smallest birds.*

*Wide margins and an open situation provide a better degree of safety for birds.*

*The material and shape of a birdbath must blend in with the style of the garden.*

*In a rock garden or Japanese garden, a rock with a natural cavity can be used for a birdbath.*

## MINIPOOLS

For a miniature water garden, a wide variety of small growing aquatic plants can be installed in a small PVC or polyester pool. Raised containers of various kinds can also be used : fibreglass reinforced cement or waterproofed reconstituted stone containers, wooden or metal tubs, etc. Any container selected should be free from residual chemicals which could foul or kill fish or plants.

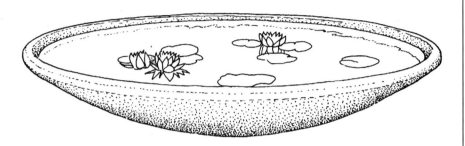

*A miniature water garden requires little care, but regular attention must be paid to the water level, especially during hot summer weather. Unlike birdbaths, which should be placed in a secluded part of the garden, miniponds can be placed to best advantage alongside a pathway, or on a terrace or balcony.*

### PLANTS SUITABLE FOR A MINIPOND

| | |
|---|---|
| *Acorus calamus* | *Menyanthes trifoliata* |
| *Aponogeton distachyos* | *Nymphaea pygmaea tetragona* |
| *Azolla* spp. | *Nymphaea* 'Pygmaea Rubra' |
| *Butomus umbellatus* | *Nymphaea* 'Aurora' |
| *Calla palustris* | *Nymphaea* 'Graziella' |
| *Ceratophyllum demersum* | *Nymphaea* 'Paul Hariot' |
| *Drosera* spp. | *Nymphaea* 'Somptuosa' |
| *Equisetum* spp. | *Nymphaea* 'Pygmaea Helveola' |
| *Hippuris vulgaris* | *Pistia stratiotes* |
| *Hottonia palustris* | *Pontederia cordata* |
| *Hydrocharis morsus-ranae* | *Salvinia* spp. |
| *Hydrocleys nymphoïdes* | *Typha minima* |
| *Juncus effusus* 'spiralis' | *Trapa natans* |
| *Lemna* spp. | *Utricularia vulgaris* |

▼ *Resolutely modern in style, this courtyard paved with granite has a small square pool in the centre. The water flows from an old hand pump painted vermillion through a narrow channel to a small pool in the background.*

▲ *This traditional little pool hollowed out of the granite receives a thin trickle of water. This simple and natural scene, fruit of the imagination of the landscape artist Jean Mus, brings a touch of magic to its surroundings.*

# A WILD GARDEN

The presence of a garden pond is an excellent point of departure for creating a wild corner which will provide shelter for a wide range of fauna. A garden of this style requires relatively little attention, since the plants can be allowed to develop freely without spoiling the composition.

F IT IS TO SEEM NATURAL, a pool must be shaped in a way that follows the contours of the site. Its margins are abundantly planted, to accentuate the "wild" look. To ensure a certain seclusion, the pool will be surrounded by large wetland trees (black alder, willow, bald cypress) or, if space is limited, by giant grasses, such as the Japanese miscanthus (*Miscanthus sinensis*) or giant reeds. A wooden platform or several large flat rocks will provide a place for relaxation and easier observation of the fauna.

## A stylised imitation

Even if your main ambition is to "hold a mirror up to nature" in its wild state, there is no reason why you should not associate plants for their colour and form. You need not necessarily restrict your choice to native plants arranged exactly as they would appear in their natural state. Local rushes and sedges can be used in association with the most decorative horticultural or foreign varieties, to enhance the wild look of the pond. But avoid scattering a large number of species haphazardly all round the garden. Instead, choose a few plants which you will group in large clumps at several places around the pool. The effect produced by these two or three dominant species will be highlighted by small groups of other species planted here and there.

▼ *A few carefully-selected species are all that is required to bring a wild feeling to a garden. Seen here, the distinctive shape of the sumach* (Rhus typhina), *thick clumps of yellow flag* (Iris pseudacorus) *and the broad leaves of the yellow skunk cabbage* (Lysichiton americanus).

▲   *Water in a garden attracts all kinds of wild life. The clumps of grasses* (Glyceria maxima, Phalaris arundinaceae, Phragmites communis) *provide shelter for a number of aquatic birds which like to nest there. Here, a small wooden platform is used for feeding the freshwater turtles which live in the pool.*

▶   *Even around a pond with an informal, wild appearance, horticultural and foreign varieties can be included for their decorative value.*

### PLANTS FOR THE WILD GARDEN

| | |
|---|---|
| *Acorus calamus* | *Lysimachia thyrsiflora* |
| *Alchemilla mollis* | *Lythrum salicaria* |
| *Alnus glutinosa* | *Matteuccia struthiopteris* |
| *A. incana* 'Aurea' | *Miscanthus sinensis* |
| *Arundo* spp. | *Miscanthus japonicus* |
| *Butomus umbellatus* | *Osmunda regalis* |
| *Caltha palustris* | *Phalaris aquatica* |
| *Carex* spp. | *Pontederia* spp. |
| *Glyceria maxima* | *Salix exigua* |
| *Hippuris vulgaris* | *Scirpus* spp. |
| *Hosta* spp. | *Taxodium distichum* |
| *Iris pseudacorus* | *Typha* spp. |
| *Juncus* spp. | *Zizania aquatica* |

# A ROCK GARDEN

The plastic beauty of a garden will be enhanced by associating mineral and liquid elements. The attractive sound of a cascade and the sparkle of flowing water form a pleasant contrast with the motionless, compact mass of the rocks, whose colour and texture are enhanced by the transparent mirror effect of the water.

I N A ROCK GARDEN THE pool must look as natural as possible and blend perfectly into its surroundings. Whatever technique is used for the construction, the edges of the pool must be masked by overhanging rocks and large stones, giving the impression that the water has accumulated naturally in a hollow. Good results can be obtained with concrete, which allows rocks to be incorporated in the margin during construction.

## Site

For a rock garden, the site should be sloping or irregular, allowing some of the underlying rock to appear here and there in outcrops, as though by natural erosion. On flat ground, a rock garden can seem very artificial. It is better to shift some earth to make a few hollows and hillocks, taking care that they are not too regular and rigid in shape. Use fairly large blocks or groups of rocks of the same nature but of different sizes, and anchor them deeply in the ground to avoid accidental tipping. Whatever you do, avoid mixing different kinds of material and accumulating masses of little stones. Some guidelines for building articifial rocks from reinforced concrete are given on page 81.

As far as possible, base your construction on photographs or sketches of examples. Fill the free spaces with small carpeting plants (*Sagina* spp., *Soleirolia*) and small grasses (blue fescues, lyme grass) which can do well in pockets of soil among the rocks. Plant in groups of the same species.

▼ *The sloping stony ground of a rock garden lends itself well to the creation of a cascading stream feeding a number of small pools.*

▲ *This magnificent garden created by Jean Mus shows artistic vision and poetic sensitivity. The sides of the pool are masked by rocks and luxuriant vegetation.*

▶ *The rocks which make the cascade are underlined completely with butyl rubber (or flexible) liner to eliminate leakage and sealed in place with mortar to provide increased stability.*

### PLANTS FOR THE ROCK GARDEN

| | |
|---|---|
| *Ajuga reptans* | *Molinia* spp. |
| *Armeria maritima* | *Parnassia palustris* |
| *Bergenia cordifolia* | *Phalaris arundinacea* |
| *Campanula carpatica* | *Pleioblastus fortunei* |
| *Elymus arenarius* | *Arundinaria pumila* |
| *Festuca glauca* | *Pleioblastus viridistriatus* |
| Ferns | *Sagina subulata* |
| *Soleirolia soleirolii* | *Santolina* spp. |
| *Hosta* spp. | *Sasa palmata* |
| *Kœleria glauca* | *Sasa veitchii* |
| *Lavandula* spp. | *Saxifraga* spp. |
| *Hypericum* spp. | *Sedum* spp. |
| *Mimulus* spp. | *Sisyrinchium* spp. |

# STREAMS AND CASCADES

The creation of a stream or a cascade can bring a dramatic element to a garden, but the utmost care must be taken to ensure that the movement and sound of the water are not obtrusive. Often a mere thread of water will be enough to transform the whole atmosphere of a garden.

A SLIGHT SLOPE (2-5 cm per metre (1-2 in per foot) lends itself very well to the creation of a stream, while a steep bank will be better suited to a waterfall. If your site is flat, you can add earth to create a slope, but do not build a hillock or mound with water flowing from the top, as this will appear totally artificial. It is better to create several gently sloping hillocks of different sizes, and allow the water to find its natural path among them. The whole course of a stream should not be visible at a glance : if possible, the head and the foot should be masked by a shoulder of ground or by plants, to preserve an air of mystery. The size of the watercourse must be in keeping with the size of the garden. The water is generally circulated by a submerged pump in the base pool which drives it back to the header pool. You may wish to provide some form of level regulator to make up for water evaporation.

▶ *The choice of pump depends on the distance and difference in height (head) between the top of the cascade and the surface of the base pool, and the desired output. Choose an appropriately sized pump for best aesthetic results and maximum pump life.*

▼ *The appearance, the flow and the sound of a cascade depend on the material used to construct it. In this stylized pool created by the landscape designer Guy Lainé, a sheet of galvanized metal creates a fine veil of water whose refined shape harmonizes with the strong outline of the thalias (Thalia dealbata) and arrowheads (Sagittaria sagittifolia).*

◄ ◄ *Pebbles and aquatic plants* (Acorus calamus, Myriophyllum proserpinacoides) *help to shape and give character to a watercourse.*
*(Designer : Guy Lainé)*

◄ *The margins of this stream are made of pebbles, carefully fitted and fixed in place with mortar to prevent erosion of the banks.*
*(Designer : Jean Mus)*

# A HARDY EXOTIC GARDEN

Even if you live in a region where winters are cold, you can still create a garden with something of the tropical jungle about it, and indulge your escapist fantasies. Among the most exotically-shaped plants, there are hardy or half-hardy species which will enable you to create a decor worthy of the Douanier Rousseau.

An atmosphere of fantasy can be created by a careful selection of plants with boldly-shaped, decorative leaves which are used in association to provide a contrast in form and a variety of shades of green. Preference should be given to the more exotic shapes, such the *Chamaerops humilis* (half-hardy) and hardy forms of papyrus (*Cyperus longus* and *Cyperus eragrostis*. If you have sufficient space, use "giant" plants, grouping several members of the same species chosen from among the most spectacular : *Gunnera manicata, Heracleum mantegazzianum, Macleaya cordata*. For a year-round impression of dense jungle, use a majority (about 70%) of evergreen species (*Magnolia grandiflora, Choisya ternata, Bergenia, Yucca filamentosa, Phormium, Aucuba japonica*) or semi-evergreens such as ornamental grasses (*Elymus, Miscanthus, Phalaris, Arundo donax, Phragmites communis, Zizania latifolia, Cortaderia*). Bamboos offer a wide choice of species which are perfectly hardy down to -22 °C (-7.6 °F), in a good range of sizes, shapes and colours.

For a seasonal note of fantasy and colour, introduce some of the more exuberant flowers : lysichitons (American skunk cabbage), cannas, arums, the castor-oil plant (*Ricinus communis*), red-hot pokers (*Kniphofia*). To complete the picture, a few ornamental trees can also be included : *Catalpa, Paulownia, Rhus typhina, Salix matsudana, Albizzia julibrissin*.

The shape of the pool must be as natural as possible and the margins will be completely masked by natural elements : rocks or evergreen foliage, beaches of pebbles. One or two accessories will provide a little local colour : an old tree stump at the water's edge, a bamboo or rope bridge, a group of rocks.

▼ *Large clumps of bamboo give an Asian jungle look to this informal pool, bordered with sedges and ferns. Shown here are* Arundinaria tessellata *and* Pseudosasa japonica, *two hardy species which are frost resistant, the first to -18 °C (-0.4 °F) and the second to -24 °C (-11 °F).*

▲   *A warm, tropical atmosphere, against a background of pointed-leaved* Phormium *and dwarf palms. Here,* Chaemerops humilis *and* Sabal minor *(half-hardy). Duck weed* (Lemna minor) *and water hawthorn* (Aponogeton distachyus) *have colonized the stream which is bordered with sagina and sedges. The red of* Lobelia cardinalis *adds a stimulating note of colour to the dominant green.*

▼   *This shallow pool installed in a closed courtyard of 40 m² (48 sq yd) is surrounded by dense vegetation reminiscent of a tropical forest. Among the plants are a* Chamaerops humilis *and a* Fatsia.

**PLANTS SUITABLE FOR AN EXOTIC GARDEN**

*Aucuba japonica*
*Azalea*
*Canna* hybrids
*Chamaerops excelsa*
*Choysia ternata*
*Crocosmia* 'Lucifer'
*Eucalyptus gunnii*
*Fatsia japonica*
*Gunnera manicata*
*Hosta* spp.
*Ilex pedunculosa*
*Macleaya cordata*
*Kniphofia* spp.
*Mahonia* spp.
*Matteuccia struthiopteris*
*Miscanthus* spp.
*Phormium* spp.
*Phyllostachys* spp.
*Pieris japonica*
*Rhus typhina*
*Sasa* spp.
*Yucca filamentosa*
*Zantedeschia aethiopica*

# A TROPICAL GARDEN

Whether it is used as a cold conservatory, a winter garden or a tropical house, the greenhouse or veranda is an ideal place for an inside pool. It is warm and light, two essential conditions for cultivating tropical species. If it is heated in winter, you can have your own tropical paradise all the year round.

THE GLASSED-IN ROOM MUST be high enough, at least 4 m (13 ft) to allow space for the tallest plants to develop. Fresh air must be allowed to circulate, and a mechanical ventilation system will provide temperature control according to seasonal requirements. A slight current of moving air also helps to control humidity.

Maintaining a higher degree than normal of air humidity will help plants thrive and ward off pests and diseases, particularly when temperatures rise. An inside pool naturally provides a moist atmosphere, by evaporation, but this may be supplemented by spraying the leaves of the plants when the temperature rises above 18-20 °C (64-68 °F). Automatic misting systems provide constant, controlled humidity.

### A pool in an unheated greenhouse

A pool in an unheated conservatory or lean-to greenhouse can be of very great use in the cultivation of certain garden plants. It provides a means of protecting from frost the less hardy species : *Salvinia braziliensis, Pistia stratiotes, Eichhornia crassipes, Thalia dealbata, Cyperus papyrus*, tropical water lilies, *Hydrocleys nymphoides*. The pool can also be used for goldfish (*Carassius auratus auratus*), Koï carp, or native species which will tolerate water temperatures down to 3-5 °C (37-41 °F).

### A tropical greenhouse

To cultivate tropical plants, a summer temperature of 20-25 °C (68-77 °F) is required, with about 75% humidity. An efficient shading system will be necessary to protect the large tender leaves being scorched by direct sun. In winter, most exotic plants will be content with a temperature of 15-18 °C (59-64 °F) provided the atmosphere is not too damp. Good insulation with double glazing will increase energy efficiency; a heating system with thermostat control is also recommended.

◄ *A very large poo l, at least 30 m² (36 yd²), is required for the huge leaves of the* Victoria regia. *From May a succession of flowers open for three consecutive nights, each aging from pure white on the first night to deep ruby on the third.*

▲ An admirable tropical scene in the Papiliorama at Marin, in Switzerland. This extraordinary garden of more than 1000 m² (1200 sq yd) under glass contains a large pool and luxuriant vegetation among which superb tropical butterflies can be observed.

◄◄ To develop fully, the variegated evergreen foliage of the different varieties of Codiaeum variegatum *need a great deal of light and a high degree of humidity.*

◄ In a hothouse pool, many tropical aquatic species can be cultivated in good conditions, such as the water lettuce, Pistia stratiotes, *which appreciates water at a temperature of 20-25 °C (68-77 °F).*

### The inside pool

A number of techniques can be used for building an inside pool : preformed PVC or synthetic resin, masonry lined with ceramic tiles, polyester resin coating, or flexible PVC or butyl rubber liners. The latter two methods allow greater freedom of form, and enable the heating system to be incorporated in the masonry, making it completely invisible.

An inside pool can also be used to create a particularly favourable environment for a number of species of animal. Depending on the water temperature, native or exotic fish, Koï, amphibians or freshwater turtles can be introduced. All these animals easily get used to the presence of the inhabitants of the house, and will eventually become very tame. This makes them easier to observe and care for. The high temperature, strong light and small volume of water make it essential to provide a filtration system to keep the water clear and clean, especially if the pool contains Koï or turtles. A level control device or easy access to a tap are also required, because the high temperature of the room at certain times of the day can cause considerable evaporation.

▶ *Plants and pebbles can create a decorative look while at the same time masking the liner and the submerged pump which recirculates the water constantly*

▼ *The main elements of this splendid design are ferns (Polystichum tsussimense, Nephrolepis exaltata, Adiantum raddianum) and papyrus (Cyperus albostriatus, Cyperus alternifolius). A carpet of Soleirolia soleirolii gives a certain unity to the composition, while the rocks and the cascade add to the lively, natural appearence of the scene.*

## PLANTS FOR THE
### TEMPERATE GREENHOUSE

Agapanthus umbellatus
Alocasia macrorrhiza
Callistemon citrinus
Brugmansia chlorantha
Dracaena fragrans
Fatsia japonica
Grevillea banksii
Hibiscus spp.
Leucodendron argenteum
Ludwigia grandiflora
Myriophyllum proserpinacoides
Pilea cadierei
Sasa spp.
Sorghum halepense
Strelitzia reginae
Thalia dealbata

## PLANTS FOR THE HOTHOUSE

Alternanthera ficoidea sessilis
Pistia stratiotes
Chamaedorea elegans
Chlorophytum comosum
Clerodendrum speciosum
Cordyline terminalis
Dracaena sanderiana
Euryale ferox
Hydrocleys vulgaris
Hygrophila spp.
Hypoestes phyllostachya
Maranta leuconeura
Nelumbo spp.
Nymphaea tropical
Salvinia braziliensis
Spathiphyllum spp.

## A heated pool

Tropical fish and freshwater turtles need a water temperature of 23-26 °C (73-78 °F) so heating must be provided, either by circulating hot water through pipes, or by means of heating cables. The heating should ideally be incorporated in the foundations of the pool, which must then be isolated from the ground by an efficient insulating material. Always include a thermostat.

▶ *The yellow inflorescences of the* Pachystachys *are in fact bracts from which emerge the real flowers, which are pure white.*

▼ *In strong light and humid conditions, and a temperate atmosphere, plants with a wide range of special requirements will grow strongly and vigorously.*

# Chapter 2

# The Ecology of Water Gardens

# WETLANDS UNDER THREAT

Among all the natural environments, marshes have certainly been the most extensively transformed or detroyed by human activity. In spite of vast rehabilitation programmes, this unique and irreplaceable ecosystem is still under threat today. By creating an aquatic biotope in our gardens, whether in town or in the  country, we can play a part in preserving the extraordinary range of flora and fauna of our wetlands.

I N 1971, NATURALISTS AND scholars from all over the world met at Ramsar, in Iran, in a conference intended to draw public attention to the urgent need to safeguard wetlands. An agreement was drawn up - and ratified - providing for the protection of wetlands or zones having such characteristics, which are of particular importance in that they are the typical habitat for aquatic and swamp birds.

## DIFFERENT TYPES OF WETLANDS

Wetlands are characterized by the presence of water, but also by a specific and homogeneous fauna, principally birds. They are sometimes artificial in origin, more often natural. But artificial or natural, their future and their survival depends on man.

### Natural wetlands

Marshes and other wet zones such as swamps, bogs, tidal marshes, are of the greatest interest, for the richness of their fauna and flora which often gives them a wild, somewhat primitive atmosphere. It is often difficult to make a distinction between the different types of wetland, since there is a considerable amount of overlap, but some definitions can be attempted :

*Ponds* are expanses of still, permanent water;

▼   *Unlike the large dragonflies (Anisoptera), damselflies (Zygoptera) can not hover: Here, the male Coenagrion puella.*

▶   *Beyond the zone formed by the maces, the iris and the water grasses, the centre of the pond is the home of the yellow water lily and the water soldier.*

*Marshes*  are zones of wet ground with ponds and pools and primarily herbaceous vegetation;

*Swamps* are similar to marshes, but have shrubs and trees (willows, poplars, alders, etc.);

*Peatbogs* are formed by the accumulation of vegetable debris in depressions in poor-draining terrain;

*Mangrove swamps* are the characteristic vegetation of tidal zones in many tropical and subtropical regions.

*Lagoons* are stretches of salt or brackish water surrounded by dry land with permanent or temporary access to the sea.

Other natural zones offer conditions quite similar to those of swamps and marshes, with which they are often associated : *lakes, river beds and river banks, deltas* (triangular river mouth zone created by silt deposits resulting in diverging outlets) and *estuaries* (undivided river mouth). These also play an important part in the survival of many species.

### Formation of wet zones

Wet zones are created by the gradual accumulation of rainwater on impermeable or poorly draining ground. Shallow stretches of water form in hollows and on the shores of lakes, rivers and seas. Such zones can also be formed by the dead arm of a watercourse, or by a build-up of silt slowing the flow of a river, forming a bog.

### Artificial wet zones

Other types of wet zone have been created by man for economic reasons, and can play a part in the survival of wetland flora and fauna. These include canals, salterns, fish-farm ponds, hydro-electric reservoirs or other reservoirs for flood control or irrigation.

In the Middle Ages, monasteries were expert in the management of *fish ponds*. The water supply was controlled through a system of canals and sluice-gates and the pond could be drained completely to harvest the fish. Ponds of this type are still used in fish farms, where they also provide a suitable habitat for numbers of insects, frogs, toads, and water birds. But the presence of fish and the relative lack of vegetation mean that these zones are of limited ecological interest. They are drained completely every two or three years and this operation is often followed by liming, to eliminate any fish parasites, which means that the biological balance of the pond

▲    *This frog* (Rana lessonae) *never ventures far from the water and leaps in at the slightest alert.*

▶    *The narrow-leaved reed mace* (Typha angustifolia) *and duckweed* (Lemna minor) *do well in nutrient-rich water.*

is regularly disturbed, and fauna and flora cannot develop normally. A certain number of wild species manage to adapt to the conditions in fish-farm ponds, migrating from one to another when drainage operations are carried out.

Old *gravel-pits* make better recreational areas than wild-life habitats. They are too deep 6-15 m (20-50 ft) for light to penetrate and the water cannot warm up sufficiently. In addition, the sides are steep, high and unstable, and the soil is poor in nutrients. It is sometimes possible, however, at relatively little cost, to create a gently-sloping shallow zone where plants can develop, by filling part of the gravel-pit with soil.

*Hydroelectric reservoirs* are of little value as wildlife habitats. Constructed in mountainous regions, they are very deep, the banks are steep, and the water level is subject to considerable fluctuation.

*Flood-control reservoirs,* generally constructed on the plain, are not so deep as mountain lakes. Their situation and surface area make them useful resting-places and assembly points for migratory birds, but the extreme variations in water level constitute a handicap for numerous species of animals and plants.

## Ornamental lakes and ponds

The ornamental lakes and ponds found in public parks and gardens are often quite large, and play an essential part in the preservation of some species of urban and suburban wild life. These stretches of water should be kept under regular surveillance (notably during periods of drought) and so provide a stable habitat for the species which live there.

Unlike waterholes, which may dry up completely, and fish ponds, which are drained periodically, there are some very small pools which retain water all the year round, even though the level may fluctuate. These provide an environment which is sufficiently stable for wild life to develop satisfactorily both in the water and around it.

And of course *the small ponds and pools in private gardens* play a very efficient part in preserving and encouraging wild life in urban surroundings. They are well-cared for by their owners, and although they are sometimes very small indeed they all form part of a vast network, providing shelter and resting places for numerous animals.

## A RICH AND COMPLEX ECOSYSTEM

The formation of a pond or a marsh is accompanied by the appearance of a wide range of plants preferring damp or submerged sites. In the moist, nutrient-rich soil at the margins there rapidly develops a very specific vegetation including *Juncus, Phragmites, Spartina, Typha.* Some plants such as peat mosses *(Sphagnum)*, salvinias *(Salvinia)*, water ferns *(Azolla)*, duckweed *(Lemna)* float on the surface. Other species, like *Myriophyllum, Elodea, Hottonia palustris* or *Ceratophyllum* are partially or completely submerged. And certain plants are bottom-rooted but have floating leaves *(Nuphar, Hydrocharis, Potamogeton, Nymphaea).*

### Zones of occupation

Marsh plants adapt perfectly to their environment and settle in the zone which is best suited to their requirements. Each species is adapted to a certain depth of water, and tends to populate zones having the same characteristics. The different species grow in concentric circles from the edge of the pond to the centre, creating several bands of vegetation which are known as zonations.

• *The outer zone* is made up essentially of reedmaces *(Typha)*, with long narrow leaves and brown, cigar-shaped inflorescences. Apart from the reedmaces, the inner part of the zone, nearest to the water, almost always contains the common reed *(Phragmites communis)*. Though the reedmaces may be absent, the common reed will always be found, forming dense colonies often referred to as reedbeds.

• *The intermediate zone,* nearer to the centre, is composed of members of the rush family, including the plaiting rush *(Schoenoplectus lacustris)* and

*Juncus conglomeratus*, often in association with the yellow flag (*Iris pseudacorus*).

• *The interior zone* usually consists of pond lilies (*Nuphar lutea*), pondweeds (*Potamogeton*), water lilies (*Nymphaea*) and knotweeds (*Polygonum*).

### Stages in evolution

Few natural habitats are transformed as rapidly as the marsh. After its formation, it evolves gradually and plant debris accumulates. The marsh silts up progressively, and finally disappears. This process, which is completed in a very short time, on the geological scale, can be divided into several phases :

**During the first phase** (called the oligotrophic stage), the pond is simply an expanse of clear water with no vegetation on the banks. Gradually, plant debris, dead leaves and insects, carried by the wind, drop to the bottom of the water, where they are decomposed by bacteria and transformed into humus and mineral substances. The organic elements enrich the soil and the minerals bring nutrients to the water. These are absorbed by free, unicellular algae which multiply rapidly in the presence of sunlight, then die and drop to the bottom where they decompose. The nutrient content of the water increases, causing a further increase in the number of algae.
Next, several generations of aquatic plants will colonize the zone, which will be enriched as they die and decompose. Other fertile elements will be provided by the droppings of resident or transient animals (migrating water birds). The accumulation of organic debris at the bottom of the pool also causes a progressive rise in the water level.

**During the next phase**, aquatic plants emerge from the water : reeds, maces, rushes, arrowheads, flags. As the plants increase and their spreading roots become intergrown, vegetable debris accumulates and forms a layer of soil rich in organic matter which can be several metres thick : this phase sees the progressive silting up of the pool.

**Subsequently the marsh extends** over the surrounding ground. The depression in which the pool formed at the start is gradually filled in and eventually disappears completely. At this stage the characteristic plants are sedges (*Carex*), which grow in water-logged ground.

**By the end of this process of evolution**, the milieu has been completely transformed, and has either become a peatbog or developed a dense cover of deciduous plants, with water-loving trees such as willow, alder and poplar.

## BIOLOGICAL CYCLES OF POND LIFE

### A fertile environment

The paludal milieu, or marsh, is characterized by the vigorous growth of its vegetation. The production of vegetable matter, called primary production, is brought about by assimilation of air, sunlight, water and the chemical elements contained in the soil and the water. The primary production of marshes, lagoons and brackish ponds is very considerable (fifty times greater than that of a meadow or a mountain forest). It may be estimated to be three to eight times greater than the primary production of cultivated ground or tropical forest.

### A nutrient-rich environment

This environment is remarkably favourable to the development and

proliferation of unicellular plant organisms (cyanophytes or blue-green algae, diatoms, and chlorophytes or green algae). It provides an abundance of dissolved mineral salts and shallow water, which is essential if light is to penetrate and bring about photosynthesis. Unicellular algae are extremely rich in energy-producing and nutrient elements, which gives them a caloric protein rating six times higher than that of rice, and a vitamin content five hundred times that of cow's milk. Phytoplankton is used by the animals forming the zooplancton (larvae of crustaceans, molluscs and copepods, etc.). The proliferation of plant plancton is the first element of a complex food chain.

▲ *The iridescent yellow-green colouring of this zygoptera shows that it is a female* Calopteryx. *The male has bluish colouring. After fertilization, the female deposits her eggs in the tissues of an aquatic plant, dipping her abdomen into the water as far as the thorax.*

## The food chains

The marsh is a classic example of an ecosystem, which is a complete, complex, living entity. As we have seen, its abundant biological resources are based on an extremely rich primary production, which is the first link in the food chain.

*The producers* are represented by plant plancton and superior plant life. The plentiful supplies of algae are eaten by bacteria and numerous animals : molluscs, worms, crustaceans and vertebrates, including various species of fishes and birds.

*The primary consumers* feed directly on the producers; they are the zoo-plancton and crustaceans (tiny shrimps, daphnia), gastropods (leeches and water-snails), plant-eating insects, herbivorous fish and birds (coots, ducks and moorhens) and a very few mammals, such as the muskrat. From the unicellular algae and plant plancton in general, to the more evolved plant species, a wide range of food is available to the herbivorous animals (primary consumers) at the start of more or less complex food chains. The larger plant-eaters (crustaceans, molluscs, insects, birds and mammals) feed directly on the superior plant forms.

*The secondary consumers* feed on herbivorous animals : these secondary consumers include coleoptera (water beetles, water boatment, whirligigs), most dragonflies, carnivorous and omnivorous fish such as carp. Also part of this group are the amphibians, insectivorous birds and fish-eating birds (grebes, herons). Zooplancton in its turn provides food for larger animals, and the chain goes on up to the birds and predatory mammals.

*The tertiary consumers* feed on the secondary consumers, and therefore on carnivorous animals. They include pike, marsh harriers, water-snakes or fresh-water turtles.

*The detritivores* complete the biological cycle. Waste produced by the fauna settles to the bottom of the pond, and forms a fine layer of foul-smelling mud, rich in organic matter. This accumulation of decomposing organic matter forms the basis for another food chain, on which the detritivores depend. These are bacteria and fungi, and also those crustaceans and molluscs which feed on dead animals and plants of all kinds which they transform into mineral matter.

Obviously, many animals can belong to more than one level of the food chain : this is the case, for example, of the freshwater crayfish and the water turtle. And any marsh dweller can be in turn predator and prey.

### A melting pot of animal life

Such a plentiful production of organic matter constitutes a reserve of food resources which is essential for an intensive development of animal life. The marsh environment is ideal for this purpose. A great part of the evolution of species is closely linked to the paludal milieu, which is still a melting pot of animal and vegetable life.

◀ *The pool in the botanical gardens in Nancy is a fine example of a "natural" biotope created by man for wildlife conservation.*

▲ *The* anisoptera, *like this male dragonfly* (Libellula depressa), *keep their wings spread out when at rest.*

## A precarious habitat

As was described earlier, in the course of the natural evolution of a pond or marsh, the reedbeds are invaded by sedges, which form meadows that are colonized in their turn by trees. In the natural course of events, the precarious nature of such marshland is counterbalanced by the formation of new wetlands. Floodwater from rivers and lakes creates new habitats. The survival of fauna and flora is assisted by the migration of species from one stretch of water to another : swimming birds, dragonflies, aquatic coleoptera such as whirligigs, water beetles and water boatmen are capable of flying considerable distances to colonize new sites, often very far from their starting point. Seeds and the spawn of certain animals (water snails, amphibia, fish) can cling to the feathers of aquatic birds and be dispersed by this means. Wind is also important, carrying the seed of certain plants (*Typha, Phragmites*), as well as tiny living organisms in the form of dry and encapsulated spores. This is the case, particularly, with protista, small crustaceans, and worms.

## A habitat under threat

But the natural evolution of ponds and marshes is frequently disturbed by human activity, as when marshes are drained or ponds used as dumps for landfill, as is all too often the case. The banks of lakes and rivers are organized and "improved", preventing the formation of new wet zones which used to counterbalance natural drying-up.

Clearly, the only way to prevent the wetlands from disappearing is to preserve the marshes as they are now, with all their diversity of size and character. Various means may be used, such as controlling the development of vegetation to prevent drying out. When possible, ponds can be preserved by limiting the development of part of the sedge land and reedbeds, and stabilizing the limits of the adjoining woodland.

If necessary, we should take part in decision-making at local and national level in order to preserve our environment. The future of numerous species of animals and plants is closely linked to decisions that each of us makes every day.

# THE ECOLOGICAL VALUE OF WATER GARDENS

Well designed garden pools and ponds are real wild-life sanctuaries. In the suburbs or in intensively cultivated zones, their presence will certainly encourage the development of local species whose natural habitat is shrinking very fast.

## A garden for wild life

Help animals to settle into your garden by creating natural shelter : the indispensable compost heap, a heap of dead wood or some large stones piled up in a sheltered corner. Their requirements are varied. Amphibians appreciate the warm, sunny places which are essential for their metabolism. Outside their periods of rest and reproduction, they also venture quite a long way from their home pond to hunt. They need space to find food and choose a shelter. In a large pond, birds will appreciate appropriate nesting places and baskets and a supply of plants suitable

for nest-building. Certain species require winter feeding if they are to survive. Consider the zone around the garden as an extension of the garden. If you can encourage and conserve wild life in your local environment, you will increase the chances of survival of garden animals.

## Another style of gardening

How can the ornamental garden be made to co-exist with wild life? The presence of water is almost essential if you wish to attract wild life. Choose some plants to provide food for animals, and cultivate your local species (especially if they are endangered). These are fully acclimatized and their nectar attracts numerous insects. Put vegetable waste on the compost heap, and do not destroy dead leaves (unless they are diseased). The compost heap is a good place to put the silt you remove from the pond, and any surplus aquatic plants, which always make a lot of growth. Do not try too hard to tame nature. A little disorder in part of the garden will make life easier for the more timid animals. Since they feed mostly on

▲ *By managing the reedbeds and installing nest boxes, man can make a valuable contribution to the preservation of wetland flora and fauna.*

insects and fruit, animals are often killed by herbicides, insecticides and fungicides. Chemicals destroy some parasites, but their natural predators may be poisoned or starved as a result. Chemicals may also pollute your pond after a heavy shower of rain, even brief. They can transform your garden into a biological desert where only a few selected species can survive. Try to use only natural, home-made fertilizers (such as your own compost or a decoction of nettles).

By creating a water garden, you will enrich and diversify the wild life in and around your garden. You take an active part in nature conservation. Even if a garden can not·fully replace a natural habitat, it will contribute to the well-being and preservation of some species, and help to give a better understanding and appreciation of the wonders of nature.

Chapter
3

# From
# Concept
## to
# Creation

- PRELIMINARIES
- A WELL-DESIGNED POOL
- WATERPROOFING TECHNIQUES
- ESSENTIAL EQUIPMENT
- ORGANIZATION
- AERATION AND FILTRATION

# PRELIMINARIES

Whether you decide to create your pool yourself or have a professional do it, the most important thing is to have a clear idea of what you want of a water garden. Allow yourself time to define the style and atmosphere which best suit your requirements, and to draw up a precise plan.

BUILDING A POOL CAN involve a great deal of construction work and take a considerable amount of time. In some cases, it will prove difficult and expensive to undo what has already been done. If you plan to start work in spring, start planning several months before, in autumn.

### The garden of your dreams

Before starting to plan your garden, you should try to define as precisely as possible what you expect from it. This will increase your chances of success. Do you have visions of an ornamental pond of superb Japanese carp, or do you want to create a "natural" pool with plants which will provide shelter for a variety of amphibians and aquatic birds? Make a list of your preferences, or of the things you would certainly not want. If you like both the calm water of natural ponds and the murmuring of streams and cascades, there is no reason why you should not design a garden which includes both.

### Choice of style

The examples given in this book can serve as a source of inspiration, but will need to be adapted for your own garden, since no two gardens are alike. The most difficult thing will be to choose from among the many possibilities offered. You will have to respect a certain unity of style and certainly sacrifice a number of interesting ideas, in favour of one main guideline for the whole project. Avoid at all costs a garden which is an incoherent collection of bits and pieces - a Japanese bridge flanked by a barbecue and a summer-house. In general, a judicious choice of details in harmony with the overall style will help to ensure a coherent and pleasing result.

### Choice of site

Several factors must be taken into account in choosing the site for the pool.

• Sunlight is an essential element for the biological cycle of the pond, especially if it is to contain plants and animals.

• If it is situated close to the house, a terrace, or the main entrance to the garden, the pond will be a focal point of general interest. If, on the other hand, it is situated in a secluded position, at the end of the garden, it will be more a place for quiet contemplation.

• The point offering the best view of the pond : this may be the terrace, or a window, or any other position which suits your requirements.

• The nature of the terrain will of course impose certain logical constraints : a stream flows down from a high point to feed a pool at the lowest point of the garden.

• The presence of trees may limit the amount of sun the pond receives, and will also have an influence on winds. Leaves can be a problem in autumn, especially for small pools.

• Safety : if there are young children, always place the pool within view of the house; consider appropriate fencing.

• Water and power supplies, together with evacuation of overflows, may pose technical or financial problems.

### Orientation

For biological equilibrium, sunlight is vital : higher water temperatures accelerate the metabolism of fish and amphibians, and strong light activates the chlorophyll function of submerged plants, increasing the oxygen content of the water, which is essential for all the pond life. The pond must receive the

### PLAN FOR AN INFORMAL POOL TO CONTAIN AQUATIC FAUNA

By taking advantage of the contour lines and the general shape of the site, it is possible to create a sinuous outline, with bays, promontories and islands, which not only improve the general appearance of the pond, but make it more attractive to water birds and certain species of fish, which like to have a well-defined territory, an isolated, private area where they find shelter, protection from wind, and a certain degree of security.

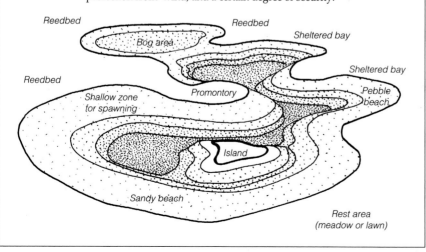

## CUT-AWAY DRAWING OF A WELL-DESIGNED POOL

sun for at least 6 hours per day, since flowering plants need large quantities of light. In summer, during the hottest hours of the day, the light shade provided by birch trees or albizzia, for example, will attenuate the intense radiation. Avoid having conifers near the water, however, since they can create dense shade at all seasons.

### Dimensions

Try to use available space to best advantage, since the bigger the pool, the more stable its biological equilibrium. If you wish to install plants and animals, make sure that you know their specific requirements - space, depth, etc. Certain plants such as some water lilies need a great deal of room if they are to flourish, about 2 m² (22 ft²) per plant. A small pool requires constant care, whereas a pond with a capacity of 5 m³ (175 ft³) or more requires comparatively little attention.

### Shape

The chosen outline depends on the style of the garden or the house. A

formal ornamental pool, which is usually of a regular geometrical shape, must harmonize with its environment. The shape of an informal pool, however, usually depends on the contours of the terrain. An informal pool will be more attractive to wildlife if its banks are long and sinuous, with sheltered bays where animals can find refuge.

### Depth

The depth of the pond also has a considerable influence on the biological process. 80-100 cm (30-40 in) of water are enough to create a degree of temperature stability sufficient to limit the damaging effects of abrupt temperature changes. The water remains cooler in summer and oxygenation is better, providing more favorable conditions for fish, which are also protected in winter when the surface of the pond freezes.

It is a good idea to vary the depth of the pond, to create a suitable biotope for all species of wildlife. But the maximum depth, in the centre, should not be more than 1.5 m (5 ft), if the water is to warm up thoroughly in spring.

The depth also has an influence on the aesthetic aspect, since it determines the

▲ *Whatever its style, a pool constructed with shelves at different levels makes planting easier, and offers a variety of biotopes for aquatic fauna.*

"colour" of the water, the degree of bottom visibility, the quality of sound of a waterfall. A purely decorative ornamental pond can be nothing more than a sheet of water a few centimetres deep.

### Shape of the sides

The sides of an ornamental pool in a frost-free site can be perfectly vertical. In temperate or cold climates, however, they should be slightly sloped, to absorb the thrust of the ice in winter. Ponds which are to be planted can be built with shelves at different levels, every 20-30 cm (8-12 in), for planting a variety of species in the best possible conditions.

Such an arrangement also suits aquatic fauna, offering a choice of depth according to the temperature of the water. A pond with stepped sides makes it easier to enter the water and to leave it. Moreover, the presence of a shallow zone all round the pool is a safety factor.

## Waterproofing techniques

A range of waterproofing material is available on the market. The choice will depend on the reliability of the material, its cost, and ease of use. It is necessary, also, to take into account its life expectancy, and technical or aesthetic consequences of the final choice. Keep an open mind, and examine the specific characteristics of each type of material before makinga final decision. The table below summarizes the most frequently-used materials, with their main characteristics.

## Extent and duration of work

If you intend to carry out the work yourself, thorough preparation will help you to evaluate the time required for each stage, and you will then be able to plan the job, spreading the tasks over as long a period as you wish. The best time to start excavations is early spring. Do not be daunted by the magnitude of the task : prepare each stage carefully, spend all the time necessary and employ all the required means.

Get help for the hardest jobs, and you will find that two people can do the work of three! Digging is very hard work, and not to be undertaken lightly. It will almost certainly be worth your while to hire a small mechanical digger or excavator, with a driver, especially for an area of more than 10 m² (110 ft²). Even if you have to hand-finish the job with pick and shovel, you will have saved a lot of time and energy.

## Budget

Because it modifies the very structure of all or part of the garden, the cre-ation of a water garden is a complex undertaking, requiring the application of a number of techniques whose cost can vary considerably from one case to another.

It may be said, in general, that the greater the expenditure the better the result, and it would be foolish to try to save costs, for example, by reducing the size of the pond. Biologically and aesthetically, this would be a mistake and would very soon be regretted.

Moreover, it would be much more expensive to try to extend the pond at a later stage. The best solution consists in retaining the whole project, and spreading the work and the expense over a period of two or three years. For example, carry out the excavation and the construction during the first year, then put in paths and do the planting over the following two years.

| WATERPROOFING TECHNIQUES | | | | | | | |
|---|---|---|---|---|---|---|---|
| MATERIAL | COST | STRENGTH | HANDLING | | | TYPES OF POOL | CHARACTERISTICS |
| | | | LAYING | THICKNESS | REPAIRS | | |
| CLAY | Variable | Mediocre | Easy | 100-300 mm (4-12 in) | Easy | All sizes | Natural appearance but vulnerable (frost, drought) ; can be damaged by roots and burrowing animals. |
| POLYANE | Low | Mediocre | Very easy | 0.2-0.5 mm (to 50th in) | Impossible | Temporary | Very limited resistance to UV (one season). Tears easily. |
| POLYTHENE LINER | Low | Poor | Very easy | 0.2-0.5 mm (to 50th in) | Impossible | Temporary | Sensitive to UV and tears easily. |
| PVC LINER | Medium · | Good | Easy | 0.5-1.2 mm (to 20th in) | Easy | Up to 1000 m² | Good resistance to UV and tearing, very flexible. Good value for money. |
| BUTYL RUBBER LINER | Medium | Good | Easy | 0.75-1 mm (to 25th in) | Easy | All sizes | As PVC, but more flexible, more expensive, more durable. Virtually unlimited life expectancy. |
| PREFORMED POOLS | High | Good | Easy | 2-8 mm (to 3rd in) | Easy | Small pools | Limited choice of shape, sides steep and smooth. Even stronger than PVC. |
| REINFORCED CONCRETE, SHUTTERED | Medium | Good | Difficult | 100-150 mm (4-6 in) | Difficult | All sizes | Very strong, but installation requires skill and expertise. Not for beginners. |
| REINFORCED CONCRETE, NOT SHUTTERED | Medium | Good | Difficult | 100-150 mm (4-6 in) | Difficult | All sizes | As above, but easier to vary shape. |
| POLYESTER RESINS | High | Very good | Difficult | 2-8 mm (to 3rd in) | Easy | All sizes | Light and indestructible, allows complete freedom of form, but installation is costly and difficult. |

## How will neighbours react?

Although you find your pond a source of endless pleasure and discovery, your neighbours will not necessarily share your enthusiasm, and may object, for example, to the sound of a waterfall or a *shishi odoshi (see p. 15)* or the croaking of frogs during the mating season.

Of course it is not just a simple question of volume of noise. The way a sound is perceived is highly subjective : what is a source of pleasure to one individual is thoroughly aggressive to another. Talk to your neighbours about it. It is often easy to find a solution to a problem of this sort if it is taken into account right from the start. People who are wary of ponds may raise the question of mosquitos, but the presence of amphibians and fish (which are very fond of the insect and its eggs) is a very natural and efficient method of eliminating this pest.

## Safety

The presence of water in a garden immediately rouses interest and curiosity, and is an obvious attraction to young children. Safety must be a major consideration. To eliminate the risk of drowning, a certain number of preventive steps can be taken :

• Teach children how to behave alongside water, and warn them clearly of the danger of falling in.

• Children under 7 have very little notion of danger. If they escape supervision for a few minutes, they·can go dangerously near to the edge of a pool (especially one that is out of sight of the house). This is almost inevitable when guests are present and the adults are engaged in conversation.

•It may be possible to prevent access to the danger zone by means of a barrier of some sort and a gate which can be locked. This barrier must be discreet, and blend naturally into the surroundings. It could take the form of a hedge,

a shrubbery, or a wall of local stone.

• All round the edge of the pond there should be a shallow zone, less than 20 cm (8 in) deep and at least 60 cm (24 in) wide, so that a person who falls into the water can get out easily. As was mentioned earlier, a shelved pond also has numerous advantages from the ecological viewpoint.

• Gently-sloping sections of bank will save from drowning a number of imprudent small animals : dogs, cats, hedgehogs.

• The pool must be clearly visible by day and by night (make provision for lighting, early in the planning stage), and the banks and margins must be regularly maintained.

• Paths around the pond should be sufficiently wide and stable.

• Finally, whatever precautions have been taken, it is very wise to take out insurance specifically against the unforeseeable dangers which your pond might present to a third party.

▲ *The safety factor must be taken into account right from the start. Children must be warned of the danger, and the youngest should not be allowed in the pool area without an adult. Take special care when guests are present.*

## Legislation

No special planning permission is required for building a pond in your garden. If you obstruct or divert a stream or river which crosses your property, you are operating within the zone of application of legislation concerning the management of free waterways, and the relevant authorities should be consulted.

If your pool should rupture or overflow, you would be responsible for any flood damage caused.

# ESSENTIAL EQUIPMENT

Although it is true to say that a well-designed pond creates its own biological balance, it may be useful or necessary, in certain cases, to make use of devices for stimulating the natural biological processes. A certain number of accessories can also be used to improve the general appearance of the water garden, or for ease of maintenance.

THE ESSENTIAL EQUIPMENT for the good management of a pool includes a supply of running water, generally coupled to a level compensator and a rain-water overflow system. In addition, filter and aerating equipment may be necessary, together with lighting for the pond and surrounding area. If at all possible, these should be planned from the beginning.

## WATER SUPPLY

### Choice of water

The water used to fill the pool must have satisfactory physical and chemical properties.

• **Town supply water :**  it is reliable, the quality being regularly controlled by local water authorities. The chlorine that it may contain is not a serious problem, since it is eliminated on contact with the air, if a spray jet is used for filling the pool. Chloramine, if used in your water district, would need to be neutralized with a proprietary, according to instructions.If the pool is some distance from the house, the pipes should be 60 cm (24 in) down to avoid freezing in winter. On a sloping site, it is simple to drain the pipes in autumn by means of a drain-cock installed at the lowest point. The water supply can safely be cut off in winter, since rainfall is usually sufficient for normal requirements.

• Spring water : a spring is an an excellent source of good quality running water. Check its chemical composition, and make sure that its output will be adequate for summer requirements.

Spring water,being at a constant temperature all the year, will raise the temperature of the pool noticeably in winter, and will tend to cool it in summer. If this is the case, it is always possible to divert part of the flow, retaining only the essential minimum. Spring water can also be heated up by directing it down through a series of sunny, shallow pools.

• **Well water :** its physical and chemical properties must be checked at regular intervals, because of the risk of pollution by the infiltration of various products : hydrocarbons, fertilizers, pesticides, etc. Its temperature is relatively low, all the year, and some precautions may be needed if it is used.

• **Rain water (run-off from roofs) :** this is soft water, but may contain pollutants. Its irregular, sometimes torrential flow is not always good for a pool; a heavy rain storm may make the water temperature fall abruptly. Make sure that zinc spouting is lined, to avoid any pollution of the run-off.

• **Stream water :** any diversion of public water must be subject to obtaining permission from the relevant authority (water board, municipal council, etc). Because of the fluctuating flow of streams, the pool should be fed from a partial diversion, so that the flow can be controlled. But there is always a risk of accidental pollution, unless the source of the stream is close by.

### Evaporation

Loss due to evaporation each year varies with climatic conditions. Although this loss is partially made up from rainfall, the biological balance of the pond can be upset and some compensation may be required from time to time. The ideal solution, of course, is a continuous supply.

• **Water from a spring or stream :** this may suffice to compensate losses, provided a constant flow can be maintained throughout the summer.

• **Well water :** this must be supplied to the pool by means of an electric pump. For reasons of economy, and in order not to cool down the pool unnecessarily, calculate the quantity of water to be replaced, according to the season, and arrange for the pump to turn on automatically, to supply the required quantity each day.

• **Roof run-off :** this is necessarily irregular and difficult to control, and will not be sufficient to replace loss from evaporation. But it can be used to supplement another source of supply and is not to be neglected in dry regions where water is scarce and expensive.

•**Town supply water :** control the flow with a ball-cock (level compensation). To avoid noises in the pipes, this device should be installed in a closed compartment where the float does not bob about in the wind.

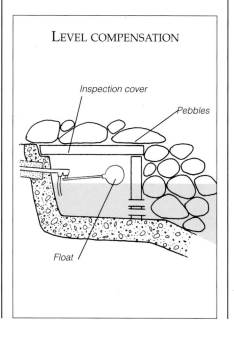

LEVEL COMPENSATION

Inspection cover

Pebbles

Float

# *EVACUATION OF WATER*

## When is a drainage pipe useful?

Paddling pools and small ornamental pools sometimes need to be emptied and cleaned. Specialist suppliers have systems suitable for all ponds, with drain fittings equipped with a vertical tube serving as an overflow pipe. Cut the tube to the desired height (usually 1-2 cm (half to 1 inch) less than the height of the pond margin, to determine the water level. The drainage hole opening and the overflow pipe should be covered with very fine netting, or a strainer.

A natural pool is never emptied completely (except if repairs are necessary), since such an operation would ruin all your efforts to build up a balanced biological environment. If it is absolutely necessary to drain water from a pond, it should be pumped or siphoned out. This method may also be used for smaller pools lacking modern drains.

## Overflow shoot or pipe

Some kind of overflow device might be provided in all pools, for two reasons :

• to prevent the pond from overflowing during heavy rain and erroding surrounding soil;

• to maintain a constant level when the pool is fed from a continuous source (spring, stream, piped water).

In one wall of the pond, make a horizontal opening, 20 cm (8 in) wide, at waterlevel i.e. 1-2 cm (half to 1 inch) below the level of the pond margin).

## Stormwater drain or sump

If the pool has an area of more than 15 m² (160 ft²), water from the overflow and from emptying operations must be directed into a sump or stormwater drain. Build a channel or instal a PVC pipe 5 cm (2 in) in diameter with a gradient of 3 cm (1 in): 1 m (3 ft). Be sure that the connection between the pond liner and the pipe or drainage channel is perfectly leak-proof. The sump is a hole about 80 cm (30 in) deep and 60 cm (24 in) square, filled with gravel, with an inspection cover over it.

# *PUMPS*

For water spouts, cascades and fountains you will need an electric pump on which different nozzles can be adapted according to the effect desired. One pump with two outlets can supply a cascade and a jet in the pool, but it is preferable to have one pump for each feature.

## Choice of pump

The choice of the pump will depend on the output required, the gradient and the length of the water column (the distance between the point from which the water is pumped and the head of the water-course or cascade). Always choose a pump which is correctly sized.

## Installing the pump

Surface-mounted pumps will be housed in dry, ventilated chambers, for increased protection against accidental shocks, freezing and corrosion.

Submersible pumps must be placed as close as possible to the surface of the water, but not so close as to suck in air. The water-pipe should be made of PVC, without any sharp elbows or narrowed sections. Remember never to let a pump run dry.

---

SEALING THE DRAINAGE PIPE

Whether PVC, fibreglass, or concrete is used for the pool, the drainage pipe must be perfectly leak-proof. Specialist water gardening centres supply drainage pipe installation kits.

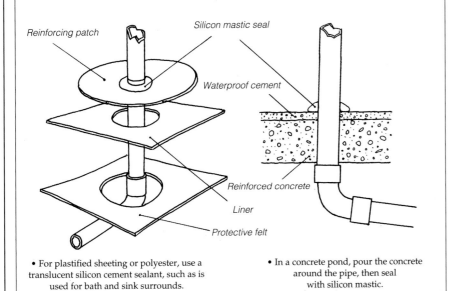

Reinforcing patch · Silicon mastic seal · Waterproof cement · Reinforced concrete · Liner · Protective felt

• For plastified sheeting or polyester, use a translucent silicon cement sealant, such as is used for bath and sink surrounds.

• In a concrete pond, pour the concrete around the pipe, then seal with silicon mastic.

## LIGHTING AND ELECTRICAL INSTALLATIONS

Electricity is essential for the operation of pumps, aerating equipment, lighting, etc, and the installation must be carried out with rigorous attention to detail. If the pool is more than 30 m (100 ft) from the house, or if there are a considerable number of accessories to be connected (three elements per circuit, at most), it is a good idea to install, close to the pool, a waterproof compartment to house the distribution panel for all the connections. This panel will be connected to the main switchboard by a cable under armoured PVC sleeving (with three cores of at least 4 mm² (5th in²) section, to avoid overheating) buried 50 cm (20 in). The size of the cable should be calculated on the total wattage/ampage of the equipment to be installed with an allowance for distance and possible future requirements. **N.B. If the house has no earthing system, or a defective system, it is vital that it be installed or replaced.**

### Pool lighting

**Submerged spotlights** use powerful bulbs (100-150 W), since water absorbs a fair proportion of the light; they must be perfectly waterproof.

• Equipment fixed into the pool wall (pumps, built-in spotlights) can be powered directly from mains (220-240 V) provided there is an equalizing link between the lighting equipment and any metal elements simultaneously accessible, less than 2 m (7 ft) away.

• Equipment not permanently fixed should be weighted before being submerged. It operates on low voltage (12 V), and can be powered from the mains through a step-down tranformer. Metal parts of the objects are connected to one another, but not earthed.

• **Non-submerged elements :** these are placed behind waterproof portholes and can be powered from mains (220-240 V). Metal parts must not be connected to conductive elements of the portholes; units are very expensive.

▲ *Lighting at ground level enhances the attraction of the pool and its surroundings. For outside use, a very low voltage (12 V) is required.*

### Garden lighting

If the pond is at some distance from the main path, make provision for some lighting of the surrounding area, for ease of movement at night. If it is well designed, this lighting will also enhance the interest of the pool itself, and the surrounding garden.

### Type of equipment

The area immediately surrounding the pool can be lit by spotlights with incandescent bulbs (21 W) or lamps with a built-in reflector (100-1000 W). They should be spaced as required, and concealed among the plants.
General lighting is provided by low bollards or standard lamps with one or several bulbs for 180° (356 °F) or 360° (680 °F) lighting, slightly directed towards the ground.
Lighting equipment must comply with official regulations, covering weatherproofing, stability of the beam and resistance to shocks and corrosion.

### Some safety rules

**N.B. A good electrical installation is a delicate undertaking. If you are not sure of your own ability in this field, it is preferable to entrust the installation of pumps and lighting to a professional who is familiar with regulations and safety standards.** Outside, especially near a pool, plugs and connecting boxes must be fully waterproof. Cables must be armoured. In general, outside lighting equipment

can be powered from mains (220-240 V). Efficient protection will be provided by equipping each circuit with a high sensitivity (30 mA) residual current device (RCD). Keep a plan of the electrical installation showing the position of spotlights, path, and depth of power supply cables. This will make it easier to locate the source of a breakdown, or change the lighting plan. It also reduces the risk of accident during subsequent digging operations.

## AERATION AND FILTRATION

The oxygenation provided by plants and the interchange between air and water determines the number and size of fish which can be introduced into the pool. The quantity of dissolved oxygen depends to a large extent on the water temperature : it is greater in cold water and in daylight hours. In summer, when the water heats up, the fish feed more, and this increases the quantity of organic matter, whose decomposition makes the dissolved oxygen content decrease. Some kind of mechanical or biological recycling must then be provided, to prevent accidents in overstocked pools or those in which conditions are unsatisfactory : pools which are too small and too shallow, lack of aquatic plants, excessive sunlight, etc.

### Recirculation

Apart from its aesthetic appeal, a fountain, stream or cascade serves a practical purpose: aerating the water and thus increasing its oxygen content, provided it flows continuously. If this is not the case, oxygenation can be carried out efficiently by means of a submerged pump equipped with a venturi. This device can be replaced by a heating element for melting ice in winter, making possible the escape of the fermentation gases produced by the decomposition of organic material.

## Biological filtration

For large pools, more than 5 m³ (175 ft³) capacity, biological filtration is preferable. The filter, occasionally built of brick or concrete but usually purchased ready-made, is composed of two or three compartments filled with filtering material. The pool water must circulate continuously through the filter, kept moving by a submerged pump. The material in suspension in the water settles on the filters, where it is decomposed by aerobic bacteria. These need the oxygen present in the water to transform the organic matter into non-toxic products. When the oxygen content is too low, anaerobic bacteria develop, but the organic matter is then transformed into toxic products. These exchanges of oxygen and carbon dioxide take place at the surface of the water, and it is therefore important that movement be maintained by fountains, cascades, sprays, etc. to renew the oxygen supply in the water passing through the filter.

**EXAMPLE OF A BIOLOGICAL FILTRATION SYSTEM**

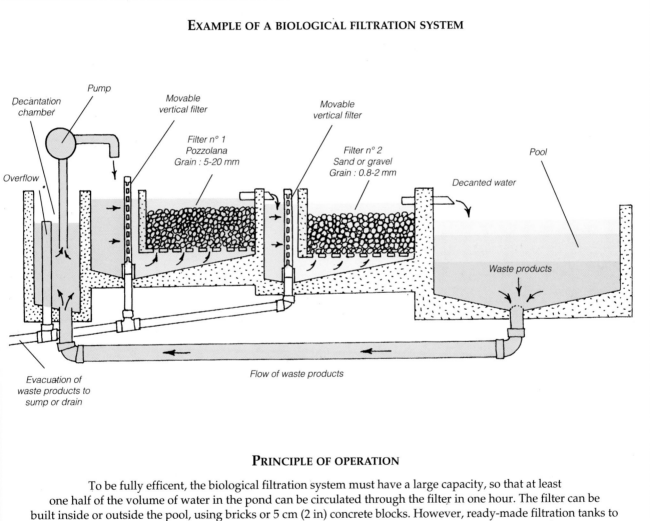

### PRINCIPLE OF OPERATION

To be fully efficent, the biological filtration system must have a large capacity, so that at least one half of the volume of water in the pond can be circulated through the filter in one hour. The filter can be built inside or outside the pool, using bricks or 5 cm (2 in) concrete blocks. However, ready-made filtration tanks to filter pools from 500-600 gallon capacity can be obtained from most good water garden centres. The pond water circulates continuously through the three compartments filled with gravel, pozzolana, river sand, etc, with a gauge of 0.8-20 mm (to 1 in). The particles in suspension in the water settle on the filters, and are decomposed by aerobic bacteria. These need the oxygen which is present in the water, in order to transform organic matter into non-toxic waste. Oxygen and carbon dioxide exchange takes place principally at the surface of the water, and the constant movement of the water through the filtration system ensures the best possible oxygenation.

# ORGANIZATION

To create a garden which will fulfil your expectations and give you satisfaction over a long period, it is best to carefully consider your site and your design ideas, and to draw up a proper plan, so as not to omit the important details. To help you with this work, here is an example of planned progression by stages which you can follow step by step.

FIRST MAKE A PERSPECTIVE drawing of your garden and a detailed design plan showing the position and size of the main permanent features of the site.

This will take a little time, but a well-prepared project will be more easily followed through to completion, and will enable you to avoid certain pitfalls.

Make sure that there are no private or municipal drains or other conduits in the area where you intend to dig your pond. If necessary, consult the appropriate authorities (water board, power board, telephone company, etc.)

## STAGE 1 : A PERSPECTIVE DRAWING

A perspective drawing of the garden will serve as a basis for a draft project. It should give a general view of the main features of the garden, from a particular viewing point.

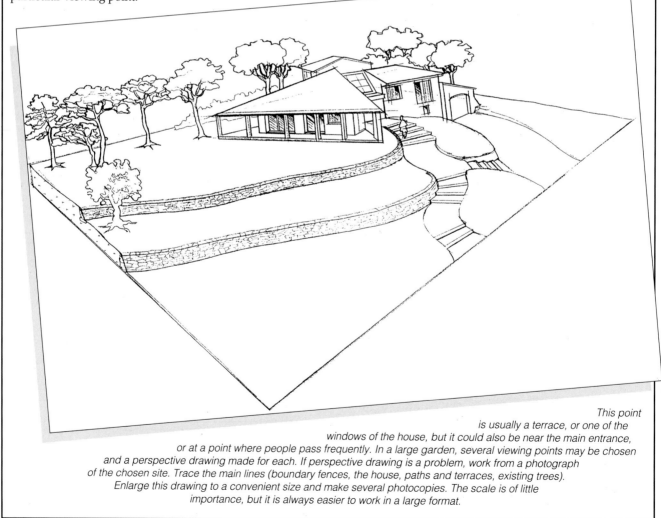

*This point is usually a terrace, or one of the windows of the house, but it could also be near the main entrance, or at a point where people pass frequently. In a large garden, several viewing points may be chosen and a perspective drawing made for each. If perspective drawing is a problem, work from a photograph of the chosen site. Trace the main lines (boundary fences, the house, paths and terraces, existing trees). Enlarge this drawing to a convenient size and make several photocopies. The scale is of little importance, but it is always easier to work in a large format.*

## STAGE 2 : THE DESIGN PLAN

The design plan gives an overall view of the garden in two dimensions. Draw it on squared paper, which will make it easier to calculate the dimensions which you will need for the construction.

**1 - Make the measurements :** first make a very rough sketch on which you will note all the measurements you make. Use a measuring tape and note the dimensions of the garden and of the house, including the width of any openings (doors, windows). Note the distance between the house and different elements of the garden (fences, paths, trees, etc). If your property is on a slope, measure the different levels, starting from the highest point. Indicate the zones shaded by the trees, the house, and fences or walls, at different hours of the day.

**2 - Drawing the plan :** trace the exact plan of the property on a sheet of squared paper 5 or 10 mm (fifth-2 fifths of an inch) squares. Choose a scale which will enable you to show clearly all the important details, for example 1 : 50  1 cm (half an inch) on the plan = 50 cm (20 in) on the ground, or 1 : 25  1 cm (half an inch) on the plan = 25 cm (10 in) on the ground. To make it easier to read the distances on the plan, mark in blue pencil the lines which represent every metre or two metres. It is a good idea to have several copies of this design plan, so that you can sketch out different ideas.

*Use a survey map or an architect's drawing of your property, if you have one. Make a copy on squared paper to the required scale (use a photocopy machine with a reduction/enlargement feature). You will then be able to calculate directly on the plan all the distances between the different features of the garden.*

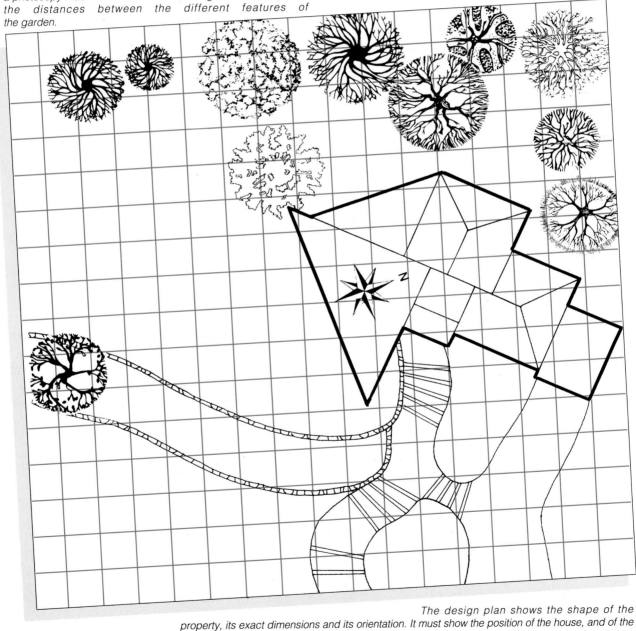

*The design plan shows the shape of the property, its exact dimensions and its orientation. It must show the position of the house, and of the doors and windows opening on to the garden, and any other hard features : paths, terrace, walls, planters, pergolas, summerhouse, etc. Do not forget to note the position and dimensions of the trees you wish to retain.*

## STAGE 3 : DRAFTS OF THE PROJECT

In the design plan and the perspective drawing, you have all the important elements for the framework of the garden. From this starting point, you can begin to get your ideas down on paper.

1- Start by making a list of the characteristics which best define your conception of what a water garden should be. This will help you to sort out your ideas and make a choice, in order of preference, from among the many possibilities offered.

2 - On the perspective drawing, pencil in the different elements of your project, starting with the outline of the future pond, which you should also draw on the design plan, in order to have some idea of its proportions in relation to the garden as a whole, and of the general effect. At this stage you can sketch out a number of projects, and make your final choice later.

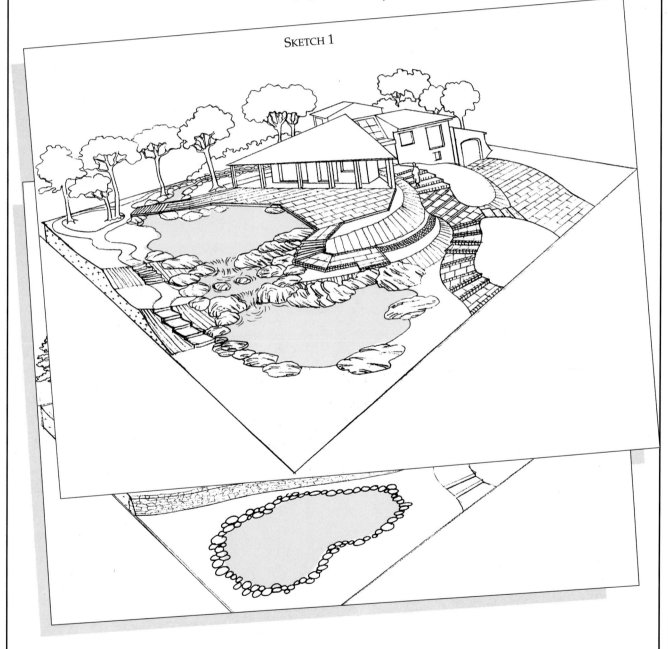

SKETCH 1

3 - Now sketch in the other important elements of the composition : bridge, groups of rocks, large trees, stream, cascades, fountains, platforms, decking, etc. Take your time over this. If you think you have found the ideal site for the pond, go into the garden and mark the outline on the ground with a thin rope or hosepipe, to obtain some idea of the general effect. In the same way, you can mark the position of paths, and see whether they will be satisfactory.

## STAGE 4 : THE WORKING PLAN

When you are sure of your choice, it will be time to draw up a detailed working plan, which is based on the design plan, and will be your principal tool throughout the construction period. It must show the precise position and final dimensions of the pool, and the main constructions : paths, stepping stones, terrace, bridges, watercourses, etc.

The working plan should also indicate the position of all the technical equipment : electrical power supply, submerged pump, overflow, water supply and discharge, sump, biological filter, level regulator etc.

It will also show the position of certain optional equipment : drains, underground irrigation, lighting, fountains, filters, aerators, drain plug, etc.

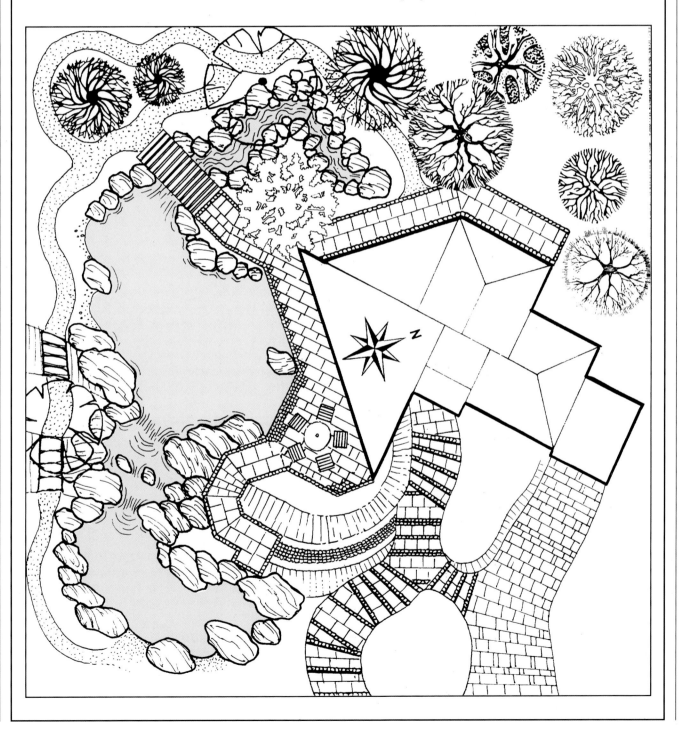

## STAGE 5 : EXCAVATION PLAN

From the working plan, draw up an excavation plan showing the contour lines which define the shape and depth of the excavation.

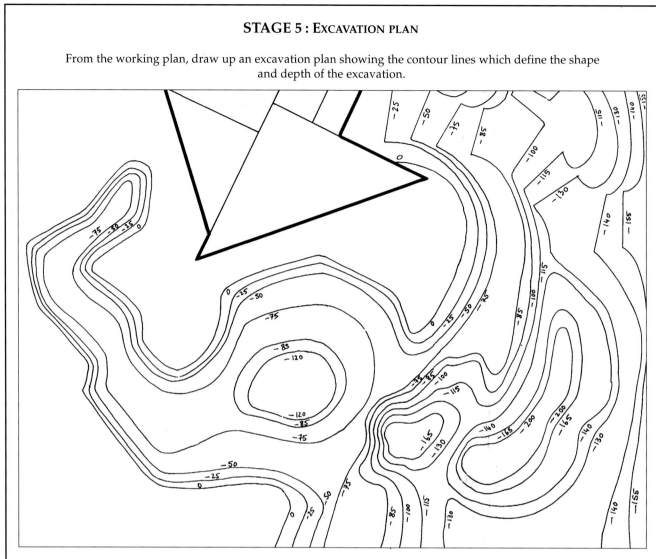

*This plan is particularly useful when the pool is a big one, with a complex shape, and will prove very helpful to the operator of the mechanical digger : it shows the different depths of the pool and takes into account the thickness of the foundation and of the construction material or liner.*

## THE EXCAVATION

### Manual or mechanical ?

If the pond is not too big, up to 15 m² (160 ft²) you can do the digging yourself, as long as you are fit. This is often a long, hard job. The advantage of hand-digging is that you can shape the hole precisely as you wish.

For a larger pool it is preferable to use a mechanical digger of some kind. Suitable machines can be hired, with or without a driver, at reasonable cost. You will save a lot of time and energy, but you will still have to use pick and shovel for the precise, finishing touches.

### How to dispose of the spoil

Because of natural expansion, the volume of earth removed from the hole will be far greater than the volume of the hole itself, 3 to 15% more, depending on the soil type. You can use the spoil to remodel your garden - build a raised area near the pool, for instance. Separate the good topsoil from the subsoil, which is relatively infertile.

You can use the latter to model the contours, then cover it with 30-40 cm (12-16 in) of good loam. Do not spread the spoil around the pond. If you can not use it all, get rid of the subsoil and keep only the quantity of topsoil you will need for future planting.

In this case, you will need means of transport to remove the spoil when the excavation is completed.

### When to start work?

If you employ a professional, it all depends on when he/she is free. If you do the digging yourself, a small pond can be started nearly any time the soil is not frozen hard, or too wet and waterlogged.

Much depends on the soil : heavy clay is sticky in winter and too hard in summer, and can best be worked in fine spring and autumn weather.

## STAGE 6 : LINER INSTALLATION PLAN

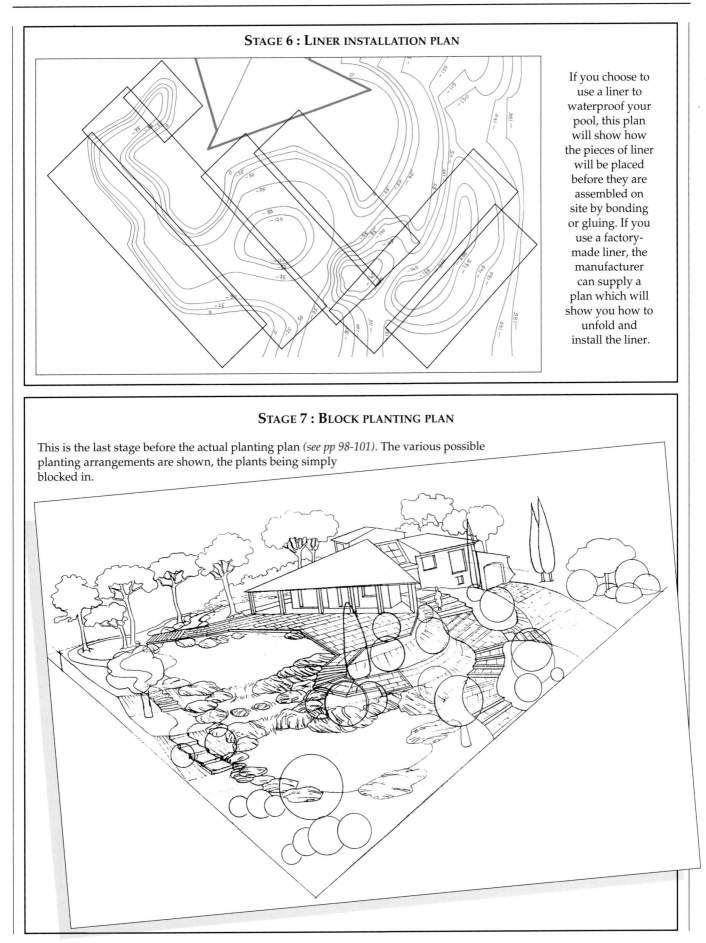

If you choose to use a liner to waterproof your pool, this plan will show how the pieces of liner will be placed before they are assembled on site by bonding or gluing. If you use a factory-made liner, the manufacturer can supply a plan which will show you how to unfold and install the liner.

## STAGE 7 : BLOCK PLANTING PLAN

This is the last stage before the actual planting plan *(see pp 98-101)*. The various possible planting arrangements are shown, the plants being simply blocked in.

# FLEXIBLE LINERS

The liner technique is used by many professionals, and it is certainly the one most accessible to the amateur, in terms of cost and ease of installation. Good material is available, with the manufacturer's guarantee of durability. Even if you are not a DIY expert, you will be able to obtain good results with this method.

THE DAYS WHEN TRUCK tarpaulins were used for making small pools or irrigation ponds are long gone. Modern technology has provided us with a wide range of different liners manufactured from synthetic materials and specially designed for the construction of garden pools.

## CHOICE OF LINER

Rectangular liners are available in a wide range of standard sizes, but can also be cut to measure, in strips from 4-8 m (13-26 ft) wide. Quality products always carry a guarantee.

### Choice of material

The material chosen must be non-toxic, and its composition should be clearly stated.

• *Polyvinyl chloride* (PVC) is a synthetic material which can be flexible (pond liners) or rigid (preformed pools). It is frostproof down to -35 °C (-31 °F) and does not rot. PVC liners can be stretched somewhat, so they can be made to fit the shape of the excavation perfectly, and provide a degree of resistance to puncturing.
Sheets of PVC are easily assembled by cementing, so it is possible to make liners for pools of any shape or size, even those measuring more than 1000 m² (10,760 ft²). To avoid any risk of water pollution, and for good durability, the PVC should be UVI-treated and contain no impregnated algaecides. PVC is a material often chosen by professionals, because it is easy to use and reliable. Depending on the manufacturer, a PVC liner has up to a 10 year guarantee.

• *Butyl rubber* is a flexible, rubber-like synthetic. It is very tough, carries a 20 year guarantee, and has a life expectancy of up to 50 years. It is relatively expensive in comparison with PVC, but far outperforms it in life expectancy, flexibilty, and puncture resistance .

• *Polyethylene* (or *polythene*) is a fine plastic film suited to friable clay. Its principal disadvantage is a lack of resistance to puncturing and cutting, since the material available for liners is very thin (0.05-0.20 mm).

• *Polyane* is a transparent plastic film. It is not suitable for waterproofing outdoor pools (unless placed between two layers of concrete), since it rots rapidly when exposed to sunlight (UV), within the space of one summer.

### Thickness

Liners are usually proposed in the following gauges : 0.5 mm (50th in), 0.8 mm (2 ply), 1.0 mm (3-ply) and 1.5 mm (4-ply). A thickness of 0.5 mm (50th in) is the minimum for a small pool, and 1 mm (25th in) is sufficient for most medium-sized ponds. On stony ground or for larger areas choose a thicker liner, even though it will be heavier and less flexible, and consequently less easy to manipulate.

## CALCULATING THE SIZE OF THE LINER

To calculate the size of the liner required, measure the maximum length and breadth of your pool. To each dimension, add double the maximum depth of the pool, then 2 x 40 cm (16 in) to allow for a flap at the edge.

• For example, for a pool measuring 6 m (20 ft) long, 3 m (10 ft) wide and 1 m (3 ft) deep, the liner must measure 8.80 m (28 ft 8 in) x 5.80 m (18 ft 8in), i.e. :

length = 6 m (20 ft)+ [2 x 1 m (3 ft)] + [2 x 0.40 m (16 in)] = 6 m (20 ft) + 2 m (6 ft) + 0.80 m (32 in) = 8.80 m (28 ft 8 in),
width = 3 m (10 ft)+ [2 x 1 m (3 ft)] + [2 x 0.40 m (16 in)] = 3 m (10 ft) + 2 m (6ft) + 0.80 m (32 in) = 5.80 m (18 ft 8 in).

You will also require a protective mat (rot-proof horticultural felt, fibreglass loft insulation) of the same dimension.

## FOR LARGE POOLS...

Butyl rubber or PVC can be used to make pools measuring more than 1000 m² (10,760 ft²), by bonding together a number of liners to obtain the required dimensions.

You can also have a liner made to your exact requirements, by supplying the manufacturer with a detailed plan of the pool. It will be delivered in a carton or on a pallet as is appropriate, and may weigh as much as 1-1.5 kg/m² (2-3 lb/ft²).

## CEMENTING AND BONDING PVC LINERS

The assembling of PVC elements by cementing or hot air bonding is a simple technique, so it is easy to use
to create pools with complex shapes and varied levels, and watercourses such as cascades and streams.
It is indispensable for fixing the liner to a solid support (wall, edge of terrace), or for installing certain accessories
such as overflow pipes, drainage plugs and level regulators. This technique can also be used to remove wrinkles
in the liner after it has been placed in the hole. Soften the PVC by heating it slightly with a hot air blower
then flatten the wrinkles by cementing or bonding them down. In some cases it may be preferable to slit
the folds with a sharp blade, then cement or bond the edges together.

### CEMENTING

PVC cement is in fact a high-density chemical solution containing a tetrahydrofuran solvent. The surfaces to be assembled are
superficially dissolved, then pressed together. Once the solvent has evaporated, the two surfaces are firmly stuck together. Since it is
difficult to apply good, even pressure on an uneven base, it is best to slide a plank under the parts to be cemented so that
strong pressure can be exerted.

*Note : A cement for rigid PVC is not suitable for a flexible liner, but the cements for flexible PVC work very well on rigid PVC.*

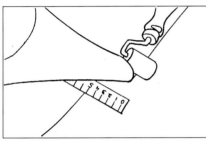 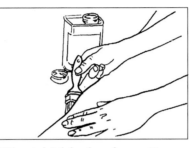 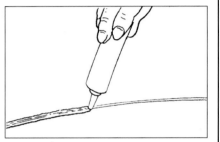

1 Put the two strips of PVC one on top of the other with an overlap of 50 mm (2 in). The surfaces to be cemented must be perfectly clean and free of grease (fingermarks). If necessary, wipe with a damp cloth then with cotton soaked in methylated spirit.

2 With a pig-bristle brush, apply cement to the two facing surfaces, over a length of about 50 cm (20 in), then press together with a paper-hanger's roller. Try to work as cleanly as possible, taking care not to let the cement run.

3 Allow the solvent to evaporate, then complete the seal by applying a strip of liquid PVC on the edge of the overlap to fix it down and prevent it from being ripped by garden tools.

**If there is a problem :**

Unlike hot air bonding, it is impossible to repeat a cementing operation, since a part of the material has been dissolved. Two solutions are
possible :
• A very small leak can be repaired with liquid PVC.
• If there is a large leak or the cement has not "taken", glue on a patch of PVC larger than the defective zone. It is important that no cement
should have been allowed to run over the area to be repaired, since it dissolves the surface. When the patch has been fixed in place, apply
a strip of liquid PVC all round the edge of the patch, to prevent it from being torn off, for example by energetic cleaning operations.

### HEAT BONDING

Two pieces of PVC can be bonded together with a controlled temperature hot air blower with a flat nozzle about 50 mm (2 in) wide.
The two sections of the liner are melted then pressed together. Put a board under the liner so that firm, steady pressure can be exerted.

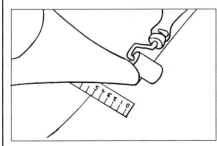 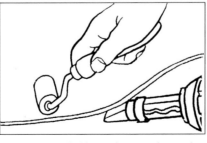

1 When the hot air reaches the desired temperature, direct the nozzle between the two layers of line, to a width of about 50 mm (2 in) keeping it flat.

2 Then move the blower along, simultaneously pressing hard with a paperhanger's roller over the section already bonded.

3 To hold down the edge of the top layer of liner (and prevent tools, etc., from catching in it) run a strip of liquid PVC along the seam.

It is a good idea to do a test on a scrap of PVC to make sure that the temperature is suitable. To keep a constant temperature,
the blower must not be turned off during the bonding operation. If necessary, the operation can be repeated several times on
badly-bonded sections. **N.B. We must stress that the above method is included for purposes of completeness and would
invalidate any supplier's or manufacturer's warranties. It is also not a technique for amateurs.**

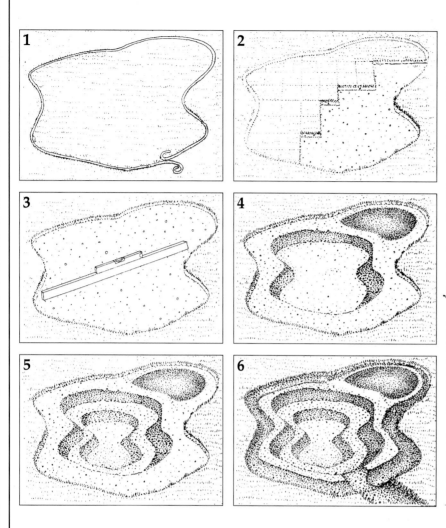

## THE EXCAVATION

1 With a cord or a hosepipe, trace on the ground the external shape of the whole water zone, including the pool and the bog area. The surface thus marked out must be perfectly level, because it corresponds to the water level in the future pond. Call this level 0.

2 Over the whole marked area, dig down to level 1, which will be 10 cm (4 in) lower than level 0. If the area was previously grassed, cut the turf out in sheets, and set aside.

3 Use a straight-edge and a spirit level to check that the bottom is perfectly flat. If the ground slopes at all, establish your level from the lowest point.

4 Mark out the pond area and the bog area, about 20 cm (8 in) apart, and dig the pond area down to level 2, which will be 40 cm (16 in) below level 0. Dig the bog area so that it slopes gently down to a depth of 35 cm (14 in).

5 At the bottom of level 2, mark out the position of level 3, which will be 80 cm (30 in) below level 0 and dig down to that point. In large ponds several further levels can be created, either by deepening the centre, down to 150 cm (60 in), or by making each level shallower. Planting shelves must be at least 35 cm (14 in) wide, so that planting baskets can be installed.

6 Dig a trench 10 cm (4 in) deep all round the wet zone. Then tamp the bottom and sides of the different levels firmly, and remove any hard or sharp objects which might damage the liner. Dig a trench 30 cm (12 in) wide and 60 cm (24 in) deep for the water supply and evacuation pipes, and for the power cables.

## INSTALLATION AGAINST A WALL

When the pond is to be at the foot of a wall or at the edge of a terrace, the liner can be cemented or bonded to the masonry, by means of PVC-coated aluminium sections. Rigid sections can be used for rectangular ponds, and flexible material is available for curved shapes.

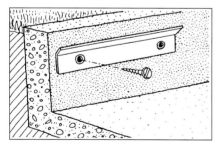

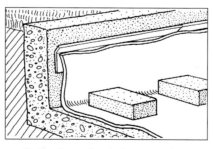

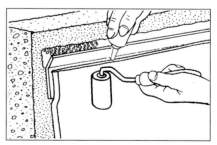

1 Use a chalk line to trace on the wall a perfectly horizontal line corresponding to the water level in the pond. Present the first section and mark the position of the screw-holes, then drill the holes in the masonry (use a bit for concrete). Insert rawlplugs then fix the section to the wall with stainless steel countersunk head screws.

2 Fix the other sections in the same way. Put the liner in place, making sure that it sits tightly against the walls and fits the bottom perfectly. To avoid the effect of tension by the water on the liner, and therefore on the aluminium sections, hold the liner in place with bricks, or any other smooth, heavy object.

3 Press the liner against the section then fix it in place (hot or cold bonding). The section can be made completely invisible under the water if the upper part is filled in with neoprene or silicone filler mixed with a little fine sand. In this case, the wall on which the section is fixed must be thoroughly water-proofed with a synthetic resin.

## *INSTALLATION*

### Shape of the pool

Flexible liners are ideal for irregularly shaped, informal pools where a natural look is required. The sides can be made to slope down very gently in places, to form pebble beaches, for example, the rest being more or less vertical, but sloping slightly outwards. Avoid sharp angles; rounded shapes are more harmonious and easier to construct. No part of the liner should be visible : in this way it will be protected from sunlight, and the pond will have a more attractive and natural appearance.

It is not necessary to make provision for a drainage plug, which would create a possible risk of leakage in the liner. You may wish to install an overflow pipe at the pool margin so that rainwater can be evacuated.

### Depth of the hole

Although the liner itself is very thin, it will be laid on a bed of sand, 5-8 cm (2-3 in) thick and this must be taken into account, as must the thickness of the layer of soil in the bottom of the pool, for planting, and the layer of pebbles on the margin, all of which reduce the depth of available water. The hole must therefore be the appropriate amount deeper than the desired depth of water.

If the pond is large, the flexibility of the liner will enable you to have as many different depths as you like. Do not forget to create a bog area as a natural extension of the pond.

### Precautions for use

Liners made of butyl and PVC are tough enough to stand up to a certain amount of trampling during the construction work, provided there are no sharp or pointed objects at the bottom of the pool or in the planting medium, which should be sieved before being placed in the pool, to get rid of any suspect objects (sharp stones, fragments of glass, nails, etc.). Be careful when handling garden tools.

Liners are usually installed on a tough undersheet of some kind, to act as a protective cushion against tree roots, burrowing animals, and so on : horticultural felt or polypropylene matting are suitable materials. It is also possible to lay a foundation composed of 5-8 cm (2-3 in) of concrete, or fine sand mixed with 15% of cement, without the addition of water, as is done for pools made of synthetic resin (see p.76).

### Other uses

Being so very easy to handle, liners are very useful for waterproofing barrels and basins, and raised ponds built of brick or concrete blocks. Use them to construct watercourses or shallow bog gardens.

### Maintenance

In normal conditions of use, flexible liners require no special maintenance. A moderate but regular drop in the water level may be due to :

• Increased evaporation caused by high temperatures and wind over the preceding days.

• The presence of cascades and fountains, which increase water loss from evaporation and splashing.

• Siphoning of water (by capillary action) out of the pool when lawn grass or certain marginal plants come in contact with the water.

All these problems can easily be overcome by installing a level regulator.

If the waterlevel drops very suddenly and noticeably, there are several possible causes :

• There may be small leaks at the junctions between cascades and

---

intermediate pools.

• The liner may have been punctured accidentally, by a garden tool or a dog's claws. The thinnest liners (polyane) can be perforated by a sharp stone in the planting medium.

Allow the water level to stabilize, and locate the leak. Holes can be repaired very easily with Patch kits available from reputable water garden suppliers.

•It may happen that water escapes from the side of the pool, because of a slight subsidence, which may occur when the edges of the liner have been buried under the bank and somebody walks there in wet weather. In this case it will be necessary to check the perimeter of the pool to find where the damage is.

• If it was badly laid in the first place, the PVC liner may have been partly exposed to sunlight for a number of years and have taken on a dull and brittle look. This will happen in any case with PVC liners. There is no remedy for this damage caused by UV radiation, but if the affected area is not too great, try cleaning it carefully and covering it with a large piece of new liner bonded over the old, damaged section.

## LAYING THE LINER

Butyl rubber and PVC liners are more flexible and easier to handle if the temperature is over 15 °C (59 °F). Have ready the necessary quantity of soil (sieved to remove stones, nails, fragments of glass, etc.) or well-washed sand for the bottom of the pond and the planting shelves. A layer of 20-30 cm (8-12 in) of soil is required for direct planting.

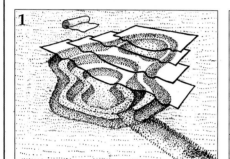

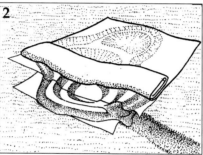

1 Lay strips of protective underfelt or matting, with an overlap of about 15 cm (6 in).

2 Place the liner in the centre of the cavity, in the correct position, and unfold it.

3 Weight the edge of the liner with smooth, heavy objects (bricks or big pebbles) placed far enough back from the cavity not to be dragged in. If the pool has sharp corners, make neat folds in the liner at the angles; it will be too late to do so once the water is in.

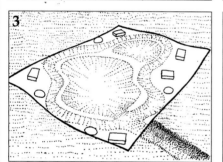

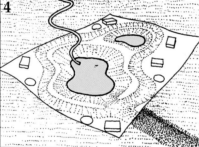

4 Start filling the centre of the liner gradually with water. The liner will stretch and mould itself to the contours of the pool, without creasing. Half-fill the pool and the bog area. If the liner is too taut at any point, remove some of the weights so that the liner can slip down a little.

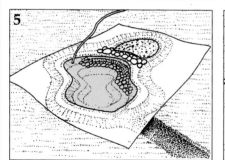

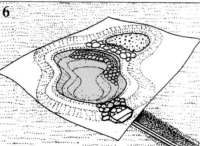

5 Stop filling when the water is a few centimetres below level 1, which is 10 cm (4 in) down. Cover level 2 with pebbles and soil covered with a fine layer of gravel. Place pebbles at water level on the zone separating the pool from the bog area (level 1). Siphon the water out of the bog area and fill with 30 cm (12 in) of good soil.

6 Put the automatic filling kit (level control) in place and weigh it down with pebbles. The housing should be surrounded with pebbles to filter organic matter in the water and prevent ripples from affecting the float. Otherwise the water pipes may make strange noises.

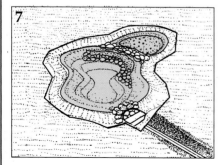

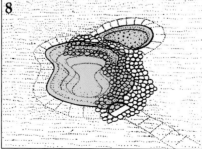

7 Complete filling to level 0. Allow to settle for a few days, then cut the liner 20 cm (8 in) above water level.

8 Fold the edge of the liner under, and push it under the surrounding grass, then cover the visible parts with the reserved turf.

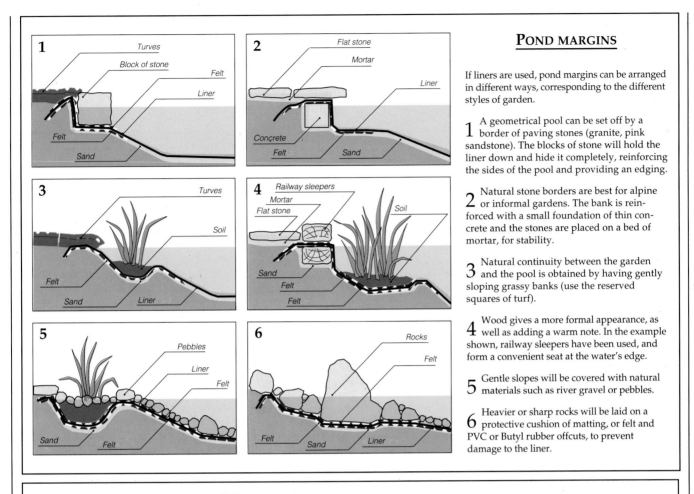

## POND MARGINS

If liners are used, pond margins can be arranged in different ways, corresponding to the different styles of garden.

1 A geometrical pool can be set off by a border of paving stones (granite, pink sandstone). The blocks of stone will hold the liner down and hide it completely, reinforcing the sides of the pool and providing an edging.

2 Natural stone borders are best for alpine or informal gardens. The bank is reinforced with a small foundation of thin concrete and the stones are placed on a bed of mortar, for stability.

3 Natural continuity between the garden and the pool is obtained by having gently sloping grassy banks (use the reserved squares of turf).

4 Wood gives a more formal appearance, as well as adding a warm note. In the example shown, railway sleepers have been used, and form a convenient seat at the water's edge.

5 Gentle slopes will be covered with natural materials such as river gravel or pebbles.

6 Heavier or sharp rocks will be laid on a protective cushion of matting, or felt and PVC or Butyl rubber offcuts, to prevent damage to the liner.

## MAKING A WATERCOURSE WITH A LINER

The stepped shape of this watercourse (see cut away diagram below) allows for bog areas at each level, with no risk of soil escaping from the planted areas. Each cascade is made of a barrage of stones over which the water must flow, each level being treated as a small pool. The liner must be completely masked by rocks, pebbles and plants.

• Trace the path of the watercourse and remove the top layer of soil.
• At each level, dig out the bed of the watercourse (central zone) and the planting trenches on either side.
• Lay the liner in the same way as for the pool. Bond any different sections together to prevent leakage.
• Fill with water temporarily to make sure that the arrangement of the stones is satisfactory.
• On the dry liner, lay a bed of mortar (3 parts fine sand to 1 part cement), then lay the stones to give a natural effect. Allow the mortar to dry for 2 or 3 days.
• Rinse abundantly to remove all trace of cement from the water. Install the soil and the plants, then cover the soil with a layer of river gravel.
Cut away drawing of a watercourse made with a liner

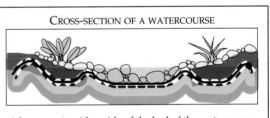

CROSS-SECTION OF A WATERCOURSE

A bog area on either side of the bed of the watercourse hides the liner completely.

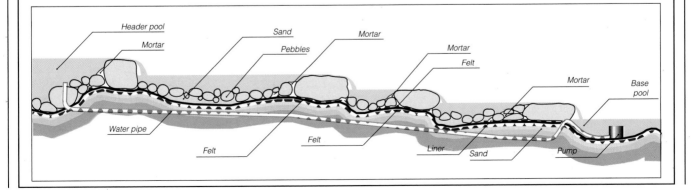

# SYNTHETIC RESINS

Robust, light and resistant, synthetic resins moulded on the pool site combine the adaptability of flexible liners with the strength of reinforced concrete. A good deal of care is required, but the task is well within the capabilities of any good DIY enthusiast, and the range of shapes and sizes that can be created is unlimited.

SYNTHETIC RESINS, WHICH ARE derived from the coal and petro-chemical industries, are very durable materials used for plasticizing. They are weather-proof, and acid and UV-resistant. The types most often used for water-proofing garden pools are epoxy and polyester resins.

### Reinforced polyester

More reasonably priced than epoxy resin, polyester resin comes in the form of a gel of a watery consistency, translucent and sometimes coloured, to which a small quantity of catalyst must be added. It is reinforced by means of one or several layers of woven glass fibre fabric (fibre-glass matting). Once it has hardened, polyester resin is a perfectly inert material representing no danger to the flora and fauna of the pond.

Polyester resin is in general use in industry, building and public works. It lends itself particularly well to the construction of pools, streams, cascades, paddling pools, swimming pools and the like, and is an ideal material for waterproofing containers of various kinds made of wood, concrete or fibro-cement.

### How to use it

After digging the hole, the first thing to do is to build a sub-base, which will also serve as a form : to model the shape of the bottom and the sides of the pool, it is customary to use a mixture of fine sand and cement, without the addition of water, which will solidify slowly when it comes into contact with the moisture in the air, and will be completely set in 48 to 72 hours. If this method is used, the shape of the form can be remodelled at will, even after the normal hardening time has elapsed. This technique makes it possible to create an infinite variety of natural, curving forms which will serve as a base for the resin, and eliminates the problems of shuttering and setting which are often encountered when traditional mortars or concretes are used. When it has set, the sub-base is covered with kraft paper to form a clean, dry base for the next operation, in which two layers of fibreglass matting are applied alternately with two layers of resin. The resin can be applied like paint, with a brush or roller, or sprayed on under pressure.

Polymerization is produced by adding a catalyst just before use. Setting will take from 15 to 30 minutes, depending on the temperature. The resin must be applied carefully, and it is important to avoid contact with the skin or eyes. The last operation consists in applying a topcoat of tinted resin. Once the resin has set completely, the pool should be filled to check that the waterproofing is perfect. Then trace a horizontal line 1-2 cm (half to one inch) above the desired water level, and cut off the excess polyester with a power tool equipped with a disc.

### Shape of the pool

Pools of any shape, regular or irregular, can be built using polyester. Depending on the style, a variety of materials can be used for the sub-base : bedding mortar (used dry), shuttered or unshuttered concrete, compacted earth covered with tar-paper, clay, polyurethane foam (which is allowed to harden, then cut or sawed into shape to form rocks), newspaper or jute sacking soaked in plaster or very liquid cement. Any of these materials can be used in combination to obtain the required shapes.

---

### MOULDED POLYESTER

#### ADVANTAGES

- Complete freedom in creation
- Its light weight about 5 kg/m² (11 lb/yd²) makes it possible to build pools even on balconies and roof terraces.
- Digging is reduced to a minimum, since the polyester shell is very thin 5 mm (fifth of an inch) and the sub-base is from 2-8 cm (1-3 in) thick : it is therefore not necessary to dig much deeper than the proposed depth of the pool.
- The mechanical resistance of polyester to puncturing, tension and compression is exceptionally good, so it is not damaged by stones, roots, garden tools or rodents.
- Fully frost and UV resistant.

#### DISADVANTAGES

- Relatively expensive.
- The moulding operation can be carried out in dry weather only. It requires accuracy and speed, and several people are needed to do the job.
- When they are applied, the resin and the solvent (acetone) are both toxic, and should not be inhaled or allowed to come in contact with the eyes. It is essential to wear safety goggles.

### How to organize the work?

The application of resins is an operation which must be carried out with meticulous care and attention to cleanliness. The air bubbles which are imprisoned in the resin as it is applied must be carefully eliminated, since they could be the source of leaks in the finished construction if allowed to remain. Because polyester hardens very rapidly, the latter operation requires the presence of an assistant or two working in coordination with the person who is applying the resin. This is the only way of making sure that no area is omitted.

## Renovation with resin

A pool made with masonry may fissure in the long term. Whether it is made from reinforced concrete, bricks or natural stone, leaks can be prevented or repaired by applying a layer of polyester resin directly on to the support material, as long as this is pe rfectly clean. If the concrete is fresh, wait until it has dried out thoroughly (about 3 weeks) before applying the resin, or use a layer of tarpaper to isolate the resin from the moisture in the concrete. This technique can be used to renovate old pools. As a general rule, it is preferable to apply two layers of resin reinforced by fibreglass matting, which will make it possible to keep the resin separate from the support.

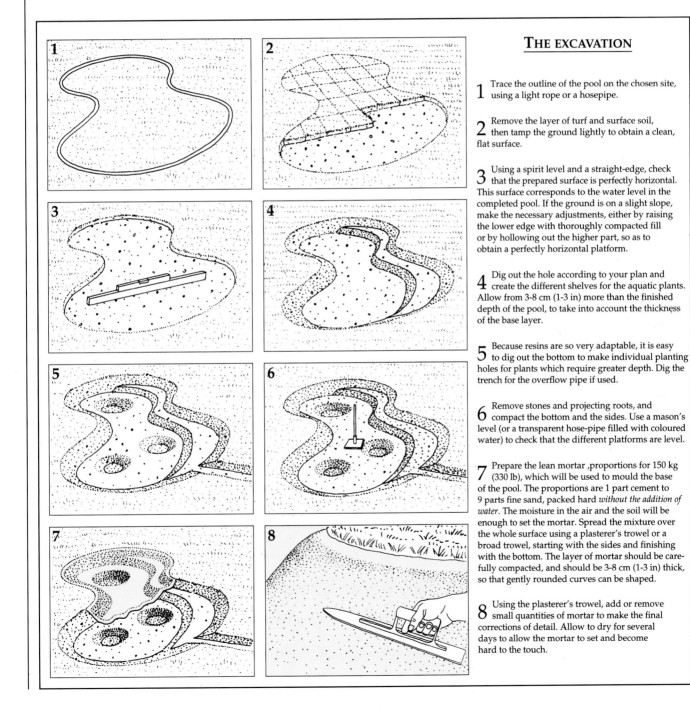

## THE EXCAVATION

1 Trace the outline of the pool on the chosen site, using a light rope or a hosepipe.

2 Remove the layer of turf and surface soil, then tamp the ground lightly to obtain a clean, flat surface.

3 Using a spirit level and a straight-edge, check that the prepared surface is perfectly horizontal. This surface corresponds to the water level in the completed pool. If the ground is on a slight slope, make the necessary adjustments, either by raising the lower edge with thoroughly compacted fill or by hollowing out the higher part, so as to obtain a perfectly horizontal platform.

4 Dig out the hole according to your plan and create the different shelves for the aquatic plants. Allow from 3-8 cm (1-3 in) more than the finished depth of the pool, to take into account the thickness of the base layer.

5 Because resins are so very adaptable, it is easy to dig out the bottom to make individual planting holes for plants which require greater depth. Dig the trench for the overflow pipe if used.

6 Remove stones and projecting roots, and compact the bottom and the sides. Use a mason's level (or a transparent hose-pipe filled with coloured water) to check that the different platforms are level.

7 Prepare the lean mortar ,proportions for 150 kg (330 lb), which will be used to mould the base of the pool. The proportions are 1 part cement to 9 parts fine sand, packed hard *without the addition of water*. The moisture in the air and the soil will be enough to set the mortar. Spread the mixture over the whole surface using a plasterer's trowel or a broad trowel, starting with the sides and finishing with the bottom. The layer of mortar should be carefully compacted, and should be 3-8 cm (1-3 in) thick, so that gently rounded curves can be shaped.

8 Using the plasterer's trowel, add or remove small quantities of mortar to make the final corrections of detail. Allow to dry for several days to allow the mortar to set and become hard to the touch.

## Quantities of Materials Necessary for Making 1 m² (1 yd²) of Moulded Polyester :

Carefully measure the area of the pool in order to calculate the exact quantities of materials required to waterproof it. If the pool is irregularly shaped, the easiest method is to square off the design plan, making each square represent 1 or 0.5 m² ( 10 or 5 ft²). The sum of the whole squares and half squares is the total area of the bottom of the pool, to which must be added the area of the sides, obtained by multiplying the height of the walls by the perimeter of the pool.

### THE SUB-BASE

·The sub-base for the pool is made from thin mortar composed of fine sand and cement, at the rate of 150 kg/m³ (330 lb/ft³)of mortar. In practice, this mortar is obtained by mixing 1 part of cement and 9 parts of well packed fine sand, without the addition of water. To calculate the volume of mortar required, multiply the area to cover (bottom and sides of the pool) by the thickness of the sub-base :

*Example : the sub-base of a pool with a total surface of 35m² (380 ft²) to be waterproofed, with an average thickness of 6 cm, will require a volume of mortar equal to : 35 x 0.06 = 2.1 m³ (74 ft³)*

- **Cement :** use a Portland cement containing 65% clinker. At the rate of 150 kg/m³ (330 lb/ft³), the weight of cement required, for our example, is :

*2.1 x 150 = 315 kg (700 lb), or 6.3 50-kg (110 lb) bags of cement*

- **Sand :** choose a fine, soft sand (builder's sand) which is easily moulded (the sand forms a compact ball when squeezed in the hand). At the rate of 150 kg/m³ (330 lb/ft³), the volume of sand corresponds to 9/10 of the total volume of mortar.

In our example, the volume of sand is equal to :

*2.1 / 10 x 9 = 1.89 m³ (65 ft³)*

**Note :** the volume of bulk sand (not compacted) is considerably increased by the presence of air pockets between the grains of sand, which can represent up to 38% of the total mass. This expansion phenomenon can be overcome by packing down the sand when measuring quantities (so as not to overdo the quantity of cement). It is therefore necessary to have 38% more bulk sand than the volume of compacted sand which will actually be required.

*In our example, taking into account the expansion phenomenon, the quantity of sand to be delivered is : 1.89 + 38% = 2.6 m³ (90ft³)*

### THE POLYESTER SHELL :

- **Kraft paper :** this tough paper is used as a support for the resin, isolating it from the soil and the moisture of the sub-base. If the latter is very damp, tarpaper can be used. The paper can also be replaced by jute sacking soaked in cement rendering or liquid plaster, in which case the support must be thoroughly dry before the resin is applied. The amount of paper or sacking required is equal to the area of the surface to be covered, plus 10 % for overlapping the strips.

- **Adhesive plastic tape, 5 cm (2 in) wide :** this is used to hold the strips of kraft paper together. The quantity required can be calculated by totaling the length of the rolls of kraft paper used.

- **Fibreglass mat :** just as concrete is reinforced with steel rods, so polyester resin is reinforced by woven glass fabric (fibreglass mat).For each layer of resin, a mat of 450 gr./m² (1 lb/yd²) will be required. If two layers of resin are applied, two mats of 450 gr./m² (1 lb/yd²) will be needed for each square metre of pool surface. To increase the reinforcement, the edge of each mat must overlap the preceding one. The quantity required is equal to the total area to be waterproofed plus 10 %, multiplied by the number of layers.

- **Polyester resin :** the resin is applied like paint, with a brush made of pure pig bristle or a mohair roller, in a uniformly thick layer, on which the glass mat is placed immediately. More resin is then applied, till the fibreglass has become translucent. The airbubbles imprisoned in the resin must be eliminated without delay, with a rubber roller or brush. A second layer of glass mat is applied in the same way. For each square metre of pool, allow 1.5 kg (3.3 lb) of polyester resin per layer of glass mat. Add 1.5 % of catalyst.

- **Finishing coat or topcoat :** this is a tinted·resin which is applied (without a glass mat) to complete the waterproofing. Allow between 300-500 gr. (2 3rds to 1 lb) of topcoat per square metre of pool. Add 1.5 % of catalyst.

- **Catalyst :** remember to add the exact quantity of catalyst, 1.5 %, i.e. 15 gr. per kilo (quarter oz/lb) of resin used, each time you prepare a new lot of resin or topcoat. For each square metre of shell comprising two layers of glass mat and one topcoat, you will need 1.5 + 1.5 + 0.5 = 3.5 kg of resin, i.e. :

*3.5 x 0.015 = 52 g of catalyst per square metre.*

- **Broad brushes and rollers :** choose pure pig bristle or mohair (nylon would be dissolved by the solvent). A rubber roller will enable you to exert more pressure on the resin to eliminate the air bubbles.

- **Acetone** is the solvent which is indispensable for cleaning brushes, removing stains, washing hands, etc.

- **Essential tools :** cord, square shovel, straightedge, spirit level,broad trowel, protective goggles, gloves, transparent hosepipe filled with coloured water (for checking levels), electric concrete mixer, buckets for measuring sand, cement and resin, etc.

# RESIN AND FIBREGLASS

Application of resin and fibreglass matting of the pool must be carried out in dry weather, at an ambient temperature above 15 °C (59 °F). Prepare very small quantities of resin at a time, 1.5 to 3 kg (330-660 lb), adding the catalyst at the last minute. Apply the resin over small surfaces, 1-2 sq m (1-2 sq yd) using a broad brush or a mohair roller. It is essential to wear goggles to protect the eyes from all contact with the catalyst and resin.

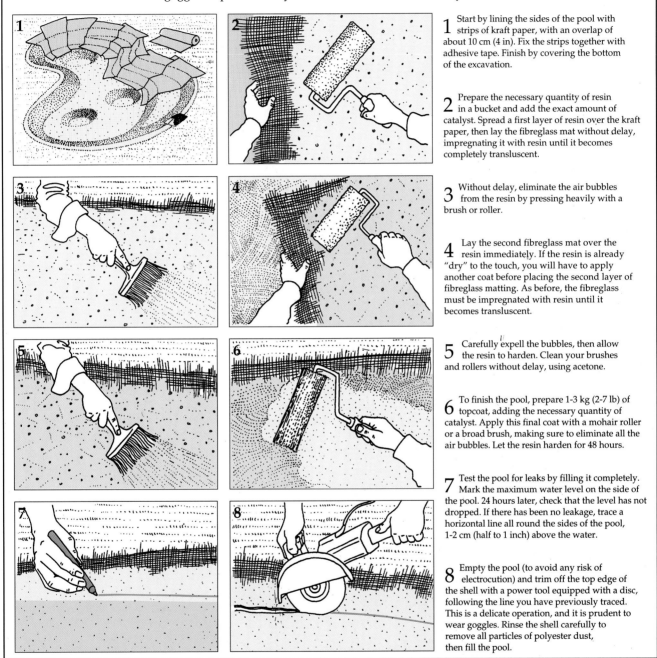

1 Start by lining the sides of the pool with strips of kraft paper, with an overlap of about 10 cm (4 in). Fix the strips together with adhesive tape. Finish by covering the bottom of the excavation.

2 Prepare the necessary quantity of resin in a bucket and add the exact amount of catalyst. Spread a first layer of resin over the kraft paper, then lay the fibreglass mat without delay, impregnating it with resin until it becomes completely transluscent.

3 Without delay, eliminate the air bubbles from the resin by pressing heavily with a brush or roller.

4 Lay the second fibreglass mat over the resin immediately. If the resin is already "dry" to the touch, you will have to apply another coat before placing the second layer of fibreglass matting. As before, the fibreglass must be impregnated with resin until it becomes transluscent.

5 Carefully expell the bubbles, then allow the resin to harden. Clean your brushes and rollers without delay, using acetone.

6 To finish the pool, prepare 1-3 kg (2-7 lb) of topcoat, adding the necessary quantity of catalyst. Apply this final coat with a mohair roller or a broad brush, making sure to eliminate all the air bubbles. Let the resin harden for 48 hours.

7 Test the pool for leaks by filling it completely. Mark the maximum water level on the side of the pool. 24 hours later, check that the level has not dropped. If there has been no leakage, trace a horizontal line all round the sides of the pool, 1-2 cm (half to 1 inch) above the water.

8 Empty the pool (to avoid any risk of electrocution) and trim off the top edge of the shell with a power tool equipped with a disc, following the line you have previously traced. This is a delicate operation, and it is prudent to wear goggles. Rinse the shell carefully to remove all particles of polyester dust, then fill the pool.

## WHAT TO DO IN THE EVENT OF LEAKAGE

If the water level drops significantly after the first filling (taking into account the amount of evaporation which is normal for the season), this is a sign of leakage. Wait until the water level stabilizes, to locate the leak. For greater precision, pour into the middle of the pool a small quantity of water to which a non-toxic colouring agent has been added (methylene blue) : the flow of water towards the precise point of leakage will be slowly visible. Drain the pool completely and allow the shell to dry. Before making the repairs, smooth the area with sandpaper, then apply another layer of topcoat. If there are a number of leaks, it is best to apply a finishing coat over the whole surface of the pool, having first dried it and sanded it down all over. Then test again for leaks.

# REINFORCED CONCRETE POOLS

The strength and remarkable plastic qualities of concrete are well known. Modeled by hand or projected under pressure, it lends itself to the creation of natural, free forms, whilst the use of shuttering makes it possible to build pools of strict geometrical shapes. But great care is required if its qualities are to be used to best advantage.

CONCRETE IS MADE BY mixing a binding agent (cement) and aggregates (sand, gravel) with water, in varying proportions. For a pool, a waterproofing compound, in liquid or powder form, will be added at the mixing stage.

## A resistant material

Reinforced concrete is poured over a framework of steel rods, the combination of steel and concrete offering a good degree of resistance to compressive and tensile stress. The steel must be completely embedded in the concrete, to prevent rusting through contact with air, water or the soil. Concrete sets (or hardens) in about three hours, but takes about 3 weeks to dry out completely. The inside of the pool is generally finished with a waterproofing layer of cement and fine sand, but this can be replaced by a coating of epoxy or polyester resin.

## Precautions for use

To preserve all the mechanical properties of concrete, it is important to respect the proportions of the components as closely as possible. If too little cement is used, the concrete will become porous and friable, whilst an excess of cement or water causes excessive shrinkage, and numerous minute fissures will appear. Concrete and mortars must be allowed to dry slowly, protected from wind or excessively hot sun. This is why the work should be carried out preferably in overcast weather, in spring or autumn, rather than in the middle of summer. The site must be prepared carefully so that the concrete can be poured in the most favorable conditions and as rapidly as possible. The base must be homogeneous and perfectly tamped down, to prevent the concrete from cracking.

▼ With non-shuttered concrete it is possible to build informal pools which blend naturally into a design where the rock dominates.

## The importance of being fit

It is preferable not to be a complete novice in construction work, to undertake this job. Even for a small pool, a considerable amount of concrete will be required : one cubic metre weighs close on 2.5 tonnes, and represents the equivalent of 25 100-kilo (220-lb) barrow-loads. Do not forget that you will have to mix, transport and spread the concrete, all within less than three hours (the period during which the concrete remains workable in average conditions of temperature and humidity). In other words, the operation is a real marathon, requiring perfect planning and excellent physical fitness. If you have any doubts about it, do not take any unnecessary risks. Get somebody with more experience to help you, or have a contractor in to do the job.

## Getting organized

For a very small pool, up to 5 m² (55 ft²), the amount of concrete required will not be more than 1.5 m³ (50 ft³). You can reasonably plan to do the job on your own, provided you have a small electric concrete mixer (which can be hired for the occasion). For a larger pool up to 15 m² (160 ft²) about 3.5 m³ (125 ft³) of concrete will have to be handled, and you will need at least two helpers : one person will load the concrete mixer and the other two will spread the concrete. In a mixer with a capacity of 140 litres (36 gallons), one load will take about 8 minutes to mix thoroughly, which represents a total of 1050 litres (280 gallons) per hour so mixing and spreading 3.5 m³ (125 ft³) of concrete will take about 4 hours. It is a good idea to delay the normal setting time (2 to 5 hours) by adding a retardant agent to the mix. With an area larger than 15 m² (160 ft²), the only reasonable solution is to use ready-mixed concrete which is delivered ready to lay. In this case you will have to be specially well-organized and have everything fully prepared, because you are going to have to handle a large quantity of concrete in a very limited time.

## SHUTTERED CONCRETE

### Shape of the pool

The rigidity of the materials used for the formwork makes it possible to build pools· which are simple and regular in shape, in a combination of straight lines and curves. That is why this technique is most suitable for ornamental pools whose geometrical shapes are harder to build by other methods such as those using liners and resins. When the sides of the pool are vertical, as is often the case in shuttered constructions, they should be made to slope slightly outwards, so that as ice forms in winter it can expand upwards and outwards.

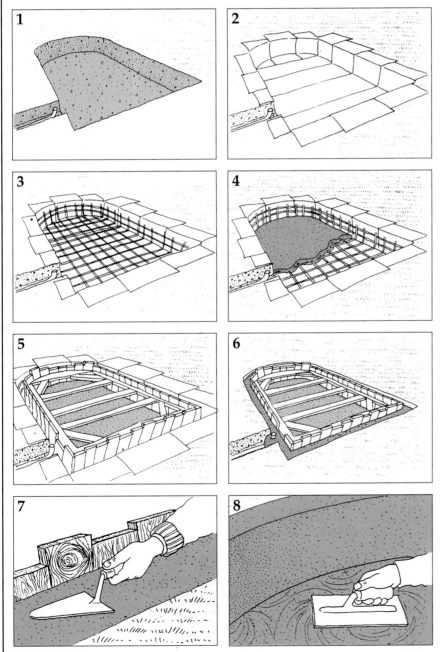

## SHUTTERED CONCRETE

1 Dig the hole according to your plan, but make it 15 cm (6 in) deeper to allow for the thickness of the concrete. Dig the trench for the overflow pipe leading to the sump, and put the pipe in place.

2 Compact the bottom and sides of the hole. Spread a sheet of builders' plastic over the whole surface to isolate the fresh concrete from the soil of the sub-base. This will prevent the mixing-water from penetrating the soil, and will ensure that the concrete dries slowly, without shrinking or cracking.

3 Fit in the reinforcing steel. This must go up to about 5 cm (2 in) from the rim of the pool. Put pebbles or small concrete chocks under the mesh, to enable the concrete to penetrate all round the reinforcing material and enclose it completely.

4 Make the bottom of the pool by spreading a layer of concrete containing a waterproofing compound (*see* **mix n° 2**, *page 80*), about 12 cm (4 in) thick. This concrete should be on the wet side, for easier spreading. Allow to set for 48 hours, spraying it from time to time and protecting it from the sun.

5 Build the shuttering for the sides of the pool : these will be 10-15 cm (4-6 in) thick and will slope outwards for good resistance to frost, a slope of 1-3 cm/m³ (half to 1 inch/ft³) is sufficient. For rounded forms, use narrow planks placed vertically, or plywood 4-5 mm (fifth of an inch) thick which is bent into a curve and fixed to a wooden form. The shuttering must be strong, reinforced and blocked with thick planks so that it will not be deformed by the strong pressure exerted by the concrete-this can exceed 2 tonnes per metre (2 tons/yard). Check that the reinforcing material stays properly centred between the sides of the formwork.

6 Inside the shuttering, trace a horizontal line marking the upper rim of the sides of the pool 1 or 2 cm (half to 1 inch) above the intended water level). Pour the sides of the pool, using concrete (*see* **mix n° 2** *page 80*) of a fairly wet consistency (when rolled into a ball in the hand, it collapses immediately). Vibrate to eliminate air pockets.

7 Level the upper rim of the sides at the required height. Remove the shuttering after 10 days, and allow the concrete to set for 3 weeks, wetting it from time to time and protecting it from the sun.

8 Prepare the finishing coat (*see* **mix n° 3**, *page 80*). Apply in a layer 2-3 cm (1 in) thick, using a trowel or a plasterer's hawk, over the whole surface, starting with the sides. Let this grouting dry for at least 1 week, wetting it frequently and protecting it from the sun to prevent it from drying too rapidly.

## READY-MIXED CONCRETE

For a big job, ready-to-use concrete delivered in a lorry-mixer is certainly the best option, for anybody who has a certain amount of experience with masonry. When you order, specify the quantity and the quality you require, and do not forget to ask the supplier to add a waterproofing agent. Generally, a lorry-mixer has a capacity of up to 6 m³ (210 ft³), 9 m³ (320 ft³) for articulated trucks, and the driver will add the necessary quantity of water at the last minute, according to the consistency you require.

But before making a decision, consider the following points :

- The quantity of concrete you will need will have to be calculated very accurately : if it is insufficient, it will be impossible to pour the pool in one operation. If you have over-estimated your requirements, you will be left with the excess. This may not be a problem if you have other work in progress or planned (the foundation for a terrace or garage, garden paths, etc) for which the surplus can be used.

- The laying must be carried out very rapidly, since setting time is from 2 to 5 hours. If you delay starting, or have last-minute problems, you cannot stop the process. To help you, you will need at least one person for each 1.5 m³ (50 ft³) which has to be spread. The site must be perfectly prepared to receive the concrete on the agreed delivery day, and time. Check that everything is in place : reinforcing steel, shuttering, formwork, piping, wiring, etc.

- There must be easy access to your garden for the truck. Will it be able to pour the concrete directly into the excavation, or will a conveyor belt or pump be required (at extra cost)? Such large quantities of concrete cannot be shifted by wheelbarrow.

- Think of the ruts the truck, which weighs more than 30 tonnes, will inevitably leave in your garden, especially if there has been recent rain. Since you have to order concrete several days in advance, you will have to take weather forecasts into account.

## NON-SHUTTERED CONCRETE

### Hand-moulded concrete

This technique can give interesting results in a relatively short time, without the use of formwork (which represents a considerable saving, both in the materials required for the shuttering and in the time it would have taken to build it). It is very suitable for informal pools with an irregular shape and gently sloping sides. The concrete must be of a smooth consistency, not too liquid, so that it can be easily applied and modeled by hand.

As with pools made from synthetic resins, the sub-base serves as a mould for the concrete shell. The thickness of this shell depends on the size of the pool, but it will be between 10-20 cm (4-8 in). The steel reinforcing material for pools of this type (especially the smaller models) must be flexible enough to adapt itself to very irregular shapes. It is best to choose, for example, galvanized wire reinforcing mesh which can easily be twisted into shape by hand, or cut into sections which will be wired together.

### Projected concrete

This other technique also has the advantage of not requiring shuttering. The concrete is projected with considerable force from a compressed air cannon on to a steel reinforcement which is gradually covered under the successive layers of concrete.

The various dry constituents of the concrete (sand, gravel, cement, water-proofing compound) are transported by compressed air to the cannon, which is equipped with a high pressure water supply. The concrete obtained by this method is very homogenous in quality and practically exempt from shrinkage. The total thickness of the concrete will be from 10 cm (4 in) for a medium-sized pool to 15 cm (6 in) for a very large pool). Projected concrete lends itself very well to the construction of irregularly shaped pools, and of artifical rocks. The projection operation can be carried out very rapidly, even over very large surfaces.

### For large pools

Pools which are 5 m (15 ft) or more in width must have an expansion joint. The pool is then composed of several distinct blocks, generally strips 3-4 metres (10-13 ft) wide, separated by a gap of 5-15 mm (5th to 3 5ths of an in). This space will subsequently be filled with a special elastic luting material. This expansion joint allows the concrete to expand when the temperature rises. To make the joint, place a thin plank of the required thickness, 5-15 mm (5th to 3 5ths of an in) in the appropriate position before pouring the concrete. Be careful to fix the plank to the ground so that it does not start to float when the concrete is poured, but make sure that you will be able to remove it after the concrete has set. Wet the

wood to expand the fibres before you pour the concrete, otherwise the plank will adhere to the concrete.

### Edges of the pool

The edges of the pool can be left as they are, or masked in some way. Choose the same material as is used for the paths leading to the pool (wooden decking, natural or reconsti-tuted paving stones) to preserve a certain continuity. The edging material will overhang the edge by a few centimetres, and be firmly fixed in place on a bed of mortar. A fairly wide, flat stone will serve mask to mask the overflow.

### Filling the pool

After the three-week setting period, the concrete must be brushed hard and rinsed several times to get rid of all the traces of free lime produced by the cement, since it is highly toxic to the flora and fauna of the pool. When you first fill it, the pond can serve as a paddling pool for your children and those of your neighbours. It will be an occasion for them to become familiar with this new centre of interest and for you to introduce them to a variety of topics concerning it. After a further rinsing, you will be able to introduce the plants in their baskets and/or tubs into the appropriate section of the pool before releasing fish into the pool water.

## Maintenance

Concrete pools do not require any special maintenance. Any tiny fissures can be repaired with a paste of pure cement and water, applied with a brush, preferably in the evening or on an overcast day so that drying will take place more slowly. For larger cracks, clean the concrete with a high pressure hose, chisel out the crack so that it is wide and clean and apply a filler of expansive cementaceous repair compound. If the cracking is caused by an unstable foundation, it is preferable to repair the damage by means of a flexible liner which will not be affected by the movements of the masonry and be perfectly water-tight. If the pool has not been designed to stand up to winter temperatures, it will be necessary to install electrical frost protection.

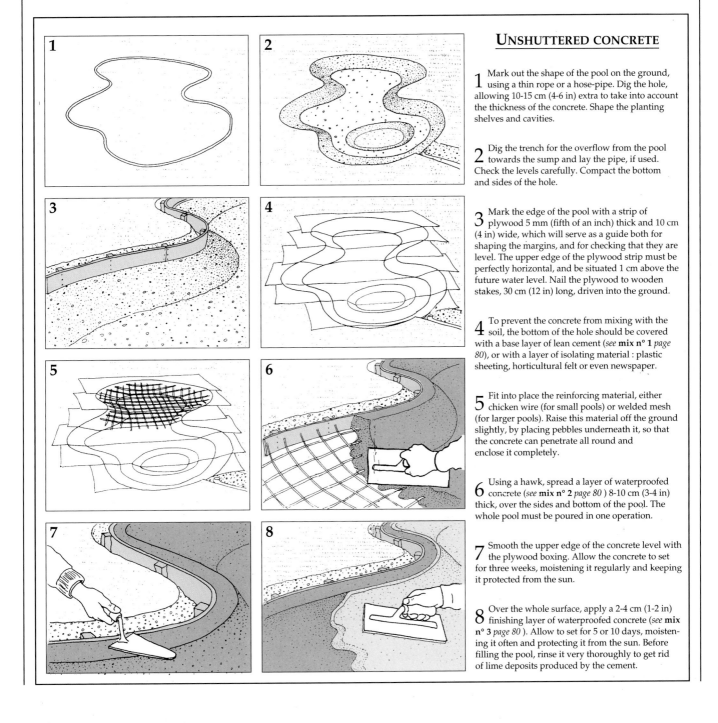

## UNSHUTTERED CONCRETE

1 Mark out the shape of the pool on the ground, using a thin rope or a hose-pipe. Dig the hole, allowing 10-15 cm (4-6 in) extra to take into account the thickness of the concrete. Shape the planting shelves and cavities.

2 Dig the trench for the overflow from the pool towards the sump and lay the pipe, if used. Check the levels carefully. Compact the bottom and sides of the hole.

3 Mark the edge of the pool with a strip of plywood 5 mm (fifth of an inch) thick and 10 cm (4 in) wide, which will serve as a guide both for shaping the margins, and for checking that they are level. The upper edge of the plywood strip must be perfectly horizontal, and be situated 1 cm above the future water level. Nail the plywood to wooden stakes, 30 cm (12 in) long, driven into the ground.

4 To prevent the concrete from mixing with the soil, the bottom of the hole should be covered with a base layer of lean cement (*see* **mix n° 1** *page 80*), or with a layer of isolating material : plastic sheeting, horticultural felt or even newspaper.

5 Fit into place the reinforcing material, either chicken wire (for small pools) or welded mesh (for larger pools). Raise this material off the ground slightly, by placing pebbles underneath it, so that the concrete can penetrate all round and enclose it completely.

6 Using a hawk, spread a layer of waterproofed concrete (*see* **mix n° 2** *page 80* ) 8-10 cm (3-4 in) thick, over the sides and bottom of the pool. The whole pool must be poured in one operation.

7 Smooth the upper edge of the concrete level with the plywood boxing. Allow the concrete to set for three weeks, moistening it regularly and keeping it protected from the sun.

8 Over the whole surface, apply a 2-4 cm (1-2 in) finishing layer of waterproofed concrete (*see* **mix n° 3** *page 80* ). Allow to set for 5 or 10 days, moistening it often and protecting it from the sun. Before filling the pool, rinse it very thoroughly to get rid of lime deposits produced by the cement.

## HOW TO PREPARE CONCRETES AND MORTARS

If making your own concrete, a concrete mixer will give you a homogeneous product with considerable a saving of time and energy. First the dry aggregates and the cement (Portland with 65% clinker) are well mixed, then the water is added gradually until the required consistency is obtained. Use a bucket to measure the sand and cement. Quantities of sand and gravel indicated are for bulk aggregates (not compacted).

### CONCRETES AND MORTARS FOR BUILDING THE POOL

• **Mix n° 1 - lean concrete proportions for 200 kg (440 lb) :** this is used for making the protective base to isolate the concrete from the earth. It can be replaced by a sheet of plastic, which will reduce the loss of water during setting. This keeps the concrete clean during the construction, and slows down the drying.
*Proportions : 1 part cement for 3.5 parts sand and 7 parts gravel calibre 10/40 mm (up to 1.5 in).*

• **Mix n° 2 - waterproofed concrete proportions for 350 kg (770 lb) : (**350 kg cement will obtain 1000 kg of finished concrete, i.e. around a third of bonding material for 1000 kg of concrete. This is used for the main construction work and enclosing the reinforcing material.
*Proportions : 1 part cement to 2 parts sand and 3 parts gravel. The concrete is rendered waterproof by the addition of a proprietary product in the proportions recommended by the manufacturer.*

• **Mix n° 3 - waterproofed finishing mortar proportions for 400 kg (880 lb) :** this is applied in a layer 2-4 cm (1-2 in) thick, and provides improved impermeability.
*Proportions : 1 part cement for 4 parts bulk sand (or 2.5 parts well packed fine sand). Add a waterproofing product in the proportions indicated by the manufacturer.*

### MORTARS FOR BUILDING ROCKS

• **Mix n° 4 - rough-casting mix or daub proportions for 500 kg (1100 lb) :** this is a mortar with a high proportion of cement offering very good adhesive properties. It is used to reinforce the bonding between the support and the finishing layer. Thickness : from 5-20 mm (5th to 1 in).
*Proportions : 1 part Portland cement for 3 parts bulk sand (or 2 parts well-packed fine sand). Add the waterproofing product in the proportions recommended by the manufacturer.*

• **Mix n° 5 - for finishing proportions for 350 kg (770 lb) :** a lime mortar gives the rock a natural look, with the colour of the sand showing through. It can also be tinted.
*Proportions : 1 part fat lime and 1 part white cement for 10 parts bulk sand (or 6 parts well-packed fine sand). Hydraulic lime can be used in place of fat lime.*

### REINFORCED CONCRETE

#### ADVANTAGES :
• Great freedom of shape.
• Remarkably resistant and durable in good conditions of use.
• The use of formwork makes it possible to build shapes which can only be obtained with difficulty by other methods.

#### DISADVANTAGES :
• Relatively high cost, includes reinforcing steel, concrete, wood for shuttering...
• Quite a long time is required for preparing the formwork, and for drying the concrete (4 weeks).
• It is hard work : handling bags of cement and barrow-loads of concrete requires a certain amount of experience.
• Lorries delivering building materials (sand, cement, concrete) may cause damage to the site, especially in soft ground and bad weather.
• Work may be delayed in certain weather conditions (frost, rain, very hot weather).

## CALCULATION OF QUANTITIES OF MATERIALS FOR MAKING CONCRETE

If you know the exact dimensions of your pool, it will be easier to calculate with accuracy the quantity of materials required.
• **Reinforcing steel :** galvanized chicken wire for small pools or 10 cm (4 in) welded steel mesh for areas greater than 25 m² (30/yd²).
• **Volume of concrete required :** to calculate this, multiply the total area to be covered by the thickness of the shell 10-20 cm (4-8 in), depending on the size of the pool.

*Example : for a pool of 15 m² (18/yd²) with a surface of 30 m² (35/yd²) covered with 15 cm (6 in) of concrete, vol. of concrete required=30 x 0.15 = 4.5 m³*
• **The quantity of cement** given for each mix is calculated for 1 m³ (35 ft³) of concrete.
*In our example, 4.5 m³ (160 ft³) of concrete on the basis of 350 kg (770 lb) require : 4.5 x 350 = 1575 kg (3500 lb) of cement i.e. 31.5 bags of 50 kg (110 lb).*
• **The total volume of aggregates** corresponds to the volume of concrete minus the volume of cement.
Given that 1 kg of cement occupies a volume of 0.66 litres (3 pt), the volume of cement used in our example is :
*1575 x 0.66 = 1039.5 litres (275 gallons).*
*The volume of aggregates is therefore :*
*4500 - 1039.5 = 3460.5 litres (915 gallons) 3.46 m³ (120 ft³)*
*This volume must be increased by 38 % to compensate for the expansion phenomenon in bulk aggregates (non-compacted).*
*3460.5 + 38 % = 4775.5 litres (1260 gallons) 4.77 m³ (170 ft³)*
For a finishing coat or rendering mortar, the aggregate is soft sand (builder's sand).
For concrete, use 1/3 sharp sand and 2/3 gravel gauge 20 mm-40 mm (1-2 in).
**The waterproofing agent** will be added in the proportions indicated by the manufacturer. It is usually packaged in quantities corresponding to the requirement for 50 kg (110 lb) of cement.

## BUILDING ARTIFICIAL ROCKS

The presence of rocks near the water opens up a wide range of possibilities for creating interesting designs and increases the natural look of the pool. If you have no rocks in your garden, you can always have some delivered from a local quarry. In this case, it will be a good idea for you to go there yourself and choose the rocks whose shapes fit best into your design.

However, this solution may not be as simple as it appears : it is not always easy to find rocks of pleasing shape and the right size. Then the transport of blocks of stone may prove very expensive, or pose insuperable technical problems. In your garden, heavy transporting vehicles and lifting equipment can dig ruts into the ground and damage plants.

For all these reasons, the construction of artificial rocks offers a number of advantages : for a small financial outlay and with limited means, this technique allows great freedom of creation and can be adapted to most situations. It is also an alternative to the systematic pillaging of certain natural sites.

The operation consists in projecting a lime- and sand-based mortar on to a rigid framework made of strips of galvanized steel. On to this supporting structure are applied successive layers of tinted mortar, to model a rock of the desired shape and colour.

**1** Make a sketch of the scene you wish to create. You may find that photographs of natural sites are a help. Try to make a harmonious composition, in which the rock structures and the masses of plants are well balanced. A block plan, with a scale of 1:25 or 1:50, will help you to situate each element in relation to the whole.

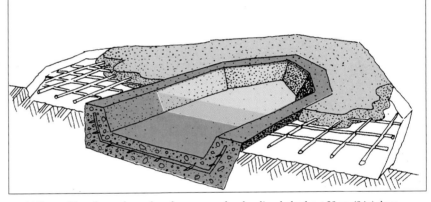

**2** At the position chosen for each rock or group of rocks, dig a hole about 20 cm (8 in) deep. Put metal reinforcement in the bottom e.g.10 cm (4 in) welded mesh then fill the foundation with lean concrete (*see* **mix n° 1** *page 80* ). This concrete sole will provide a strong, stable base for the rock construction.

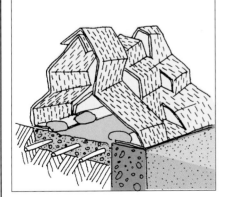

**3** The strips of steel, 60 cm (2 ft) wide and 2.5 m (8 ft) long, can be obtained from builders' suppliers. Cut them to the required dimensions and fix them to the foundation with blobs of cement, then bend and fold them into shape by hand. The slits in the metal make it much easier to carry out this task. For very big rocks, a double framework can be constructed if necessary.

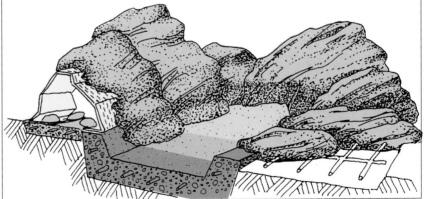

**4** Cover the framework with a layer or layers of rough-cast mortar (*see* **mix n° 4** *page 80* ) fairly wet in consistency and applied with a trowel. This first layer will be 5-20 mm (5th to 1 inch) thick. Allow it to dry for 3-5 days, then moisten the surface and apply the second coat (*see* **mix n° 5** *page 80* ), which will be of a firmer consistency, and 2-3 cm (1 in) thick. Allow to dry for 48 hours. Add one or more layers of the same mortar to model shapes and surface texture in greater detail. If desired, the mortar can be tinted by adding a colouring agent to the mix. These pigments must be used in minute quantities if the result is to appear natural. It is essential to make several preliminary colour tests, allowing the mortar to dry thoroughly to see what the final result will look like.

# PREFORMED POOLS

Pools preformed from rigid PVC or polyester resins are technically very reliable, and have the advantage of being easily and quickly installed. Many models are available on the market, but since only a limited number of shapes and depths are on offer, the choice of a preformed pool may restrict the scope for creativity, to a certain extent.

USING A PREFORMED POOL is probably the easiest way of creating a small pond. Even if you have little DIY experience, you will be able to obtain results quickly and without too much effort. Preformed pond shells are particularly useful for geometrical shapes, which are harder to build with flexible liners or resins, or in concrete which requires shuttering.

## A limited choice

Although it can certainly be considered a safe option, the choice of a preformed pool may well present a number of disadvantages, especially if you have particular requirements as to size or esthetic qualities.

When you have decided on the dimensions of your pool, you will probably find that there are in fact only a limited number of models which really have the volume you require.

## Criteria for choice

If your pond is to be viable (see pp 52-53 and 176-177), it is always preferable to choose the the largest pool that you can fit into the space available. Make sure that the depth in the centre is between 60-80 cm (24-30 in).

The volume of preformed pools ranges from 500-5000 litres (130-1300 gallons), but models of up to almost 8000 litres (2100 gallons) are available on special order from some manufacturers.

The shape you choose will of course depend on your personal preferences and the style of your garden, but you should pay particular attention to the planting shelves incorporated in the various models. Are they wide enough and deep enough to contain planting baskets? Are they situated at points corresponding to the places you have chosen on your plan? If you want to be able to plant exactly what and where you wish, it is better to choose a flat-bottomed pool without any planting

shelves at all. You will have an increased volume of water, and you can create your own planting shelves by placing the baskets on piles of bricks, making it easy to change the position of plants as often as you want to. Make sure that the slope of the sides is compatible with the type of material you intend to use to mask the margins (pebbles, slabs, rocks, etc.). Check that there is an overflow pipe (if one is desired). A drainage plug in the bottom of the pool may be a source of leakage, and is, in any case, unnecessary if you have a pump.

## Materials

**Rigid PVC pools** are generally dark in colour (grey or black). They are strong, will not rot and have a high resistance to ultra-violet rays and to frost. They do not stand up to shocks and stresses as well as pools made of reinforced polyester, but they are less expensive. The excavation must be perfectly leveled and well compacted, to avoid all risk of cracking or deformation.

**Pools made of polyester** reinforced with fibreglass are virtually indestructible and have a certain flexibility which enables them to withstand some minor deformation (frost). They come in a range of colours, some of which,

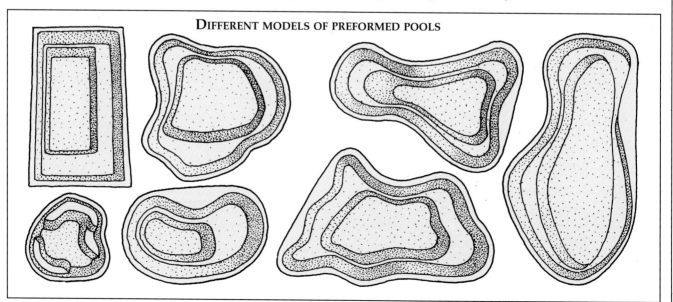

DIFFERENT MODELS OF PREFORMED POOLS

like swimming-pool blue, are too garish and artificial to blend in to the garden. Some manufacturers can supply colourless, translucent pools through which the colour of the bed material, soil or sand, is visible.

**Fibro-cement pools** are heavier than PVC or reinforced polyester and completely rigid, but remarkably shock-proof. The sides must have a slight slope to resist the pressure of ice. Although fibro-cement is little used for pools, its rigidity makes it very suitable for basins in starkly simple shapes, like the "Chinese hat", which can be used as raised miniponds. These can be used on a terrace or patio for dwarf varieties of waterlilies. Like fresh concrete, fibro-cement must be thoroughly rinsed several times before the final filling. Whatever the material, search for a pool with at least a ten-year guarantee.

### Modular elements

Some manufacturers offer a range of modular pools which can be used in combination, together with elements for streams and cascades. With this system, a complex installation can be created in a relatively short time, with several pools, streams and cascades. It can be extended or altered at any time, since each element can be moved, even after a number of years. Modules are assembled on site and bonded or screwed together (the material necessary having been supplied by the manufacturer).

---

**Advantages:**
- Perfectly waterproof.
- Quick to install.
- Easy to install.
- Strong.

**Disadvantages:**
- Limited choice of shape and size.
- Planting shelves often narrow and not deep enough.
- Steep sides are difficult to mask, whether with stones or other material, and the general appearance is artificial.

---

## MODULAR UNITS FOR BUILDING STREAMS AND WATERCOURSES

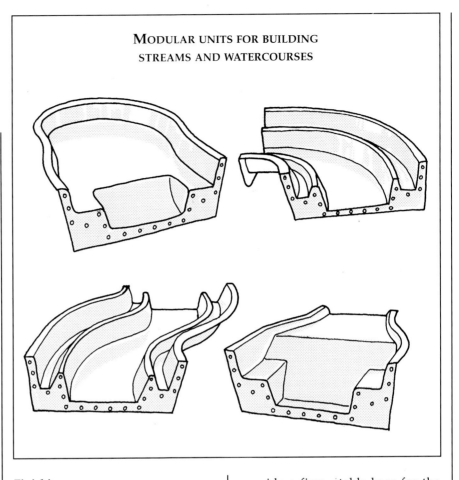

### Finishing

The edges of preformed pools can be covered with a margin of natural paving stones or with lawn. In either case, it will be necessary to pierce holes in the rim of the pool to offer a better hold for the mortar used to set the stones in place or to enable the grass to take root more easily. The edges of the pool can also be masked by plants with creeping or weeping foliage, preferably evergreen. With most preformed pools the sides are too steep for the creation of pebble beaches or rocky banks.

### The excavation

Unless you choose to build a raised pool, you will inevitably have to face the tedious task of excavating the site. This may require a greater degree of accuracy than is necessary when working with flexible liners, resins, or concrete especially if the pool is of a complicated shape. The hole will need to be 10-15 cm (4-6 in) bigger than the actual size of the pool, to allow room in the bottom for a bedding layer of sand which will provide a firm, stable base for the pool and make it easier to level it. Backfill around the sides with damp soil or sand, tamping it well down, and start filling the pool with water at the same time as you backfill.

If you have a big pool, i.e. one that is more than 2 m (7 ft) wide, it is a good idea to mix a little dry cement (about 15%) with the sand, so that the foundation will gradually harden.

### Maintenance

It is unnecessary to clean the sides of a preformed pool every year, since by doing so you deprive its inhabitants of the living micro-organisms which settle on the sides. In the (very unlikely) event of leakage, check that any drainage system is well sealed. In PVC pools, a violent shock caused, for example, by a falling stone, may provoke leaking. Repair kits are available from suppliers. Since preformed pools are most often used to create small ponds (with a capacity of less than 3.5 m³ (125 ft³), it is consequently more difficult to achieve biological balance, and a filtration and aeration system will be advisable.

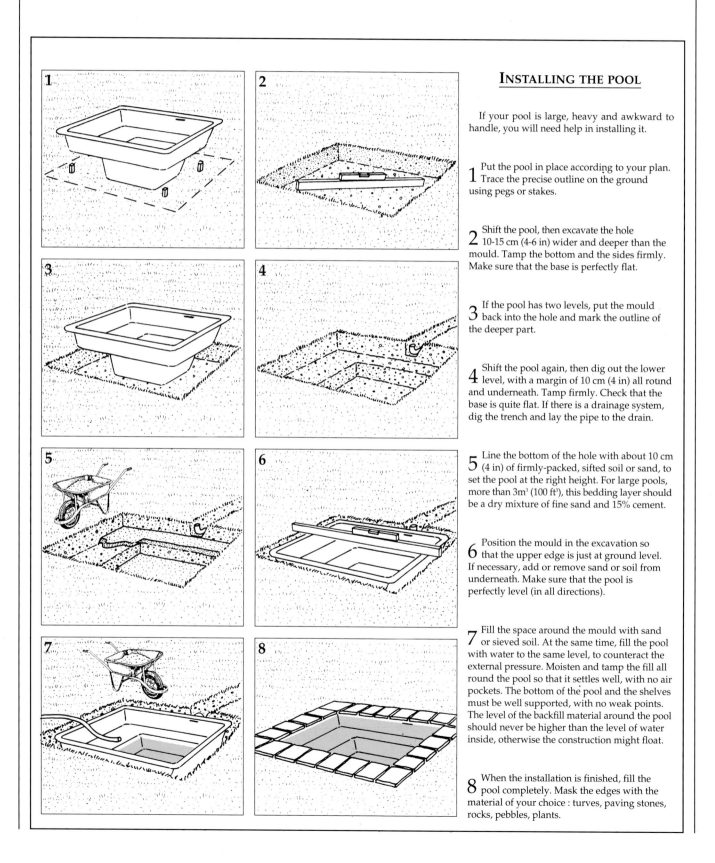

## INSTALLING THE POOL

If your pool is large, heavy and awkward to handle, you will need help in installing it.

1 Put the pool in place according to your plan. Trace the precise outline on the ground using pegs or stakes.

2 Shift the pool, then excavate the hole 10-15 cm (4-6 in) wider and deeper than the mould. Tamp the bottom and the sides firmly. Make sure that the base is perfectly flat.

3 If the pool has two levels, put the mould back into the hole and mark the outline of the deeper part.

4 Shift the pool again, then dig out the lower level, with a margin of 10 cm (4 in) all round and underneath. Tamp firmly. Check that the base is quite flat. If there is a drainage system, dig the trench and lay the pipe to the drain.

5 Line the bottom of the hole with about 10 cm (4 in) of firmly-packed, sifted soil or sand, to set the pool at the right height. For large pools, more than 3m³ (100 ft³), this bedding layer should be a dry mixture of fine sand and 15% cement.

6 Position the mould in the excavation so that the upper edge is just at ground level. If necessary, add or remove sand or soil from underneath. Make sure that the pool is perfectly level (in all directions).

7 Fill the space around the mould with sand or sieved soil. At the same time, fill the pool with water to the same level, to counteract the external pressure. Moisten and tamp the fill all round the pool so that it settles well, with no air pockets. The bottom of the pool and the shelves must be well supported, with no weak points. The level of the backfill material around the pool should never be higher than the level of water inside, otherwise the construction might float.

8 When the installation is finished, fill the pool completely. Mask the edges with the material of your choice : turves, paving stones, rocks, pebbles, plants.

## STREAM AND CASCADES IN PREFORMED UNITS

Some manufacturers offer a range of preformed units for building streams and watercourses, and header pools with a capacity of 100-500 litres (25-130 gallons) designed on the same lines as the main pool (base pool). Before you make a final decision as to the layout of your watercourse, you should check the exact shapes and dimensions of the units you think you will need. You will find that illustrated catalogues can be valuable when you are planning your garden : photocopy the pictures of the different units proposed by the manufacturers, cut them out and position them on a plan of your garden drawn to the same scale. The basic method of installation is the same as for a preformed pool. Start by positioning the lowest element (the base pool), then install the watercourse units, working upwards to the header pool. After positioning and blocking each unit, turn on the water and check that there are no leaks and that the flow path is satisfactory. Then backfill with damp soil or concrete. As with pools, the preformed watercourse units must be carefully camouflaged with pebbles, rocks and plants.

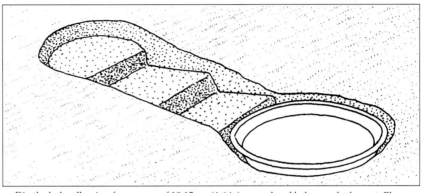

1 Dig the hole, allowing for a space of 10-15 cm (4-6 in) around and below each element. Place the units on a bed of sand, and adjust their position by adding or removing sand as required. Install the pump and the pipe for circulating the water to the header pool.

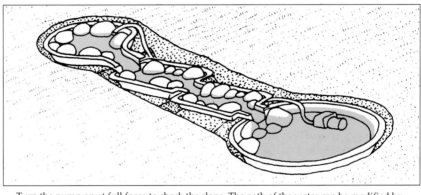

2 Turn the pump on at full force to check the slope. The path of the water can be modified by placing pebbles or rocks in the stream bed. Check for leaks in the water circuit, paying special attention to the curves and the junctions between units.

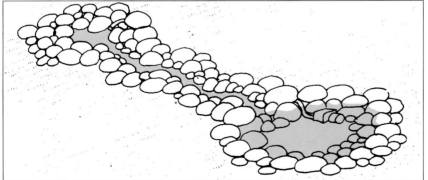

3 Backfill with damp sand, damp soil, or concrete, making sure that it settles well in. Make a final test with the pump at full force, and change the position of some stones if necessary. Use a thin mortar to seal in place those stones which might be shifted by the water, and especially those which retain the soil for planting, alongside the watercourse.

4 Install the plants beside the stream, so that they will mask the edges of the units. Each level of the cascade is treated as an individual pool. Be sure they are placed so as not to act as wicks and drain water out of the system.

# CLAY

Clay is a plastic, naturally impermeable material, which has been used for many centuries to make a waterproof lining for canals and natural ponds. It is comparatively inexpensive, and can be used to construct a garden pond, but it is much less reliable than flexible liners, synthetic resins or concrete, because it is fragile and easily ruptured.

DEPENDING ON THE REGION, clay can be obtained more or less easily from certain builders' supply firms. It can be delivered in bulk by the truck load, about 15 tonnes, or supplied in the form of unfired bricks or in a powdered form (bentonite). The price of clay can be very reasonable in certain regions, according to the distance from the point of production.

## Bulk clay

Moderately priced and easy to use, bulk clay is very useful for improving the impermeability of large areas (such as those used for fishing and water sports), where the base layer is made of compact, relatively impermeable and unfissured earth (avoid chalky or sandy soils). The usual method is to have a bulldozer spread a layer of clay 10-30 cm (4-12 in) thick over the whole area before the pond is filled.

## Clay over fabric

Clay becomes soft and malleable when wet, and the water-tight surface can easily be damaged if it is necessary to walk on the bottom of the pool for routine plant care. This why it is often used in association with other materials in order to increase its mechanical resistance to accidental deterioration. An underlay of agricultural felt or matting will prevent the clay coating from being damaged by burrowing animals.

More recently, a technique has been devised which makes use of strips of rotproof fabric specially impregnated with clay. The bottom and the sides of the pond are simply covered with two crossed layers of the material, with the strips overlapping one another by 10-20 cm (4-8 in). This forms a fairly thin, uniform layer of clay which becomes impermeable on contact with water.

| CLAY |
|---|
| **Advantages :** |
| • Technique easy to use. |
| • Cost can be low. |
| **Disadvantages :** |
| • The water-proofing layer must be very thick, so the excavation must be deeper. |
| • Easily damaged by roots and rodents. Fissures if allowed to dry out. |
| • Impossible to walk in pool without damaging the bottom. |
| • Impossible to install an overflow or a level controller. |

## Bentonite and raw clay bricks

Bentonite is a special type of clay which increases its volume 14 to 18 times when water is added to it. It is quite easily obtainable from specialist suppliers, in bags containing 50 kg (110 lb). Use it to transform a hollow area in your garden into a bog or a small pool by spreading a thick layer of bentonite over a well-tamped soil base.

Clay is sometimes used in association with a flexible polythene liner, in the form of unfired clay bricks which are obtainable from brickworks and are delivered on pallets. By this method it is easy to cover the sides and bottom of the excavation with a homogeneous, even layer of clay (see the description of the process on the oppostie page). Then a sheet of

◄ *Evergreen plants provide good protection against erosion of the banks of clay ponds, which are more vulnerable to wave action and to damage from run-off and from burrowing animals. The banks can also be protected with blocks of stone, or by driving treated wooden posts into the clay.*
*Designer : Gilbert Galloché.*

polythene is spread over the whole surface of the pond, extending well beyond the edges. Next, the planting medium for the aquatic plants is put into the centre of the liner, and the pool is filled slowly, so that the liner adheres perfectly to the clay surface. A few days later, when everything has settled into place, the excess liner at the edge of the pool is cut away so that the margins can be completed.

## Special uses for clay

Powdered clay or bentonite is sometimes used to waterproof a pool made with a liner or concrete which is leaking, if you do not wish to empty it to carry out the necessary repairs.
To do so, broadcast the contents of a few bags of bentonite over the surface of the water, at the rate of 2-10 kg/m² (2-20 lb/yd²). In some cases this can be sufficient to stop the leaks.

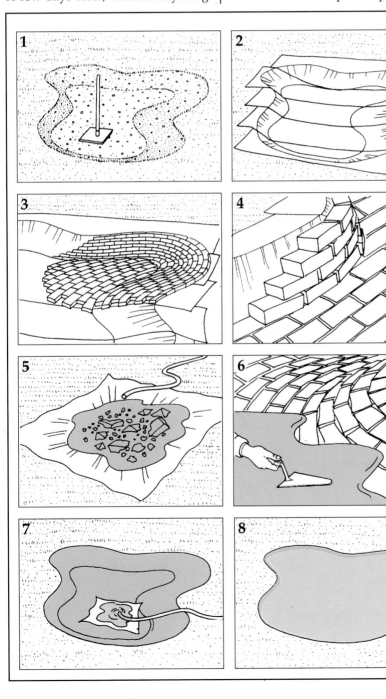

## CLAY PONDS

1 Dig the excavation according to your plan, allowing a margin of 15 cm (6 in) for the layer of clay. Tamp the base and sides thoroughly, removing roots and sharp stones.

2 Line the bottom of the excavation with horticultural felt, polyester matting, or plastic matting, to protect the clay from being damaged by spreading roots and burrowing animals (moles, earthworms, mole crickets).

3 At the bottom of the hole and around the gently sloping sides, arrange the clay bricks, tapping them tightly into place with a mallet. The bricks are laid flat, and form a layer 10-15 cm (4-6 in) thick. Water them lightly from time to time to prevent premature drying out, which would cause shrinkage and cracking of the water-proof coating.

4 Line the steeper sections of the sides with bricks laid in horizontal rows one on top of the other.

5 Damaged bricks should be set aside, and can be used for making a finishing coat. Put them on a sheet of plastic and break them up. Water abundantly and puddle by treading vigorously, to obtain a smooth mixture. The same result can be obtained by mixing bentonite with water.

6 Coat the base and sides of the pool with this puddled clay to fill all the gaps between the clay bricks.

7 To fill the pond, lay the end of the hose pipe on a piece of plastic sheeting so that the jet of water does not dig into the clay. Cut off the surplus liner around the edges of the pond. Set in plants in their planting containers

8 Set in plants in their planting containers. Plants with creeping roots might damage the water-proof coating. For the first days after the pond has been filled, the water will be cloudy, because of particles of clay in suspension. As these drop to the bottom, the water will clear.

# MILLSTONE FOUNTAINS

Millstone fountains or pebble fountains, easy to install in whatever space is available, provide a focal point for the terrace, patio, or garden, however large or small. They combine the structural harmony of a piece of sculpture and the sensual attraction of the texture of the stone with the sound and sparkle of water in continuous movement.

N OT MUCH SPACE IS required to install a millstone or pebble fountain on a terrace or in a garden, and it can be a charming and very welcome addition to an otherwise unattractive, confined space. It is simple to install, and the operation provides excellent training for carrying out a more ambitious project at a later date.

## Installation

The installation of fountains of this type presents no particular problems. The pool which will contain the submersible pump can be built using one of the methods described for pond-building. In most cases, a simple, round, flat-bottomed preformed pool will suffice. You may wish to use a pump linked to a simple computerized control panel, so that you can program usage times in advance. The programme control equipment will be installed in a weatherproof housing at the power source and readily accessible at all times. The water supply could have an automatic filling system with a level controller which may be concealed by a custom-built housing and/or rockery. To limit loss of water from splashing, the height of the jet should not be greater than 50% of the width of the pool.

▼ *Whatever the style, symbolic, natural or figurative, a composition based on stones and rocks is always effective. It is important to place each element carefully in order to obtain a dynamic balance.*

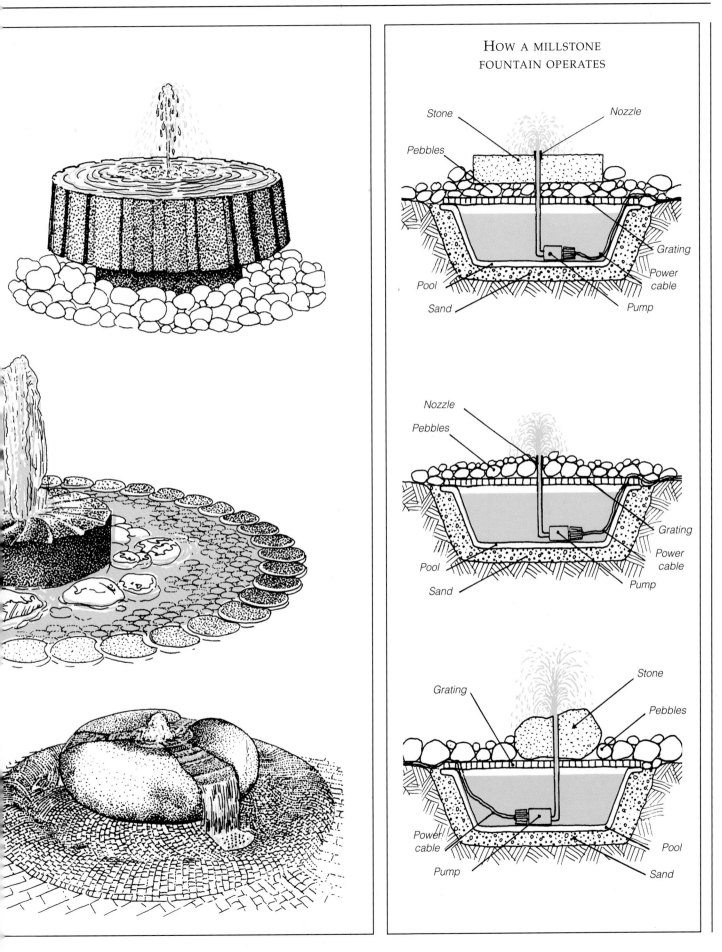

HOW A MILLSTONE
FOUNTAIN OPERATES

Stone    Nozzle

Pebbles

Grating

Power
cable

Pool

Sand    Pump

Nozzle

Pebbles

Grating

Power
cable

Pool

Sand    Pump

Grating    Stone

Pebbles

Power
cable    Pool

Pump    Sand

# BUILDING A BRIDGE

Whatever its style, a bridge is always an attractive feature of a garden, inviting the visitor to pause and admire the scene around him, and appreciate its charms. This makes it a major element of a water garden, and the greatest care must be taken, both in designing it and in the actual construction.

MUCH OF THE CHARM of a bridge resides in the impression of solidity produced by the construction. Safety of use must, of course, be a primary consideration. At the design stage, particular attention must be given to the strength of the decking and the handrails, and to the quality of the materials used.

### Strength : the first essential

A bridge must be designed to bear a load greater than the total weight of the number of people which the deck can hold at any one time. The materials and methods of anchoring must be chosen with care, so that the structure will be as robust as possible. If the span of the bridge is greater than 4 m (13 ft), build piles from wood, 15 x 15 cm (6 in), or in masonry, every 2 m (7 ft). Always allow an adequate safety margin. For stability, each side of the bridge and each pile will be firmly anchored in concrete. Any visible part of these foundations can be masked by evergreen plants.

### Style

While strength is a primary consideration, the aesthetic aspect of the construction must not be neglected. The range of shapes and styles is considerable, and the simplest forms are often the most elegant. Two telephone poles or beams covered with wooden planks can make a very attractive footbridge.

A flat stone or a concrete slab suspended a few centimetres above the surface of the water can be very effective. The more complex structures attract greater attention, and introduce into the garden an architectural element which will enhance a particular style.

A bridge made from logs will stress the rustic aspect of a garden, while an arching, red-lacquered bridge spanning the water brings an unmistakably oriental note. A bridge suspended between banks covered with luxuriant, exotic-looking vegetation will evoke childhood dreams of adventure.

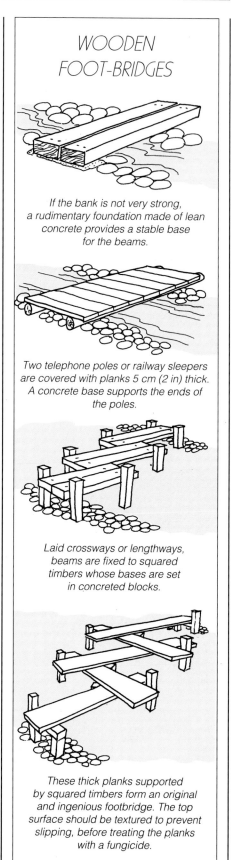

## WOODEN FOOT-BRIDGES

If the bank is not very strong, a rudimentary foundation made of lean concrete provides a stable base for the beams.

Two telephone poles or railway sleepers are covered with planks 5 cm (2 in) thick. A concrete base supports the ends of the poles.

Laid crossways or lengthways, beams are fixed to squared timbers whose bases are set in concreted blocks.

These thick planks supported by squared timbers form an original and ingenious footbridge. The top surface should be textured to prevent slipping, before treating the planks with a fungicide.

◀ The austere shape of this granite bridge suits both a traditional Japanese garden and a more contemporary style of architecture (Japanese garden at Unesco Headquarters, Paris).

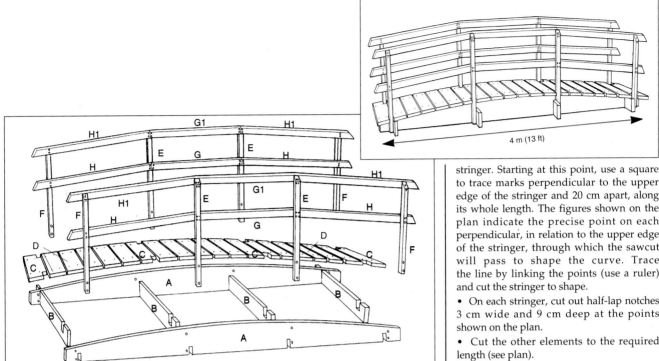

4 m (13 ft)

## BUILDING A BRIDGE

This easily-constructed rustic bridge is made of oak or pine planks which are assembled without gluing, so that the wood can work and not be deformed by heat and moisture. The rigidity of the whole is provided by 4 crossbeams (B) fixed to 2 stringers (A) by half-lap joints, reinforced by angle-irons. It is a good idea to test-assemble the construction in the workshop before carrying out the definitive assembly work.

• To trace the upper edge of the 2 stringers (A), first make a mark halfway along each stringer. Starting at this point, use a square to trace marks perpendicular to the upper edge of the stringer and 20 cm apart, along its whole length. The figures shown on the plan indicate the precise point on each perpendicular, in relation to the upper edge of the stringer, through which the sawcut will pass to shape the curve. Trace the line by linking the points (use a ruler) and cut the stringer to shape.

• On each stringer, cut out half-lap notches 3 cm wide and 9 cm deep at the points shown on the plan.

• Cut the other elements to the required length (see plan).

• On the 4 crossbeams (B) cut out half-laps 8 cm from each end, 5 cm wide and 8 cm deep.

• Drill and countersink all the holes for the 80 5x60 mm screws in the 20 planks (C, D) making up the deck, at a distance of 105 mm from each end. Striate the surface of each plank with a saw or a chisel, for protection against slipping.

• As shown on the plan, cut out a rectangle 7x8 cm at the corners of the planks (C) to fit the uprights of the handrails (E, F).

• Bevel the top end of the uprights of the handrails (E,F).

• Bevel the extremities of the end sections of the handrails (H1, H).

• On each stringer, place the uprights E and F (use a square) in position, to the left or right of the notches; drill mounting holes for 6x110 mm carriage bolts.

• Plane the upper edge of the handrails (H1, G1) to give them a rounded shape.

• Drill the screw-holes 5-75 mm in the handrail sections (E, F, G, G1, H, H1). Note that the bottom rails are midway between the top of the uprights and the level of the deck.

• After sanding, treat all the wood pieces to protect them from insects and fungal attack, then apply two protective coats of clear stain or varnish, leaving 24 hours between each coat. (The third coat is applied once the bridge has been installed). Allow to dry for three days.

• At least one week before installing the bridge, lay two concrete foundations 30 cm thick to support the ends of the bridge. These will isolate the wood from the damp ground and increase the stability of the construction.

### LIST OF MATERIAL (dimensions in mm)

| Ref. | Quant. | Name | Lgth. | Width. | Thk. |
|------|--------|------|-------|--------|------|
| A | 2 | Stringers | 4 000 | 300 | 50 |
| B | 4 | Crossbeams | 1 000 | 200 | 30 |
| C | 4 | Planks | 1 000 | 200 | 30 |
| D | 16 | Planks | 1 000 | 200 | 30 |
| E | 4 | Central uprights | 1 130 | 60 | 40 |
| F | 4 | External uprights | 1 010 | 60 | 40 |
| G, G1 | 4 | Central handrails | 1 260 | 80 | 40 |
| H, H1 | 8 | External handrails | 1 430 | 80 | 40 |

### Hardware

16 angle irons, 100 mm (4 in), with 5x50 mm (5thx2 in) screws (or 8 square angle blocks).
80 countersunk head screws, 5x60 mm (5thx2 in). 16 carriage- bolts, 6x110 mm (5thx4 in), with nuts and washers. 64 countersunk head screws, 5x75 mm (5thx3 in) hand rail.

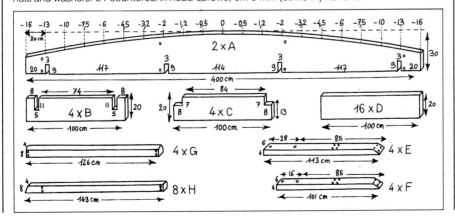

## Dimensions

The bridge is a natural extension of a pathway, and must be of corresponding width. For safety and for comfort, the width of the deck should be between 80-120 cm (3-4 ft), but never less than 60 cm (2 ft). If the span is greater than 4 m (13 ft) and it is impossible to install intermediate piles, the task of designing it should be entrusted to a specialist. If the space to be bridged is very narrow, it is a good idea to increase the importance of the construction by extending it beyond the edge of the banks. Railings are usually from 85-100 cm (30-40 in) high. They must be strong enough to withstand the pressure exerted by all the persons using the bridge simultaneously. If this is not the case, the false sense of security created by the presence of parapets is potentially more dangerous than their complete absence. Remember to allow sufficient height between the water and the deck, if boats are to pass.

## Position

The bridge is a place where it is pleasant to linger and enjoy a general view over the water : its surroundings must therefore offer year-round interest. A large tree or an arbour will provide welcome shade in summer.

If it is not to appear too artificial, a bridge must be seen to answer a need : in most cases, it will link opposite banks of a small pool, a stream or a bog area, but it can also be used to cross a dry pebble stream or a steep, little gully. It may provide the best means of observing from a safe distance the fragile flora of a peat-bog. Being a point of transition from one zone to another, a bridge will always arouse the curiosity of the visitor. It may be the only means of access to an islet whose shores are completely hidden by vegetation, helping to bring an air of mystery to the garden.

## Masonry bridges

Masonry constructions are much more durable than wooden bridges, and require no special maintenance. Their shape and proportions must be chosen with care, in order to avoid the ponderous look which sometimes results from the use of concrete and stone. For the facings, choose a material in keeping with the style of the garden : brick fits well into an urban environment. If you choose natural stone, whether rough or dressed, make sure that it is of local origin if possible, of the type seen in the walls of old houses. In a rock garden, the bridge should be made of the same stone as that used for the rest of the garden, mortared unobtrusively to give a dry-stone effect resembling that of a traditional mountain bridge. Ironwork can also be used to good effect : the deck of the bridge can be made of a slab of reinforced concrete or wooden planking fixed to a metal support, while railings made of wrought-iron are extremely decorative. This type of bridge, like those made of wood, requires regular maintenance.

## Wooden bridges

Wood is a noble material, and relatively easy to work. Even the simplest wooden structures have a certain charm. Hardwoods, such as beech, chestnut, elm or oak are the longest-lasting, while the softer types, such as pine and fir, although easily worked, are also less durable. Regular maintenance is required with a wooden bridge : the wood selected must have been treated to prevent damage from damp, insects or fungi, and could be painted or varnished, to weatherproof it. Stains are useful because they colour the wood without masking the texture. Unlike paints and varnishes, a surface treated with this type of product does not need to be sanded before a new coat is applied : a good washing down is all that is necessary. You can also use exotic hardwoods such as iroko and meranti which are more expensive but rot-proof, and have been pressure-treated to make them weatherproof and immune from attack by insects.

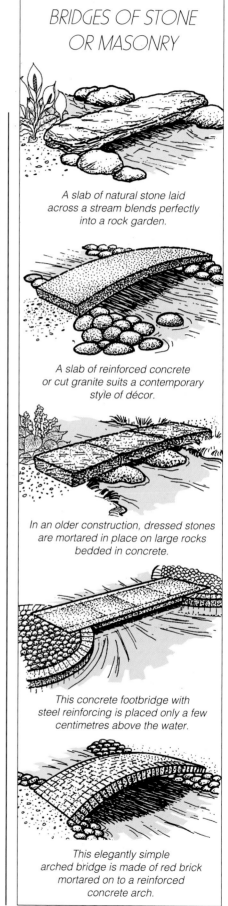

### BRIDGES OF STONE OR MASONRY

*A slab of natural stone laid across a stream blends perfectly into a rock garden.*

*A slab of reinforced concrete or cut granite suits a contemporary style of décor.*

*In an older construction, dressed stones are mortared in place on large rocks bedded in concrete.*

*This concrete footbridge with steel reinforcing is placed only a few centimetres above the water.*

*This elegantly simple arched bridge is made of red brick mortared on to a reinforced concrete arch.*

## HOW TO BUILD A BRIDGE IN MASONRY

The use of shuttered, reinforced concrete makes it possible to reduce the thickness of the deck of a bridge : it might be only a few centimetres, since the steel reinforcing makes the load-bearing structure remarkably strong and resistant. On this base, the railings of the bridge will be constructed from materials best in keeping with the general style of the garden : rough or dressed stone, bricks, slates, pebbles, etc. A certain know-how is required to work with these different materials, but the rudiments are quickly learned. To accustom oneself to the technique best adapted to the chosen material, it is a good idea to practise on some small jobs (a low wall, for example, or a planting trough). If the completed bridge is to be a success from the aesthetic point of view, you must have a very precise picture of what you want the finished result to look like. This implies that you will have made one or several sketches before preparing a detailed, dimensioned drawing.

1 On each bank, dig a foundation 40 cm (16 in) deep, to anchor the ends of the bridge. Following your plan, trace and cut out from thick plywood two patterns of the arch profile. Assemble these two pattern pieces parallel to each other with several crossbars, whose length will be equal to the width of the deck minus the width of a railing.

2 Nail plywood 8-10 mm (half an inch) thick on to this curved support, which will serve as shuttering for the arch. Fit the shuttering in place, bracing it strongly and checking that it is level. See that the planks on the sides which will retain the concrete are firmly fixed in place.

3 The metal reinforcing of the deck is composed of 10 mm (half an inch) steel rods placed length-wise over the structure, at 20 cm (8 in) intervals. These rods must be long enough to touch the bottom of each of the foundation cavities. Place small chocks of stone cement under the rods, so that the reinforcement will be completely embedded in the concrete. Wire 10x10 welded mesh (or wire netting) over the rods.

4 Fill the foundations with concrete (*see mix n°2 p 80*) and allow to set for 24 hours. Pour the concrete for the deck, 5-12 cm (2-5 in) thick, taking care that the reinforcement is completely embedded in the concrete. Allow to harden for 21 days; moisten frequently and protect from strong sun.

5 Remove the side boxing, then shift the shuttering of the arch over sideways till it extends 10-15 cm (4-6 in) out from one side of the deck. Using the shuttering and the concrete arch as a base, build the first parapet, using the facing material chosen for the finishings. In this way, the concrete structure of the arch will be completely masked by the facing, which is assembled with a lime and cement mortar (*see mix n°5 p 80* ).

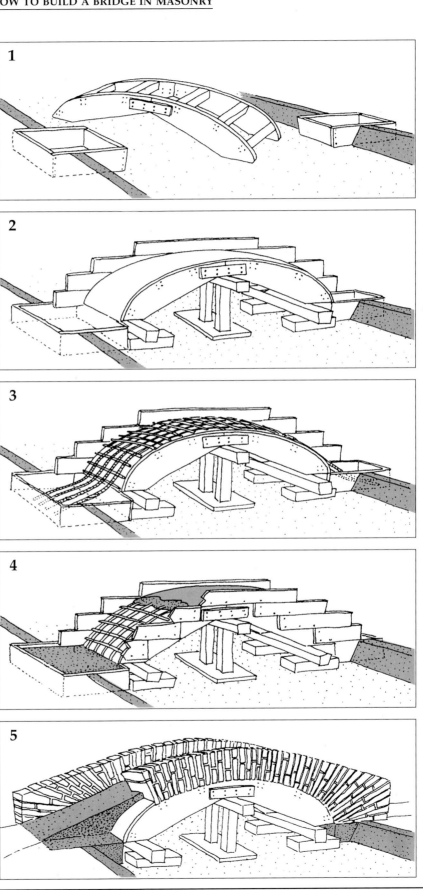

# FORDS AND STEPPING STONES

While a bridge usually provides an overall view of the pond and its surroundings, stepping stones draw the attention down towards the water. The subtle rhythm created by the position and shape of the stepping stones leads the visitor on in a gradual progression, from one point of interest to another.

STEPPING STONES ARE AN important element in the composition of a water garden and crossing a pool by this means can give the visitor an agreeable illusion of walking on the water, as well as enabling him to have a better appreciation of the beauty and perfume of the aquatic plants most distant from the shore. Sometimes, stepping stones are seen as a kind of game, or a personal challenge, in which there is a certain element (hopefully very slight) of risk : "Can I get across without getting my feet wet?"

### Size and arrangement of the elements

The elements must be big enough to make crossing easy, and the minimum width should never be less than 35 cm (14 in). If there is enough space to do so, some larger stones can be placed at a strategic point in the crossing so that the visitor is virtually obliged to pause and appreciate the scene which is revealed to him.

The distance between the elements must not be too great, so that no visitor, tall or short, need take unnecessary risks in crossing.

A distance of 50-60 cm (20-24 in), centre to centre, corresponds to an average stride. When the stones are closely spaced, there is a natural tendency to linger and appreciate the view, whereas if they are rather far apart one is more likely to cross over more rapidly. In moving water, the distance between the stones can be reduced to a few centimetres, in order to create eddies in the current.

Give some thought, too, to the height of the elements above the water : if they are set at different levels, a further dimension is added, creating a contrast with the horizontal plane of the water, opening up new angles of vision and new sensations.

### What materials can be used?

Many types of material are suitable for stepping stones : slates, rough or faced natural stone, shuttered concrete and concrete with a surface of exposed aggregate, reconstituted stone, wood. Oak will last for many years if it is treated with a fungicide (with a non-toxic product) then given a coating of stain.

The section of wood to be immersed can be charred with a flame and covered in a bituminous based product or a synthetic resin. The surface of the elements must be sufficiently rough and flat to avoid risk of falls. If you use railway sleepers or sections of tree-trunk, the top surface should be striated to make it slip-proof.

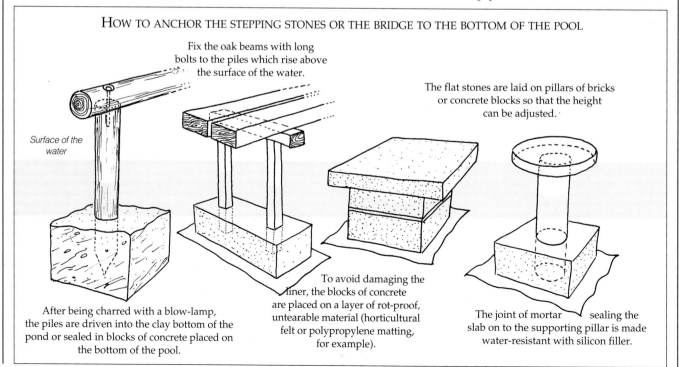

HOW TO ANCHOR THE STEPPING STONES OR THE BRIDGE TO THE BOTTOM OF THE POOL

Fix the oak beams with long bolts to the piles which rise above the surface of the water.

The flat stones are laid on pillars of bricks or concrete blocks so that the height can be adjusted.

*Surface of the water*

After being charred with a blow-lamp, the piles are driven into the clay bottom of the pond or sealed in blocks of concrete placed on the bottom of the pool.

To avoid damaging the liner, the blocks of concrete are placed on a layer of rot-proof, untearable material (horticultural felt or polypropylene matting, for example).

The joint of mortar sealing the slab on to the supporting pillar is made water-resistant with silicon filler.

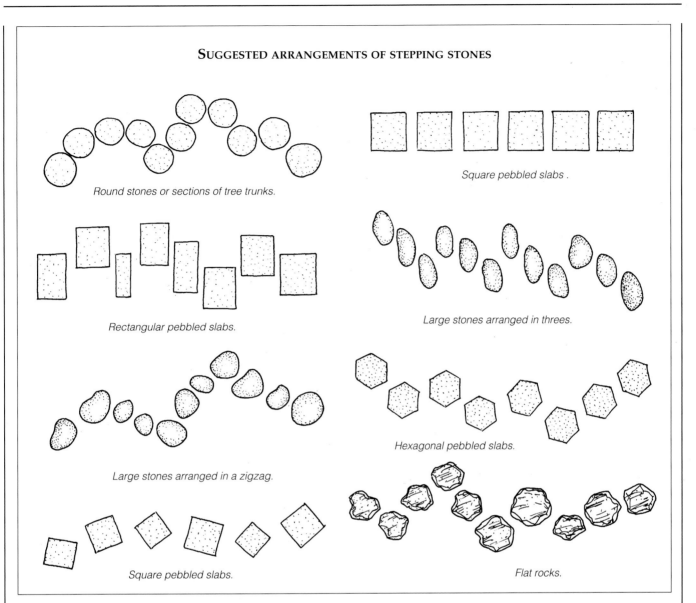

**SUGGESTED ARRANGEMENTS OF STEPPING STONES**

Round stones or sections of tree trunks.

Square pebbled slabs .

Rectangular pebbled slabs.

Large stones arranged in threes.

Large stones arranged in a zigzag.

Hexagonal pebbled slabs.

Square pebbled slabs.

Flat rocks.

## Style

The aesthetic effect produced by a passage of stepping stones, which depends on the number, the shape and the positioning of the elements, can make a considerable contribution to the general ambience and style of the pool. In a garden of a "contemporary" style, regularly-shaped elements will be chosen, made of natural or reconstituted stone, or shuttered concrete. The natural look of a rockery or a garden inspired by Oriental models will be enhanced by the use of flat, rough stones. Whenever possible, use the same materials as those employed to make the paths, and preserve a certain unity of outline. Considerable care is required in choosing the shape and size of the stones and the way they are arranged in the pool, in order to create a balanced and harmonious composition, pleasing from a number of different angles.

## Position

The stepping stones can be arranged in such a way that the visitor is led to discover one or more of the focal points of the pool : a piece of sculpture, a cascade, lotus flowers or water-lilies at a distance from the bank, and so on. A larger stone (or several stones placed close together) can form a resting place, or a kind of crossroad offering two or more alternative routes. Always try to preserve (or to create artificially) a logical continuity between the layout of the garden path on the one hand and the position and layout of the stepping-stone passage on the other. If necessary, obstacles such as flower beds, groups of rocks or clumps of shrubs can be installed, to justify the arrangement which has been selected.

## Construction

It is always preferable to plan to include a passage of stepping stones right from the beginning, so that the method of building and the depth of water surrounding the stones can be selected with due regard to people's safety.

Moreover, the sub-base of the pool at this point must be sufficiently strong and stable to support the weight of the stepping stones and their foundations. The latter may be built of bricks or concrete blocks, or made from fibro-cement pipes. Alternatively, blocks of the required dimensions can be made from waterproofed concrete (*see page 80, mix n° 2*). The pillars, whose width will correspond to the size and weight of the stepping stones, must not be visible from the surface. Bricks and concrete blocks must be laid so that the vertical joints do not line up with one another. For increased stability and resistance to frost, the concrete blocks and fibro-cement pipes should be filled with water-proofed concrete.

For safety, always seal the stepping stones on to their foundation, which must be perfectly stable. The mortar used for sealing is composed of 2 parts cement and 4 parts fine sand, with a waterproofing agent added. The joint should be about 2 cm (1 in) thick. To prevent water from penetrating through any microscopic fissures between the stepping stone and its foundation, apply a waterproof finishing coat of epoxy or silicon filler over the joint. The upper surface of the lowest stepping stones must be at least 2 cm (1 in) above the surface of the water.

**Safety measures**

Stepping stone passages (and many foot bridges) do not have handrails or railings, so precautions must be taken to ensure the safety of users, especially of young children. When designing the pool, incorporate a very shallow safe zone, less than 15 cm (6 in) deep, extending 1.5 m (5 ft) on each side of the passage. If it is impossible to do so, see that a barrier or other device is installed to prevent access to the pool when it is not under surveillance.

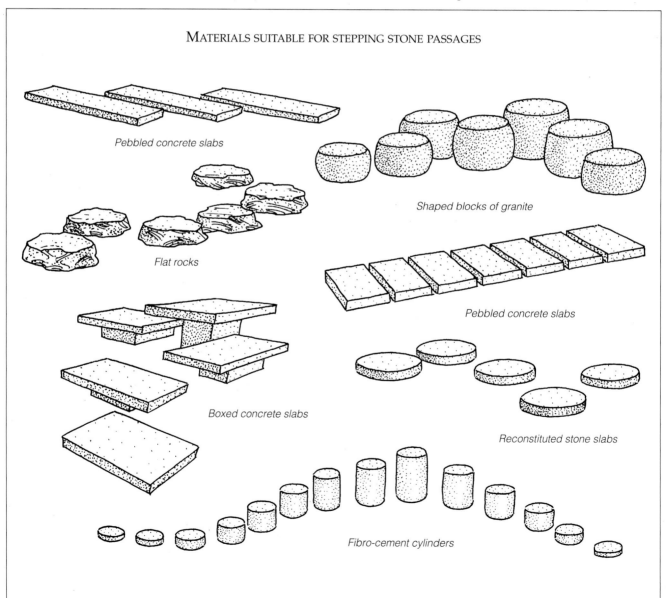

MATERIALS SUITABLE FOR STEPPING STONE PASSAGES

*Pebbled concrete slabs*

*Shaped blocks of granite*

*Flat rocks*

*Pebbled concrete slabs*

*Boxed concrete slabs*

*Reconstituted stone slabs*

*Fibro-cement cylinders*

# Chapter 4

# Plants and Planting

# A PLANTING PLAN

An ornamental garden is not just a collection of pretty plants, but a real composition requiring thought and planning. A design plan will help to provide some idea of the general effect, while a precise planting plan will enable you to draw up a complete list of the plants required and their exact position.

TO DRAW UP A DESIGN PLAN or the block planting plan for an existing garden, refer to the detailed explanations given in pages 60 to 65.

## The block planting plan

The scale of the plan must be such that the smallest plants can be shown, and their names inscribed legibly : for small gardens a scale of 1:20 is satisfactory (1 m [3 ft] on the ground is represented by 5 cm [2 in] on the paper) or 1:25 (1 m [3 ft] = 4 cm [under 2 in]). For big gardens, a scale of 1:50 (1 m [3 ft]= 2 cm [1 in]) is more suitable. Enlarge plans with a photocopier equipped with a reduction or enlargement facility. If you make several copies of the plan, you can sketch out a variety of ideas. If you use squared paper 5x5 mm (5thx5th in) it will be easier to calculate the distances for planting.

## The design plan

This is a perspective drawing of the garden showing all the important features : pool, paths, trees, walls and fences, etc. Make several photocopies so that you can experiment with different arrangements of the plants you have chosen.

**GARDEN DESIGN PLAN WITH PLANTS**

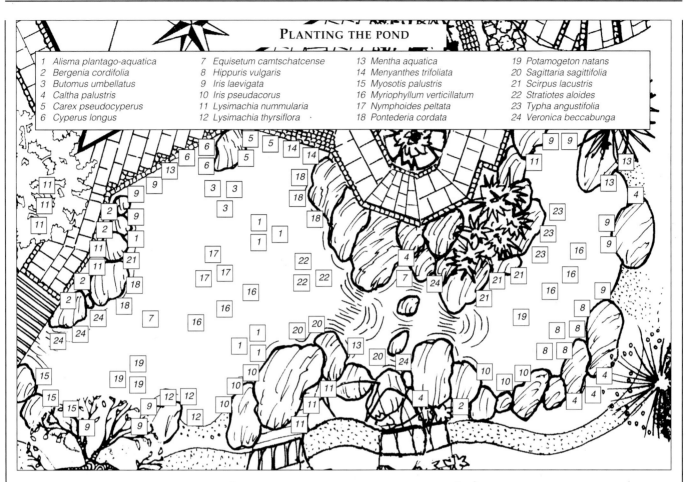

PLANTING THE POND

| | | | | | |
|---|---|---|---|---|---|
| 1 | Alisma plantago-aquatica | 7 | Equisetum camtschatcense | 13 | Mentha aquatica |
| 2 | Bergenia cordifolia | 8 | Hippuris vulgaris | 14 | Menyanthes trifoliata |
| 3 | Butomus umbellatus | 9 | Iris laevigata | 15 | Myosotis palustris |
| 4 | Caltha palustris | 10 | Iris pseudacorus | 16 | Myriophyllum verticillatum |
| 5 | Carex pseudocyperus | 11 | Lysimachia nummularia | 17 | Nymphoides peltata |
| 6 | Cyperus longus | 12 | Lysimachia thyrsiflora | 18 | Pontederia cordata |
| 19 | Potamogeton natans |
| 20 | Sagittaria sagittifolia |
| 21 | Scirpus lacustris |
| 22 | Stratiotes aloides |
| 23 | Typha angustifolia |
| 24 | Veronica beccabunga |

## Unity of style

Unless you have a very large garden in which you can create several distinctive scenes, it is better to keep to a single style for the whole garden. Choose plants according to your personal preferences, and in keeping with the atmosphere you wish to create (e.g. a garden dominated by foliage chosen to produce a jungle-like effect, a garden of flowers, a rock garden, etc.). Make a complete list of the plants selected and note carefully the characteristics and requirements of each : colour, shape, size, planting distance, situation, nature of the soil, planting depth, etc.

## Work in volumes

It is easy to obtain balanced volumes by following a few simple principles, whatever the size of your garden. Plants which take up a great deal of space will be placed in the background, and smaller plants further forward, nearer to the viewer, beside the paths or the terrace. When you are selecting trees, make sure you know their adult height and spread, and take this into account in planning your

garden, to avoid creating problems for yourself in the future. Start by choosing the position of the trees and the most voluminous plants (Gunnera, Heracleum, Macleaya), which will form the framework of the garden, respecting planting distances and taking into account the particular requirements of each species. Mark the size of each plant on your block plan and sketch in its shape on the design plan, to obtain some idea of the general effect. Represent each plant as a simple geometrical shape (cone, sphere, etc.,) and consider your garden as a harmonious combination of volumes. Do not try to include all the plants that please you : be selective. Now introduce the medium-sized plants, positioning them so as to obtain effects of harmony or contrast : tall, narrow shapes alongside large, rounded leaves, luminous colours placed against a background of dark foliage, contrasting textures, etc. Complete the composition with some smaller plants. If you place 3, 5, 7 or 9 plants of the same species in a triangular arrangement, you will obtain balanced and homogeneous groups which will blend gently into one another.

▲ The pond planting plan shows the position of aquatic and semi-aquatic plants.

## A garden for all seasons

Check on your plan that deciduous plants make up about 2/3 of the total. The remaining third, the evergreen plants that make up the winter framework, will be distributed over the whole of the garden. Place colours (flowers, foliage, bark) to harmonize or, on the contrary, to create contrasts. The most difficult thing is to create a succession of scenes which will provide decorative interest all the year round.

## Do not forget the animals

Before finalizing your plan, make sure that you have included a certain number of plant species of use to the animals that will be in your pond. Do not overlook the native species. For hundreds of thousands of years, these have provided the familiar habitat for the local fauna, and are indispensable for its survival and reproduction.

## PLANTING PLAN

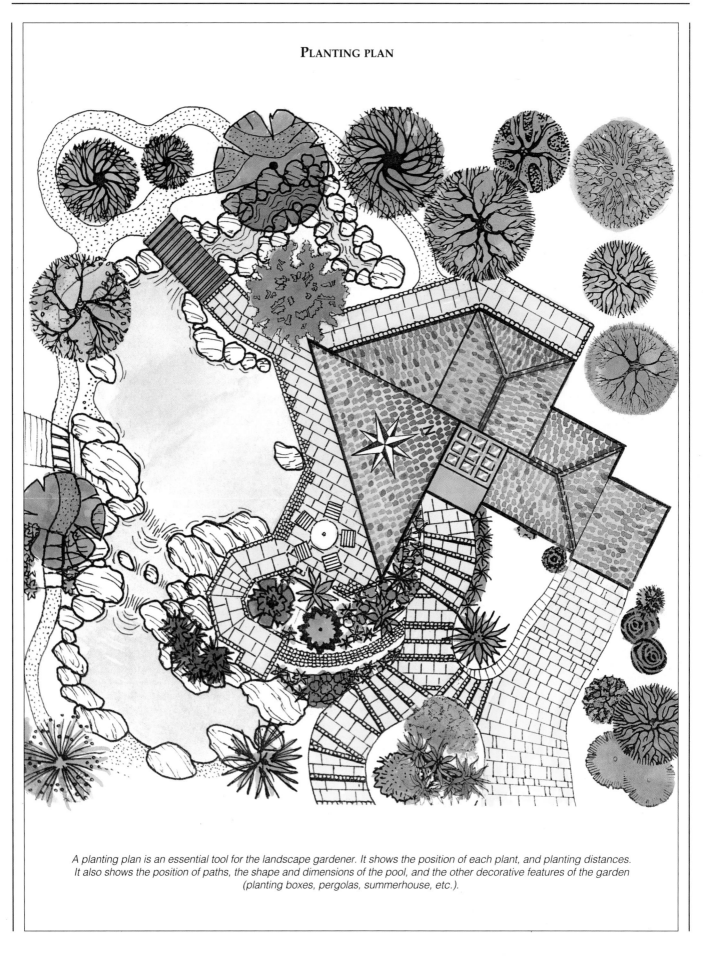

*A planting plan is an essential tool for the landscape gardener. It shows the position of each plant, and planting distances. It also shows the position of paths, the shape and dimensions of the pool, and the other decorative features of the garden (planting boxes, pergolas, summerhouse, etc.).*

### The water plants

Check how much space you really have on the planting shelves and the bottom of the pool. It is a good idea to buy your planting containers in advance, so that you will be sure of having the number you need, and the right sizes. As in the rest of the garden, the taller water plants should be placed in the background. Plants should not cover more than two thirds of the surface of the pool, to enable light to penetrate more easily and gas exchange to take place satisfactorily at the surface of the water.

### Streams and cascades

The rocks and pebbles used on the margin of pools, streams and cascades can shelter a number of plants. Pockets for planting, made of concrete or flexible liner, can be positioned under the pebbles and filled with earth. The space between stones and rocks can be filled with soil and planted with ferns.

### Situation

Most aquatic plants need full light, or dappled light filtering through the surrounding foliage. When you are designing your pool, make sure that it is correctly exposed to the sun, and avoid placing it in the shade of a wall or building. If there is too much sun, it is always easier to create shade by adding a few plants or shrubs beside the water. Flowering plants, such as water lilies, for example, need much sunlight to develop properly.

### Test your ideas

After this preparatory work, you may find that you have to exclude certain plants that you like, for lack of space or in order to preserve a unity of style. In some cases you may have to modify your original plan (for example, the position of the pool or paths) because of the requirements of certain plants you have selected.

All the preparatory work will be justified if it enables you to foresee and solve in advance the main problems involved in creating a garden. It

▲ *In this attractive stream-bank composition, the tall silhouette of the bright yellow loosestrife (Lysimachia punctata) contrasts with the spherical mauve inflorescence of the flowering onion (Allium giganteum). Creation Gilbert Galloché.*

is always better to take time to think about a project before making a final choice.

### The planting plan

When you are satisfied with the result, all that remains for you to do is to mark on the planting plan the position of each plant, using the squares on your plan to make sure that planting distances are corrrect. For marginal plants, the planting distance must also be established in relation to the edge of the pool or pond. Now that your plan is completed, you can draw up a full list of all the plants you will require. As soon as the basic construction work is finished, you will have to prepare the position for each plant with appropriate organic material and fertilizer.

# WHERE TO FIND PLANTS

You now have a complete planting plan, with the help of which you have drawn up a full list of the plants you have chosen for your garden. When conditions are right you will be ready to start the main construction work, and prepare the ground and the pool to ensure the best possible conditions for planting.

DEPENDING ON THE SIZE of the job, the main construction work can be done at the beginning of spring or in the preceding autumn, so that the garden will be ready for planting at the beginning of May.

### Where to find the plants

It is increasingly easy to find plants for ponds and bog gardens in garden centres. But for the greatest choice of species, including a number of lesser-known ones, you should address yourself to a water garden specialist. Find out early in the planning stage what is available from different suppliers, so that you will have time to consider your choice of plants while you are creating your plan.

### When to buy plants

The best time to order plants is be tween October and April. They will then be delivered to you in April-May, or later, if that suits you better. Depending on the supplier, the plants will be delivered in containers or with bare roots. In the latter case, the

roots will be protected with plastic or damp paper, to prevent them from drying out.

### Containers or bare roots?

Container-raised plants have compact root-balls, formed with the compost in which they have been grown. Containerized plants can be transplanted virtually all the year round, provided they are well watered. If buying by mail order, of course, the weight of the containers may increase the cost considerably, especially if the plants are well-developed. Bare-rooted plants are more economical in this respect, since without the weight and bulk of the rootball in its container, the cost of transport will be lower. The roots should be handled carefully when transplanting bare-rooted plants.

### Before ordering...

If you decide to buy your plants by mail order, ask for details about the age and the size of the plants which will be delivered, and the method and cost of shipment. Ask the supplier whether plants will be replaced in the event of damage during transport, or failure to strike. If certain plants ordered should be unavailable and you do not wish to receive the supplier's replacement choice, specify on your order form your own choice of substitute plants or ask that your account be credited for a later purchase. Be sure to keep a copy of your order.

### Delivery

The plants will be delivered,whether by mail or special parcel delivery, carefully protected and packed in a carton. First check that the outer wrapping is in good condition and

▶ The Joe Pye Weed (Eupatorium purpureum) is a vigorous perennial which can reach a height of 2 m (7 ft) in the first year. Here it provides a background for the composition formed by the lobelias (Lobelia cardinalis 'Queen Victoria'), arrowheads (Sagittaria sagittifolia), and knotweeds (Polygonum bistorta 'Superbum'). Creation Colette Sainte-Beuve/Plantbessin.

that the package has not been crushed or torn open during transport. If there is any sign of damage, note the details on the delivery docket before signing it. You should also make a note of the length of time between the date the parcel left the supplier and the date it was delivered, in case any delay has resulted in damage to the living plant material Open the parcel immediately and inspect the contents for damage or error, and notify the supplier immediately if there are any. If you cannot plant immediately, keep your plants cool, shaded, and damp, for no more than a couple of days, when you may then plant them out.

### Unpacking the plants

Plants should always be unpacked in a shady place (or in overcast weather), since large-leaved varieties (*rodgersias, rhubarbs, petasites,* ferns) are particularly sensitive to sun during transplantation. Check and save the plant labels. Bare-rooted plants should immediately be placed in water, in a shady place, but the protective wrapping will not be removed until the moment of planting either in the ground or in the pool. If temperatures are on the cool side and there is still a risk of spring frost, or your garden is not quite ready, put the plants into pots for the time being, in a mixture composed of 1/3 compost and 2/3 good garden soil. Water the plants well, and keep the pots in a light, sheltered place until you are ready to plant.

### Permanent labelling

Use plastic labels and write on them the Latin name of each plant, and where it comes from. Use an ordinary lead pencil - you will find it is more weatherproof. These plastic labels will replace the paper ones which usually accompany the plants, but which finally become completely illegible, if they do not totally disintegrate. Bear in mind the fact that many perennials die down completely in the autumn, and if

their position is not marked by a clearly visible label, the crown can easily be damaged during routine digging operations.

### After planting

If you find that your plants seem rather sickly during the first months after planting, do not be too concerned. Some aquatic plants may die down well before the autumn, but will reappear the following spring. (This is where good labeling is useful). This is quite normal behaviour, since plants require a certain time to acclimatize. The least vigorous (*Hosta, Lysichitum, Gunnera*) will not really start to develop and flower before the second or third year. All you can do is make sure that growing conditions are right (watering, site) and be patient.

During this period, it is important that plants for damp or wet soil be kept well watered. A good mulch of grass clippings or compost will help to keep the ground moist. Remember to stake those plants which require support. During the growing period, once the plant has settled down, make a monthly application of dilute-fertilizer (except for the pond plants).

▲ *Around a small pool, an attractive composition associating the leaves and colours of a willow* (Salix sachalinensis 'Sekka'), *loosestrife* (Lythrum salicaria), *Ligularia* (Ligularia dentata) *and* Pontederia cordata.

### PRESERVE OUR NATURAL HERITAGE

Unless a natural habitat and its flora are about to disappear under the treads of earth-moving equipment, avoid gathering plants from the wild, or their seeds, however tempting this may be. There are too many examples of species becoming very rare or even extinct because they are gathered by passers-by who find them attractive. As for the "protected" species (many of which are available from specialist nurseries), removing the plants, or their seed, is severely punished by law. It is preferable to address yourself to a specialist grower or professional collector, or to other water garden owners. By doing so, you will be encouraging the cultivation and conservation of rare species, and you will certainly have the opportunity of meeting other enthusiasts and exchanging plants and ideas.

# ADVICE FOR PLANTING

In some books, and in specialist catalogues, aquatic plants are usually classified according to the position they occupy in the pond or the depth at which they grow. This is quite a convenient classification, but it tends not to take into account the fact that many of these wet zone plants adapt themselves very easily to other situations.

AQUATIC PLANTS ARE generally grouped into three main categories : submerged plants, or "oxygenators" such as the Canadian pondweed, plants with floating leaves (whether they are bottom-rooted, or free-floating like duckweed), and plants whose leaves emerge above the surface (reedmace, arrowhead). To these are usually added the bog plants, which grow in the immediate vicinity of the pond in ground which is more or less water-logged.

### Limitations of the usual classification

This classification tends to under-estimate the adaptability of many species. Certain plants can grow in a variety of conditions at different depths and in more or less wet soils. For example, in what category should one place creeping Jenny (*Lysimachia nummularia*), the common reed (*Phragmites communis*) or water grass (*Glyceria aquatica*), which grow just as well under water as on dry land? And the arrowhead? Its leaves are submerged, then floating, and finally erect. Plants whose leaves are at one period or another beneath the surface of the water must surely all be "oxygenators". We have therefore chosen, in this book, to set aside the arbitrary classifications and to present the plants in the alphabetical order of their Latin names. The requirements of each are indicated, so that the reader can make his own decision as to how to use a particular plant.

## PLANTING IN THE POOL

Bottom-rooting aquatic plants, whether submerged, floating or emerging above the surface, can either be grown in containers or planted directly into the pool. Each method has its advantages, and both can be used in the same pool.

### Container planting

Container planting offers a number of advantages : it simplifies control of creeping rootstocks, and makes it easy to vary the position and depth of planting. Once past their best, flowering plants can be removed and replaced by others, for a continuous display. With more tender species, the containers are placed just beneath the surface in summer or in the deepest part of the pool in winter, to protect them from frost. If the pool is shallow, it is easy to remove the plants and winter them over in a heated greenhouse. Finally, if a plant needs to be divided, or the compost renewed, it is easy to withdraw the container from the water and carry out the operation on the bank.

Container growing is especially useful in a small pool : water lilies may have smaller leaves and flowers when grown in containers than when directly planted on the bottom. Stand containers on one or more bricks placed in the desired situation and at the right height for the plants' requirements.

### Bottom planting

The bottom of the pool can be covered with a layer of good garden soil (loam) 20-30 cm (8-12 in) thick. The advantage of this method of direct planting is that it allows plants to grow vigorously in conditions similar

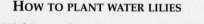

## HOW TO PLANT WATER LILIES

• Allow at least 1 m² (10 ft²) per plant. Large varieties need at least 4 m² (45 ft²) of surface area.

• A sunny situation encourages flowering (flowers open from approximately 10 a.m. to 5 p.m.).

• According to the species, plant in 20-50 cm (4-20 in) of good garden soil (heavy loam) at a depth of from 30-200 cm (1-7 ft). Add no manure.

• The rhizome should be planted at a 45° angle, with the top of the crown showing.

• Baskets or crates can be used, and many shapes and sizes are available. The advantage of plant-ing in containers is that the root can be kept under control, and plants shifted easily.

• For best development, place the container near the surface on a pile of bricks, for example. As the young leaves start to float on the surface, lower the container progressively by removing bricks until the final planting depth is reached.

• Hardy water lilies, will not need lifting in the winter as long as they are under at least 30 cm (12 in) of water. While it is not necessary to remove faded flowers or leaves, the appearance of smaller pools is certainly improved with this minor maintenance, and you may then observe the health and condition of the pool and its plants.

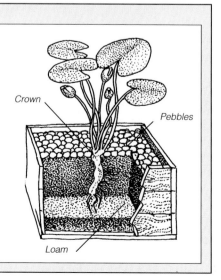

*Crown*

*Pebbles*

*Loam*

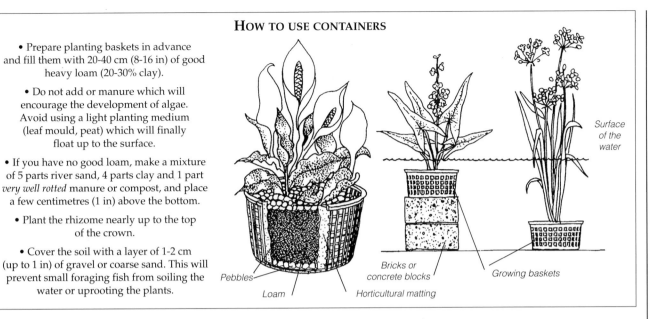

## HOW TO USE CONTAINERS

• Prepare planting baskets in advance and fill them with 20-40 cm (8-16 in) of good heavy loam (20-30% clay).

• Do not add or manure which will encourage the development of algae. Avoid using a light planting medium (leaf mould, peat) which will finally float up to the surface.

• If you have no good loam, make a mixture of 5 parts river sand, 4 parts clay and 1 part *very well rotted* manure or compost, and place a few centimetres (1 in) above the bottom.

• Plant the rhizome nearly up to the top of the crown.

• Cover the soil with a layer of 1-2 cm (up to 1 in) of gravel or coarse sand. This will prevent small foraging fish from soiling the water or uprooting the plants.

*Surface of the water*

*Pebbles*

*Loam*

*Bricks or concrete blocks*

*Horticultural matting*

*Growing baskets*

to those of the natural habitat. But it is difficult to keep plants with strong root growth under control (*Nymphaea, Typha, Glyceria,* etc). For maintenance work it will sometimes be necessary to lower the level of the water.

### Floating plants

These are simply placed on the water and require no other attention, except cutting back from time to time, since they can take over all the available surface as long as the water provides sufficient nutrients, which they absorb directly through their roots.

### Water quality

Aquatic plants do not usually have any special requirements as to the quality of the water, apart from temperature : water lilies do best in calm, warm water. In pools fed from

a subterranean spring or a well, water temperature should be checked at intervals. If the water is too cold in summer, a deviation will be needed. In winter, spring or well water is relatively warm, which is an advantage.

## BOG PLANTS

### Preparing the soil

Bog plants need a well-worked, weed-free soil enriched by well-rotted manure. Heavy clay soils retain moisture. In these circumstances, avoid planting perennials in autumn, since there is a risk that the crown may rot during the winter. Plant in spring, or improve the soil by adding sand and compost, which will help to prevent crusting and cracking in summer. A

very light soil can be improved by adding small quantities of clay.

### Bog perennials

These reappear each spring, and should be planted when there is no danger of frost or freezing. Spring frosts may damage buds and young shoots, but in most cases after a slight check new buds will be produced.

### Ferns

These prefer shade to direct sunlight, and are happiest in the shelter of plants with light foliage such as birches, the twisted willows, and bamboos. They also like a moist to wet soil, neutral to acid (pH 7-4.5), which can be achieved by adding leaf mould, ericaceous compost, or sulphur chips. Cut down the dry fronds at the beginning of winter to use as mulch. Ferns can be used to very good effect among rocks.

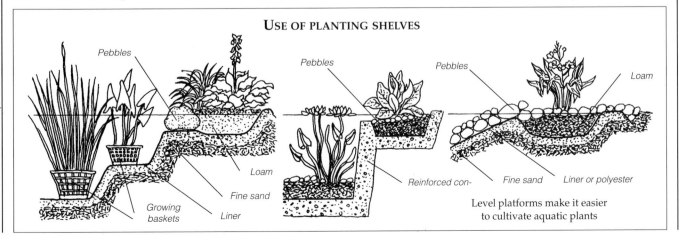

## USE OF PLANTING SHELVES

*Pebbles*

*Pebbles*

*Pebbles*

*Loam*

*Loam*

*Fine sand*

*Growing baskets*

*Liner*

*Reinforced con-*

*Fine sand*

*Liner or polyester*

Level platforms make it easier to cultivate aquatic plants

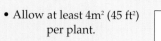

## HOW TO PLANT LOTUSES

- Allow at least 4m² (45 ft²) per plant.

- The planting medium, rich in organic matter, will contain 20% well rotted manure for 80% garden soil.

- Limit the planting zone by using a wooden crate or large planting basket, such as a perforated laundry basket, lined with hessian.

- Lay the rhizome horizontally onto the soil surface and carefully weight it between its nodes with stones or wire pegs.

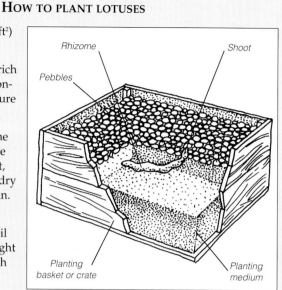

Rhizome

Shoot

Pebbles

Planting basket or crate

Planting medium

## EXOTIC PLANTS

### In an outside pool

Tropical plants are, of course, a very attractive addition to a pool in a veranda or a heated greenhouse. In an outside pool they must be grown in containers, since our European winters are too cold for permanent planting. They will be lifted at the end of summer and sheltered through the winter. The containers can be installed in a pool in a greenhouse where the air and water temperatures never fall below 8°C (46 °F). Alternatively, transplant into a watertight container filled with a mixture of 1/3 compost and 2/3 garden soil, and store in a cool place, keeping it moist.

Cannas must be placed in trays or in pots of damp sand and stored in a light place, unheated, but protected from frost. Prevent the roots from drying out by watering the sand every 10 days.

In a mild climate, the hardier species can spend the winter outside provided the crown is kept below freezing level. To provide satisfactory protection, it may be worth your while to install a thermostatically-controlled electrical heating system around the containers.

In summer, the temperature of the water can be raised appreciably by means of pipes carrying hot water, heated by solar or heat exchangers power. This system also makes it possible to extend outdoor cultivation of exotic species well into autumn.

## GENERAL CARE

### Growing from seed

The seed of aquatic and marsh plants must be harvested at the end of summer and conserved in permanently wet or moist compost. The young plants will be pricked out into larger containers and kept (out of reach of the fish) in an aquarium, preferably equipped with a filtration system to limit the development of algae and fungi.

### Dividing plants

Spring is the best time to divide pond plants. With rhizomatous plants, use a sharp knife to cut sections bearing one or several buds. Avoid using secateurs, which crush the tissues and increase the risk of rotting. The cut surfaces may be dusted with charcoal as a protection against fungal infection. The most vigorous shoots or runners are at the outside part of the crown, and these can be separated and planted up individually. When plants reach a certain size, after 3-5 years, it is advisable to divide them into two or three sections, to prevent the plant from becoming exhausted, or from bursting the container (water lilies). Each section can be planted separately in new compost. Exotic water lilies produce, on certain leaves, tiny plantlets which throw out roots. Detach the leaf with the plantlet and plant under water.

### Disease prevention

Respecting the requirements of each plant (situation, planting depth, type of soil) is an essential part of disease prevention. Do not be too concerned if the young plants seem slow to develop. Some transplanted material takes two or three years to reach maturity and produce flowers. Healthy plants are much less subject to attack from parasites and fungal diseases. If this does occur, it is preferable to look for the cause (is the plant correctly positioned, for example?) rather than simply treating the symptoms with a pesticide. After a certain time, natural predators will probably restore things to normal. No chemical pesticides should be used near the pool, because of the risk of destroying all forms of life, by interrupting the food chain and poisoning other species (ladybirds, dragonflies).

### Dead leaves

The smaller your pool, the more the water may be saturated by dead leaves in autumn. During this period, remove most of the dead leaves which drop in or around the pool, or place a protective net over the water (2-4 cm [1-2 in] mesh). But do not be too ruthless; allow a few dead leaves to lie here and there, to preserve a natural look, as the Japanese do so very well.

### Algae

The presence of large quantities of filamentous algae, or blanket weed, is a sign that the plants are not absorbing all the nutrients in the water. Check that the soil in your submerged containers is properly covered with a layer of gravel or sand. Remove the algae with a pond net. The weeds can also be wound around a stick - rather like spaghetti - which avoids damaging the plants. The most efficient way to combat them is to introduce floating plants (*Lemna* spp., *Azolla* spp., *Pistia stratiotes, Potamogeton, Hydrocharis,*

▲ *Like most rhizomatous plants,* the yellow pond lily (Nuphar lutea) *can be propagated by dividing the rhizome into fragments about 12 cm (5 in) long.*

Stratiotes aloides, *Callitriche*, etc) or plants which spread rapidly (*Ludwigia, Hydrocotyle, Nymphoides peltata*, etc.) whose roots draw their food directly from the water. The algae will disappear once biological balance is achieved. Also check that the runoff from the garden is not entering the pool adding unwanted excess nutrients.

## Duckweed

Duckweed absorbs the nutrient material in suspension in the water to the detriment of algae, which it is much harder to get rid of. It is only a problem if it is allowed to spread freely, since it will easily cover all the surface of the water, limiting the gaseous exchanges and preventing light from reaching the submerged plants. Remove part of the duckweed periodically, without eliminating it completely. Its growth will slow down as the nutrient content of the water diminishes.

## Divide to control...

Aquatic and bog plants grow vigorously and must be kept firmly under control. To prevent certain plants from taking over the garden, you should cut back ruthlessly those which spread beyond their allotted zone. Divide plants on average every three years, keeping the younger sections (nearest the outside) and eliminating the old part, which will be past its best.

## Silting up of the pond

The formation of silt at the bottom of the pond is normal, and it is essential to the life of the flora and fauna. Decomposing vegetable matter and the various elements in suspension in the water (zooplancton, phytoplancton) drop to the bottom and will, over a long period, cause the water quality to deteriorate appreciably. This phenomenon can be avoided by thinning out invasive plants in summer and removing dead leaves in autumn. A reasonable quantity of plant matter in

the water will be sufficient to preserve the food chain for the pond fauna. Excess silt can be removed. To preserve the biological balance, spread the cleaning operation over three successive years, cleaning one third of the bottom at a time. Do the work at the end of summer, before the amphibians have had time to settle in to the mud for the winter. Avoid draining your pool completely to clean it. This complete drainage operation is commonly used in fish farming to destroy germs and parasites by liming, but it is incompatible with the establishment of a durable and natural biological balance.

## Chemical treatments

If there is a problem, always look for the root cause behind the symptoms. The use of chemical remedies (anti-algal treatment) or mechanical methods (filters, pumps) will at best provide a temporary solution. When treatment is stopped, the problem may reappear.

## How to use vegetable matter

All the vegetable matter withdrawn from the pond (algae, duckweed, dead leaves, silt, etc.) contains a great quantity of nutrient material. As it rots down, this organic material forms an excellent manure which you can use on your flower beds or make into a compost heap. The compost will be of good quality, and will also provide shelter for numerous pondside animals : insects, tritons, toads, etc.

## Are fertilizers necessary?

Aquatic plants usually grow rapidly. The water of the pool and its inhabitants produce organic matter, so it is not always necessary to add fertilizer when planting or during the growing period. Certain aquatic plant varieties obtain all the nutrient they need from fresh soil every 3-5 years. Others, however, notably *Nymphaea*, may require the application of aquatic fertilizer tablets, pressed well into the root zone of the planting container, several times during each growing season.

## The pool in winter

Check that the containers of the least hardy plants are below freezing level. A well-designed pool with at least one sloping side will allow ice to expand upwards and outwards, and prevent damage. When the ice is covered with snow, the oxygenating plants do not receive sufficient light for efficient photosynthesis.If the pool contains fish, it is therefore a good idea to sweep the snow off without breaking the ice, or else install an aerator. Never empty the pool in winter, because it would then be subjected to strong pressure from the outside which could cause damage. In a very wet winter, water pressure from below could even cause an empty pool to lift.

# CALENDAR FOR ROUTINE CARE

| | WATER | POOL, ACCESSORIES | ANIMALS |
|---|---|---|---|
| JANUARY | | • If the pool freezes over, check that the oxygenating equipment is working satisfactorily. | |
| FEBRUARY | | • If you do not have such a system, and if the frost lasts longer than a few days, make an air-hole in the ice with a pan of hot water. Do not smash the ice. Lower the level of the water to create a layer about 3 cm (1 in) of air beneath the ice, so that gaseous exchanges with the atmosphere can take place. | • As soon as the water temperature rises above 5 °C (41°F), start feeding the fishes, which have been fasting throughout the winter. Give small quantities which will be consumed immediately. |
| MARCH | | | • Now is the time to observe the metamorphosis of dragonflies and tadpoles. |
| APRIL | • Put back the level regulator and turn on the water supply to make up winter losses. | • This is a good time to start digging operations if you are building a water garden. The ground is easy to work and temperatures are rising.   • Turn on the fountains, cascades, etc.   • Put the pump back into place in small pools. | • Check the health of your fish, and look for parasites (fish lice, leeches). |
| MAY | | | |
| JUNE | • Check the quality of the water regularly (dissolved oxygen) as it starts to warm up.   • Check that the water level remains constant in spite of evaporation loss.   • If there is no automatic level control, add fresh water from time to time. | • The vegetation and the microscopic fauna of the pool are now sufficiently well-developed to provide food for the fish (unless there is a population explosion). Extra feeding is no longer essential. | • The water in the pool is now warm enough, 15 °C (59°F) or more, for the tropical fish which have spent the winter in the aquarium. |
| JULY | | | |
| AUGUST | | | |
| SEPTEMBER | | • Take out the pump, perform normal pump maintenance, and clean the filter and store in a dry place.   • This is also a good time to start digging operations. | • The biomass of the pool is starting to diminish. Provide a little supplementary food for the fish, which need to build up reserves for the winter. |
| OCTOBER | • If there is no heating device, check for frost damage.   • During a long spell of frost, remove any snow from the ice, to allow light to penetrate. | | • As soon as the water temperature falls below 15 °C (59°F), return your tropical fish to the aquarium for winter. |
| NOVEMBER | | • To absorb the thrust of ice in a concrete pool with vertical sides, anchor some soft floating objects (plastic bottles, blocks of polystyrene, small bundles of reeds or rushes). | • Stop feeding the fish as soon as the water temperature falls below 5 °C (41°F). |
| DECEMBER | | | |

# PLANTS AND PLANTING

• If you intend to purchase new plants, study the catalogues and send off your orders.

• As soon as temperatures rise above freezing, deciduous ornamental trees with bare roots can be planted.

• Make plans now for planting.

• The earliest plants are starting to show signs of life : *Caltha, Darmera* …

• Plant the perennials alongside the pool (*astilbes*, ferns, *primulas*) and the evergreen shrubs (conifers, aucuba, bamboos, choisya).

• Cut back the faded flowers and leaves of marginal and aquatic plants if this was not done in autumn.

• This is the best time to visit garden centres and buy new plants.

• Plant out the tender bulbs which have been wintered under cover : *canna, arum, agapanthus.*

• When the risk of spring frost is passed, uncover the tender species.

• Return to the pool the tropical plants which have spent the winter under cover : tropical water lilies, water hyacinth, lotus, papyrus, canna, *Zantedeschia, Pistia, Thalia*, etc.).

• Divide the marginal or aquatic plants. Sections of rhizome should be 12 cm (5 in) long and carry at least one bud.

• Apply fertilizer to plants that have been in place for at least 3 years.

• Limit the development of floating plants so that light can enter the pool and stimulate the growth of oxygenating plants.

• Make sure that growing plants are healthy : yellowing leaves (chlorosis) are a sign of an iron deficiency, which needs correction.

• Check the water lily leaves for aphids : do not use chemical treatments, but spray the leaves with a strong jet from a hose pipe.

• Cut back the faded flowers and leaves on the marginal and aquatic plants. Divide clumps which are too large.

• Thin out the pond plants and remove algae if necessary to prepare good winter conditions for the oxygenating plants.

• Remove shoots or fragments of fragile plants (*Eichhornia, Pistia, Salvinia,* tropical water lilies) and place them in an aquarium sheltered from frost (veranda or heated greenhouse).

• Remove the foliage of floating plants and cut back to below water level those plants whose leaves are completely brown.

• Protect fragile plants ( *Gunnera, Pennisetum, Gynerium, Zantedeschia*) from frost by covering the crown with dead leaves or a clay pot filled with straw. The plant can also be wrapped in straw securely tied in place.

• Remove the dead leaves from the water with a fork covered with fine netting. A net can be placed over the pool to prevent leaves from dropping in.

• In cold regions, if your pool is less than 60 cm (24 in) deep, bring the containers of water lilies inside and keep them in a tub of water, after cutting back the leaves.

1

*Acer* spp.

# MAPLE

ACERACEAE

**Origin :**
**Northern Hemisphere**

*Acer palmatum* 'Dissectum Atropurpureum'

The *Acer* genus contains numerous trees or shrubs which are prized for the elegance of their form and the beauty of their foliage. Among the most decorative are the small or medium sized varieties, most of which originated in the Far East. From spring to autumn, their finely-cut leaves offer an extraordinarily rich range of colours, from palest yellow to deepest purple. Certain cultivars have coloured trunks and stems, or interesting bark texture. They are not difficult as to situation, and their slow rate of growth makes them useful in the small garden.

Plant maples in cool or damp soil, in light shade, with hostas and ferns. A single specimen or a small clump, planted by the side of a pond so that the coloured foliage is reflected in the water, is a happy addition to any garden.

**Position :** light shade, sheltered from cold winds and very hot sun.

**Planting :** moist or damp soil, especially during growing period.

**Care :** protect against hard frosts.

**Propagation :** from seed in autumn, cuttings in summer, air layering in spring and summer.

**Species or varieties :**

• *Acer griseum*, the paper bark maple, is a small tree, originally from China, whose very decorative orange-brown bark peels in winter. The leaves have three leaflets and turn red in autumn. Height : 7.5 m (25 ft).

• *Acer japonicum*, the Japanese maple, is a deciduous variety with 11-lobed, fan-shaped leaves, bright yellow, orange and red in autumn. Full sun, but prefers light shade in summer. Height : 2 m (7 ft).

• *Acer shirasawanum aureum*, the golden Japanese maple, has superb golden yellow palmate leaves, turning garnet-red in autumn. Slow grower. Height : 2 m (7 ft).

• *Acer negundo*, the ash-leaved maple or box elder, a North American native, has pale green leaves with 3-5 lobes. It is a fast grower but can be cut back every 2 years. It likes moist soil and full sun or light shade. Height : 8-10 m (26-32 ft). Spread : 6 m (20 ft).

• *Acer negundo* 'Flamingo' is a cultivar with pink and white marginate foliage.

• *Acer negundo variegatum* is a less vigorous cultivar with green leaves margined with silvery-white.

*Acer palmatum* 'Atropurpureum'

*Acer palmatum*

• *Acer palmatum*, or Japanese maple, of which there are more than 250 cultivars, has been cultivated in Japan for centuries. Its pale green foliage, with 5 or 7 finely-cut lobes, has an upright habit, then spreads out and turns reddish-copper in autumn. Over time, the bark takes on a silvery tint. It is a fast grower and prefers a moist, acid soil, with summer shade and protection from the wind. Requires protection against hard frosts. Height : 2 m (6 1/2 ft). Spread : 2 m (7 ft).

• *Acer palmatum atropurpureum*, the Blood Leaf Japanese maple, has deeply-lobed, reddish-purple foliage which turns bright red in autumn. Flared shape. Hardy and sun-resistant. Height : 3 m (10 ft). Spread : 2 m (7 ft).

• *Acer palmatum* 'Aureum' has yellow foliage in spring, becoming more and more golden. Height : 3-4 m (10-13 ft).

• *Acer palmatum* 'Butterfly' is particularly decorative, having grey-green leaves with pink and cream borders. Slow grower. Height : 1.5 m (5 ft). Spread : 1.2 m (4 ft).

• *Acer palmatum* 'Crimson Queen' is a cultivar with dense, bushy foliage, fine and deeply indented, light crimson in spring and deeper crimson in autumn. Height : 1.5 m (5 ft). Spread : 2 m (7 ft).

• *Acer palmatum* var. *dissectum*, the laciniated Japanese maple, is a very elegant tree, with finely-cut leaves, pale green in spring and turning orange in autumn. Height : 1.5 m (5 ft). Spread : 2 m (7 ft).

• *Acer palmatum* 'Dissectum Atropurpureum' differs from the preceding variety in that it has crimson foliage in spring, turning orange in autumn. Height : 1.5 m (5 ft). Spread : 2 m (7 ft).

• *Acer palmatum* 'Senkaki' has pale green spring foliage, turning yellow in autumn. Height : 3-4 m (10-13 ft).

*Acer palmatum*      *A. p.* 'Butterfly'      *A. p.* 'Deshôjô'      *A. shirasawanum aureum*

| 2 |
| --- |
| *Achillea ptarmica* |

## ACHILLEA

ASTERACEAE
Origin:
Northern Hemisphere

*Achillea ptarmica*

A hardy perennial with a creeping rootstock, this plant does well in the wet, acid soil of marshes and peat-bogs. The tall stems have numerous long, fine-toothed, fern-like leaves, and white umbellate flower heads in July and August. It is a vigorous grower and will flower again in autumn if cut back after the first flowering.

**Position:** sunny.
**Planting:** damp, acid soil. 3 to 5 plants per sq.m.
**Height:** 60-120 cm (2-4 ft).
**Decorative interest:** white flowers, June to August.
**Propagation:** division of rootstock every three years, in autumn.

**Other species or varieties:**
• *Achillea filipendulina*, the dropwort-leaved achillea, a very hardy species from the Caucasus, has very fine, silvery foliage and flat, golden flowerheads, up to 15 cm (6 in) in diameter, from June to September. Planted in largish groups, it is very suitable for big, natural gardens. Good for cutting, lasts well when dried. Height: 1-1.3 m (3-4 ft).
• *Achillea millefolium*, or yarrow, has sturdy, branching stems with numerous very finely-cut, deep green leaves, and corymbs of small, pinkish-white flowers from June to August. Height: 20-100 cm (8 in-3 ft).

*Achillea filipendulina* 'Cloth of Gold'

| 3 |
| --- |
| *Acorus calamus* |

## SWEET FLAG

ACORACEAE
Origin:
Asia, introduced into Europe

This marsh plant, a native of South-East Asia, forms colonies beside nutrient-rich, stagnant water. The long, narrow leaves of the *Acorus,* somewhat similar to those of the iris, sprout from a creeping rhizome and form a thin tuft about 1.5 m (5 ft) tall. Between May and July, a thick spike of numerous small, yellowish flowers grows sideways out from the top of a leafless stalk. At the base of the spike there appears a vertical spathe which resembles a leaf prolonging the stem. Since seeds rarely ripen in this climate, vegetative propagation methods must be used. It is a hardy perennial, with no special requirements. The *Acorus* was introduced into Europe in the 16th century and cultivated for its medicinal properties, which had been known for many centuries in India and Greece. The rhizome has a pleasant, camphor-like perfume, and was used in a number of ways, most notably in confectionery. It is still used today in the preparation of certain liqueurs or perfumes.

*Acorus calamus*

**Position:** sunny, but the plant is quite happy in shade.
**Planting:** very wet soil, or in water up to 20 cm (8 in). 8 to 10 plants per sq.m.
**Height:** 80-160 cm (3-5 ft).
**Decorative interest:** yellow flower spike, 8-15 cm (3-6 in) tall, May to July.
**Care:** divide the clumps every 3 to 4 years, in spring.
**Propagation:** division of rootstock in spring, or pieces of rhizome, 5-10 cm (2-4 in) long.
**Other species or varieties:**
• *Acorus calamus* 'Variegatus', the myrtle flag or sweet flag, is a cultivar with superb, yellow-striped foliage. The young shoots have a pink tinge. Height: 80-100 cm (31-39 in).

*Acorus calamus* 'Variegatus'

Immersion: 10 cm (4 in).
• *Acorus gramineus*, a native of China and Japan, is a small plant suitable for shallow ponds. Persistent, narrow, sword-like leaves form a fan shape. Height: 20-30 cm (8-12 in).
• *Acorus gramineus* 'Variegatus' is a decorative cultivar with persistent green leaves with a white variegation. Somewhat less hardy, it does well in semi-shaded positions. Plant in very wet soil, or immersed 10 cm (4 in). Height: 20-30 cm (8-12 in).
• *Acorus gramineus* 'Ogon', 20 cm (8 in) tall, has attractive, fine, yellow-striped foliage. Damp soil.
• *Acorus gramineus* 'Pusillus' is a dwarf cultivar, no more than 20 cm (8 in) tall, with fine, drooping foliage.

*Acorus gramineus*

## 4

### *Agapanthus africanus*

# AGAPANTHUS

LILIACEAE
Origin :
South Africa

*Agapanthus africanus* 'Albus'

This magnificent plant has beautiful, strap-shaped leaves forming a thick clump from which emerge smooth, leafless stems, up to 1.2 m (4 ft) tall, which carry large umbels of bright blue flowers, 20 cm (8 in) in diameter.

**Position :** full sunlight.
**Planting :** in rich, loamy soil, damp to very damp in summer, dry and well-drained in winter. 3 plants per sq.m.
**Height :** 80-120 cm (3-4 ft) .
**Decorative interest :** blue flowers, July to September.
**Care :** tuber requires winter protection.
**Propagation :** division, between March and September.
**Other species or varieties :**
• *Agapanthus africanus* 'Albus' smaller cultivar, numerous umbels of white flowers, about 12 cm (5 in) in diameter.
Height : 60-100 cm (2-3 ft).

## 5

### *Ajuga reptans*

# COMMON BUGLE

LABIATAE
Origin :
Europe, Asia, North Africa

This hardy perennial is an excellent ground-cover plant, with bright, evergreen foliage which offers a useful alternative to lawn grass.

*Ajuga reptans* 'Burgundy Glow'

**Position :** any.
**Planting :** moist, humus-rich soil. 8 plants per sq.m.
**Height :** 10-15 cm (4-6 in).
**Decorative interest :** blue or white flowers, May-August.
**Propagation :** division and cuttings.
**Other species or varieties :**
• *Ajuga reptans* 'Alba' has pretty white flowers on dark foliage.
• *Ajuga reptans* 'Burgundy Glow' is a very decorative cultivar, whose purple leaves have cream, pink and green variegations. The pale blue flowers grow in spikes.

## 6

### *Alisma plantago-aquatica*

# WATER PLANTAIN

ALISMATACEAE
Origin :
Temperate zones, Northern Hemisphere

*Alisma plantago-aquatica*

The water plantain is an attractive, hardy bog plant which grows on the margin or in the shallow waters of lakes, ponds, and slow-moving streams. It is happiest in muddy, slightly acid, nutrient-rich soil. It has a thick rhizome from which sprouts a rosette of submerged, ribboned leaves which gradually develop into long-stemmed, spear-shaped, floating or aerial leaves. The numerous flowers, which appear from June to September, are borne on a large and graceful conical panicle at the end of a stalk 1 metre long. They are pinkish or white, 2-3 cm (1 in) in diameter, with three rounded sepals and petals. The seeds (akenes) are dispersed by water.

**Position :** sun or half-shade, accepts full shade.

**Planting :** for best results, needs a loamy, nutrient-rich soil, very wet or immersed 40 cm (16 in). 8-10 plants per sq.m.

**Height :** foliage 30-50 cm (12-20 in), flower stems 70-100 cm (2-3 ft).

**Decorative interest :** white flowers, June-September.

**Care :** good resistance to cold. Remove dead flowers to avoid self-seeding.

**Propagation :** from seed, or root division in spring.

**Other species or varieties :**

• *Alisma lanceolatum* has aerial leaves tapered at each end. Height : 20 cm (8 in).

## 7

### *Alternanthera sessilis*

# ALTERNANTHERA

AMARANTHACEAE
Origin :
South America

*Alternanthera ficoidea sessilis*

This bog plant, a native of Brazil, grows half-immersed in shallow, stagnant or sluggish water. Its narrow, persistent, spear-shaped leaves are remarkable for their colour, from reddish copper to dark green, sometimes touched with bright pink. It is a fast grower and hardy in mild climates. Its mat-forming habit makes it useful cover for banks of streams or bottoms of ponds. It is easily cultivated in a heated greenhouse, in water at temperatures of 18-26 °C (64-78 °F) in summer and 8-12 °C (46-53 °F) in winter.

• *Alternanthera sessilis* 'Rubra' is a cultivar with all-red, very decorative foliage.

**Position :** full sun, but is shade-tolerant.

**Planting :** wet soil, or submerged 50 cm (20 in).

**Height :** stems 20-100 cm (8-39 in).

**Decorative interest :** foliage, all the year.

**Care :** in cold regions, some plants should be brought in under cover for the winter.

**Propagation :** tip cuttings.

---

| 8 |
|---|
| *Ammania senegalensis* |
| AMMANIA |

LYTHACEAE
Origin :
South Africa

*Ammania senegalensis* 'Rubra'

This marsh plant has erect stems, 40-60 cm (16-24 in) tall, bearing stalkless, opposite, smooth-edged leaves in pinkish-tinted clumps, forming a thick mat, half-immersed, in calm, shallow water. It needs a bright, hot situation, in rather warm water, 18-26 °C (64-78 °F) and prefers sandy soils.

• The most generally used cultivar is *Ammania senegalensis* 'Rubra', whose vegetation is a handsome purplish-red when immersed, becoming green when it emerges from the water.

**Position :** full sunlight.

**Planting :** in 10-50 cm (4-20 in) of water, poor, sandy soil.

**Height :** 40-60 cm (16-24 in).

**Decorative interest :** foliage, May-November.

**Care :** the root must be kept below frost-level.

**Propagation :** from seed and cuttings.

---

| 9 |
|---|
| *Aponogeton distachyos* |
| APONOGETON |
| Cape Pondweed, Water Hawthorn |

APONOGETONACEAE
Origin :
South Africa

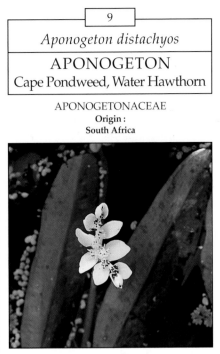

*Aponogeton distachyos*

This attractive, floating-leaved perennial, naturalized in the South of France, does well in shallow water in ponds and slow-moving streams. Its bulbous rhizome is held in the mud by thick roots. In spring, long-stemmed, lance-shaped floating leaves appear on the surface of the water. They are bright green, glossy, sometimes tinged with brown, and measure 8-15 cm (3-6 in) in length. In spring and autumn, fragrant white flowers appear on the surface of the water. They are most remarkable, with pur-plish-brown stamens surrounded by two V-shaped white spikes, 10 cm (4 in) long, to which their scientific name refers ("*dis-tachys*" means "having two spikes"). It is a robust plant, easily cultivated, and flowers freely from April till the end of October discontinuing flowering at the height of summer, complementing the flowering period od *Nymphaea*. It does well in cool or moderately warm water, and also flowers out of direct sunlight. Generally, the *Aponogeton* lies dormant for 2-4 months in winter, and is frost-hardy to -18 °C (-0.4 °F), coming rapidly back into growth at the beginning of spring. Plant it in small, isolated clumps, in association with *Azolla filiculoides* for an interesting colour-contrast.

**Position :** semi-shade.

**Planting :** accepts wide range of soil ph, 5-40 cm (2-16 in) of water. 3-5 plants per sq.m. If winters are severe, plant below freezing level, or in baskets which can be lifted before winter.

**Length of stems :** 30-80 cm (1-3 ft).

**Decorative period :** April-October, though excess light during the hottest months may interrupt flowering.

---

**Care :** bulbs can be wintered in the pool or under cover, in a box of damp sand, kept in a cool, dark place 5-18 °C (41-64 °F).

**Propagation :** separation of lateral shoots or division of rhizome. The flowers are hermaphrodite, and can be pollinated with a brush; they often self-pollinate. Gather the seeds which float on the surface and germinate them in a container holding 10 cm (4 in) of sand under 10 cm (4 in) of water, in a well-lit position, at a temperature between 18-25 °C (64-77 °F). After two months, when the seedlings are about 5 cm (2 in) tall, transplant into a larger container in garden soil.

**Other species or varieties :**
• *Aponogeton distachyos* 'Grandiflorum' is a cultivar with large white flowers.

---

| 10 |
|---|
| *Armeria maritima* |
| ARMERIA |
| Thrift, Sea-pink |

PLUMBAGINACEAE
Origin :
Temperate zones of Europe, Andes

*Armeria maritima*

This rhizomatous plant provides excellent ground cover, and resembles grass when not in flower, with its fine, evergreen foliage forming a thick, bright carpet. Its flowers, which appear in May, are grouped in bright pink, round heads, 2-3 cm (1 in) in diameter.

**Position :** sun or semi-shade. Sun- and drought-resistant, suitable for coastal regions.

**Planting :** dry or well-drained, light, sandy or gritty soil. 12 plants per sq.m.

**Height :** 15-20 cm (6-8 in).

**Decorative interest :** pink flowers, May-July. Will reflower at end of summer if dead-headed.

**Propagation :** division.

**Other species or varieties :**

• *Armeria alpina*, or Alpine Thrift, grows at higher altitudes. It is hardier, and prefers stony, non-alkaline soils.

## 11

### *Aruncus dioicus*
### Syn. *A. sylvestris*

## GOAT'S BEARD

ROSACEAE
Origin :
Temperate zones, Northern Hemisphere

*Aruncus dioicus*

This hardy native, with its elegant foliage and majestic flower, does best in cool, damp sites - open woodland, by streams and in peat-bogs - and at higher altitudes. Its denticulate, long-stemmed leaves may be as long as 1 m. The limb is broadly triangular and double-tripinnate in form, with deeply serrated leaflets. The stems are erect, with few branches, and may be up to 2 m (7 ft) high; panicles of white flowers appear in June and July. Plant the *Aruncus* in full or half shade, in isolated groups of 4 or 5, or in association with astilbe and hosta, by the waterside.

**Position :** full or half shade, but is tolerant of sun.

**Planting :** deep, moist soil, acid, rich in humus or peat. 6 plants per sq.m.

**Dimensions :** 1.5-2 m (5-7) tall, 1.2 m (4 ft) wide.

**Decorative period :** flowers in June and July.

**Propagation :** from seed, or division of roots in early spring.

## 12

### *Arundo donax*

## GIANT REED

GRAMINEAE
Origin :
Southern Europe, Asia

This attractive perennial grass, which is fairly hardy in spite of its southern origins, produces strong stalks which may grow as tall as 12 m (40 ft). It likes a sunny position, in damp, sandy soil close to water. Its broad,

*Arundo donax*

ribbon-like leaves, pale bluish-green in colour form thick clumps and have a rather exotic, bamboo-like appearance. Although it is often used simply as a windbreak or a background plant, the giant reed is highly decorative in its own right. Use it in isolated clumps, in association with other decorative-foliaged plants, such as *Miscanthus*, *Gunnera*, *Rodgersia*, *Papyrus*...

• *Arundo donax* 'Variegata' is a cultivar with magnificent cream-striped foliage, which does well in semi-shade. It is less hardy than the species, and may require protection in winter.

**Position :** sun or semi-shade.

**Planting :** for best results, damp, sandy or peaty soil should be used. Tolerant of drought, and temporary immersion. 1 or 2 plants per sq.m.

**Dimensions :** height : 2-4 m (7-13 ft). Spread : 1 m (3 ft).

*Arundo donax* 'Variegata'

**Decorative interest :** thick spikes of purplish-blue flowers, July-September.

**Care :** rootstock will require protection in hard winters. In autumn, cut the dry stems down, shred, and mix with peat or straw as a protective mulch.

**Propagation :** from seed, or division of rhizome. Like the bamboos, the giant reed can easily become invasive if conditions suit it. It is readily contained by means of root barriers.

## 13

### *Astilbe* spp.

## ASTILBE

SAXIFRAGACEAE
Origin :
China, Japan

*Astilbe* x *arendsii* 'Bressingham Beauty'

There are more than 30 identified species of astilbes, all native to South-East Asia, and these have given rise to numerous hybrids. They vary in height from 15-200 cm (6-78 in), and produce magnificent feathery panicles of flowers from June till September. They come in a wide range of deep or pastel colours, from carmine to pure white, and all the intermediate tones of pink and mauve. Their fine, light foliage, sometimes tinged with red or brown, is decorative throughout the growing period. They are hardy perennials, and do best in semi-shade, in cool or damp non-alkaline soil. They fit well into a natural-style garden, alongside a stream or pond. For best results, plant them in groups of blending colours. They mix well with ferns, hosta and water iris and are excellent for cutting, with a long vase-life.

**Position :** full or semi-shade, but will do well in full sun provided the root is kept very damp.

**Planting :** early autumn, neutral to acid soil, rich in humus and nutrients and kept moist or very damp. Will tolerate temporary flooding. 6-8 plants per sq.m.

*Astilbe* x *arendsii* 'Lilli Goos'

**Height** : 15-200 cm (6-78 in) by variety.

**Decorative interest :** feathery flower-heads, May to September.

**Care :** cut back foliage in autumn. Every two years, in early spring, topdress with well-rotted manure. Divide the clumps every three years or so, to rejuvenate the plants. Cover the roots of old-established plants with compost or peat, since they tend to lift out of the ground.

**Propagation :** division, in spring or autumn.

**Species or varieties :**
• *Astilbe* x *arendsii* is the group of hybrids most often cultivated. Smooth foliage, panicles of flowers between June and August. Height : 50-150 cm (20-60 in).

• *Astilbe* x *arendsii* 'Bressingham Beauty', salmon pink flowers. Height : 70 cm (28 in).

• *Astilbe* x *arendsii* 'Cattleya', violet flowers, August-September. Height : 60 cm (24 in).

• *Astilbe* x *arendsii* 'Diamant', white flowers, June-July. Height : 60 cm (24 in).

• *Astilbe* x *arendsii* 'Else Schluck', erect, pink flowers, July-August. Height : 60 cm (24 in).

• *Astilbe* x *arendsii* 'Erica', pink flowers and purple foliage. Height : 1 m (3 ft).

• *Astilbe* x *arendsii* 'Fanal', thick panicles of purplish-red flowers from June to August, red foliage in spring. Height : 50 cm (20 in).

• *Astilbe* x *arendsii* 'Federsee', bright pink flowers. Very early. Height : 60 cm (24 in).

• *Astilbe* x *arendsii* 'Hyazinth', large mauve spikes in August-September. Height : 1 m (3 ft).

• *Astilbe* x *arendsii* 'Irrlicht', white flowers and purple foliage, very early. Height : 50 cm (20 in).

• *Astilbe* x *arendsii* 'Lilli Goos', very thick, bright pink panicles, attractive, finely-cut foliage. Height : 50 cm (20 in).

• *Astilbe* x *arendsii* 'Snowdrift', white flowers,

pale green foliage. Height : 70 cm (28 in).

• *Astilbe* x *arendsii* 'Spinell', red flowers, June to August. Height : 60 cm (24 in).

• *Astilbe* x *arendsii* 'Weisse Gloria', tight spikes of pure white flowers, pale green foliage. Height : 50 cm (20 in).

• The *Astilbe chinensis*, whose erect, branching pink inflorescences appear later (August-September), have spear-shaped leaves. Height : 30 cm (12 in).

• *Astilbe chinensis* var. *pumila*, a slow grower, has mauve flowers. Its coloured foliage forms low tufts and provides decorative ground-cover. Height : 20-30 cm (8-12 in).

• *Astilbe chinensis taquetil* 'Superba', has tight spikes of purplish-red flowers from August to October, and is a more drought-resistant cultivar. Height : 1.25 m (4 ft).

• *Astilbe* x *crispa* is a group of dwarf hybrids with dark, denticulate leaves and miniature panicles well-suited to pool-side rockeries. Height : 15-20 cm (6-8 in).

• *Astilbe* x *crispa* 'Perkeo', pink flowers.

• *Astilbe japonica* includes small and medium sized varieties, early, with erect panicles in June and July. Height : 50-60 cm (20-24 in).

• *Astilbe japonica* 'Deutschland', white flowers, June-July. Height : 50 cm (20 in).

• *Astilbe japonica* 'Etna', red flowers. Height : 70 cm (28 in).

• *Astilbe japonica* 'Rheinland', pink flowers and green foliage. Height : 60 cm (24 in).

• *Astilbe simplicifolia* is a group of small cultivars with bronze, slightly crimped leaves and airy panicles with curving tips. Flowers July-August. Height : 30-40 cm (12-16 in).

• *Astilbe simplicifolia* 'Atrorosea', large, pale pink flower heads.

• *Astilbe simplicifolia* 'Bronce Elegans', pale pink flowers and bronze foliage.

• *Astilbe simplicifolia* 'Delicata', erect, pink flower heads.

*Astilbe chinensis pumila*

• *Astilbe simplicifolia* 'Elegans', graceful, drooping pink panicles.

• *Astilbe simplicifolia* 'Sprite', pink flowers and gleaming purple foliage, crimped leaves.

• *Astilbe* 'Straussenfeder', also called "Ostrich Feather", has graceful, curving, pink panicles. Height : 80 cm (3 ft).

• *Astilbe thunbergii*: late-flowering cultivars with large, drooping panicles. Height : 1-2 m (3-7 ft).

---

**14**

*Astilboides tabularis*
Syn. *Rodgersia tabularis*

# ASTILBOIDES

---

SAXIFRAGACEAE
**Origin :**
**China**

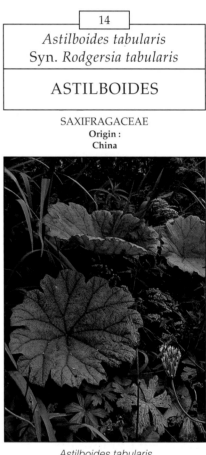

*Astilboides tabularis*

This attractive and unusual shade-loving perennial has large round leaves of a handsome green, whose long stalks are attached to the centre of the leaf. They have jagged edges, and measure from 60-90 cm (24-35 in) diameter. Between June and September, light panicles of creamy-white flowers appear, about 30 cm (12 in) tall, at thetop of an erect stem. It is a hardy, slow-growing plant which thrives in a damp, rich soil.

**Position :** full or semi-shade, sheltered from strong winds.

**Planting :** rich loam, damp to very wet.

**Height :** 60-100 cm (23 1/2-39 in).

**Decorative interest :** white flowers, June-July.

**Propagation :** from seed, or root division.

## 15

### *Azolla* spp.

## AZOLLA
## Fairy Moss, Water Fern

AZOLLACEAE
Origin :
Temperate and tropical America

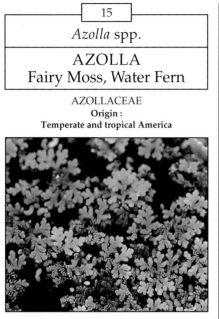

*Azolla filiculoides*

These graceful little aquatic ferns were introduced into Europe and have been acclimatized. They float freely on the surface of still water and form large colonies. They are annuals, and grow rapidly as the water warms up in summer, after a slow start in spring. They are killed off by frost, but the spores remain dormant throughout the winter, under the water.

• *Azolla filiculoides* has a branching stem, 1-10 cm (up to 4 in) in length, with threadlike roots and minute leaves which are tightly overlapped, 2 by 2. Each leaf has a lower, submerged lobe and an upper, floating lobe which is bigger and very rounded, and has a large, whitish marginal marking. Exposure to bright sunlight in summer, or cold autumn weather, causes the plant to turn an attractive brick red colour, due to anthocyanin.

• *Azolla caroliniana*, a native of North America, is often confused with *Azolla filiculoides*, but is rarely more than 1 cm (half an in) long; rounded, pale green lobes with very little overlap, do not turn red when exposed to cold or bright light.

**Position :** sheltered from wind.

**Planting :** from April-May, allow the plant to float freely on calm, nutrient-rich water.

**Height :** less than 5-10 mm (half an inch) above the water.

**Decorative interest :** blue-green foliage from May, becoming red in sunny positions and from September to December.

**Propagation :** spontaneous, since branches are broken up by wind and rain, and the plant easily becomes invasive. Reduce spread by removing portions as required.

## 16

### *Bambusoideae*

## BAMBOO

POACEAE-BAMBUSOIDEAE GRAMINEAE
Origin :
Asia, Africa, the Americas

*Phyllostachys pubescens*

*Phyllostachys nigra* 'Boryana'

Always decorative beside a pond, the elegant and exotic bamboos are a useful addition to any garden. They are perennial grasses, with persistent or deciduous foliage, of which more than 1000 species have been identified. The varieties available from nurseries are easy to grow, coming for the most part from temperate regions where they may be subjected to winter temperatures as low as - 20 °C (-4 °F).

**Position :** young plants require sufficient shade to keep the shallow roots and tender shoots cool. After a few years, the adult plant provides sufficient shade for the young shoots. Some varieties require full sun for best stem colour, and certain types of foliage do better in shade.

**Planting :** any cool or moist soil, provided there is good winter drainage. Plant in March-April, after the last spring frosts, or in August-September. Moisten the existing root ball, taking care not to destroy it, and plant in well-worked soil enriched with compost or well-rotted manure. Cover with 10 cm (4 in) of mulch, to avoid drying-out.

Tall varieties will require staking at first (with bamboo canes, of course!). Water well during the first summer, about once a week. To avoid having your lawn completely taken over by the very invasive root system, create a barrier with sheets of rigid, non-perishable material (e.g. fibreglass reinforced cement or very thick plastic) 1m (3 ft) high, driven into the ground all around the plant.

**Height :** 0.2 m to 35 m (8 in-115 ft), depending on species and climate.

**Decorative interest :** whether they are evergreen or deciduous, bamboos are decorative throughout the year. Those which flower do so rarely, at intervals of several years, and all individuals of the same species then flower simultaneously.

**Care :** apply fertilizer in spring, unless the soil is very rich. Cut dead or damaged stems down to ground level at the beginning of autumn.

**Propagation :** divide the clumps as needed in June-July. Reproduction in bamboos is largely asexual, by means of buds which sprout from the rhizome.

*Sasa tessellata*

*Pleioblastus auricomus*

**Species or varieties :** here is a selection of bamboos in order of adult height. The figures in brackets indicate the average length and breadth, respectively, of the leaves. The degree of frost-hardiness is also stated.

**Dwarf bamboos :**
The slender stems of the dwarf bamboos reach their adult height 80-100 cm (2-3 ft) in the second or third year. Plant them in isolated clumps, or in association with ferns, beside the water. They are also very useful ground cover plants, which can be trimmed every three or four years, in early spring, to obtain a regular surface.
Planting distance : 60 cm (2 ft).

• *Pleioblastus variegatus* provides year-round interest, with its white-striped green leaves 12/2 cm (5/1 in). It likes a sheltered situation in any type of soil, preferably damp, in shade or semi-shade. Cut it back every year or two years to maintain good bright leaf colour. Hardy to - 20 °C (-4 °F).
Height : from 20-100 cm (8-39 in).

• *Pleioblastus humilis* var. *pumilus* has long, narrow, dark green leaves 8/2 cm (3/1 in), which develop best in full or semi-shade. It will tolerate sun, but not prolonged drought. Hardy to - 20 °C (-4 °F).
Height : 10-100 cm (4-39 in).

• *Sasaella ramosa* has attractive, mid-green leaves 15/3 cm (6/1 in) with a white edge in winter. It stands up well to cold, and settles rapidly in to any situation. Frost-hardy to - 24 °C (-11 °F). Height : 60-100 cm (2-3 ft).

• *Pleioblastus auricomus* has variegated leaves 16/2 cm (6/1 in), of a luminous green striped with yellow. Does best in shade or semi-shade. Frost-hardy to - 22 °C (-7 °F). Height : 60-20 cm (2-4 ft).

**Small bamboos :**
These take from 3 to 5 years to reach adult height up to 3 m (10 ft). They do not lend themselves so well to trimming, but can be cut back to the desired height as long as this is done in June-July, after the growth of the young shoots.

• *Sasa veitchii* is very decorative. Its leaves 20/4 cm (8/2 in) brilliant dark green in summer, develop a white border in winter. The fine green stem is often tinged with purple. It is useful for brightening a dark

*Sasaella ramosa*

*Phyllostachys aurea*

corner of the garden, in a damp situation. Frost-hardy to - 20 °C -(4 °F).
Height : 1-1.5 m (3-5 ft).

• *Sasa tessellata* is remarkable for its very big 50/8 cm (20/3 in) leaves, bright green and persistent, with a graceful arching habit. The stems are green, 1 cm (half inch) in diameter. This species spreads quite readily and likes a semi-shaded position. It is frost-hardy to - 20 °C (-4 °F). Height : 2 m (7 ft).

• *Sinarundinaria nitida* forms thick, graceful clumps of slender, arching stems, of a purplish-green. The bright green, persistent leaves are small and fine 7/1 cm (3/.5 in). This species does not spread to any great extent, does well only in shade or semi-shade, and is frost-hardy to - 25 °C (-13 °F). Height : 2.5 m (8 ft).

**Medium-sized bamboos :**
These reach adult size, between 3-6 m (10-20 ft) in 5 or 6 years.

• *Arundinaria murielae* (Muriel bamboo) is a slow spreader, and has soft green leaves 10/2 cm (4/1 in) on fine, arching green stalks. It does not tolerate too much sun, and prefers a shady or semi-shady position. Frost-hardy to - 24 °C (-11 °F).
Height : 4-5 m (13-17 ft).

• *Pleioblastus chino* has dark green, narrow leaves 20/2 cm (8/1 in) and purplish-green stalks, up to 2 cm (1 in) in diameter. It prefers sun or semi-shade, and is frost-hardy to - 22 °C (-7 °F).
Height : 3-4 m (10-13 ft).

*Pleioblastus* Variegatus

*Phyllostachys edulis* 'Bicolor'

• *Pseudosasa japonica* (Arrow bamboo, Metake) has erect stalks and shiny dark green leaves 30/4 cm (12/2 in), forming dense clumps which spread out at the top. Stems are green, with persistent sheaths, and up to 1 cm (1 half in) in diameter. A slow spreader, it does well in any situation, being tolerant of cold and of drought. Frost-hardy to - 24 °C (-11 °F). Height : 4-6 m (13-20 ft).

**Tall bamboos :**
These are mainly *Phyllostachys*, recognizable by the internodal groove on the stems. They spread into large clumps over a period of years, and are good specimen plants.

• *Phyllostachys aurea* has very supple stems, 3-5 cm (1-2 in) in diameter. They are bright green and turn golden yellow in the sun. At the base, the internodal sections are sometimes short and swollen. It spreads very little, stands up well to cold, drought, and accepts all types of soil, and any situation. Its leaves 12/2 cm (5/1 in) are green with a bluish underside. Frost-hardy to - 20 °C (-4 °F). Height : 4-9 m (13-30 ft).

• *Phyllostachys aurea* 'Albovariegata' is a handsome cultivar with white-striped foliage.

• *Phyllostachys nigra* f. *punctata* is an attractive bamboo whose gracefully arched stalks become black from the third year. They are 3-5 cm (1-2 in) in diameter, and have brilliant green, fine leaves 8/1 cm (3/1 half inch). Does well in any damp soil. Frost-hardy to 18 °C (64 °F).
Height : 6-8 m (20-26 ft).

*Pleioblastus humilis* var. *pumilus*

## 17
### *Bergenia* spp.
## BERGENIA

SAXIFRAGACEAE
**Origin :**
**Eastern Asia**

*Bergenia cordifolia*

These robust hardy perennials, native to Siberia and the Altai, stand up to the coldest weather. They have large, round leaves, of a shining dark green, with a purple underside. In cold weather they turn red, and are an excellent cover-plant for the pond-side. The flowers are grouped in bunches, pink, mauve or white, at the end of the stalk, and appear between March and May.

**Position :** shade and semi-shade.
**Planting :** likes poor soils, cool or damp, but stands up well to drought.
**Height :** 30-40 cm (12-16 in).
**Decorative interest :** pink flowers, March to April, decorative leaves all the year.
**Propagation :** division, and separation of spring shoots.
**Other species or varieties :**
• *Bergenia* 'Abendglut' (S. 'Evening Glow'), with very brilliant bright green foliage turning plum-colour in autumn, and bright red flowers. Height : 35 cm (14 in).
• *Bergenia* 'Baby Doll', with light green foliage and pale pink flowers. Attractive purple foliage in winter. Height : 30 cm (12 in).
• *Bergenia cordifolia* 'Purpurea', has green foliage turning purple in winter, and dark pink flowers. Height : 40 cm (16 in).

## 18
### *Bletilla striata*
## JAPANESE ORCHID

ORCHIDACEAE
**Origin :**
**Japan**

A beautiful, hardy bulb, with long, ribbon-like leaves and bright pink flowers in July-August. There is a white-flowered cultivar, *Bletilla striata* f. *gebina*.

*Bletilla striata*

**Position :** sun and half-shade.
**Planting :** cool or damp soil.
**Height :** 40 cm (16 in).
**Decorative interest :** flowers in July-August.

## 19
### *Butomus umbellatus*
## FLOWERING RUSH

BUTOMACEAE
**Origin :**
**Temperate zones of Europe and Asia**

*Butomus umbellatus*

This very attractive perennial, with a creeping rhizome, likes a hot position in shallow, still or sluggish water, in the north of Europe and Asia. It is often found with reeds and arrowheads, beside pools and ponds with a stable water-level. From its thin rhizome, with lateral roots, there sprouts a bunch of radical leaves, long and narrow, triangular at the base but flattening out towards the top. At first they are purplish-green, but they take on an olive green colour. They may grow as tall as 1.2 m (4 ft). In the centre of the tuft there appear several cylindrical flower-heads, branchless and leafless. They are always taller than the leaves, and are crowned by 20 to 50 pink flowers in an umbel.

The flowers are 2-3 cm (1 in) wide and appear between June and August. They have greenish-pink sepals and pink petals, which grow in threes, around nine red-anthered stamens. The fruits contain numerous seeds, about 1 cm (half an inch) in length, which can float on the water.

The flowering rush is very decorative when cultivated in fairly thick clumps of 5 to 10 plants. It is perfectly hardy, and appreciates a sunny position and a nutri-ent-rich soil. Plant it in a large container, to allow sufficient room for the vigorous root system to develop.

In numerous parts of Asia, the rhizome of the flowering rush is eaten, raw, dried or baked. It is rich in proteins, fats and starch, which is sometimes transformed into flour for bread-making. It can be torrefied, for use in the preparation of certain hot drinks.

It is also an attractive plant for dried flower arrangements.

**Position :** sun or half-shade.

**Planting :** muddy soil in 5-50 cm (2-20 in) of water. About 12 plants per sq.m.

**Height :** 50-150 cm (20 in-5 ft).

**Decorative period :** pink flowers, June-August.

**Care :** divide clumps in spring to give them room to develop if crowded.

**Propagation :** propagation from fragments of rhizome.

## 20
### *Calla palustris*
## BOG ARUM

ARACEAE
**Origin :**
**Northern Hemisphere.**

The bog arum once formed extensive colonies in the warm, shallow water of peat bogs and forest pools, but it has tended to become more rare as its natural habitat is destroyed. Its thick, heart-shaped leaves, about 8-10 cm (3-4 in) wide, on the end of a long stem rise above the water from the creeping rhizome. They are shiny pale green and form a thick mat, ideal for masking the edge of a pond. The flowerhead is

*Calla palustris*

formed of numerous small yellow-green florets, grouped in a cylindrical spike (or spadix). This is enclosed in a white, funnel-shaped spathe, 6-7 cm (2-3 in) tall. After pollinisation, (most frequently by snails), brilliant red fruit appear, providing decorative interest till the end of autumn. This hardy perennial is attractive throughout the growing period, but it should be noted that the fruits are toxic, and dangerous for very young children.

**Position :** full sun or half-shade.

**Planting :** 8 to 10 plants per sq.m., extremely wet soil or immersed - 15 cm ( - 6 in).

**Height :** 15-45 cm (6-18 in).

**Decorative interest :** white flowers, May to August, red fruit, August to November.

**Propagation :** from seed, or division of rhizomes.

---

| 21 |
| :-: |
| *Callitriche palustris* |
| **CALLITRICHE** **Water Starwort** |

CALLITRICHACEAE
**Origin :**
**Northern Hemisphere.**

*Callitriche palustris*

Callitriches are hardy, submerged or floating plants, which do well in the clear water of ponds or slow-flowing rivers. Their form may vary slightly with the habitat. Their creeping, fragile, thread-like stems are fixed at the bottom of the water by fine, lateral roots which may penetrate to a depth of 1 m. At the other end of the stem, on the surface of the water, is a star-shaped rosette of numerous oval leaves. The submerged leaves are opposite, narrower and spear-shaped. Between May and October, very discreet, small, greenish flowers appear at the axil of the upper leaves. Callitriches are perennial plants (sometimes annual), and do best in cold water. They are a precious addition to any pond, because of their oxygenating properties.

**Position :** sun and semi-shade.

**Planting :** wet soil, or under 20-60 cm (8-24 in) of water. 1 to 5 plants per sq.m.

**Size :** length of stem, 40-60 cm (16-24 in).

**Propagation :** fragments of stem take root in the mud.

---

| 22 |
| :-: |
| *Caltha palustris* |
| **MARSH MARIGOLD** **Kingcup** |

RANUNCULACEAE
**Origin :**
**Europe, Asia, North America**

*Caltha palustris*

*Caltha palustris* is a hardy perennial, common throughout the cold and temperate regions of the northern hemisphere.
It flowers very early in spring, providing a touch of colour at the edge of streams and ponds. The erect or creeping stalks take root when they touch the soil. The dentate leaves are heart-shaped, deep, bright green in colour, and form a rounded, spreading clump. A vast number of small, brilliant golden flowers, about 4 cm (2 in) diameter, appear in April-May. They are generally made up of 5 to 10 large sepals surrounding a number of stamens. The fruits are brown, pod-shaped follicles containing numerous seeds which sow themselves very readily. Easy to cultivate, *Calthas* are very effective in small colonies beside "wild" ponds.

**Position :** sun or semi-shade.

*Caltha palustris* var. *alba*

**Planting :** March-April, in deep, rich, damp soil, or down to 20 cm ( 8 in) under water. 6 to 8 plants per sq.m.

**Height :** 20-50 cm (8-20 in).

**Decorative interest :** golden-yellow flowers, April to July.

**Propagation :** from seed, or division of roots after flowering.

**Other species or varieties :**
• *Caltha leptosepala* is a mat-forming variety with small leaves and white flowers, in April-May. Height : 10 cm (4 in).
• *Caltha palustris* var. *alba* (white marsh marigold) is a compact cultivar, ideal for small ponds. Its white flowers appear early (April-May). Height : 20-30 cm (8-12 in).
• *Caltha palustris* 'Flore Pleno' (double marsh marigold) is an attractive horticultural variety, flowering generously from March to June. A second flowering sometimes occurs in September-October. Height :10-20 cm (4-8 in).
• *Caltha palustris palustri* is a large, vigorous species 40-80 cm (16-32 in) from the Himalayas. It is notable for its large yellow flowers, 5-6 cm (2 in), which appear in May-June, and its large leaves. Suitable for large ponds, planted to a depth of 35 cm (14 in).

## 23

### *Canna* spp.

## CANNA

CANNACEAE
Origin :
Tropical Asia and America

*Canna indica*

This superb tropical herbaceous plant can reach an impressive height up to 2 m (7 ft) within a few weeks. It is a highly decorative marsh plant, with its large, coloured flowers and big, pointed, blue-green or purple leaves which are often more than 50 cm (20 in) long. Cannas are planted out for the summer, in rich, very wet soil.

**Position :** full sun.

**Planting :** at the beginning of June, in very damp, well-worked soil with plenty of well-rotted manure, or down to 20 cm (8 in) under water.

**Height :** 1-2 m (3-7 ft).

*Canna flaccida*

**Decorative period :** flowers from June till October.

**Care :** make regular applications of fertilizer or manure throughout the growing period. In autumn, let the tubers dry and store in a cool, dry place 5-10 °C (41-50 °F).

**Propagation :** division, after flowering.

**Species or varieties :**

• *Canna glauca*, 1.5-2.5 m (5-8 ft) tall, has pale green foliage and yellow or orange flowers, June to October.

• *Canna flaccida*, 80-120 cm (3-4 ft), yellow flowers from May to October.

• *Canna* 'J. B. van der Schoot', 1.5 m (5 ft), speckled flowers and green foliage.

• *Canna rubra*, 2 m (7 ft), purple foliage and scarlet flowers.

## 24

### *Cardamine pratensis*

## CARDAMINE
### Bitter cress, Lady's mantle

CRUCIFERAE
Origin :
Temperate zones of northern hemisphere.

*Cardamine pratensis*

This is a charming hardy perennial with a creeping rhizome, commonly found in damp or marshy meadows. It has long-stemmed, composite leaves, and sprays of delicate little pink flowers from April to June. The young leaves are rich in vitamin C and can be used in salads.

**Position :** sun and half-shade.

**Planting :** damp or wet soil.

**Height :** 30-40 cm (12-16).

**Decorative interest :** pink flowers, April to June.

**Propagation :** from seed, and leaf tip cuttings.

**Other species or varieties :**

• *Cardamine pratensis* 'Flore Pleno' is a very decorative, double-flowered cultivar.

## 25

### *Carex* spp.

## CAREX

CYPERACEAE
Origin :
Cold and temperate zones

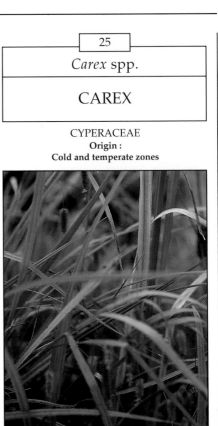

*Carex pseudocyperus*

There are about 2000 species of *Carex*, distributed throughout the cold and temperate zones of our planet. They are hardy perennial sedges with matted root systems and prefer poor, water-logged, peaty soils. They are slow growers, and look somewhat like grasses, but their leaves, stiff and sharp-edged, grow up from the base of the stem, which is solid, nodeless and triangular in section. *Carex* with their persistent, often brightly-coloured foliage, provide year-round interest in any garden.

**Position :** hot and sunny, accepts semi-shade.

**Planting :** from October to April, moist to damp soil. (Will stand temporary dryness).

**Height :** 15-150 cm (6 in-5 ft), according to species.

**Decorative interest :** fairly inconspicuous brown inflorescences, May to September.

**Care :** cut back dry foliage towards late March.

*Carex riparia* 'Variegata'

Carex comans 'Bronze Form'

Carex acutiformis

**Use :** the creeping roots help to stabilize pond margins.
**Propagation :** spreads readily (stolons). Divide clumps between May and July.
**Species or varieties :**
• *Carex acutiformis* has relatively wide leaves 7-10 mm (half an inch) which are blue-green, turning red in autumn. Height : 1.5 m (5 ft).
• *Carex buchananii*, or leatherleaf sedge, a New Zealand native, forms dense tufts of fine, airy foliage, reddish-brown in summer and yellow in winter. Frost hardy only to -10 °C. Height : 40-50 cm (16-20 in).
• *Carex comans* 'Bronze Form', another New Zealand native, has coppery, persistent, arching leaves. Height : 40 cm (16 in).
• *Carex elata* (syn. *C. stricta*), tufted sedge. Height : 50-120 cm (2-4 ft).
• *Carex elata* 'Bowles Golden' (syn. *C. elata* 'Aurea'), golden sedge, has long, bright yellow leaves, sometimes edged with green. Spectacular in association with irises. Height : 80 cm (3 ft).
• *Carex grayi*, (mace sedge) has fine, pale green leaves and very attractive brown spicules. Height : 60 cm (2 ft).

• *Carex morrowii* 'Evergold' (syn. *C. haschijænsis* 'Aurea Variegata'), has handsome persistent green foliage with a creamish-yellow variegation. Height : 40 cm (16 in).
• *Carex ornithopoda* has fine, light green leaves 1-3 mm (1/5 in). Chalky soil. Height : 25 cm (10 in).
• *Carex ornithopoda* 'Variegata', is a dwarf form, with white-marked foliage. Height : 15 cm (6 in).
• *Carex pendula* (*C. maxima*) or pendulous sedge forms dense tufts of wide leaves 15-20 mm (1 in), which are yellowish green with a bluish underside. Decorative long, cylindrical, arching spikes. Height : 1.5 m (5 ft).
• *Carex pseudocyperus* has broad, gracefully-arching leaves 5-12 mm (half an inch), bright greenish-yellow in colour. Pendent flower spikes, autumn. Height : 1.2 m (4 ft).
• *Carex riparia* (greater pond sedge) has broad, blue-green leaves (5-15 mm). Height : 1.3 m (5 ft).
• *Carex riparia* 'Variegata' has green foliage with creamy-white stripes. Height : 50 cm (20 in).

Carex curta

Carex pendula

Carex montana

Carex morrowii 'Evergold'

Carex ornithopoda

---

### 26

### *Ceratophyllum demersum*

# HORNWORT

CERATOPHYLLACEAE
Origin :
Subcosmopolitan

*Ceratophyllum demersum*

*Ceratophyllum demersum* is a native perennial which floats freely in calm or stagnant, nutrient-rich water. It has long, totally submerged, rootless stems. These are fragile and easily broken, but remain rigid even when out of the water (which is not the case with the stems of the *Myriophyllum*) The leaves, which are grouped in whorls at each node, have the form of tapering, toothed segments, dividing once or twice into a Y-shape. They are dark green, turning reddish-brown in autumn. The minute flowers are produced under water, between June and September. In autumn, scaly winter buds separate from the parent plant and spend the winter under water. Propagation takes place principally from fragments of stalk, which means that the plant can easily become invasive. But it is simply controlled, by removing the surplus plants.

• *Ceratophyllum submersum* is a rarer species, identifiable by its 3- or 4-lobed leaves.

C. demersum          C. submersum

These plants are perfectly hardy and are a precious addition to any pond, because of their oxygenating and cleansing properties. They provide shelter and food for aquatic animals, as well as a depository for spawn.

**Position :** any.

---

**Planting :** allow the plant to float freely, or else weight some branches with a small stone and place them in the water at a depth of 30-80 cm (1-3 ft).

**Dimensions :** stems are 10-150 cm (4 in-5 ft) in length.

**Care :** easy to control by removing surplus vegetation. If it is allowed to become invasive, in a small pond, excess carbon dioxide may be produced at night.

**Propagation :** occurs naturally. To ensure rapid growth in the spring, pinch the ends of the shoots in autumn and let them fall to the bottom of the pond.

---

### 27

### *Chamaedorea elegans*

# DWARF PALM

PALMAE
Origin :
Mexico, South America

*Chamaedorea elegans*

The dwarf palm is a shrubby plant from Central America, which grows no taller than 1.2 m (4 ft). Its elegant, exotic shape makes it a good subject for the heated greenhouse. The root must be kept moist, especially during the summer. Its long, divided, glossy leaves have stalkless leaflets, tapering at each end, which grow in pairs and can reach 15 cm (6 in) in length.

• *Chamaedorea tenella* is a smaller species, no taller than 80 cm (3 ft).

**Position :** light, but out of direct sun.

**Planting :** soil rich in humus, damp or very damp.

**Height :** 1.2 m (4 ft).

**Care :** does well with a minimum summer temperature of 18 °C (64 °F) and a rest period in winter at a temperature between 12-14 °C (53-57 °F). Apply diluted fertilizer every two weeks.

**Propagation :** from seed in spring; soak seed in tepid water about 25 °C (77 °F) for two days, then sow in light compost, at 24-28 °C (75-82 °F).

---

### 28

### *Chlorophytum comosum*

# SPIDER PLANT

LILIACEAE
Origin :
South Africa

*Chlorophytum comosum* 'Variegàtum'

This very decorative hardy evergreen hot-house plant is particularly robust and vigorous. Its long green ribbon-like leaves, with pointed tips, form a gracefully arching clump 30-40 cm (12-16 in) tall. It has a creeping root system, and flower stems up to 60 cm (24 in) long. The little white flowers produce plantlets, complete with leaves and roots, which will produce new plants.

• *Chlorophytum comosum* 'Variegatum' is a cultivar whose green leaves have a thin white line down the middle.

**Position :** light, but out of direct sun.

**Planting :** damp compost, a mixture of garden soil and peat.

**Height :** 30-40 cm (12-16 in).

**Care :** keep at 18-20 °C (64-68 °F) in summer, and apply fertilizer once a week. Browning of the leaftips may be caused by too dry an atmosphere, over-wet compost or lack of light.

**Propagation :** cultivate the plantlets, or divide old-established plants.

---

### 29

### *Clerodendrum* x *speciosum*

# CLERODENDRUM

VERBENACEAE
Origin :
Indonesia, Polynesia

This fine hothouse plant from the Sunda Islands is particularly decorative, with its large, persistent, heart-shaped leaves of a brilliant, deep green which make a happy

*Clerodendron speciosum*

contrast with the clusters, 20-30 cm (8-12 in) long, of superb scarlet flowers which appear between May and July.

**Position :** light, but not in direct sun.

**Planting :** moist or wet soil, humus-rich, slightly acid.

**Height :** 60-80 cm (2-3 ft).

**Care :** requires a humid atmosphere and moisture at the roots, especially in summer. Keep at 18-24 °C (64-75 °F) in summer, 10-15 °C (50-59 °F) in winter.

**Propagation :** from seed in spring, or cuttings in spring and summer.

---

30

### *Cordyline fructicosa*
### Syn. *Cordyline terminalis*

## TI-TREE

**AGAVACEAE**
**Origin :**
**South-East Asia, Australia, New Zealand.**

*Cordyline fructicosa*

---

The Cordyline is a small, palm-like tree or shrub with broad, spear-shaped leaves of a bright dark green. It is an excellent plant for the heated greenhouse, and sometimes produces pink or white flowers. It requires a moist atmosphere and plenty of light, especially in winter.

• *Cordyline fructicosa* 'Firebrand' is a cultivar remarkable for its red-bordered foliage.

• *Cordyline fructicosa* tricolor has very attractive variegated leaves, pink, green and white.

**Position :** light, but out of direct sun.

**Planting :** in moist soil, or submerged 10 cm (4 in). Use a nutrient-rich mixture of leaf-mould, peat and garden soil.

**Height :** 30-60 cm (1-2 ft).

**Care :** apply ordinary fertilizer every fortnight. Keep at 18-24 °C (64-75 °F) in summer, 10-12 °C (50-53 °F) in winter.

**Propagation :** from seed, January-February, or stem cuttings in spring and summer.

---

31

### *Cortaderia selloana*
### Syn. *Gynerium argenteum*

## PAMPAS GRASS

**GRAMINEAE**
**Origin :**
**Argentina, Southern Brazil**

*Cortaderia selloana*

This superb ornamental perennial grass is a relatively undemanding plant, forming a clump of bluish-green ribbon-like foliage throughout the growing period, but it is at its best in September when the long, silky, silver-white panicles appear. It requires well-drained soil, dry to moist, and a hot, sheltered position, and can be used to good effect in an isolated group, or in association with other tall grasses such as *Miscanthus zebrinus* and *Arundo donax*.

**Position :** sun or semi-shade.

---

**Planting :** dry or moist soil in summer, but with good winter drainage.

**Height :** 2-3 m (7-10 ft in).

**Decorative interest :** flowers, August to October.

**Care :** before the first frosts, lift up the leaves and attach them around the flower stems, then protect the whole plant, including the root area, with straw matting, for example. Cut back to 30 cm (12 in) in spring.

**Propagation :** from seed or by division.

**Use :** the panicles last well, for dry flower arrangements.

**Other species or varieties :**

• *Cortaderia selloana* 'Alba', green foliage and white flowers.

• *Cortaderia selloana* 'Aureolineata', foliage streaked with golden-yellow and silvery flowers.

• *Cortaderia selloana* 'Pumila', dwarf cultivar for small gardens, maximum height 1.2 m (4 ft).

• *Cortaderia selloana* 'Rendatieri', green foliage and pink flowers.

• *Cortaderia selloana* 'Albolineata', green and white variegated foliage and silvery flowers.

---

32

### *Cotula coronopifolia*

## COTULA
## Brass buttons

**ASTERACEAE**
**Origin :**
**South Africa**

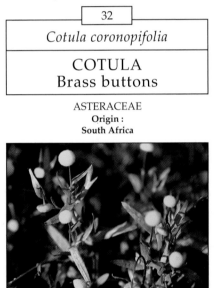

*Cotula coronopifolia*

This pretty perennial, from Natal, produces surprising little button-shaped, yellow flowers, from June to October. The fine, shining, serrated leaves form thick tufts, ideal for filling spaces between rocks or masking pond margins. It is self-seeding but not invasive. Fully hardy only in damp soil and in a mild climate.

**Position :** sun or semi-shade.

**Planting :** damp soil or under water 10 cm (4 in).

**Height :** 15-20 cm (6-8 in).

**Decorative interest :** yellow flowers, June to October.

**Propagation :** from cuttings, or seed sown in April.

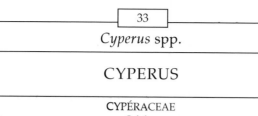

33

*Cyperus* spp.

# CYPERUS

CYPÉRACEAE
Origin :
Hot and temperate zones

*Cyperus longus*

There are more than 300 species of this graceful and exotic-looking perennial. Its creeping roots can become invasive, so it is advisable to install a root barrier or cultivate the plant in a container, unless, of course, it is used to stabilise a pond margin.

**Position :** hot and sunny.

**Planting :** in heavy soil with plenty of nutrients (manure or dried blood). Use sufficiently deep containers and place 5-50 cm (2-20 in) below the surface of the water.

**Dimensions :** tuft is 0.3-4 m (1-13 ft) tall.

**Decorative interest :** green or brown flowers, June to October.

**Care :** divide clumps to limit their spread and remove dry stems. Tender plants should be sheltered from the end of September.

**Propagation :** division of clumps in spring, or cuttings : cut a tuft of leaves on a young stem. Reduce leaves and stem to about 5 cm (2 in). Place the tuft on a glass of water, or in clean, moist sand. Pot up the young plant when the first roots appear.

**Hardy varieties or species :**
• *Cyperus asper* has narrow leaves and tight, blackish-brown spikelets of flowers. Height : 50 cm (20 in).
• *Cyperus badius* has globular spikelets. Height : 40-100 cm (16-39 in).
• *Cyperus dives* has broad leaves and spikes of flowers. Height : 1.5 m (5 ft).
• *Cyperus eragrostis* (syn. *C. vegetus*) is a native of tropical America, but has become acclimatized in southern Europe. Its pale green leaves, 5-10 mm (half an inch) wide, are arranged in a single or composite umbel with 8-10 branches. The flower is composed of 8-13 tight, yellowish-green spikelets. Height : 90-120 cm (3-4 ft).
• *Cyperus flavescens* has narrow leaves and sparse, sessile spikelets or umbels with up to 4 branches. Height : 30-40 cm (12-16 in).
• *Cyperus longus* (sweet galingale), a native of southern Europe and Asia, has dark green shining leaves 2-3 mm (fifth of an inch) wide. The flowers are carried on a composite umbel with up to 10 branches, each of which has 4-25 spikelets. Very hardy, not demanding, sometimes invasive. Height : 1.5 m (5 ft).
• *Cyperus rotundus* has branching stems and numerous spikelets. Height : 50 cm (20 in).

*C. rotundus*    *C. serotinus*    *C. badius*    *C. longus*    *C. eragrostis* (syn. *C. vegetus* )

*Cyperus eragrostis* (syn. *C. vegetus*)

*Cyperus papyrus*

*Cyperus rotundus*

*Cyperus flavescens*

• *Cyperus serotinus*, with reddish-brown spikelets, is indigenous to the south of Europe. Height : 1.2 m (4 ft).

**Tender species or varieties :**

These are plants of tropical origin, and should be brought outside only after the last frosts. They will also be happy all year round in a patio or conservatory pond, and will grow vigorously, provided the ambient temperature (air and water) is maintained at a minimum of 10 °C (50 °F) in winter.

• *Cyperus involucratus* (syn. *C. alternifolius* (umbrella plant) comes from Madagascar. It has umbels of leaves up to 25 cm (10 in) long, and rosettes of greenish-white flowers. It is hardy if the root is sufficiently deep in the water to be below frost-level. Stands up to short periods of dryness. Height : 1.5 m (5 ft).

• *Cyperus alternifolius* 'Gracilis' is a smaller cultivar, no more than 50 cm ( 20 in) tall.

• *Cyperus albostriatus* has broad, curving leaves. Resistant to short periods of drought. Height : 30 cm (12 in).

• *Cyperus C. papyrus* 'Nana' (syn. *C. haspan*) is a dwarf form, no more than 30-50 cm (12-20 in) tall.

• *Cyperus isocladus* has stems bearing long, slender leaves 8-10 cm (3-4 in) terminating in a dense umbel of brown spikelets which, when it touches the water, produces a new plant. Height : 1 m (39 in).

• *Cyperus papyrus*, a native of tropical Africa,is the famous papyrus of the ancient Egyptians. It forms long, erect stems terminating in tufts of fine leaves. The inflorescences take the form of star-shaped umbels, 40-50 cm (16-20 in) diameter. Height : 2-4 m (7-13 ft).

---

| 34 |
|---|

### *Dactylorhiza majalis* Syn. *Orchis latifolia*

## MARSH ORCHID

ORCHIDACEAE
Origin :
Europe, Near East, Siberia

The *Orchis* family contains a number of closely-related species which produce hybrids that are often difficult to identify with certainty. The broad-leaved orchid is a hardy perennial, frequently found in marshes and very wet meadows in temperate zones of Europe and Asia. From a bulbous root sprouts a rosette of 6 to 8 spear-shaped leaves which are blue-green in colour with strong brown markings. Between May and July, at the top of a tubular stem, there appears a cylindrical spike of pink to purplish-violet flowers.

**Position :** sun and semi-shade.

**Planting :** neutral or slightly acid soil, rich in nutrients, very damp. Or in up to 10 cm (4 in) of water.

**Height :** 30-60 cm (1-2 ft).

---

*Dactylorhiza majalis*

**Decorative interest :** purplish-pink flowers, May to July.

**Propagation :** root division in spring.

**Other species or varieties :**

• *Dactylorhiza fuchsii* (common spotted orchid), 60-80 cm (2-3 ft) tall, has leaves with dark, elliptical markings and prefers chalky soil. The central lobe of the flower is narrower and longer than the other two.

• *Dactylorhiza maculata* prefers an acid soil, dry to moist. It has round leaves with paler markings. The central lobe of the flower is smaller than the other two.

---

| 35 |
|---|

### *Darmera peltata* Syn. *Peltiphyllum peltatum*

## DARMERA
### Umbrella Plant

SAXIFRAGACEAE
Origin :
North America

*Darmera peltata*

This hardy perennial, with its unusual and decorative foliage, is an excellent poolside plant. The leaves, like up-turned parasols, 30-40 cm (12-16 in) wide, are fixed at the middle at the end of long, up to 1.5 m (5 ft), erect stalks. From the end of summer till the first frosts they take on an attractive coppery colour. In April-May, before the leaves, tight umbels of pearly-pink flowers appear, at the end of a stem 50-80 cm (20-32 in) tall. The

---

vigorous creeping rhizome makes the *Darmera* an excellent ground-cover plant for damp sites, where it can be used in association with ferns, astilbes or hostas.

• *Darmera peltata* 'Nana' is a dwarf cultivar, no taller than 40 cm (16 in).

**Position :** accepts full sun or semi-shade.

**Planting :** deep, moist or damp soil, rich in humus. 2 plants per sq.m.

**Dimensions :** forms a clump about 1 m (39 in) wide and up to 1.5 m (5 ft) tall.

**Decorative interest :** white or pale pink flowers, April-May. Handsome green foliage, turning a coppery colour from late August to December.

**Propagation :** root division in spring.

---

| 36 |
|---|

### *Deschampsia cespitosa*

## TUFTED HAIR GRASS

GRAMINEAE
Origin :
Europe and North America

*Deschampsia cespitosa*

This is a hardy perennial grass, commonly found in marshland, damp meadows and undergrowth. It forms a thick tuft of narrow, evergreen leaves from which emerge long flower stalks, up to 2 m (79 in) tall, with elegant silvery or bluish plumes in June-July. It is a good ornamental plant for sun or shade, and provides decorative interest throughout the winter, with its wind-resistant, dry stalks.

• *Deschampsia flexuosa* 'Tatra Gold' is a golden species forming a small tuft of very fine leaves, 10-30 cm (4-12 in) tall. Dryer soil.

**Position :** any.

**Planting :** moist or very wet soil.

**Height :** from 80 cm (32 in) foliage, to 2 m (79 in) flower stems.

**Decorative period :** flowers, June-July.

**Propagation :** divide clump in spring.

37

*Dracaena sanderiana*

## RIBBON PLANT

DRACAENACEAE
Origin :
Tropical Africa

*Dracaena sanderiana*

This attractive variegated plant forms
a small, palm-shaped tuft, 60 cm (2 ft) tall.
The arching, spear-shaped leaves are 20 cm
(8 in) long and 2-3 cm (1 in) wide, brilliant
green with thin, silvery-white stripes and a
pale yellow edge. It is a plant for the heated
greenhouse, requiring constant humidity
and slightly cooler temperatures in winter.

**Position :** light, or semi-shade.

**Planting :** in humus-rich soil with a peat or
compost base. Wet, or submerged 20 cm (8 in).

**Height :** 40-60 cm (16-24 in).

**Care :** summer temperature 20-23 °C
(68-73 °F), winter 15-18 °C (59-64 °F). Lack of
light causes leaves to lose their variegation.

**Propagation :** take tip or stem cuttings,
about 8 cm (3 in) in spring or summer.

38

*Drosera* spp.

## DROSERA
Sundew

DROSERACEAE
Origin :
Cold and temperate zones,
Northern Hemisphere.

These are hardy perennial, insectivorous
plants, which do well in moist, acid soil.
At the base is a rosette of long-stemmed
leaves, more or less broad, according
to the species, and covered with sticky red
hairs, each of which has at the end a droplet
of mucilage. Between June and September,
small white flowers appear at the end
of a flexuous, reddish stem, 20 cm (8 in)
long. When an insect lands on a leaf,
it is immediately captured by the long,
sticky hairs which slowly enclose it.

Enzymes then dissolve the prey, which
provides the plant with the nitrogen nutrients lacking in the poor, acid soil of its
natural habitat. The droseras, or rossolis
(from the Latin, meaning "sundew") were
once common in the peat-bogs, heaths and
acid marshes of Europe. Small colonies can
still be found floating around ponds, but
their existence is threatened by the exploita-
tion and destruction of the peat-bogs.

**Position :** sun and semi-shade.

**Planting :** damp, peaty or sandy soil, acid to
very acid.

**Height :** 5-30 cm (2-12 in).

**Decorative period :** small white flowers,
June-September.

**Propagation :** division of clumps.

*Drosera longifolia*

**Species or varieties :**
• *Drosera intermedia* has moderately long
leaves 7-10 mm (half an inch) on hairless
stems. Height : 10 cm (4 in).

• *Drosera anglica,* syn. *Drosera lingifolia*
(long-leaved drosera) has leaves 2-5 cm (1-2
in) long and 5 mm (fifth of an inch) wide, on
hairy stems. Height : 20 cm (8 in).

• *Drosera rotundifolia* (round-leaved drosera)
easily recognizable, with round or oval leaves
on long, hairy stems. Height : 30 cm (12 in).

39

*Duchesnea indica*

## DUCHESNEA

ROSACEAE
Origin :
India

This is a hardy ground-cover plant
with attractive yellow flowers and red,
strawberry-like fruit, tasteless but not toxic,
which are produced in close succession from
June to November. Plant in moist or damp
soil, out of direct sun, under small trees or
beside a pond. The duchesnea is not fully
hardy in a colder climate, but some plants
may be wintered over in a cool greenhouse.

**Position :** shade or semi-shade.

*Duchesnea indica*

**Planting :** moist or damp soil, rich in
humus.

**Height :** 5-10 cm (2-4 in).

**Decorative interest :** red fruit and yellow
flowers, June-November.

**Care :** frost-tender.

**Propagation :** sow in cold frame in autumn,
or separate runners at the end of summer.

40

Syn. *Baldellia ranunculoides*
Syn. *Alisma ranunculoides*
*Echinodorus Ranunculoides*

## ECHINODORUS

ALISMATACEAE
Origin :
Temperate regions of Europe, North Africa

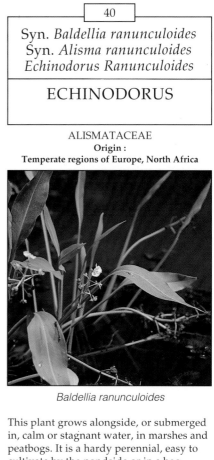

*Baldellia ranunculoides*

This plant grows alongside, or submerged
in, calm or stagnant water, in marshes and
peatbogs. It is a hardy perennial, easy to
cultivate by the pondside or in a bog
garden, in sun or shade. From May to
September it produces white or pinkish
flowers, 3-4 cm (1-2 in) in diameter.
Propagate from seed or by division.

**Position :** sun, but is quite happy in shade.

**Planting :** wet soil, or immersed 50 cm
(20 in). Use a compost made of peat, clay

and sand, rich in nutrients and in iron.

**Height :** 40-50 cm (16-20 in).

**Propagation :** division of clumps, and from runners.

---

| 41 |
| --- |

## *Eichhornia crassipes* Syn. *Pontederia crassipes*

### WATER HYACINTH

PONTEDERIACEAE
**Origin :**
Tropical and sub-tropical zones

*Eichhornia crassipes*

This is a superb floating plant with a rosette of shining round leaves carried on stems whose swollen bases serve as floats. From June to September, sprays up to 30 cm (12 in) tall of splendid pale lavender-blue flowers with a darker, yellow-marked throat appear above the water. In cold or temperate climates it can be cultivated as an annual in an outside pond, from mid-June onwards. Some plants can be brought inside and wintered over in a cold aquarium. It can also be cultivated as a perennial in a pool in a well-lit conservatory or heated greenhouse, with a water temperature of 12 °C (53 °F) in winter and 18 °C (64 °F) in summer. The water hyacinth is used in ponds to remove certain pollutants, and especially heavy metals such as chrome, copper, etc.

**Position :** hot and sunny.

**Planting :** allow the plant to float freely, in shallow, nutrient-rich water with a muddy bottom. Temperature, about 18 °C (64 °F).

**Height :** about 20 cm (8 in) above the surface of the water.

**Decorative interest :** pale lavender-blue flowers, June-September.

**Propagation :** throws out runners, very prolific, but is really invasive only in hot climates.

---

| 42 |
| --- |

## *Elodea canadensis* Syn. *Anacharis canadensis*

### WATER WEED Water thyme

HYDROCHARITACEAE
**Origin :**
North America,
acclimatized in Europe, Asia, Australia

*Elodea canadensis*

This is a hardy, submerged, bottom-rooting perennial. Of Canadian origin, *Elodea canadensis* (from the Greek *hêlodes* "of the marshes") was introduced into Ireland in 1836. One single female plant multiplied so rapidly that it became a hazard to navigation and fishing. But this "population explosion" occurs in a number of species of plants when they are introduced into a new habitat, and tends to disappear as the plant becomes integrated with the native flora, which seems to be the case at present with the *Elodea*. It has become very common in calm or stagnant waters in the temperate zone. The thread-like, branching stems spread rapidly and form large matted colonies, with numerous small, lance-shaped leaves, dark, translucent green in colour and arranged three by three, in whorls. It has small flowers, borne singly at the end of a long stem, from May to August. It is a dioecious plant, but is sterile in Europe, since only female flowers have been acclimatized here, but it multiplies rapidly from natural cuttings. The stems are fragile and easily broken, and each fragment gives rise to a new plant which floats freely on the surface at first, then takes root at the bottom of the water. Nutrients are absorbed by the

*Elodea crispa*

fine, isolated lateral roots, and by the plant's leaves, which appear at certain stem nodes. Easily cultivated in cool, clear water, the elodea, with its evergreen leaves, is valuable all year for its oxygenating and purifying action. It provides a depository for the spawn of aquatic fauna, as well as shelter and food. It can also help to soften very hard water, by absorbing the lime.

**Position :** any, but oxygenation is more efficient in very bright conditions.
**Planting :** weight the plants with a small stone, and throw into 30-150 cm (1-5 ft) of water. 1-5 bunches per sq.m.
**Dimensions :** length of stem varies from 30-200 cm (12- 79 in).
**Care :** to keep the vigorous growth in check, remove excess vegetation with a fork or rake.
**Propagation :** stem cuttings, 10 cm (4 in).

**Other species or varieties :**
• *Elodea crispa* of gardens, syn. *Lagarosiphon muscoides major,* is native to South Africa, and has more closely-set, curved leaves.
• *Elodea densa* (syn. *Egeria densa* or *Anacharis densa*) is a longer-leaved species from South America.

---

| 43 |
| --- |

## *Elymus arenarius* Syn. *Leymus arenarius*

### LYME GRASS

GRAMINEAE
**Origin :**
Europe

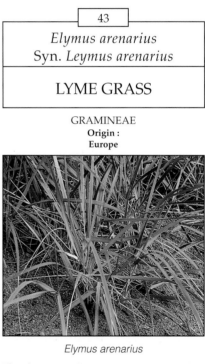

*Elymus arenarius*

This decorative rhizomatous grass spreads readily and colonizes sandy ground and coastal dunes. Its bluish leaves, 10-15 mm (half an inch) wide, form a dense clump up to 1.5 m (5 ft) tall. Pale green inflorescences, similar to ears of wheat, appear between June and August. It is a hardy perennial and can be used to good effect in the "wild" garden.

**Position :** sun or semi-shade.
**Planting :** light, sandy soil, well-draining.
**Height :** 1-1.5 m (3-5 ft).
**Decorative interest :** pale green ears, June to August.

## 44
### *Epilobium palustris*
### WILLOW HERB

ONAGRACEAE
Origin :
**New Zealand and all temperate regions**

This is a hardy perennial with a stoloniferous root, common in wet meadows, marshes and peat-bogs. It has light mauve flowers between June and September, and narrow, spear-shaped, stalkless leaves. Height : 60 cm (2 ft).

• *Epilobium hirsutum*, or hairy willow herb, is a more decorative species. From its creeping rhizome rises a very hairy, branching stem, 1.5-2 m (5-7 ft) high, with markedly dentate, hairy leaves.
It appreciates chalky clay soils and does well in running water, near springs and streams, forming large clumps with attractive reddish-purple flowers in summer.

*Epilobium hirsutum*

**Position :** any.

**Planting :** damp soil, or immersed 10 cm (4 in).

**Decorative interest :** flowers, June-September.

**Propagation :** from stolons.

## 45
### *Equisetum* spp.
### HORSE-TAIL
### Scouring rush

EQUISETACEAE
Origin :
**Cold and temperate zones, Northern Hemisphere.**

*Equisetum hyemale* (syn. *E. hibernale*)

*Equisetum* (from the Latin *equus*, horse and *setum*, bristle), or horse-tail, is a genus of hardy perennials which form large colonies in wet or flooded ground.
They are very ancient plants, dating back to the Carboniferous era, at which time they grew several dozen metres tall.
Like the ferns, they have no flower, and are reproduced by vegetative methods or by the emission of spores collected in ears situated at the top of the stems. These are cylindrical in form and hollow, and retain large quantities of silica, which gives them an abrasive quality which was formerly put to use for scouring barrels or polishing metals. The erect stems grow from buds on the creeping rhizome, which can reach more than 10 m (30 ft) in length, in unrestrained conditions. At the stem nodes are whorls of fine, narrow, rudimentary leaves, depending on variety.

**Position :** sun or semi-shade.

**Planting :** in wet soil, or immersed to 15 cm (6 in). Plant small colonies, either in containers or in open ground with an effective root barrier. The stolons spread rapidly and the plants can become most difficult to control.

**Height :** 15-150 cm (6 in-5 ft), according to species.

**Decorative period :** all the year.

**Propagation :** division of stolons, May to September.

**Species or varieties :**
• *Equisetum americanum*, or American horse-tail, withstands hotter climates. Year-round decorative interest. Height : 50-150 cm (20 in-5 ft).

• *Equisetum arvense*, the least aquatic

*Equisetum maximum* (syn. *E. telmateia*)

of all, does well in moist ground. Its green stalks carry numerous whorls of undivided leaves. Height : 30-60 cm (1-2 ft).

• *Equisetum fluviatile* (syn. *E. limosum*) is the most aquatic variety. It spreads rapidly in marshy land or when submerged, down to 30 cm (1 ft). Its semi-persistent stems, which are striated and have few ramifications, are of a yellowish green, often tinged with orange. Height : 50-150 cm (20 in-5 ft).

• *Equisetum hyemale* (syn. *E. hibernale*),

*Equisetum fluviatile* (syn. *E. limosum*)

the Dutch or scouring rush, is a native of the subarctic and northern temperate zones. It has thick, erect, blue-green stalks which have no ramifications and which bulge out slightly between the sheaths. The latter are black at the base with a green or whitish central line. Height : 50-150 cm (20-5 ft).

• *Equisetum maximum* (syn. *E. telmateia*)is the tallest European species. It has whitish stems with single branches and 20 to 40 ribs. It likes a damp, clay soil (even chalky) and a mild climate. Height : 1.5-2 m (5-7 ft).

• *Equisetum palustre* is a truly aquatic plant which can be submerged to 20 cm (8 in). Its slender, branching stems are deeply grooved, with 6-10 ribs. The sheaths have serrated black marking with a wide white border. Height : 40-60 cm (16-24 in).

• *Equisetum ramosissimum* has a stem with a slightly branching at the top and 8 to 20 ribs with numerous small "branches" in whorls. The sheaths are green or brown with a black band at the base and a finely serrated border. Height : 80-100 cm (30 in-5 ft).

• *Equisetum scirpoides* is a low-growing species native to arctic and subarctic zones. Its stems, which are always green, are solid and have only 3 or 4 ribs. It forms persistent, handsome dark green colonies. Submerge to 5 cm (2 in). Height : 15-20 cm (6-8 in).

• *Equisetum sylvaticum* forms colonies in moist undergrowth and acid peat-bogs. Its stems carry numerous whorls of branches, always divided in pairs and with drooping tips. Height : 20-60 cm (8-24 in).

• *Equisetum variegatum* does well in very wet or flooded ground, even chalky. Its arched, evergreen stems have 4-10 ribs. Its sheaths are black at the top, green below, sometimes tinged with orange. Height : 80 cm (30 in).

*Equisetum variegatum*

---

| 46 |
|---|

## *Eriophorum* spp.

## COTTON GRASS

CYPERACEAE
**Origin :**
**Northern Hemisphere**

*Eriophorum angustifolium*

The cotton grasses are elegant, slow-growing hardy perennials found in marshy moorland and acid peat-bogs. From the base of their rounded, erect stems grow long, drooping, linear leaves forming thick, dark green tufts. In April-May the flowers appear, with bright yellow anthers. These are followed, between May and July, by brown seed pods enclosed in the very characteristic tufts of shining white long, silky fibres.

**Position :** sun and semi-shade.

**Planting :** acid soil, wet and peaty, or submerged to 30 cm (12 in). 6-10 plants per sq.m.

**Height :** 50-75 cm (20-30 ft).

**Decorative interest :** flowers in April-May, white plumes from May to July.

**Propagation :** division of clumps.

**Species or varieties :**

• *Eriophorum angustifolium* (narrow-leaved cottongrass) has a stoloniferous, creeping rootstock. It has hairless stems and fine, keeled, linear leaves, 3-5 mm (fifth of an inch) wide, sometimes tinged with violet. Several spikelets, with long, cotton-like fibres, 3-4 cm (1-2 in) long, appear between April and June.

• *Eriophorum latifolium* (broad-leaved cotton grass) is the only species which appreciates chalky soil and alkaline water. It has a spreading root, broader leaves 5-8 mm (third of an inch) and rough stalks. The branching, silky fibres are 2 cm (1 in) long.

• *Eriophorum vaginatum* (sheathed cotton grass) forms large, dense tufts; threadlike leaves 1 mm wide (25 th of an inch) and a single seed head.

---

| 47 |
|---|

## *Eupatorium cannabinum*

## HEMP AGRIMONY

ASTERACEAE
**Origin :**
**Eurasia, North Africa.**

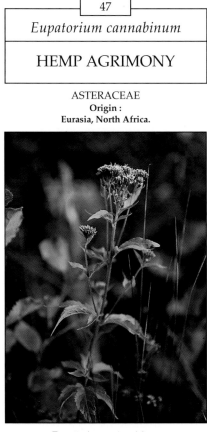

*Eupatorium cannabinum*

This very attractive hardy perennial does well in marshy fields and damp forests. Its reddish, erect stems bear numerous serrated-edged, spear-shaped leaves. The pink or red flowers are tubulous and grouped in downy-looking false umbels. They appear between July and September, and are an excellent source of pollen and nectar. Pollinization is carried out by butterflies.

**Position :** sun and semi-shade.

**Planting :** in damp, rich, even chalky soil, or submerged to 10 cm (4 in).

**Height :** 80-150 cm (30 in-5 ft).

**Decorative interest :** pink flowers, August-October.

**Propagation :** sow under cover in April, prick out in May. Selfsows readily.

**Other species or varieties :**

• *Eupatorium purpureum* (purple agrimony) is a native of the Great Lakes region of North America. The umbels of pinkish-purple flowers, 30 cm (12 in) in diameter, appear between July and October. The stems are purplish in colour, up to 2.5 m (8 ft) tall and covered with dark green, pointed leaves with purplish stems. Spread : 2 m (7 ft).

• *Eupatorium purpureum* 'Atropurpureum', has purplish-white flowers in August. Height : 1-1.5 m (5 ft).

• *Eupatorium rugosum album* is a smaller cultivar 80-120 cm (30 in-4 ft) with white flowers.

## 48

### *Euphorbia palustris*

## MARSH SPURGE

EUPHORBIACEAE
**Origin :**
**Eurasia**

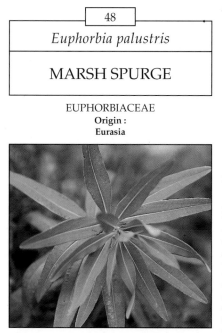

*Euphorbia palustris*

This rhizomatous hardy perennial has blue-green foliage with remarkable, large flower-like bracts turning yellow in May-June. It is found in marshy meadows and beside calm or still water, and forms a thick, bushy clump, 80-150 cm (3-5 ft) high, with a slightly exotic appearance.

**Position :** sunny.
**Planting :** in very wet soil, or submerged to 20 cm (8 in). 4 plants per sq.m.
**Height :** 80-150 cm (3-5 ft).
**Decorative interest :** yellow bracts, May-June.
**Propagation :** from seed, or cuttings in spring. (Be careful when handling this plant since the sap is a toxic irritant. Gloves are advisable).

## 49

### *Festuca glauca*

## BLUE FESCUE

GRAMINEAE
**Origin :**
**Cold and temperate zones,**
**Northern Hemisphere**

The *Festuca* genus comprises about 100 species, for the most part perennial, which grow in dry, well-draining soils without much nutrient. The blue fescue, a native of the Alps, is a hardy grass with fine, stiff foliage of an attractive silvery blue colour. It forms compact, evergreen tufts, 15-20 cm (6-8 in) high and is an excellent groundcover plant for dry gardens where a dry or Mediterranean look is desired, or the areas of water are surrounded by sand, pebbles and rocks.

*Festuca glauca*

• The cultivar *Festuca glauca* 'Blaufuchs' is a particularly remarkable shade of blue.
**Position :** hot and sunny.
**Planting :** for poor, dry soils; sandy or stony.
**Decorative interest :** creamy-white spikes, June-July.
**Propagation :** division of clumps.

**Other species or varieties :**
• *Festuca altissima* (syn. *Festuca sylvatica*) is a larger species, which prefers damp, shady sites. Its smooth leaves, 1 cm (half an inch) wide, can be up to 1.2 m (4 ft) long.
• *F. gigantea* forms a fairly large tuft 30-40 cm (12-16 in) high, with wide, drooping leaves, and prefers semi-shade.

## 50

### *Filipendula ulmaria*
### syn. *Spiraea ulmaria*

## MEADOWSWEET

ROSACEAE
**Origin :**
**Eurasia**

*Filipendula ulmaria*

This attractive, native, hardy perennial grows in damp meadows, near springs and ponds. It has a creeping rhizome from which sprout a number of very slightly branching stems, at whose base are dark green, composite,

imparipinnate leaves. The top of the stem carries a large spray of numerous small, perfumed creamy-white flowers.

**Position :** sun or semi-shade.
**Planting :** moist or damp soil.
**Height :** 1-2 m (3-7 ft).
**Decorative interest :** creamy-white flowers, June-September.
**Propagation :** cuttings, or fragments of rhizome.

**Other species or varieties :**
• *Filipendula ulmaria* 'Aurea' has very handsome golden foliage. Prefers shade or semi-shade. Height : 1 m (3 ft).
• *F. vulgaris*, or dropwort, is a native species with plumes of white flowers. Height : 60-100 cm (2-3 ft).
• *F. vulgaris* 'Multiplex' is an interesting cultivar with double, pinkish flowers. Fine, evergreen foliage. Height : 80 cm (30 in).

## 51

### *Filicineae*

## FERNS

PTERIDOPHYTES
**Origin :**
**Subcosmopolitan**

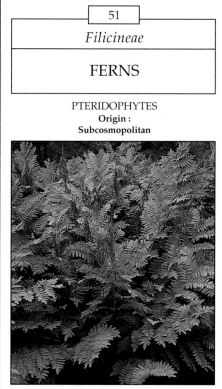

*Osmunda regalis*

Ferns are perennials with a general preference for cool, shady conditions.The wide variety in colour and shape of their leaves, evergreen in cases, makes them a valuable addition to any garden.
**Position :** shade.
**Planting :** moist or damp soil, neutral or acid.
**Decorative period :** April till the first frosts.
**Care :** cut back dry fronds at end of autumn.
**Propagation :** divide, or sow spores in spring.
**Species or varieties :**
• *Adiantum pedatum* is a hardy, maidenhair fern, with pale green, spreading fronds and black stalks. Deciduous. Height : 50 cm (20 in).
• *Asplenium scolopendrium*, the hart's tongue fern, has bright green, tongue-shaped, narrow leaves. It is a vigorous evergreen, likes moist

Dryopteris erythrosora

Asplenium trichomanes

Asplenium scolopendrium

Gymnocarpium dryopteris

Athyrium nipponicum metallicum

Onoclea sensibilis

conditions and tolerates chalky soil.
Height : 40-60 cm (16-24 in).
• *A. s.* 'Cristatum' is a superb cultivar with frilled foliage. Height : 40 cm (16 in).
• *A. trichomanes* or maidenhair spleenwort, is an evergreen fern with tufts of fronds varying from grey-green to yellowish green, on shiny black or brown stems. Cool rockeries.
Height : 30 cm (12 in).
• All the *Athyriums* are deciduous :
• *A. filix-femina* , the lady fern, forms tufts of long, finely-cut, pale green leaves.
Height : 80 cm ( 30 in).
• *A. f.-f.* 'Minutissimum'has very fine, dense foliage. Height : 20 cm (8 in).
• *A. f.-f.* 'Vernoniae Cristatum' has green fronds; fluted, triangular pinnules. Height : 1 m (3 ft).
• *A. f.-f.* 'Victoriae' has leaflets with dentate edges in a 'V' formation. Height : 1 m (3 ft).

• *A. nipponicum metallicum* (painted fern) has attractive, spreading, silver-grey fronds. Height : 50 cm (20 in).
• *Blechnum spicant*, or hard fern, has persistent dark green foliage, divided into long, fine, linear segments. Height : 50 cm (20 in).
*Dryopteris* are robust, hardy ferns which are sometimes evergreen.
• *Dryopteris erythrosora* has persistent, light green foliage. Young shoots have a remarkable copper colour. Height : 60 cm (2 ft).
• *D. filix-mas*, or male fern, has erect, semipersistent, indented fronds, bright green and turning golden in autumn. Height : 1 m (3 ft).
• *D. thelypteris*, is a very pretty hardy fern with light green, indented fronds. Its creeping roots develop even under 5-10 cm (2-4 in) of water. Likes light shade and does not tolerate dry conditions. Height : 70 cm (28 in).

• *Matteucia struthiopteris*, ostrich fern or ostrich feather fern. Bright, evergreen leaves, forming a funnel-shape. Height : 1.5 m (5 ft).
• *Onoclea sensibilis*, the sensitive fern, is a North American native acclimatized in Europe. Has deciduous, light green, triangular, pennate leaves. Root spreads easily in damp soil.
Height : 60 cm (24 in).
• *Osmunda regalis*, or royal fern, is among the largest. Decorative, with copper-brown crook-shaped shoots which open out in spring into tender green fronds turning yellow or brown in autumn. Happy in sun or semi-shade, in wet, peaty soil. Deciduous. Height : 2 m (7 ft).
• *O. r. purpurascens* is a cultivar whose young stems are coppery-red in spring, then take on a violet shade which lasts till the first frosts. Height : 1.2 m (4 ft).

Thelypteris palustris      Dryopteris filix-mas      Polypodium interjectum      Athyrium filix-femina      Onoclea sensibilis      Blechnum spicant

## 52

*Geranium* spp.

### PERENNIAL GERANIUM
### Cranesbill

GERANIACEAE
**Origin :**
**Europe**

*Geranium* sp.

This large family of herbaceous annuals and perennials includes a number of hardy species appreciated for their long flowering period and their denticulate foliage. Geraniums (not to be confused with the very popular *Pelargonium,* wrongly referred to as a geranium) grow vigorously in any moist to damp soil. They are cold-and drought-tolerant. They are often cultivated in clumps, in sun or shade, and provide good, marginal ground-cover for pools. The smaller species can be used to excellent effect in rockeries.

**Position :** shade and sun.

**Planting :** October to April, moist or damp soil, even chalky. 8-10 plants per sq.m.

**Height :** 10-80 cm (4-30 in) according to species.

**Decorative interest :** flowers, May-October.

**Propagation :** from seed, or division of roots.

**Species or varieties:**

• *Geranium endressii,* excellent ground cover plant with green foliage, pale pink flowers from June till August. The cultivar 'Al Johnson' has deeper pink flowers. Height : 20-40 cm (8-16 in).

*Geranium palustre*

• *G. palustre* (marsh cranesbill) has 7-lobed palmate leaves and does well at the water's edge. Its flowers, with their heart-shaped pinkish-mauve petals, appear in June-July. Height : 50-60 cm (20-24 in).

• *G. phaeum,* (mourning widow) has white flowers ('Album'), pinkish lilac (var. *lividum*) or purplish brown (*Phaeum*). Height : 30-60 cm (12-24 in).

• *G. rivulare* is a species which does well in damp, relatively chalk-free soil. The white flowers with purplish-violet veins, appear in July-August. Height : 30-60 cm (12-24 in).

• *G. sanguineum* (bloody cranesbill) is a native species, 20-50 cm (8-20 in) tall, with reddish-purple flowers, May-July.

• *G. sylvaticum* (wood cranesbill), 20-60 cm (8-24 in) tall, has blue flowers in June-July. It enjoys a shady position in heavy, damp soil. There is a whiteflowered cultivar (*G. s. albiflorum*), and another with china-blue flowers (*G. s.* 'Mayflower').

## 53

*Geum rivale*

### WATER AVENS

ROSACEAE
**Origin :**
**Cold and temperate zones,**
**Northern Hemisphere.**

*Geum rivale*

This rhizomatous, hardy perennial grows in clumps near springs, on stream-banks and in marshes or water-meadows in cool or mountainous regions. It has numerous, erect, hairy stalks from which hang heads of small, orange flowers. The lyre-shaped leaves are divided and irregularly dentated. The water avens accepts any position, but appreciates moist or very damp soil. It can be used to good effect in low beds at the pondside, in association with Japanese primulas and hostas, for their foliage interest.

**Position :** sun and shade.

**Planting :** plant in soil enriched with well-rotted farmyard manure.

**Height :** 30-50 cm (12-20 in).

**Decorative interest :** flowers, May-July.

**Propagation :** division of clumps in March, or after flowering.

**Other species or varieties :**

• *Geum* 'Coppertone' is a cultivar with double yellow flowers. Height : 50 cm (20 in).

• *Geum* 'Borisii' is an excellent ground cover plant, orange-red flowers, June-August. Height : 40 cm (16 in).

• *Geum rivale* 'Leonard's Variety', a very prolific bloomer. Coppery-pink flowers, June-July. Height : 30 cm (12 in).

• *Geum* 'Lionel Cox' has yellow flowers with a brown calix. Height : 30 cm (12 in).

## 54

*Glyceria maxima*
Syn. *G. aquatica, G. spectabilis*

### GLYCERIA

GRAMINEAE
**Origin :**
**Europe, Asia Minor**

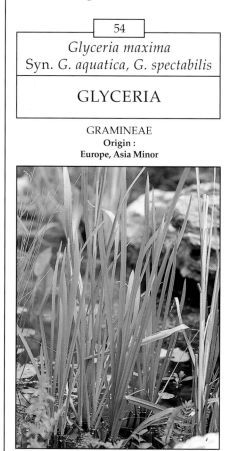

*Glyceria maxima*

This *Glyceria* is one of the grasses commonly found alongside calm or still, nutrient-rich water, in company with the *Phragmites* and *Phalaris* which compose the reedbeds. It has gracefully arching, luminous green leaves, 15-20 mm (half to 1 inch) wide. The erect, rigid stalks, which were formerly used for thatching, can grow as long as 2.5 m (8 ft), and have a loose, very branching panicle of yellowish flowers. It is a hardy perennial, whose creeping roots make it useful for stabilizing pond margins. Its strong, flexible foliage provides nesting places for swimming birds, which also eat the seed.

The submerged parts provide shelter for fish and a depository for their spawn. In large ponds, it can be used as a windbreak or as a background plant.

• For a spectacular decorative effect, choose *Glyceria maxima variegata* whose variegated foliage, pink-tinged in spring, is really magnificent, with its pale yellow and

*Glyceria maxima Variegata*

light green stripes. It is smaller than the species 80-120 cm (3-4 ft) but has the same habit. Suitable for even small gardens, as an isolated specimen or in groups.

**Position :** sun and semi-shade.
**Planting :** wet soil, or submerged to 50 cm (20 in). 10 plants per sq.m., preferably in containers, if pool is small. Is tolerant of dry soil, but does really well only in a very wet site.
**Height :** 1.5-2.5 m (5-8 ft).
**Decorative interest :** foliage from May to November. Flowers between June and August
**Care :** divide the clump every 4-5 years if necessary.
**Propagation :** from seed, and division of clump.

---

55

*Glyceria fluitans*

# GLYCERIA

GRAMINEAE
Origin :
Northern Hemisphere.

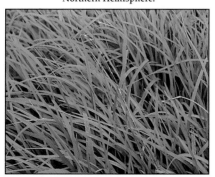

*Glyceria fluitans*

This glyceria is an amphibious grass quite commonly found in wet zones, beside non-limy, still or running water. It is a hardy perennial with a rhizomatous though non-stolon-forming root, and flexible stems

reaching 1.5 m (5 ft). The terrestrial form has green or blue-green leaves, first flat to the ground, then becoming erect. From May to August, the greenish flowers form a long, loose, one-sided panicle. The aquatic form is bottom-rooting, sometimes in quite deep water, and the leaves are submerged or float on the surface, very close together. In this form the plant is sterile, and reproduction is by root division. It is a hardy, though not very decorative grass, whose floating leaves serve as rafts for basking water-snails and frogs, while the seeds are eaten by birds.

**Position :** sun and semi-shade.
**Planting :** in wet ground, or submerged to 1 m (3 ft).
**Length :** 40-150 cm (16-60 in).
**Decorative period :** flowers from May till August.
**Propagation :** from seed, or division of clump.

---

56

*Gunnera manicata*

# GUNNERA
## Giant Rhubarb

GUNNERACEAE
Origin :
South America

*Gunnera manicata*

This enormous plant, a native of the lower slopes of the Andes, has vast, indented and serrated leaves up to 3 m (10 ft) in diameter. Flowering takes place in June-July, in the form of large, pale green, conical spikes which give rise to orange-brown pods. Alone or in a group, *Gunnera manicata* always produces a spectacular effect beside a large pool. If you have sufficient space 4-5 m (13-16 ft), even in a smaller garden, it will help to create an exotic atmosphere if used in association with plants remarkable for their foliage, such as *Astilboides, Petasites, Miscanthus, Rodgersia*. *Gunnera manicata* likes a deep wet soil, well-worked and enriched with well-rotted manure. Give it a sunny position, sheltered from strong winds. The crown will require frost protection in winter, in colder climates.

**Position :** sun or semi-shade, in a sheltered position.
**Planting :** in April-May, in a deep, rich soil, constantly wet or even sodden.

**Height :** 2-3 m (7-10 ft). **Spread :** 5 m (16 ft).
**Decorative interest :** foliage, May till October.
**Care :** a vigorous grower, it requires an annual application of manure each spring. In autumn, cut back the dry leaves and mulch the crown with peat or straw to a depth of about 30 cm (12 in), completing the cover with the dry leaves, to ensure good winter protection.
**Propagation :** division of the crown or separation of suckers, in spring.

**Other species or varieties :**
• *Gunnera tinctoria chilensis* (syn. *G. scabra, G. chilensis*), or giant Chilean rhubarb, is somewhat smaller than *G. manicata*, with leaves 1 m (3 ft) in diameter. Slightly more hardy, but still requires winter protection. Height : 2 m (7 ft).

• *Gunnera magellanica* is a dwarf, carpeting species; bright, crinkled foliage, scarcely more than 10 cm (4 in) tall. Spread : 80 cm (3 ft).

## 57
### *Hemerocallis* spp.
## HEMEROCALLIS
### Daylily

LILIACEAE
**Origin :**
**Eastern Asia**

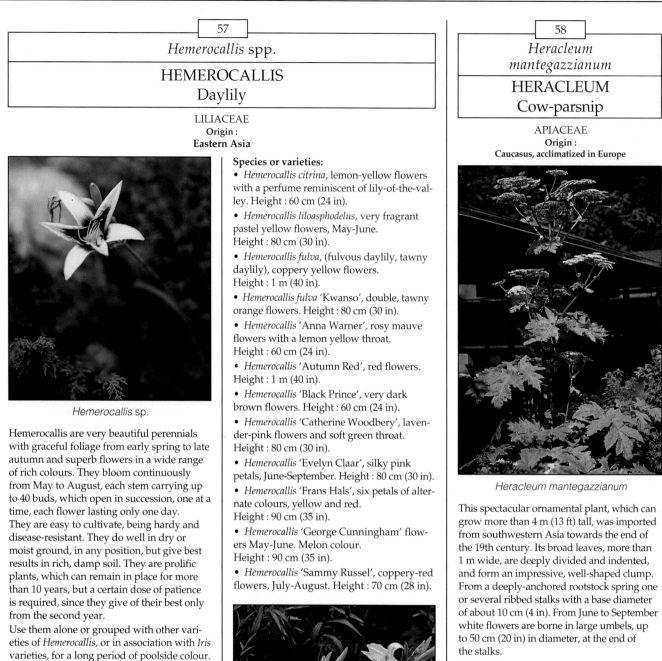

*Hemerocallis* sp.

Hemerocallis are very beautiful perennials with graceful foliage from early spring to late autumn and superb flowers in a wide range of rich colours. They bloom continuously from May to August, each stem carrying up to 40 buds, which open in succession, one at a time, each flower lasting only one day.
They are easy to cultivate, being hardy and disease-resistant. They do well in dry or moist ground, in any position, but give best results in rich, damp soil. They are prolific plants, which can remain in place for more than 10 years, but a certain dose of patience is required, since they give of their best only from the second year.
Use them alone or grouped with other varieties of *Hemerocallis*, or in association with *Iris* varieties, for a long period of poolside colour.

**Position :** sun or semi-shade.

**Planting :** between September and mid-April, plant in deep, nutrient-rich, dry or moist soil, or even submerged in 5-10 cm (2-4 in) of water. Incorporate well-rotted manure or a fertilizer rich in phosphate and potassium, and a little peat, and water generously. Use 5 plants per sq.m., 50-80 cm (20-30 in) apart, since daylilies form vigorous clumps over the years. For container planting, use a mixture composed of 1 third good garden soil, 1 third compost, 1 third fertilized peat.

**Height :** 60-80 cm (24-30 in).

**Decorative period :** June-September

**Care :** in the spring, cut back the dry foliage and give a light application of a complete fertilizer.

**Propagation :** divide clumps in autumn.

**Species or varieties:**
• *Hemerocallis citrina*, lemon-yellow flowers with a perfume reminiscent of lily-of-the-valley. Height : 60 cm (24 in).
• *Hemerocallis liloasphodelus*, very fragrant pastel yellow flowers, May-June.
Height : 80 cm (30 in).
• *Hemerocallis fulva*, (fulvous daylily, tawny daylily), coppery yellow flowers.
Height : 1 m (40 in).
• *Hemerocallis fulva* 'Kwanso', double, tawny orange flowers. Height : 80 cm (30 in).
• *Hemerocallis* 'Anna Warner', rosy mauve flowers with a lemon yellow throat.
Height : 60 cm (24 in).
• *Hemerocallis* 'Autumn Red', red flowers. Height : 1 m (40 in).
• *Hemerocallis* 'Black Prince', very dark brown flowers. Height : 60 cm (24 in).
• *Hemerocallis* 'Catherine Woodbery', lavender-pink flowers and soft green throat. Height : 80 cm (30 in).
• *Hemerocallis* 'Evelyn Claar', silky pink petals, June-September. Height : 80 cm (30 in).
• *Hemerocallis* 'Frans Hals', six petals of alternate colours, yellow and red.
Height : 90 cm (35 in).
• *Hemerocallis* 'George Cunningham' flowers May-June. Melon colour.
Height : 90 cm (35 in).
• *Hemerocallis* 'Sammy Russel', coppery-red flowers, July-August. Height : 70 cm (28 in).

*Hemerocallis* sp.

## 58
### *Heracleum mantegazzianum*
## HERACLEUM
### Cow-parsnip

APIACEAE
**Origin :**
**Caucasus, acclimatized in Europe**

*Heracleum mantegazzianum*

This spectacular ornamental plant, which can grow more than 4 m (13 ft) tall, was imported from southwestern Asia towards the end of the 19th century. Its broad leaves, more than 1 m wide, are deeply divided and indented, and form an impressive, well-shaped clump. From a deeply-anchored rootstock spring one or several ribbed stalks with a base diameter of about 10 cm (4 in). From June to September white flowers are borne in large umbels, up to 50 cm (20 in) in diameter, at the end of the stalks.

It is a hardy perennial which provides a spectacular effect in the large garden, either isolated or planted in a group beside a large area of water. It is a valuable source of nectar, and re-seeds itself quite readily. Note that the sap can have an irritant action on the skin if the latter is exposed to the sun after contact.

**Position :** semi-shade.

**Planting :** deep rich soil, damp to wet.

**Dimensions :** height 2.5-3.5 m (8-12 ft), spread 4 m (13 ft).

**Decorative period :** white flowers, June-September.

**Care :** remove faded flowers before the seeds ripen, to avoid self-seeding. Wear gloves.

**Propagation :** from seed.

## 59
### *Hippuris vulgaris*
### WATER HORSE-TAIL

HIPPURIDACEAE
**Origin :**
**Subcosmopolitan**

This attractive, hardy perennial plant
with its strongly-spreading rhizome forms
large colonies in calm waters in many parts
of the world. It likes cool, limy water and
can take root several metres down,
when it is totally submerged.

But in shallower water from 50 cm (20 in)
its unbranched stems, up to 80 cm (30 in)
tall, are visible. Numerous stiff little leaves,
in whorls of 6 or 12, grow perpendicular to
the stem, giving it a characteristic, fir-tree
shape. In May, very inconspicuous, greenish flowers appear at the leaf axils.

*Hippurus vulgaris* is easily cultivated
and will not escape notice in a small pond

*Hippuris vulgaris*

or basin, but regular attention is needed
to keep it from getting out of hand.
Container planting may be advisable.

**Position :** any.

**Planting :** 6-10 plants per sq.m., in
ordinary or humus-enriched soil, or in a
container, at a depth of from 10 cm (4 in)
down to several metres.

**Dimensions :** 20-80 cm (8-30 in) of stalk
may emerge. The rhizome can reach
several metres in length.

**Care :** eliminate sections of rhizome if
the plant spreads too vigorously.

**Propagation :** divide the rhizome.

## 60
### *Hosta* spp.
### HOSTA
### Funkia, Plantain Lily

LILIACEAE
**Origin :**
**Japan, China**

*Hosta* 'Golden Tiara'

The *Hostas* are splendid foliage plants, in a
range of colours from blue-green to yellow-
green, with some white-variegated cultivars.
They have delicately perfumed racemes of
mauve or white, bell-shaped flowers, between
July-August. They are hardy perennials and
make excellent groundcover for pond margins. Plant in contrasting foliage, with *Astilbes*,
ferns, and Japanese primulas. They take 2-3
years to settle in and produce their best effect.

**Position :** shade or semi-shade, but will
tolerate sun if the soil is kept moist.

**Planting:** in well-worked, humus-rich, damp
to wet soil. Plant 40 cm (16 in) apart, to avoid
having to shift the plants, which would check
their growth.

**Height :** 30-60 cm (12-24 in).
Flowers : 60-80 cm (24-30 in).

**Decorative interest :** flowers May-September,
white, blue or lilac. Foliage.

*Hosta* 'Golden Medaillon'

*Hosta sieboldiana*

**Care :** add humus at the time of planting,
and each spring. Remove faded leaves and
flowers. Slug and snail control is essential,
to prevent damage to leaves.

**Propagation :** divide crown in spring.

**Varieties or species :** All the cultivars
available on the market are highly decorative.
Only a few examples are given here.

• *Hosta* 'August Moon', has crinkled bright
yellow foliage and pretty lilac flowers.
Height : 40 cm (16 in)

• *Hosta fortunei* var. *aureomarginata* has green
leaves with creamy-yellow edges.
Height : 40 cm (16 in).

• *Hosta plantaginea* var. *grandiflora* has broad
yellow-green foliage, and handsome, fragrant
white flowers in July-August.
Height : 50 cm (20 in).

*Hosta* 'Wide Brim'

## 61
### *Hottonia palustris*
# HOTTONIA
# Water violet

PRIMULACEAE
Origin :
Northern Hemisphere

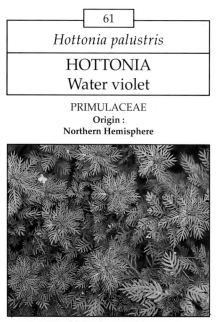
*Hottonia palustris*

This attractive native member of the primula family was christened *Hottonia* by Linnaeus, in homage to the Dutch botanist P. Hotton (d.1709). The *Hottonia* likes cold, calm, rather shallow water, nutrient-rich but not limy. Its light green leaves are deeply divided, and form a dense and graceful carpet beneath the surface of the water. Attractive white or pinkish flowers appear above the water in May-June, at several levels, while the plant frees itself from the bottom and floats freely on the surface. After pollinisation, the fruits lie ripening under water until the following spring. Perfectly hardy, this is certainly the most decorative of the oxygenating plants.

**Position :** shade or semi-shade.

**Planting :** 4-6 plants per sq.m, in 20-60 cm (8-24 in) of cold, still, relatively lime-free water.

**Dimensions :** flower stalk rising 25-40 cm (10-16 in) above the surface. Submerged stems 20-80 cm (8-30 in) long.

**Decorative period :** mauve flowers, May-June.

## 62
### *Houttuynia cordata*
# HOUTTUYNIA

SAURURACEAE
Origin :
Himalayas, China, Japan, Canada.

This vigorous plant is excellent for small gardens, as ground cover beneath shrubs or around stones at the water's edge. Its reddish stems carry mid-green, heart-shaped leaves, decorative all the year in a mild climate. In June, it produces perfumed, small, yellowish spikes of flowers with white bracts. A hardy

*Houttuynia cordata*

perennial, it rapidly sends out runners in moist or damp soil; happy to have its root in the water, provided it is below frost level.

**Position :** any.

**Planting :** 6 plants per sq.m in damp soil or submerged to 30 cm (12 in); also in ordinary garden soil. For container cultivation, use a humus-enriched compost. In regions with cold winters, keep the crown below frost level, or winter over in pots under cover.

**Dimensions :** height 40 cm (16 in), spread 30 cm (12 in).

**Decorative interest :** white flower bracts, July-September. Foliage, May-October.

**Propagation :** division of the crown, spring or autumn.

*Houttuynia cordata* 'Chameleon'

**Cultivars :**
• *Houttuynia cordata* 'Chameleon' (syn. *H.c* 'Variegata') is a superb cultivar with variegated foliage, yellow, green, bronze and bright red, at its best in autumn.
• *Houttuynia cordata* 'Flore Pleno' is a double-flowered variety.

## 63
### *Hydrocharis morsus-ranae*
# FROGBIT

HYDROCHARITACEAE
Origin :
Northern Hemisphere.

This aquatic perennial floats freely in shallow, nutrient-rich, still water, preferably warm and relatively lime-free, where it

rapidly forms extensive colonies. Its heart-shaped leaves are rarely more than 7 cm (3 in) in diameter, reminiscent of a dwarf water-lily, but the white flowers, appearing from June to August, are quite different. They are generally in groups of three (male flowers) or single (female flowers). The corolla, 2 cm (1 in) wide, is composed of three rounded petals, marked with yellow at their base.

The leaves serve as floats to support the rhizome, which throws out a small tuft of pendent roots, which increase considerably the surface in contact with the water. In autumn, bulbous buds, or hibernacles, appear at the end of shoots. They ripen under water then fall to the bottom where they hibernate in the warmer water. In spring, they float up to the surface to produce new plantlets.

*Hydrocharis morsus-ranae*

**Position :** preferably hot and sunny, but is quite tolerant of shade.

**Planting :** allow to float freely on the water.

**Dimensions :** rosettes of leaves up to 50-60 cm (20 24 in) in diameter.

**Propagation :** detach young plantlets as required. It is also possible to conserve some ripe fruit in a container of damp sand in a cool, dark place 5-15 °C (41-59 °F). Return to the water in April-May.

## 64
### *Hydrocleys nymphoides*
### Syn. *Limnocharis humboldtii*
# HYDROCLEYS
# Water poppy

LIMNOCHARITACEAE
Origin :
Equatorial America

This attractive perennial, a native of slow-moving or still waters in Equatorial America, can be cultivated throughout the year in a heated greenhouse, or outside, in summer. Place it in a container in a

*Hydrocleys nymphoides*

shallow pond where the water will more rapidly reach a temperature of 18-25°C (64-77 °F). It grows rapidly throughout the summer and produces isolated flowers with three rounded yellow petals, rising 10 cm (4 in) above the surface. The leaves are shining, dark green, and heart-shaped, forming a thick, decorative carpet on the water.

**Position :** sun.

**Planting :** in 20-60 cm (8-24 in) of water, the crown covered with 4-5 cm (2 in) of earth.

**Decorative period :** May-October.

**Care :** winter plants over in a pool in a heated greenhouse. They can also be kept inside, in damp soil, with good light and a temperature not lower than 15 °C (59 °F).

**Propagation :** divide crown in spring.

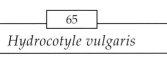

| 65 |
| :---: |
| *Hydrocotyle vulgaris* |
| MARSH PENNYWORT |

UMBELLIFERAE
**Origin :**
**Europe, North Africa**

*Hydrocotyle vulgaris*

The marsh pennywort is a fully hardy plant, naturally found in slow moving or still water in Europe. Its long, creeping stalk produces numerous, long-stemmed, little round peltate leaves, with a slightly lobed edge. The minute umbels of greenish flowers appear from June to August, but are usually hidden by the leaves. It can form large colonies, providing shade and shelter for fish, and helps to purify the water by absorbing dissolved nutrient matter even during the winter.
It also provides good ground cover in wet or sodden soil, masking pond margins or adding interest to rocky cascades and streams.

**Position :** sun or semi-shade.

**Planting :** in clayey, non-chalky soil, wet, or submerged to 30 cm (12 in).

**Dimensions :** stems reach 20-80 cm (8-30 in) in length.

**Decorative period :** inconspicuous flowers, July-August.

**Propagation :** by division of rhizome.

| 66 |
| :---: |
| *Hygrophila* spp. |
| HYGROPHILA |

ACANTHACEAE
**Origin :**
**Asia, Indian Ocean**

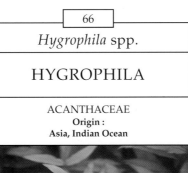

*Hygrophila angustifolia*

The *Hygrophila* are of Indian and Malaysian origin. They grow in warm, still or running water, and on the banks. There are about 100 species of varying sizes, with smooth, opposite leaves, variable in colour from blue-green to purple, according to whether they are submerged or not. They are cultivated in heated greenhouses all the year round, or in outdoor pools in summer.

**Position :** sun and semi-shade.

*Hygrophila polysperma*

**Planting :** in wet ground, or submerged to 60 cm (24 in).

**Propagation :** from cuttings.

**Species or varieties :**
• *Hygrophila angustifolia* has narrow, spear-shaped leaves; can grow to 80 cm (30 in) tall.
• *Hygrophila polysperma* is a species with shining, green, oval foliage, which can have an emerged height of 30 cm (12 in), and becomes purple when submerged.

| 67 |
| :---: |
| *Hypoestes phyllostachya* |
| HYPOESTES Freckle-face, Polka-dot plant |

ACANTHACEAE
**Origin :**
**Madagascar**

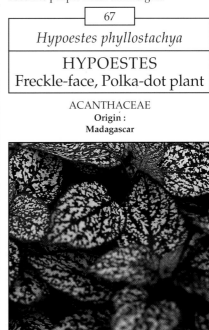

*Hypoestes phyllostachya*

This attractive, bushy plant, from the tropical rain forests of the Indian Ocean, is cultivated as a houseplant. Its abundant evergreen foliage, speckled with pink or white, can provide an interesting colour contrast, which is enhanced by the mauve flowers appearing in early autumn.

**Position :** light, but out of direct sun.

**Planting :** in moist, well-drained soil, dryer in winter, on the acid side, a mixture of leaf-mould, peat and compost.

**Height :** 40-60 cm (16-24 in).

**Care :** keep the atmosphere at a constant level of humidity, with a minimum winter temperature of 16 °C (60 °F).

**Propagation :** from cuttings in spring.

## 68

## *Iris* spp.

# IRIS

**IRIDACEAE**
**Origin :**
**Northern Hemisphere**

*Iris sibirica* 'Crème Chantilly'

The **Iris sibirica** or Siberian irises, from Northern Europe, form handsome, erect tufts of narrow leaves and violet-blue flowers, around ponds, beside streams, and in cool, wet situations. They are very hardy, but require some time to settle in.

**Position :** sun or semi-shade.

**Planting :** in a damp or wet place. Cover the rhizome with 5 cm (2 in) of neutral to slightly acid soil.

**Decorative period :** blue or white flowers, late spring to early Summer.

**Care :** in a cold climate, apply a mulch to protect the crown during the first winter. Make a first application of humus or compost in March, again in June after flowering.

**Propagation :** divide the clumps every 5 years.

• *Iris sibirica* 'Cambridge', pale blue with turquoise sheen, darker sepals. Height : 75 cm (30 in).

• *I. s.* 'Fourfold White' is the largest white variety of *I. sibirica*; flower 15 cm (6 in) in diameter with a bright yellow centre. Height : 85 cm (34 in).

• *I. s.* 'Teal Velvet', a large, velvety, violet-purple flower; white-veined throat. Height : 85 cm (34 in).

• *I. s.* 'White Swirl' is a very floriferous, pure white cultivar with a yellow throat. Height : 90 cm (35 in).

*Iris ensata*, syn. *kaempferi*, or Japanese flag, are the result of centuries of selection by Japanese gardeners. Their spreading flowers come out between mid-June and mid-July. They like moist, acid soil, and are tolerant of being submerged during the summer.

**Position :** sun or semi-shade.

**Planting :** from September till the end of March, in damp, neutral to acid soil (pH 5 to 7), or in up to 10 cm (4 in) of water (except in winter). To increase soil acidity, add an ericaceous compost of well-rotted manure, composted oak leaves and peat. Cover the rhizome with 4-5 cm (2 in) of soil. If plants are to be submerged (between March-September) cultivate them in 15-20 cm (6-8 in) pots in the following mixture : 1 third ericaceous compost, 1 third ordinary compost, 1 third light soil or peat. Put a thin gravel layer on the surface to prevent the compost escaping into the water.

**Dimensions :** 80-120 cm, according to variety.

**Decorative period :** early June-late July.

**Care :** top-dress with compost or humus every spring. Apply a general-purpose fertilizer after flowering. Make preventive applications of a soil insecticide, to control pests which attack the bulb or rhizome, and a systemic insecticide (not in pools) as needed.

**Propagation :** divide clumps every 4 years.

*Iris ensata* 'Lady in Waiting'

**Water irises** prefer a very damp or slightly submerged position to 10 cm (4 in), but can also be cultivated in an ordinary garden provided they are well-watered.

*Iris pseudacorus* (yellow flags) grow in large clumps beside ponds and rivers. They have broad leaves, and bright yellow flowers in June-July. They will tolerate alkaline soil.

• *I. p.* var. *bastardi* is a selected variety of the

*Iris pseudacorus*

native flag, with pale, yellow flowers.

• *I. p.* 'Golden Queen', soft yellow flowers.

• *I. p.* 'Flore Pleno' has a double flower.

• *I. p.* 'Roy Davidson' is a giant form with golden yellow flowers slightly veined with brown, a very long flowering period and abundant vegetation. (Plant 50 cm apart).

• *I. p.* 'Variegata' has green, yellow-edged leaves in spring, turning green in summer.

*Iris versicolor* (blue flag, wild iris) are North American natives, with violet-blue flowers and large clumps of bright green leaves.

• *I. v.* 'Berlin Versilaev', is a cross between *versicolor* and *laevigata*, with stems which grow horizontally at first then become erect. Flowers are purplish-violet with a golden-yellow claw.

• *I.* x *robusta.* 'Gerald Derby', is a cross between *versicolor* and *virginica* . Very handsome foliage, purple at the base, and large violet flowers with white and bright yellow veining in the throat.

• *I. v.* 'Kermesina', has very attractive violet-purple flowers with white and gold veining in the throat.

• *I. v.* 'Lavander', has pretty lavender flowers.

• *I. v.* 'Vernal' is a purplish-pink variety with a white-veined throat, only 50 cm (20 in) high.

*Iris virginica*, from eastern central USA, are hardy and tolerate alkaline soil.

• *I. v.* var. *Shrevei*, broad leaves, lavender blue with violet striped flowers. Height : 45-60 cm (18-24 in).

*Iris laevigata* do well in neutral to acid soil, and do not like alkaline conditions.

• *I. ensata.* 'Rose Queen' forms very handsome clumps of numerous pink flowers with purple veining and yellow throat. Height : 50-70 cm (20-28 in). Flowers mid-June to July.

• *I. l.* 'Variegata', blue flowers and superb green and gold variegated foliage.
Height : 70 cm (28 in).

| *I. p.* 'Roy Davidson' | *I. p.* var. Bastardi | *I.p.* 'Flore Pleno' | *I. v.* 'Gerald Derby' | *I. versicolor* | *I. virginica* var.shrevei | *I. versicolor* 'Kermesina' |

### 69

## *Juncus* spp.

## RUSH

JUNCACEAE
**Origin :**
**Europe, South-West Asia, North America**

*Juncus ensifolius*

*Juncus inflexus* (syn. *J. glaucus*)

*Juncus effusus*

*Juncus acutiflorus* (syn. *J. sylvaticus*)

*Juncus obtusiflorus*

These hardy perennial plants do well in wet or flooded zones. The cylindrical, semi-persistent stems and leaves are used in basketwork (*Juncus* comes from the Latin *jungere*, to join). Their brown fruit, decorative all the year round, appear at the end of the stalks, at the base of a stem-like bract. They are vigorous and undemanding plants, whose creeping roots are useful for stabilizing pond margins.

**Position :** sun or semi-shade.

**Plantation :** wet soil, or submerged to 20 cm (8 in). Plant closely to obtain dense clumps.

**Propagation :** from seed, or division of crowns in April-May. Vegetative reproduction is rapid.

**Species or varieties :**

• *Juncus anceps* has a twisted rhizome. Keeled leaves. Acid soil. Height : 100 cm (40 in).

• *J. acutiflorus*, syn. *J. sylvaticus* has a creeping rhizome. Erect stems, rounded, slightly compressed leaves. Flowers in whorls which spread out. Poor, acid soils. Height : 100 cm (40 in).

• *J. bulbosus* syn. *J. supinus* is the only typically aquatic bulbous species. Dark green stem, loose, green-brown flower head.

Peaty, acid soil. Height : 90 cm (35 in).

• *J. conglomeratus* looks like *J. effusus*, but has striated stems and very compact seed heads. Sandy, non alkaline soil, submerged to 40 cm (16 in). Height : 100 cm (40 in).

• *J. effusus* (soft rush) has a short rhizome. Numerous shining green stems, smooth or slightly striated, filled with pith. Lateral panicles of flowers, compact at first, becoming looser. Sandy or marly soil. Height : 1.2-1.5 m (45-60 in).

• *J. effusus* 'Spiralis' (corkscrew rush) has curious, spiralling cylindrical leaves. Height : 50 cm (20 in).

• *J. ensifolius*, from North America, has flat stems and ribbon-like leaves similar to the iris. Dark brown flowers in a spherical, terminal spike. Height : 30 cm (12 in). Very decorative.

• *J. filiformis*, slender stems, only slightly striated, blue-green foliage. Isolated greenish flowers at the end of short stalks. Height : 60 cm (24 in).

• *J. glaucus*, syn. *J. inflexus*, has a short rhizome and stands up well to dry summer weather. Rigid, striated, cylindrical stems with continuous pith, forming dense, bluish clumps. Lateral cluster of numerous red-brown flowers on the

upper quarter of the stem, under a long bract. Marly or chalky soils, dislikes acid conditions. Height : 50-100 cm (20-40 in).

• *J. obtusiflorus* syn. *J. subnodulosus*, with a creeping rhizome and rounded leaves. Chalky soils. Height : 1 m (40 in).

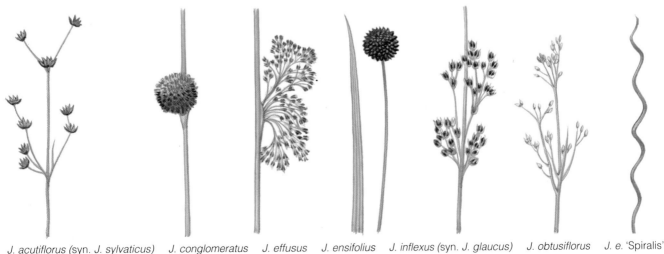

*J. acutiflorus* (syn. *J. sylvaticus*)   *J. conglomeratus*   *J. effusus*   *J. ensifolius*   *J. inflexus* (syn. *J. glaucus*)   *J. obtusiflorus*   *J. e.* 'Spiralis'

## 70

### *Kniphofia* spp.

### KNIPHOFIA
### Red-hot poker, Torch lily

**LILIACEAE**
**Origin :**
**SouthAfrica, Madagascar**

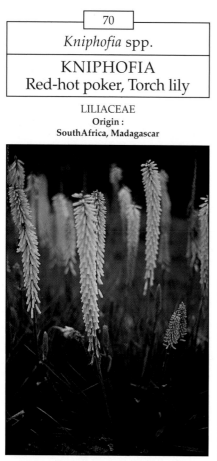

*Kniphofia* 'Little Maid'

These superb perennials are remarkable for their bunches of scarlet buds producing bright flower clusters from summer till autumn. Their flamboyant spikes grow at the end of long, rigid stems up to 2 m (7 ft) tall rising from a large tuft of tapering, narrow leaves. The vertical and parallel lines of the flower stalks contrast attractively with the curved and intersecting lines of the foliage. *Kniphofias* appreciate a moist soil in summer, but stand up well to drought. They need good drainage in winter, and protection in cold climates. They are good nectar producers, and excellent cut flowers.

**Position :** sunny, or semi-shade.

**Planting :** 6 plants per sq.m., in wet soil, even slightly flooded in summer, but dry and well-drained in winter. They will accept ordinary garden soil all year round.

**Dimensions :** height : 80 cm (30 in). Spread : 80 cm (30 in).

**Decorative period :** August-September.

**Care :** in cold winters, cover the crown with peat or other mulch.

**Propagation :** from seed, or division of the clump.

**Species or varieties :**

• *Kniphofia caulescens*, bluish green foliage, orange flower spike. Height : 80 cm (30 in).

• *K. praecox*, with its orange and yellow flower spikes. Height : 1 m (3 ft).

• *K. triangularis* (*triangularis*) with pink and cream flowers. Height : 70 cm (28 in).

**Principal hybrids :**

• *Kniphofia* 'Alcazar', garnet-red flowers. Height : 1 m (3 ft).

• *K.* 'Buttercup', golden-yellow flowers. Height : 80 cm (30 in).

• *K.* 'Candlelight', yellow flowers. Height : 80 cm (30 in).

• *K.* 'Fiery Fred', orange. Height : 80 cm (30 in).

• *K.* 'Goldelse', yellow. Height : 80 cm (30 in).

• *K.* 'Jenny Bloom', pink and cream. Flowers July-August. Height : 80 cm (30 in).

• *K.* 'Lemon Cream', lemon yellow. Flowers July-August. Height : 80 cm (30 in).

• *K.* 'Little Elf', pale orange, later flowering (October-November). Height : 70 cm (28 in).

• *K.* 'Little Maid', cream to straw-coloured. Height : 70 cm (28 in).

• *K.* 'Modesta', cream and coral. Height : 60 cm (24 in).

## 71

### *Kœlaria glauca*

### KŒLARIA

**GRASSES**
**Origin :**
**Europe**

*Kœlaria glauca*

If you are building a rockery beside the pond, or if your garden soil is dry, sandy and stony, think about using *Koelaria glauca* with its fine, persistent, blue-grey foliage. This small, hardy perennial grass is not at all demanding, and will blend naturally into a rockery, while being equally at home in more aquatic surroundings.

**Position :** sunny.

**Planting :** in poor soil, especially chalky, sandy or stony.

**Height :** 20-40 cm (8-16 in).

**Decorative interest :** cream flowers in June-July. Evergreen foliage.

**Propagation :** divide the clumps as they become crowded.

## 72

### *Lemna* spp.

### DUCKWEED

**LEMNACEAE**
**Origin :**
**Subcosmopolitan**

*Lemna minor*

Throughout the summer, duckweeds carpet the surface of warm, still, nutrient-rich water. They are hardy perennials which seem to behave as annuals, and rarely flower in this climate. The flowers are minute and composed of only one stamen and one pistil, without corolla or calix. Vegetative reproduction takes place by lateral budding and aquatic birds take care of the distribution. Duckweed has a certain decorative value in the "natural" garden, introducing a little of the disorderly element that is part of nature's charm. In nutrient-rich waters its vigorous growth hinders the development of algae, but it can also deprive the submerged and oxygenating plants of light.

However, it can be kept in check naturally by the presence of herbivorous fish, such as goldfish and Koi carp, and aquatic birds, such as ducks, which feed on it. It can also be "harvested" regularly, since it makes excellent compost.

**Species or varieties :**

• The Lemnaceae family includes a number of different species of duckweed, belonging to two genera : *Wolffia*, which are rootless plants, and *Lemna*, which have one root.

• *Lemna gibba* (gibbous duckweed) has oval leaves, 3-7 mm (a fifth of an inch) long, with a very convex lower surface and a single root.

• *L. minor* (lesser duckweed) has small, flat, oval or round leaves, 4-10 mm (a fifth to half an inch) long, with a single root.

• *L. polyrhiza*, (greater duckweed), 2-16 roots arranged in clusters; leaves are larger, flat and oval, 10-20 mm (half to one inch) long, sometimes with a reddish underside.

• *L. trisulca* (ivy-leaved duckweed) is identifiable by its pointed leaves,

6-12 mm long (a fifth to half an inch). They are pale green and translucent, usually submerged (except during the flowering period, when they float), and have a single root. The series of offshoots remain fixed to the side of the parent plants. This variety prefers clear, alkaline water.

• *Wolffia arrhiza* ,whose minute leaves 1 mm (a twentyfifth of an inch) are rootless, hence the name *'arrhiza',* is the smallest flowering plant yet identified.

*Lemna minor*   *Wolffia arrhiza*   *Lemna gibba*

*Lemna polyrhiza*   *Lemna trisulca*

73

## *Ligularia* spp.

## LIGULARIA

ASTERACEAE
**Origin :**
**South-East Asia**

*Ligularia dentata* 'Desdemona

The foliage of the *Ligularia* forms a decorative clump more than 1 m (3 ft) broad, from which emerge magnificent yellow flower spikes, up to 1.5 m (5 ft) tall, between July and September. These splendid hardy perennials like a wet soil, with regular applications of compost or well-rotted manure.

*Ligularia japonica*

**Position :** moderate sun and semi-shade, sheltered from strong winds.
**Planting :** in rich, moist to damp soil. 3-4 plants per sq.m.
**Height :** 1-1.5 m (3-5 ft). Spread : 1 m (3 ft).
**Decorative interest :** flowers, July-September.
**Propagation :** from seed, and division of clumps in spring.

**Species or varieties :**
• *Ligularia dentata* (syn. *L. clivorum*) has rounded foliage and numerous yellow daisy-like flowers. Height : 1.5 m (5 ft).
• *L. d.* 'Desdemona' has large round leaves and very decorative purple stalks, with large clusters of orange flowers. Height : 1.5 m (5 ft).
• *L. hessei* 'Gregynog Gold' has handsome conical panicles of large, star-shaped orange-yellow flowers, and rounded green leaves. Height : 1.2 m (4 ft).
• *L. hogsonii* has heart-shaped leaves and daisy-like flowers at the top of the stalks. Height : 1 m (3 ft).
• *L. japonica* has large denticulate leaves

*Ligularia dentata* 'Othello'

and long stems bearing golden-yellow, starry flowers. Height : 1.7 m (6 ft).
• *L. dentata* 'Othello' is a cultivar with purple foliage. Height : 1.7 m (6 ft).
• *L.* x *palmatiloba*, has large, very denticulated leaves and spikes of yellow flowers on stems up to 2 m (7 ft) tall.
• *L. przewalskii* forms a medium-sized clump with very denticulated greenish-bronze foliage. Its long spikes of starry lemon-yellow flowers are carried on elegant black stems. Height : 1.5 m (5 ft).
• *L.* 'The Rocket' has the finest foliage, with black stems and leaf-stalks,with large rounded toothed dark-green leaves. Long erect spikes of golden-yellow flowers. Height : 1.5-2 m (5-7 ft).
• *Ligularia tangutica* (syn. *Sinacalia*) has deeply denticulated leaves and spikes of yellow flowers. Height : 1.2 m (4 ft).
• *L. veitchiana* has perfectly round leaves which turn purple in autumn. Spikes of yellow flowers. Height : 1.5 m (5 ft).
• *L. wilsoniana*, has heart-shaped toothed leaves. The flower stalks form vertical spikes up to 1 m (3 ft) tall.

*Ligularia przewalskii*

*Ligularia wilsoniana*

### 74

## *Lobelia* spp.

## LOBELIA

CAMPANULACEAE
**Origin :**
Temperate and tropical zones

The *Lobelias* are perennials, originally from the United States of America. They are very decorative, from late summer to the first frosts, with their shining foliage crowned with a cluster of bright flowers. Lobelias are hardy in a mild climate, but in continental regions it is advisable to protect the crown during the winter, by mulching. Attractive cut flowers.

*Lobelia siphilitica*

**Position :** sunny, but accepts shade.
**Planting :** 5-6 plants per sq.m., in moist to very damp soil or submerged to 15 cm (6 in).
**Height :** 80-100 cm (30-40 in).
**Decorative interest :** flowers July-October.
**Care :** in cold climates, protect crown in winter.
**Propagation :** from seed, or division of

*Lobelia* 'Pink Flamingo'

clump in spring.

**Species or varieties :**
• *Lobelia cardinalis* (cardinal flower) has green foliage and a cluster of bright red flowers. Height :10-50 cm (4-20 in).
• *L.* 'Dark Crusader' has dark red flowers and purplish-green leaves. Height : 1.2 m (4 ft).
• *L.* 'Queen Victoria' has remarkable shining purple foliage. Height : 1 m (3 ft).
• *L. laxiflora* var. *angustifolia* is an attractive variety with narrow dark green leaves and brilliant red, tubular flowers.
Height : 50 cm (20 in).
• *L.* 'Pink Flamingo' has bright pink flowers and green foliage. Height : 1 m (3 ft).
• *L. sessiliflora*, periwinkle blue flowers, light green foliage. Height : 60-80 cm (24-30 in).
• *L. siphilitica* is a very attractive, fully hardy species with large green leaves and bright violet-blue flowers. *Lobelia siphilitica alba* is a white-flowered cultivar.
Height : 60-180 cm (2-6 ft).
• *L.* x *gerardii* 'vedrariensis' has purplish-violet flowers and green foliage.
• *L.* x *gerardii* 'vedrariensis Alba' has white flowers. Height : 90 cm (35 in).

### 75

## *Ludwigia grandiflora*
Syn. *Jussiaea grandiflora*

## LUDWIGIA

ONAGRACEAE
**Origins:**
North America, Europe

This *Ludwigia* does well in still or running water in temperate and tropical zones. It is a submerged perennial plant, with stems that float across the water,

*Lobelia* 'Queen Victoria'

before rising a few centimetres above the surface. The stalk is anchored to the bottom, whilst the adventitious roots act as floats to maintain the plant at the surface, and also absorb nutrient matter in suspension. Flowering produces an uninterrupted succession of yellow blooms, 3-4 cm (1-2 in) wide, with 5 wide-spread petals. The plant is vigorous, especially in warm water and a rich soil, but it is easily controlled by cutting back the stems through the season. Use in a hot, sunny position in large ponds, where it will have plenty of room to spread out.

The *Ludwigia* was named in honour of the German botanist, Christian Gottlieb Ludwig, a contemporary of Linnaeus. Its alternative name, *Jussiaea grandiflora*, is dedicated to the French botanist, Bernard de Jussieu.

*Ludwigia grandiflora*

**Position :** sunny.

**Planting :** about 5 plants per sq.m., in rich soil, at a depth of 30-50 cm (12-20 in). It can also be allowed to float freely on the surface, if a stone is attached to the stem to act as an anchor and stop the plant from drifting with the wind. In cold climates, plant below frost level or cultivate in a container which can be protected during winter.

**Height :** 10 cm (4 in) above the water, but stalks may be more than 5 m (16 ft) long.

**Decorative interest :** bright yellow flowers, June-September.

**Care :** cut back excessively long stems through the season.

**Propagation :** from terminal or lateral stem cuttings carrying adventitious roots. The *Ludwigia* is a spontaneous self-sower.

**Other species :**
• *Ludwigia sprengeri* is a tropical species with very big yellow flowers.
Height : up to 1 m (3 ft). Like *L. grandiflora*, it can also be cultivated outside, in a hot, sunny situation.

---

76

*Luzula* spp.

## LUZULA

JUNCACEAE
**Origin :**
**Europe**

*Luzula sylvatica*

Of the same family as the rushes, the *Luzulas* are hardy perennial plants on a creeping root, which grow in clumps in moist or wet situations. They can be identified by their flat, narrow leaves fringed with fine white hairs. Their uses are similar to those of the ornamental grasses.

• *Luzula nivea* has narrow, pale green foliage 3-4 mm (fifth of an inch) with graceful inflorescences in the form of silvery-white plumes in May-June. Height : 40-50 cm (16-20 in).

• *L. sylvatica* (greater woodrush) is the biggest of the luzulas, 1 m (40 in) tall. Its shining leaves, 15-20 mm (half to 1 inch) wide, are topped by elegant brown inflorescences between April and June.

**Position :** any.

**Planting :** in moist or damp soil, especially poor and acidic.

**Height :** 40-100 cm (16-40 in).

**Decorative period :** inflorescences, April-June.

**Propagation :** by separation of stolons.

---

77

*Lychnis flos-cuculi*
Syn. *Silene flos-cuculi*

## LYCHNIS
Cuckoo-flower

CARYOPHYLLACEAE
**Origin :**
**Europe, acclimatized in North America.**

This attractive flower of marshes and wet meadows is a hardy perennial common almost all over Europe, with the exception of the Mediterranean. It forms a rather sparse clump of narrow leaves, from which emerge long, bare, often reddish stalks bearing

*Lychnis flos-cuculi*

large, pink flowers with 5 finely-fringed petals.

• *Lychnis* x *arkwrightii* is most decorative, with its purple foliage setting off the very conspicuous orange flowers, between June and October. Height : 40-60 cm (16-24 in).

• *L. flos-jovis*, is an alpine species, 45 cm (18 in) tall, with large, pink flowers.

**Position :** sun and semi-shade.

**Planting :** all soils, rather acid, damp, or slightly submerged to 10 cm (4 in).

**Height :** 40-80 cm (16-30 in).

**Decorative period :** flowers, May-June.

**Propagation :** from seed in April, or by division of the crown.

---

78

*Lysichiton americanus*

## LYSICHITON
Skunk cabbage

ARACEAE
**Origin :**
**North America, Alaska to California.**

*Lysichiton americanus*

This unusual plant comes from the peat bog zones of the west coast of North America. It is a perfectly hardy perennial, but sometimes takes a long time to come into flower after being moved. But its spectacular flower, with a bright yellow spathe up to 20 cm (8 in) in length, makes it worth waiting for a year or two. Later in the season, its giant leaves form an equally decorative clump, about 1.2 m (4 ft) tall. Plant lysichitons in very wet soil or submerged, at the edge of a large pond (for a mirror effect) or beside a stream. They need deep, rich soil, for theyare greedy plants, and their roots can go down as far as 1.5 m (5 ft) in search of nourishment.

**Position :** sunny, but tolerates shade well.

**Planting :** 1 plant every 80 cm (30 in) in damp soil or submerged 10 cm (4 in). Appreciates deep, rich, preferably acid soil. Apply well rotted manure or compost when planting, then once a year, in spring.

**Decorative interest :** bright yellow spathe, March-April.

**Propagation :** from runners, or division of rhizome at beginning of spring. From seed in damp humus (re-seeds spontaneously).

**Other species :**

• *Lysichiton camtschatcensis* originates in north-east Asia (Kamtchatka). It is not so tall as its American cousin, and has a white spathe, which is also smaller. Height : 40-70 cm (16-28 in).

*Lysichiton camtschatcensis*

## 79

## *Lysimachia* spp.

# LYSIMACHIA
## Loosestrife

PRIMULACEAE
Origin :
Temperate and cold zones, northern hemisphere.

*Lysimachia clethroides*

These are hardy perennials with creeping roots. They are easy to cultivate by the waterside, and do well in any soil or position.
**Planting :** 6 plants per sq.m. in damp soil or slightly submerged 10 cm (4 in).
**Decorative period :** June to September.
**Propagation :** from seed, or division of the clump after flowering.
**Species or varieties :**
• *Lysimachia barystachys* has small, starry yellow flowers along the stem.
Height : 60 cm (24 in).
• *L. ciliata* is a hardy species, late-flowering.

*Lysimachia nummularia*

*Lysimachia thyrsiflora*

Its starry yellow flowers contrast with its young, brown foliage. Height : 1 m (3 ft).
• *L. clethroides*, with a creeping rhizome, has small white star-shaped flowers grouped in gracefully arching spikes. Its pure green spear-shaped leaves turn orange-red in autumn. Dislikes alkaline soil. Height : 80 cm (30 in).
• *L. ephemerum*, a less creeping species, has spikes of white flowers rising from the blue-green foliage, July-September.
Height : 80 cm (30 in).
• *L. nemorum* has small, round evergreen leaves which provide excellent ground cover for shady situations. Height : 5 cm (2in).

*Lysimachia punctata*

*Lysimachia ephemerum*

• *L. nummularia* (Creeping Jenny or moneywort), is a creeping species with small round leaves (like coins) turning golden yellow in autumn. It has star-shaped, bright yellow, isolated flowers, 2 cm (1 in) in diameter. When planted in water it floats, but among rocks it has a trailing habit. Height : 5 cm (2 in).
• *L. nummularia* 'Aurea' is a cultivar with pretty golden foliage, and star-shaped yellow flowers from June to July. Semi-shade. Height : 5 cm (2 in).
• *L. punctata* (garden loosestrife) has whorls of four, dark green, spear-shaped leaves in erect spikes covered with starry, bright yellow, bell-shaped flowers. Height : 60-150 cm (2-5 ft).
• *L. thyrsiflora* is a native variety with pale green, opposite, spear-shaped leaves. The flowers are yellow, in very dense pyramidal clusters. Height : 40-80 cm (16-30 in).
• *L. vulgaris* has a creeping rhizome and terminal clusters of yellow flowers. Height : 80-150 cm (30 in-5 ft).

*Lysimachia vulgaris*

## 80

### *Lythrum salicaria*

## PURPLE LOOSESTRIFE

LYTHRACEAE
**Origin :**
**Europe, temperate Asia,**
**Australia, North America.**

*Lythrum salicaria*

This is often found beside ponds and rivers, in wet meadows and marshes. It is a hardy perennial, easy to cultivate, and appreciates very damp, even flooded conditions. Its narrow, spear-shaped, sessile leaves are carried on long, erect, slightly downy stalks, flaring out to form a clump about 80 cm (30 in) wide. It is an excellent source of nectar, with purplish-pink flowers in spikes up to 1 m (3 ft) in length. There are a number of horticultural varieties in a range of colours from white to red.

**Position :** sun and semi-shade.

**Planting :** in damp soil, or submerged to 30 cm (12 in).

**Height :** 40-150 cm (16 in-5 ft).

**Decorative period :** June-September, pink to reddish violet flowers, according to species.

**Care :** cut the clumps back to ground level in autumn.

**Propagation :** from seed, or division of clumps in spring and autumn.
Re-seeds generously.

**Other species or varieties :**

• *Lythrum salicaria* 'Augenweide', with reddish-violet flowers. Height : 1 m (3 ft).

• *L. salicaria* 'Roseum' has pale pink flowers. Height : 80 cm (30 in).

• *L. virgatum*, has red flowers in longer, more slender spikes. 40-60 cm tall. Very suitable for small ponds.

## 81

### *Macleaya cordata*
### Syn. *Bocconia cordata*

## MACLEAYA
## Plume poppy

PAPAVERACEAE
**Origin :**
**Asia**

*Macleaya cordata*

A native of China, this is a vigorous, hardy plant with a creeping rhizome. It has large, deeply-lobed leaves, bronze-green with a downy, almond green under-side. In summer, its minute flowers form immense, pale pink, feathery panicles, up to 3 m (10 ft) tall.

• *Macleaya microcarpa* 'Kelway's Coral Plume' is a coral-pink cultivar.
Height : 2 m (7 ft).

• *M. microcarpa*, airy pink inflorescences in August. Height : 3.5 m (11 ft).

**Position :** sun or semi-shade, protected from wind.

**Planting :** in any type of soil, moist or damp. 3 plants per sq.m. In a windy situation will need staking.

**Height :** flower heads 2.5 m (8 ft), foliage 1.5 m (5 ft).

**Spread :** 1 m (3 ft).

**Decorative period :** pink flowers, July-September.

**Care :** cut back dry foliage in spring. In cold regions, protect crowns in winter with mulch.

**Propagation :** from stolons.

## 82

### *Maranta leuconeura*

## MARANTA
## Prayer plant

MARANTACEAE
**Origin :**
**American tropics**

*Maranta leuconeura*

These are evergreen plants from the tropical rain forests of Brazil. They are all suitable for cultivation in the heated greenhouse, provided a high degree of humidity is maintained. The handsome sprawling foliage of *Maranta leuconeura* makes it an excellent ground cover plant for the pond margin.

• *Maranta insignis* has a decorative, palm-like appearance. Its wavy-edged, spear-shaped leaves are pale green in colour with a dark green chevron pattern on either side of the central rib.

**Position :** light, but out of direct sun.

**Planting :** in a damp situation, or slightly submerged 10 cm (4 in). Needs a light, humus-rich, slightly acid mixture of ericaceous compost and ordinary compost.

**Height:** 40-60 cm (16-24 in).

**Care :** needs a temperature of 20-25 °C (68-77 °F) in summer, 16 °C (60 °F) at night; 18 °C (64 °F) in winter, 15 °C (59 °F) at night). Apply diluted liquid fertilizer fortnightly.

**Propagation :** by division or from stem cuttings, at the end of winter.

*Maranta insignis*

## 83

### *Marsilea quadrifolia*

### MARSILEA
### Water clover, pepperwort

MARSILEACEAE
Origin :
Southern Europe,
naturalized in North America

*Marsilea quadrifolia*

This singular, delicate and very rare floating plant is easily recognized by its groups of four leaflets which give it the appearance of a large, four-leaved clover. It is in fact an aquatic fern, moderately hardy, with a creeping, bottom-rooted rhizome. Its long-stalked fronds form a floating carpet of leaves, some of which rise about 15 cm (6 in) above the water. They turn an attractive colour in autumn. The small fruits of the *Marsilea*, called sporocarps, which look like little blackish pills, are found at the base of the leaf-stalks. The spores ripen in September-October.

This is the only European species of the genus, and is found in ponds, marshes and still waters in southern Europe. It is a protected species, having become very nearly extinct, but you may be lucky enough to find a collector willing to part with a specimen.

**Position :** sun or semi-shade.

**Planting :** in extremely wet soil, or sub-merged to 20 cm (8 in).

**Height :** emerged, 5-15 cm (2-6 in) above the surface of the water.

**Decorative period :** foliage takes on attrac-tive autumn colours, between September and November.

**Care :** cut back foliage in spring.

**Propagation :** division of rhizome, in spring.

## 84

### *Mentha* spp.

### MINT

LABIATAE
Origin :
Eurasia

*Mentha aquatica* 'Rubra'

The mints are melliferous, hardy perennials which prefer rich, moist soil. There are more than 1000 varieties, some of which do well in shallow water. It is preferable to grow them in containers, to keep their vigorously-spreading roots under control.

**Position :** semi-shade.

**Planting :** in very wet soil, or submerged to 30 cm (12 in).

**Height :** 15-50 cm (6-20 in).

**Decorative period :** flowers from July till October.

**Propagation :** by root cuttings at end of spring.

**Species or varieties :**
• *Mentha aquatica* (water mint) : flowers in compact spherical groups at the end of the stalks and branches. Foliage turns reddish in the sun. Height : 30-80 cm (12-30 in).
• *M. aquatica crispa* has curly, bright green foliage. Height : 40 cm (16 in).
• *M. aquatica* 'Rubra' is a horticultural variety with reddish-violet leaves. Height : 60 cm (24 in).
• *M. arvensis* has whorls of lilac flowers at the leaf axils. Light green, slightly downy leaves. Height : 10-60 cm (4-24 in).
• *M. cervina* (syn. *Preslia cervina*) is a Mediterranean species with long, narrow, bright green foliage. Very perfumed pale mauve flowers. Height : 15-20 cm (6-8 in).
• *M. c.* 'Alba' (syn. *Preslia cervina* 'Alba') is a cultivar with white flowers and attractive green foliage. Height : 15-20 cm (6-8 in).

*Mentha aquatica*

*Mentha pulegium*

• *M. longifolia* ssp. *palustris*, light grey foliage and lilac flowers. Height : 40-50 cm (16-20 in).

• *M. pulegium* (pennyroyal), is a sprawling plant with round whorls of flowers. Small rounded leaves, light green, strongly-scented. Not a lime-lover. Height : 10-15 cm (4-6 in).

## 85

### *Menyanthes trifoliata*

### MARSH TREFOIL
### Bog myrtle, bog bean, buckbean

MENYANTHACEAE
Origin :
Temperate and cold zones,
Northern Hemisphere.

Marsh trefoil is a native, semi-submerged plant, whose creeping root either floats or is anchored to the bottom. Its shining, pure green leaves are composed of three oval, slightly pointed petioles. They emerge a few centimetres above the surface and sometimes form large colonies, which are decorative but not invasive. In April-May, the compact clusters of star-shaped, gracefully fringed, white flowers rising above the water make a splendid sight. It is a fully hardy perennial which was once common in peat-bogs and marshes, but it has become more and more rare in the wild, due, no doubt, to excessive harvesting of the leaves for medicinal purposes. It is known to have tonic, vermifuge and antiscorbutic properties, as well as being useful in the treatment of rhumatism and skin problems.

The marsh trefoil is the only European

*Menyanthes trifoliata*

representative of the Menyanthaceae, with the exception of *Nymphoides peltata*.

**Position :** sun or semi-shade.

**Planting :** 5-10 plants per sq.m, very wet, acid soil or submerged 30 cm (12 in).

**Dimensions :** flowering stem 15-30 cm (6-12 in) above the water.

**Decorative period :** white flowers, April-June. Sometimes a second flowering in autumn.

**Propagation :** from seed, and division of rhizome in spring.

---

| 86 |
| :---: |

### *Mimulus* spp.

### MIMULUS
### Monkey Flower

SCROPHULARIACEAE
**Origin :**
**U.S.A., Chile**

*Mimulus guttatus*

---

This hardy, generously-flowering perennial grows easily in wet or flooded ground, where it self-seeds very readily. Its name comes from the Latin *mimus*, meaning 'little buffoon' and refers to the great diversity of colour found in the more than 150 known species or varieties.

**Position :** sun or semi-shade.

**Planting :** about 10 plants per sq.m. in wet soil, or submerged to 20 cm (8 in).

**Decorative period :** July to September.

**Care :** to encourage flowering, pinch out the terminal bud of young plants to cause them to branch. Dead-head the plants to avoid self-seeding.

**Propagation :** sow in spring, divide the crown or separate shoots from the base.

*Mimulus ringens*

**Other species or varieties:**

• *Mimulus cardinalis*, various shades from yellow to red. Height : 60-80 cm (24-30 in).

• *M. cupreus*, from California, has coppery red flowers. Height : 20-40 cm (8-16 in).

• *M. guttatus* has yellow flowers with reddish spots in the throat. Self-seeds readily. Height : 40 cm (16 in).

• *M. lewisii*, from the north-east United States, varies from pale pink to very bright red. Height : 45-60 cm (18-24 in).

• *M. luteus* originally from Chile, is an annual. Yellow flowers have red blotches on the petals. Height : 40-60 cm (16-24 in).

• *M. luteus alpinus*, white flowers with red blotches. Height : 40-60 cm (16-24 in).

• *M.* 'Ohrid', a very hardy cultivar with brown-marked yellow flowers. Height : 15-20 cm (6-8 in).

• *M. ringens*, lavender-blue flowers. Height : 40-50 cm (16-20 in).

---

*Mimulus tilingii*

• *M. tilingii*, starry white flowers. Height : 40-50 cm (16-24 in).

---

| 87 |
| :---: |

### *Miscanthus* spp.
### Syn. *Eulalia* spp.

### MISCANTHUS

GRAMINEAE
**Origine :**
**Eastern Asia**

*Miscanthus sinensis* 'Gracillimus'

*Miscanthus*, also called *Eulalia*, are handsome decorative grasses from China and Japan. They are hardy and easily managed, tall and fast-growing, and like a rich and sufficiently damp soil, especially during the growing period, in spring and summer,

*Miscanthus sinensis* 'Variegatus'

but will tolerate dryer conditions in winter. Their semi-persistent foliage forms graceful clumps which provide interest even throughout winter, with silky inflorescences appearing in September-October. They do not appear to best advantage until 2 or 3 years after planting. For an interesting contrast, use them in association with large-leaved plants such as *Gunnera*, *Rodgersia* or *Rheum palmatum*. The larger varieties can be used to screen part of the garden.

**Position :** sunny.

**Planting :** moist or sodden ground.

**Height :** 1-4 m (3-13 ft) according to variety.

**Decorative period :** flower heads, September to November.

**Care :** cut back to ground level in spring.

**Propagation :** divide the clump at the beginning of summer or at the end of autumn (after flowering).

**Other species or varieties :**
• *Miscanthus floridulus* 'Giganteus', (syn. *M. japonicus*) has rigid stalks and large green leaves. Good resistance to wind, so is useful for wind-breaks or decorative natural hedges. Inflorescence : silky, silver

*Miscanthus japonicus*

*Miscanthus sinensis* 'Silver Feather'

white plume. Height : 3-3.5 m (10-11 ft). Spread : 2-3 m (7-10 ft).
• *M. sacchariflorus* (Amur silver grass) is a majestic slow-growing, decorative grass which forms a very dense clump of broad, arching, dark green leaves, with silver-white plumes in summer. Height : 2-4 m (7-13 ft). Spread : 2 m (7 ft).
• *M. sinensis* 'Giganteus' has strong and graceful foliage reaching a height of 3-4 m (10-13 ft).
• *M. sinensis* 'Gracillimus' is a cultivar with narrow, flexible, gracefully-curving leaves with a yellow-marked mid-rib. Feathery inflorescences in autumn. Height : 1.5-2 m (5-7 ft).
• *M. sinensis* var. *purpurascens*, forms a clump of fine foliage turning crimson in autumn. Height : 1.3-1.6 m (4-5 ft).
• *M. s.* 'Silberfeder' (syn. 'Silver Feather'), very narrow leaves and silky, pale-pink plumes. Height : 1.5-2 m (5-7 ft).
• *M. s.* 'Variegatus' has attractive variegated leaves with long green and white stripes. Height : 1.5-2 m (5-7 ft).
• *M. s.* 'Zebrinus' has broad, erect leaves, striped with transverse white bands. Silvery white plumes in summer. Height : 1.5-2 m (5-7 ft).

*Miscanthus sinensis* 'Zebrinus Strictus'

*Molinia* spp.

# MOLINIA

GRASSES
**Origin :**
**Europe**

*Molinia caerulea* 'Variegata'

*Molinia* are attractive, hardy perennial grasses, whose supple foliage is decorative all the year, but particularly in autumn when it takes on a fine golden colour.

**Position :** sunny or shaded.

**Planting :** in any soil, even acid, moist, or even submerged to 10 cm (4 in). Stands up well to dry conditions.

**Propagation :** divide clumps in spring.

**Species or varieties :**
• *Molinia altissima* is a medium-sized species 1.5-1.8 m (5-6 ft) with very handsome autumn colouring.

• *M. caerula arundinacea* 'Karl Foerster' has thicker stems and therefore offers better wind resistance.

• *M. caerulea* is common in the acid soil of damp woodland and flooded moorland. It forms a large erect tuft with tapering stems up to 1 m (3 ft) tall. Its leaves, 4 mm (a fifth of an inch) wide, are blue-green in summer and turn golden yellow in autumn. They last throughout the winter. Flowering occurs between July and September, in the form of fine, blue-violet plumes. This *Molinia* is very tough, and will survive even if the soil dries out completely.

• *M. caerulea* 'Variegata' (variegated purple moor grass) is a very pretty variety with green and white variegated foliage. Flower heads are bluish at first, becoming whitish. Height : 80-100 cm (30-40 in).

## 89

## *Myosotis scorpioides*
## Syn. *Myosotis palustris*

### WATER FORGETMENOT

BORAGINACEAE
**Origin :**
**Northern Hemisphere.**

*Myosotis scorpioides*

This is a hardy native perennial with a creeping rhizome, common in damp clearings or marshy meadows. According to the nature of the habitat, it has a terrestrial, semi-aquatic or aquatic form, the latter being most frequent in cold water in winter. It grows rapidly, but is easily controlled by thinning. Use by the side of a stream, or to mask the edge of a pond or a submerged plant container. Its terminal clusters of minute blue flowers with their yellow centre combine very happily with the yellow flowers of *Caltha palustris*.

- *M. s.* 'Alba' is a white-flowered cultivar.
- *M. s.* 'Mermaid' has large blue flowers.
- *M. s. semperflorens* flowers abundantly and for a particularly long period.

**Position :** sunny or shaded.

**Planting :** about 20 plants per sq.m. in moist soil or submerged to 15 cm (6 in).

**Height :** 20-40 cm (8-16 in).

**Decorative interest :** sky blue flowers, May till October.

**Propagation :** from seed in autumn, plant out before winter. Divide clumps in spring.

## 90

## *Myriophyllum* spp.

### MYRIOPHYLLUM
### Water milfoil

HALORAGIDACEAE
**Origin :**
**Subcosmopolitan**

The *Myriophylla* are hardy submerged plants found in still waters in temperate and tropical regions. They are excellent oxygenating plants, helping to clear the water and serving as a depository for fish spawn. Their stems carry numerous finely-divided little leaves (*Myriophyllum* means "having innumerable leaves") forming a thick, feathery carpet which is sometimes quite deep in the water. When taken out of the water, the stems of *Myriophyllum* go limp, in contrast to those of *Ceratophyllum*, which remain stiff. Between June and September, spikes of pink or yellowish flowers emerge slightly from the water. When the water is shallow, the stem emerges and develops aerial leaves.

*Myriophyllum verticillatum*

**Position :** sun or semi-shade.

**Planting :** plant in 20-250 cm (8 in-8 ft) of water, in a mixture of 1 third garden soil, 1 third sand and 1 third compost, or let the plant float freely.

**Dimensions :** stems 1.5-3 m (20 in-10 ft) long.

**Care :** control by cutting back the clumps.

**Propagation :** in spring, remove lateral or terminal shoots about 12 cm (5 in) long and plant them in well-worked ground to encourage rooting.

*Myriophyllum aquaticum*

**Species or varieties :**
The **native species** which are perfectly hardy, do best in cold to moderately warm water 5-20 °C (41-68 °F) :

- *Myriophyllum alterniflorum* has rather branching stems, yellowish, alternate, whorled flowers and leaves in whorls of 4. Running water poor in organic matter.

- *M. spicatum* has smaller, less dense leaves, in whorls of 4. Still water, even alkaline.

- *M. verticillatum* has leaves in dense whorls of 5. Still, lime-free water, rich in nutrients.

The **tropical species** appreciate warmer water 15-25 °C (15-25 °F) and it is essential that they be protected against frost :

- *Myriophyllum aquaticum* (syn. *M. brasiliense, proserpinacoides*), from South America, has very dense, rigid stems, rising up to 30 cm (12 in) above the water. It spreads vigorously and forms large colonies. This is the most popular *Myriophyllum*

- *M. matogrossense* from the Mato Grosso in Brazil, likes slightly acid water. Leaves in whorls of 5 or 6, reddish-brown under the water.

## 91

## *Nasturtium officinale*

### WATER CRESS
### BRASSICACEAE

BRASSICACEAE
**Origin :**
**Europe**

*Nasturtium officinale*

Water cress is a hardy perennial, quite common in streams and near springs, and in reedbeds in running water. Its stems are prostrate at the base, then become erect, and spread rapidly, making it a useful ground cover plant for the edge of a pond or the side of a cascade. It can also be allowed to float freely on the water. This medicinal plant has an excellent flavour, but pregnant women should avoid eating it.

- A related species, *Rorippa amphibia*, has similar habits, but is readily distinguished by its large clusters of bright yellow flowers.
- See also p.174 *Veronica beccabunga* (brooklime).

**Position :** sunny.

**Planting :** in very wet soil or submerged, under 5-60 cm (2-24 in) of water.

**Height :** 20-90 cm (16-35 in).

**Decorative period :** white flowers, June-September.

**Propagation :** from seed and cuttings.

| 92 |
| --- |

## *Nelumbo* spp.

## LOTUS

NELUMBOACEAE
**Origin :**
**Warm temperate and tropical zones of Asia, Australia, North America and Europe.**

*Nelumbo nucifera*

Real wonders of nature, lotus are superb plants for the water garden. Their abundant flowers and large, glaucous, matt leaves are a splendidly decorative element for a patio pool, and add an element of exoticism in an informal pond. They are perennial plants with a creeping rhizome, and do best in warm situations in marshes and shallow ponds. As they require high light levels to sufficiently store energy reserves in the rhizome, they usually dwindle after the first year in the UK, where they are treated as highly ornamental annuals. Their rounded leaves, with a waxy, peltate limb, spread out on the water in spring then rise up to two metres above the surface, at the end of a long stem. The chalice-shaped flower, with its giant petals arranged in a spiral, rises above the foliage between July and October. After fertilization, the stamens and petals fall, revealing the ovary in its inverted cone-shaped receptacle, somewhat reminiscent of the rose of a watering-can. The ripe fruit falls to the water and floats upside-down, releasing the seeds, which have an extraordinarily long life - up to several thousand years. The seeds are edible while they are still green. From the most remote times, the lotus flower ("nelumbo" in the Sri-Lankan language) has been considered throughout Asia as the symbol of beauty and purity. Buddhism sees in it a symbol of the capacity of the human soul to rise above spiritual ignorance.

**Position :** very sunny.

**Planting :** early March to late May. Lay the rhizome delicately (it is fragile as glass) in a horizontal position on a layer of about 30-50 cm (12-20 in) of good loam, rich in organic material (20% well-rotted manure and 80% mud or loam). Loosely cover the root with 8-10 cm (3-4 in) of soil, to protect it from cold. Since each plant occupies an area of about 4 sq.m., a pond of at least 2 m (7 ft) x 2 m (7 ft) by 50 cm (20 in) deep will accept one plant or at the very most two. Always instal root barriers to limit the spread of the roots. It is preferable to make a clear separation between *Nelumbo* and *Nymphea*, by creating compartments with sheets of fibreglass or plastic 30 cm (12 in) high, well anchored, or cement building blocks.

**Height :** leaves 40-80 cm (16-32 in) in diameter, rising up to 2 m (6 ft 6 in) above the water.

**Decorative period :** flowers from June till October.

**Care :** like water lilies, lotus respond to regular applications of fertilizer (a general fertilizer for flowering plants, or rotted manure) every two months during the growing period.

**Winter protection :** during the winter the rhizome, covered with silt, must remain below frost level. In regions with a cold, continental climate it is preferable to lift the rhizomes at the end of October and store them in damp sand, in a frost-free place.

**Propagation :** divide the rhizome in spring, keeping two buds per segment.

**Species and varieties :**
• *Nelumbo lutea* (American or yellow lotus), from North America, has a yellow flower and large, dark green leaves.

• *N. lutea* 'Flavescens', a smaller variety. Yellow flowers with red centres.
• *Nelumbo nucifera*, the sacred or oriental lotus, has a pale pink flower.
• *N. n.* 'Alba Grandiflora' has very large, fragrant, pure white flowers with yellow stamens.
• *N. n.* 'Alba Plena' is a dwarf variety with small double white flowers.
• *N. n.* 'Alba Striata' has white petals with a distinctive fine carmine border.
• *N. n.* 'Chawan Basu' is a small variety with pink-edged white petals.
• *N. n.* 'Gigantea' has very large purplish-pink flowers.
• *N. n.* 'Kermesina' has very large, double, bright pink flowers.
• *N. n.* 'Osiris' has carmine pink flowers.
• *N. n.* 'Pekinense Rubra', the smallest carmine-flowered lotus. There is a variety with large double flowers ('Pekinense Rubra Plena').
• *N. n.* 'Pygmaea Alba', a dwarf variety with small white flowers. Leaves 20 cm (8 in) in diameter. Exists in pink ('Pygmaea Rosea') and double white varieties ('Pygmaea Alba Plena').

| 93 |
| --- |

## *Nuphar lutea*

## YELLOW POND LILY

NYMPHEACEAE
**Origin :**
**Europe, Sibéria, Africa**

*Nuphar lutea*

The yellow pond lily is a vigorous hardy perennial with a thick rhizome which takes root at the bottom of nutrient-rich, calm or still water. Its long, oval leaves are heart-shaped at the base, and can reach 40 cm (16 in) in length. Between June and August, there appears a single, very fragrant, golden yellow flower, 5-7 cm (2-3 in) in diameter, rising up to 10 cm (4 in) above the water. It is composed of 5 large yellow sepals forming a globe-shaped corolla which protects the numerous tiny petals, of the same colour. After pollinization, the stalk contracts and draws the flower under the water, where the bladder-shaped fruit ripens and floats to the surface, made buoyant by the air contained in its tissues. Finally it disintegrates and drops to the bottom, where it will sprout the following spring. Tolerant of colder and deeper water than the other water lilies, the yellow pond lily does well in very large, even shaded ponds.

**Position :** any.

**Planting :** submerged in 40-300 cm (1 ft 4 in-10 ft) of calm water.

**Decorative period :** golden yellow flower, June to August.

**Propagation :** from seed kept under water in autumn. Divide rhizome in spring.

**Other species or varieties :**
• *Nuphar advena*, a native of Central America, has larger flowers, red-tinged on the inside.
• *Nuphar japonica* has yellow flowers marked with red and arrow-shaped leaves emerging from the water. Height : 30-50 cm (12-20 in). Heat tolerant.
• *Nuphar pumila* is a dwarf species suitable for shallow water 20-30 cm (8-12 in).

94

*Nymphaea* spp.

# HARDY NYMPHAEA
## Water nymph, Water lily

NYMPHAEACEAE
**Origin :**
**Cold and temperate zones, northern hemisphere**

*Nymphaea* 'René Gérard'

From the most remote times, water lilies were admired and venerated by the peoples of Asia. The ancient Egyptians, in the frescos in temples and tombs of the early dynasties, left us exact representations of the *Nymphaea lotus* (white-flowered) and *Nymphaea caerulea*, the very famous "blue Egyptian lotus", two tropical species which inhabited the marshes of the Nile valley 5000 years ago. In a stylized form, the flower of *Nymphaea lotus* became one of the characteristic decorative motifs of architectural art under the Pharaohs.

From India to China, another species of blue lotus, *Nymphaea stellata*, was the sacred flower of the Buddhists, together with its close cousin *Nelumbo nucifera*, the sacred pink lotus of Asia. In most parts of Europe, hardy species are found, such as *Nymphaea alba* and *Nymphaea candida*, whose white flowers are at the origin of numerous myths and popular beliefs. They symbolized beauty and eloquence for the ancient Greeks, who saw in them the representation of nymphs and water sprites. For the peoples of central Europe they kept away evil spirits.

Today these splendid aquatic perennials are cultivated as ornamentals, with a preference for the many coloured hybrids. For practical purposes, it is useful to make the distinction between lilies of tropical origin (*see the entry "Tropical water lilies", p.156*) and hardy water lilies, including all the species from cold and temperate regions of the world.

**Hardy *Nymphaea* :**
Although they are completely dormant during the winter, hardy water lilies are capable of standing up to the hardest weather, provided the rhizome remains below ice level. They enjoy a sunny situation in calm water, without currents or waves, from 15-300 cm (6 in-10 ft) deep, according to the varieties. The thick rhizome is firmly anchored to the bottom, and gives rise to long stems, each bearing a

**LOTUSES AND LILIES**

The term "water lily" has been used since ancient times to designate both nympheas and nuphars, which are in fact two distinct genera of the *Nymphaeaceae* family.

The term *lotus* (from the *Nelumbo lôtos* = lotus, or bird's-foot trefoil) formerly designated several floating plants, principally the genus of the *Nelumboaceae* family, *and* the nympheas and nuphars. However, although there is a certain resemblance, these species belong to different, quite distinct botanical families.

single leaf. The young, submerged leaves are rolled in a cone, which gradually opens and spreads out on the surface of the water in a thick, shining heart or oval shape. The flowers, which float on the surface, are up to 10 cm (4 in) or more in diameter, and come out progressively, between May and October. After fertilization, petals and sepals close up to form a tough, globular receptacle containing up to 1500 seeds. When ripe, the fruit comes free and drops to the bottom of the water, where it passes the winter. In spring, the sprouted seeds rise up to the surface, and are dispersed by the wind to new corners of the water body.

**Position :** sun.

**Planting period :** from early March to mid-October, in calm or still water.

**Planting depth :** a depth of between 40-60 cm (16-24 in) is suitable for all varieties. Shallower water heats up more rapidly and favours early and abundant flowering.

*Nymphaea* 'marliacea Albida'

*Nymphaea* 'marliacea Chromatella'

For small ponds, choose smaller varieties which are quite happy in 15-40 cm (6-16 in) of water. In large pools or natural ponds, plant vigorous growers which are happy in 2 m (7 ft) and more. It should be noted that in deep water the number of flowers will be fewer during the first years.

**Nature of soil :** water lilies like an ordinary garden soil, preferably heavy loam and rich in organic matter. Avoid adding manure or fertilizer, which would stimulate the growth of foliage, but not of flowers. However, if the available soil is extremely poor, put manure or fertilizer *under* the layer of soil, not mixed in with it, so that the roots can draw up the quantity of nourishment they need.

**Method of planting :** lay the rhizome horizontally onto the soil, at a 45° angle with its growing tip exposed. Cover all but grow-ing tip with up 5 cm (2 in) of soil, then sand or gravel

• In large, natural ponds water lilies can be cultivated on a layer of earth or mud 20-30 cm (8-12 in) deep. When the water level cannot be lowered for planting, the rhizome can be rolled in a piece of turf tied round with a  string and thrown in to the desired position. It can also be planted in a container filled with soil. Choose a receptacle of about 5 litre capacity made of some.material that will gradually break down in the water - hessian, wicker or fine netting lined with newspaper - allowing the rhizome to settle itself in gradually.
• In an artificial pond, water lilies can be cultivated in the same way, provided there is a sufficient depth of soil. If the bottom is covered with pebbles, plant in plastic mesh containers 40 cm (6 in sq) square and 30 cm (12 in) deep. This makes it easy to  instal the plants in the desired position and at the right depth and to lift them for winter protection. The baskets will restrict the growth of the very

vigorous species, which will produce smaller leaves and flowers than would be the case in a natural pond.

**Dimensions :** each plant covers a surface of about 1 sq.m (1 sq yd).

**Decorative period :** flowers from May till September, or later.

**Care :** regular removal of old leaves and flow-ers. Divide and resoil or repot rhizomes every 3-5 years in most garden pools.

**Propagation :** separate the shoots which appear on the rhizome, or take root cuttings, about 10 cm (4 in) long. Seed propagation will not reliably reproduce the parent plant.

**Species or varieties of hardy water lilies :** Before choosing a variety, make sure that it is suitable for the depth of the pool where it is to be planted (suggested depths are given for each variety).

**White-flowered water lilies :**
• *Nymphaea alba* (white water lily) is the hardy species most frequently found in northern Europe. Its vigorous habit makes it ideal for ponds more than 80 cm (30 in) deep.
• *N. alba* 'Plenissima', snowy white, very vig-orous. Depth : 20-50 cm (8-20 in).
• *N. candida* comes from central Europe and Siberia. Medium sized, very elegant. Depth : 15-40 cm (6-16 in)
• *N.* 'Caroliniana Nivea', very distinguished, fragrant variety. Depth : 30-80 cm (12-30 in).
• *N.* 'Gladstoneana', large white flower, very big leaves. Depth : 20-80 cm (8-30 in).
• *N.* 'Gonnère', enormous double flower. Magnificent. Depth : 20-100 cm (8-40 in).
• *N.* 'Hermine', tulip shaped white flower. Depth : 20-60 cm (8-24 in).
• *N.* 'Lactea', fragrant, very graceful flower. Depth : 15-40 cm (6-16 in).
• *N.* 'Marliacea Alba', pure white, very vigorous. Depth : 20-60 cm (8-24 in).
• *N.* 'Marliacea Albida', robust and prolific

bloomer. Suitable for natural ponds. Depth : 20-200 cm (8-80 in).
• *N. odorata* 'Pumila', white flower, bright yellow stamens, fragrant. Very prolific bloom-er, suitable for small pools. Depth : 15-40 cm (6-16 in).
• *N. tuberosa* 'Maxima', fragrant, spherical flowers, purest white. Depth : 20-60 cm (8-24 in).
• *N. tetragona*, quite small, white flowers. Depth : 5-80 cm (2-30 in).
• *N. tuberosa* 'Alba', pure white flowers. Depth : 30-50 cm (12-20 in).
• *N. tuberosa* 'Richardsonii', very beautiful flowers, very double. Depth : 40-100 cm (16-40 in).
• *N.* 'Potslingberg', vigorous. Depth : 30-80 cm (12-30 in).

**Pink water lilies :**
• *N.* 'Amabilis', big, pale pink flowers with flesh-coloured sepals. Depth : 20-100 cm (8-40 in).
• *N.* 'American Star', pretty, star-shaped flower, petals pink at the base. Erect. Depth : 20-60 cm (8-24 in).
• *N.* 'Baroness Orczy', enormous, very beautiful flowers, very deep pink. Depth : 20-60 cm (8-24 in).
• *N.* 'Brackele Rosea', deep pink, held above the water. Depth : 30-60 cm (12-24 in).
• *N.* 'Candissima Rosea', abundant, soft pink flowers. Depth : 20-60 cm (8-24 in).
• *N.* 'Caroliniana', flesh pink, almost salmon. Depth : 20-60 cm (8-24 in).
• *N.* 'Caroliniana Rosea', beautiful pink variety. Depth : 20-60 cm (8-24 in).
• *N.* 'William Doogue', very pretty flesh pink flower. Depth : 20-60 cm (8-24 in).
• *N.* 'Fabiola', very handsome variety, large, deep pink flowers. Depth : 20-100 cm (8-40 in).
• *N.* 'James Hudson', large flowers, very pretty shade of pink. Depth : 20-60 cm (8-24 in).
• *N.* 'Laydekeri Rosea', handsome purplish-pink flower. Depth : 20-50 cm (8-20 in).

*Nymphaea* 'marliacea Rosea'

- *N.* 'Leviathan', large flowers, deep pink. Depth : 20-100 cm.
- *N.* 'Lusitania', pretty, very soft pink flower. Depth : 20-60 cm (8-24 in).
- *N.* 'Marliacea Carnea', enormous pinkish-white flowers, very attractive. Vigorous, well-suited to large ponds. Depth : 20-200 cm (8-80 in).
- *N.* 'Marliacea Rosea', large, pale pink flowers with darker sepals. Depth : 20-100 cm (8-40 in).
- *N.* 'Masaniello', large flower, pink, specked with carmine, very beautiful. Depth : 20-100 cm (8-40 in).
- *N.* 'Meteor', attractive deep pink flower. Depth : 20-40 cm (8-16 in).
- *N.* 'Mrs Richmond', large, pale violet-pink flower. Superb. Depth : 20-100 cm (8-40 in)
- *N.* 'Madame Wilfon Gonnère', large, intense pink, double flower. Depth : 50-80 cm (20-30 in).
- *N.* 'Neptune', quite large flowers with long petals, pale pink outside, slightly shaded inside, striped with crimson. Depth : 20-60 cm (8-24 in).
- *N.* 'Odalisque', delightful pink flower, turning white, rising above the water. Depth : 20-100 cm (8-40 in).
- *N.* Odorata 'Turicensis', very deep pink, fragrant flower. Depth : 40-80 cm (16-30 in).
- *N.* 'René Gérard', starry, pure pink flower. very abundant. Depth : 20-50 cm (8-20 in).
- *N.* 'Rose Arey', deep rose pink flowers, rising above the water. Depth : 20-40 cm (8-16 in).
- *N.* 'Rosea', beautiful flower, clear pink, fragrant. Depth : 20-100 cm (8-40 in).
- *N.* 'Rosennymphe', deep pink, very vigorous. Depth : 20-40 cm (8-16 in).
- *N.* 'Somptuosa', large, double, pale pink flowers. Depth : 15-40 cm (6-16 in).
- *N.* 'Suivassima', attractive double flower, light pink. Depth : 20-60 cm (8-24 in).
- *N.* 'W. B. Shaw', very beautiful pastel pink flower. Fragrant. Generous bloomer. Depth : 20-60 cm (8-24 in).

## Yellow or orange-tinted water lilies :

- *N.* 'Aurora', flower orange to red, changing

*Nymphaea* 'Candida'

colour in first days. Depth : 15-40 cm (6-16 in).
- *N.* 'Chrysanha', yellow flower turning orange, then vermilion. Depth : 20-60 cm (8-24 in).
- *N.* 'Colonel A.J. Welch', beautiful bright yellow flower riding above the water. Depth : 20-80 cm (8-30 in).
- *N.* 'Comanche', ochre, tawny yellow and orange. Vigorous. Depth : 20-40 cm (8-16 in).
- *N. Mexicana*, native to Florida, has handsome leaves with brown markings. Depth : 20-60 cm (8-24 in).
- *N.* 'Fulva', flowers are red, mixed with yellow. Rare variety. Depth : 20-60 cm (8-24 in).
- *N.* 'Graziella', coppery orange flower and handsome leaves with brown marbling. Very generous bloomer. Not too large, suitable for smaller pools. Depth : 15-30 cm (6-12 in).
- *N.* 'Indiana', yellowish orange first, turning coppery red. Unusual and decorative. Depth : 20-30 cm (8-12 in).
- *N.* 'Marliacea Chromatella', numerous, canary yellow flowers. Very robust. Good for natural pools. Depth : 40-200 cm (16-80 in).
- *N.* 'Mooeri', straw yellow. Floriferous, very attractive. Depth : 20-60 cm (8-24 in).
- *N.* 'Odorata Sulphurea', large, fragrant, sulphur yellow flowers. Depth : 20-40 cm (8-16 in).
- *N.* 'Paul Hariot', magnificent tawny yellow flowers. Depth : 15-40 cm (6-16 in).
- *N.* 'Phœbus', yellow, copper-veined flower. Depth : 20-40 cm (8-16 in).
- *N.* 'Pygmaea Helveola', small, canary yellow flowers very numerous. Not too vigorous, good for small pools. Depth : 10-15 cm (4-6 in).
- *N.* 'Sioux', large, coppery yellow flowers. Depth : 30-60 cm (12-24 in).
- *N.* 'Solfatare', abundant flowers, yellow to pinkish copper. Depth : 15-40 cm (4-16 in).
- *N.* 'Odorata Sulphurea Grandiflora', very fine, flowers high above the water, like an exotic. Depth : 20-60 cm (8-24 in).

*Nymphaea* 'Escarboucle'

## Red or purple water lilies :

- *N.* 'Andreana', quite erect flower, red tinged with ochre. Depth : 20-60 cm (8-24 in).
- *N.* 'Atropurpurea', splendid variety, deep red, 18" across. Depth : 20-60 cm (8-24 in).
- *N.* 'Attraction', very big, garnet red flowers with dark mahogany stamens. Very vigorous. Depth : 20-100 cm (8-80 in).
- *N.* 'Charles de Meurville', vermilion red flower, orange stamens. Depth : 40-100 cm (16-80 in).
- *N.* 'Conqueror', very big flowers, bright red with dark red veins. Depth : 20-50 cm (8-20 in).
- *N.* 'Ellisiana', attractive vermilion flowers, orange stamens. Depth : 15-40 cm (6-16 in).
- *N.* 'Escarboucle', amaranth, one of the most beautiful. Depth : 20-60 cm (8-24 in).
- *N.* 'Frœbelii', very abundant, small flowers light claret. Not invasive. For small pools. Depth : 15-40 cm (6-16 in).
- *N.* 'Gloriosa', splendid flower, colour of red currants. Depth : 20-60 cm (8-24 in).
- *N.* 'James Brydon' splendid double, peony-shaped pinkish crimson. Very vigorous; for large areas. Depth : 20-60 cm (8-24 in).
- *N.* 'Laydekeri Fulgens', amaranth flower. For small pools. Depth : 15-40 cm (6-16 in).
- *N.* 'Laydekeri Lilacea', lilac pink petals and red stamens. Depth : 15-40 cm (6-16 in).
- *N.* 'Laydekeri Purpurata', delightful bright crimson. Depth : 15-40 cm (6-16 in).
- *N.* 'Lucida', vermilion. Depth : 20-60 cm (8-24 in).
- *N.* 'Madame Maurice Laydeker', cherry red, peony-shaped. Depth : 20-60 cm (8-24 in).
- *N.* 'Marliacea Flammea', handsome claret flower. Depth : 20-60 cm (8-24 in).
- *N.* 'Marliacea Rubra Punctata', large variety, reddish-mauve. Depth : 40-80 cm (16-30 in).
- *N.* 'Maurice Laydeker', the smallest red flower, very floriferous. Depth : 15-40 cm.
- *N.* 'Newton', dark red. Depth : 20-40 cm.
- *N.* 'Picciola', flower purplish red, white-veined. Depth : 20-50cm (8-20 in).

N. alba

N. 'Albatross'

N. Caroliniana Nivea'

N. 'Gladstoneana'

N. 'Gonnère'

N. 'Hermine'

N. odorata

N. tetragona

N. 'Potslingberg'

N. 'Amabilis'

N. 'American Star'

N. 'Caroliniana'

N. 'Helen Fowler'

N. 'Marliacea Carnea'

N. 'Masaniello'

N. 'Newton'

N. 'Meteor'

N. 'René Gérard'

N. 'Rose Arey'

N. 'Madame Wilfon Gonnère'

N. 'Comanche'

N. 'Graziella'

N. 'Indiana'

N. 'Odalisque'

N. 'Odorata Sulphurea'

N. 'Paul Hariot'

N. 'Solfatare'

N. 'Odorata Sulfurea Grandiflora'

N. 'Atropurpurea'

N. 'Attraction'

N. 'Charles de Meurville'

N. 'Conqueror'

N. 'Escarboucle'

N. 'Froebeli'

N. 'Gloriosa'

N. 'James Brydon'

N. 'Laydekeri Fulgens'

N. 'Laydekeri Lilacea'

N. 'Lucida'

N. 'William Falconer'

## 95
### *Nymphaea* spp.

## TROPICAL WATER LILIES

NYMPHAEACEAE
Origin :
**Warm tropical zones, world-wide**

*Nymphaea* x *daubenyana*

*Victoria*

"Tropical water lilies" are the species found in tropical and sub-tropical regions. They are not hardy in our climate and must be protected from frost in winter. They are remarkable for their brilliant colours and the elegance of the flowers rising above the water. Some species flower at night, but they need a favorable environment (tropical climate, heated greenhouse or heated outdoor pool). The exotic varieties have gnarled tubers, very different from the rhizomes of the hardy lilies, on which grow easily detachable bulbils or eyes, which are readily propagated.

**Position :** sunny.

**Planting period :** June to October or later, water temperature at least 18 °C (64 °F).

**Planting depth :** plant the tuber up to the neck in 20-30 cm (8-12 in) of heavy soil or silt containing plenty of nutrients, not too deep 10-30 cm (4-12 in) in shallow water which will warm easily.

**Water temperature :** the ideal temperature is between 18-35 °C (64-95 °F), but it must on no account go below 5 °C (41 °F) in winter.

**Hothouse cultivation :** a pool in a well-lit situation, in a veranda or a heated greenhouse (or even a cool greenhouse, provided it is frost-free) can be used for year-round cultivation of tropical water lilies, provided correct air and water temperatures can be maintained.

**Outside cultivation :** possible during summer, in a sunny position and shallow water which will heat up easily. Heating the pond (by means of solar panels or heat exchanger) is sometimes the only way of ensuring that ideal temperatures are maintained.

**Winter protection :** at the end of autumn (as late as possible, but before the first frosts) the tubers formed during the summer, or the containers holding them, should be lifted from the water and stored in a frost-free place. The tubers can be stored in a tub of clean water or in a container filled with slightly damp sand. If a greenhouse pool is available, containers may be stored there in which tubers can be planted. If the greenhouse is heated, flowering will be prolonged by several months. Put the tubers back in place after the last spring frosts.

**Care :** groom spent foliage and flowers.

**Decorative interest :** succession of flowers, late July to late October.

**Propagation :** separate the eyes that develop on the tuber. In some varieties, at the base of the leaves, bulbils develop, and these can be detached as soon as they have thrown out roots. Ripe seed can be germinated in an aquarium, on a layer of sand under 10 cm (4 in) of water maintained at a temperature of 25-30 °C (77-86 °F).

*Euryale ferox*

N. 'Edward Whitaker'

N. 'After Glow'

N. 'Director George T. Moore'

N. 'Mrs Ward'

Nymphaea 'Panama Pacific'

**Day-flowering blue water lilies :**

• *N. odorata* var. *gigantea*, an immense blue-mauve flower, remarkable, from Australia.

• *N. caerulea*, or blue Egyptian lotus, large, fragrant pale blue flowers, very vigorous.

• *N.* 'Colonel Lindbergh', delightful pale blue flower.

• *N.* x *daubenyana*, pale blue, not very vigorous, very floriferous.

• *Euryale ferox*, originating in China and Vietnam, has large leaves with a spiny purple underside, up to 1 m (40 in) in diameter. Large violet flower, 5 cm (2 in) wide.

• *N.* 'Green Smoke', strange and very beautiful, fragrant, generous bloomer.

• *N.* 'King of the Blues', dark blue, fragrant.

• *N.* 'Mr Edward Whitaker', blue, fragrant, vigorous.

• *N.* 'Pamela', fragrant, pale blue.

• *N.* 'Panama Pacific', violet flower with purple sepals.

• *N.* 'Blue Beauty', very floriferous, dark blue with blue stamens.

• *N. zanzibariensis*, from South-East Africa. Sky blue, very floriferous.

**Day-flowering, red water lilies :**

• *N.* 'Afterglow', a mélange of yellow, rose and peach, vigorous.

• *N.* 'American Beauty', dark red, perfumed.

• *N.* 'Director George T. Moore', large dark red flowers.

• *N.* 'Enchantement', medium pink, large, abundant flowering.

• *N.* 'Julian Decelle', superb pink flower and very handsome serrated leaves with red marbling.

• *N.* 'Mrs C.W. Ward', very elegant, half-hardy. Pale pinkish mauve. Can stand some frost.

• *N.* 'Persian Lilac', fragrant, dark pink.

• *N.* 'Pink Pearl', large, fragrant, pure pink flowers.

*N. victoria cruziana*, from South America, has purple flowers and pale green leaves, smaller than those of *Victoria regia*, and with a lower rim. Plant at a depth of 15-40 cm (6-16 in).

**Day-flowering yellow water lilies :**

• *N.* 'Albert Greensberg', coppery yellow.

• *N.* 'Isabelle Pring', large, perfumed, yellow flowers.

• *N.* 'St Louis', small yellow flowers.

**Day-flowering, white water lilies :**

• *N.* 'Mrs George Pring', large, pure white flowers, extremely vigorous.

• *N.* 'Ted Ulber', little white flowers

• *Victoria amazonica*, syn. *Victoria regia*, has curious leaves in the shape of a tart tray, with numerous spikes on the underside. A leaf brought back from the Amazon by Bridges in 1849 measured more than 1.8 m (6 ft) in diameter. The first night flower is white and subsequent nights blooms are progressively pinker. A flower comes out every two or three days, but lasts only three days. It needs to be cultivated in a tropical climate, or else in a heated greenhouse, in a sunny pool at least 6 m wide (20 ft). Plant in a tub measuring at least 1 m (3 ft) x 1 m (3 ft) filled with rich soil and placed under 20-40 cm (8-16 in) of non-calcareous water.

**Night-flowering water lilies :**

• *N.* 'Trudy Scolum', large pure white flowers.

• *N.* 'Maroon Beauty', large deep red flowers.

• *N.* 'Mrs George C. Hitchcock', deep pink.

• *N.* 'Red Flare', starry red flower.

N. 'Persian Lilac'

N. 'Pink Pearl'

N. 'Isabelle Pring'

N. 'Red Flare'

## 96
### *Nymphoides peltata*
Syn. *Villarsia nymphoides*

## FRINGED WATER LILY

MENYANTHACEAE
**Origin :**
**Europe, China, Japan**

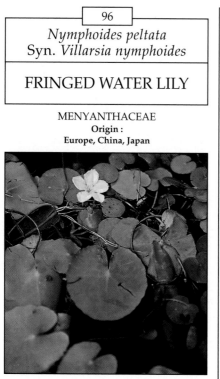

*Nymphoides peltata*

The heart-shaped leaves of the fringed water lily float on the surface of the water. They are brilliant light green in spring, becoming progressively darker, and are often marked with purple on the underside. Measuring only 3-10 cm (1-4 in) in diameter, they are smaller than those of true water lilies (though it is true that dwarf varieties of the latter do exist). The golden yellow flower, 4 cm (2 in) in diameter, has five fringed petals, and rises about 10 cm (4 in) above the water. The buds form under water then break above the surface, between June and July. The fruits have the form of capsules which ripen in the water then float free to the surface. Once released, the seeds, which have small thorns, float on the water and catch in the feathers of aquatic birds, which carry them from one area of water to another. The seeds germinate in water, or on the ground, but in the latter case flowers are rarely produced. The fringed water lily grows in still, shallow water in Europe and Asia, preferring warm, nutrient-rich situations. It is a hardy perennial with a long creeping rhizome which takes root in the mud and forms large colonies. It grows and spreads vigorously, and quickly forms a dense carpet when planted in a new pool, where it helps to keep the water pure and free of algae. It also prevents the water from heating up too quickly in summer, and provides shade and shelter for fish. It is preferable to cultivate the plant in containers, to prevent it from taking over all the available space.

**Position :** sun or semi-shade.

**Planting :** in containers, under 10-80 cm (4-30 in) of water. 5 plants per sq.m.

**Height :** from 5-10 cm (2-4 in) above the water, length of stems 80-150 cm (3-5 ft).

**Decorative period :** yellow flowers, July-October.

**Propagation :** from seed, and root cuttings in April-May.

**Other species or varieties :**
• *Nymphoides indica* is a violet-leaved species with a fine, star-shaped, tender flower.
• *Nymphoides peltata* 'Bennettii' is a cultivar with larger flowers.

## 97
### *Orontium aquaticum*

## ORONTIUM
Golden club

ARACEAE
**Origin :**
**Southern U.S.A.**

*Orontium aquaticum*

This slow-growing perennial is perfectly hardy and fully deserves a place in any water garden. Its large, spear-shaped leaves are a handsome blue-green and form a clump which emerges from shallow water or floats in deeper water 20-30 cm (8-12 in). Flowering occurs in March, when a great number of long white floating stalks appear, with erect, bright yellow spadices, like lighted candles. To obtain the best effect with this spectacular plant, isolate it in a position where it will be clearly visible, to the side of a large pond or in the centre of a small pool.

**Position :** sun or semi-shade.

**Planting :** 5 plants per sq.m.
Depth : 0-40 cm (0-16 in).

**Height :** 45 cm (18 in) above the water.

**Decorative period :** flowers, March to June.

**Care :** to protect it from competition from more vigorous species which might crowd it out, keep a clear area all round the plant.

**Propagation :** from seed, or root cuttings containing a node.

## 98
### *Parnassia palustris*

## GRASS OF PARNASSUS

PARNASSACEAE
**Origin :**
**Europe**

*Parnassia palustris*

This elegant little hardy perennial is the only European member of the *Parnassaceae*. It is found in wet, peaty, lowland meadows and also in mountainous regions, between dripping, moss-covered rocks. It has rosettes of numerous heart-shaped leaves at the base of a long stalk, which has a single, stalkless leaf halfway up, and carries a solitary, 5-petalled, veined white flower.

It is an attractive plant for an informal garden, in a bog area or between rocks.

**Position :** sun or semi-shade.

**Planting :** any soil, damp to very wet.

**Height :** 30-40 cm (12-16 in).

**Decorative period :** in June-September, white flower 2-3 cm (1 in) in diameter.

**Propagation :** from seed.

## 99
### *Pennisetum villosum*

## FEATHER TOP

GRASSES
**Origin :**
**Tropical and sub-tropical**

This is a splendid hardy ornamental grass whose tuft of fine blue-green foliage is crowned in autumn with handsome white flower spikes reminiscent of a bottle-brush. Use it in groups, either on its own or with other grasses. Requires protection in cold winters. Dries well.

• *Pennisetum alopecuroides,* syn. *Pennisetum compressum,* can be up to 1 m (3 ft) tall.

*Pennisetum villosum*

Reddish-brown inflorescence.

**Position :** sunny, sheltered.

**Planting :** moist or dry soil.

**Height :** 2-2.5 m (7-8 ft).

**Decorative period :** flower spikes, August to October.

**Care :** tie leaves and stems together, then wrap the whole thing in hessian or straw matting, not forgetting protection for the crown. Cut back the stalks in spring.

**Propagation :** divide clumps in spring.

---

| 100 |
| --- |
| *Petasites hybridus* Syn. *Petasites officinalis* |
| PETASITES |

ASTERACEAE
**Origin :**
Europe, Japan

*Petasites hybridus*

This hardy perennial, ornamental grass produces pinkish-violet, fragrant flower heads in late winter (February-March). It has large dentate leaves with a scalloped base, arranged in a very decorative whorl (*Petasites* means "parasol"). The leaves appear after the flowers, and can be as much as 60 cm (2 ft) in diameter.

**Position :** semi-shade.

**Planting :** moist soil.

**Height :** 1.2 m (4 ft).

**Decorative period :** flowers February-May.

**Propagation :** from seed, and root division.

**Other species or varieties :**

• *Petasites fragrans*, also called winter heliotrope, is a dwarf species with delighful, fragrant, pink flowers. Height : 30 cm (1 ft).

• *P. japonicus* is a low-growing species 25 cm (10 in) with large round leaves spread-ing out as much as 2 m (7 ft). Its yel-low flowers appear early in the season and are very attractive to bees.

• *P. japonicus* var.'giganteus' is a cultivar which can grow to a height of 1.6 m (5 ft). A strange, green, solitary flower appears between January and April.

• *P. japonicus* var. *giganteus* 'Variegatus' has very decorative yellow-striped foliage.

---

| 101 |
| --- |
| *Phalaris arundinacea* |
| CANARY GRASS Ribbon grass, Lady's garters |

GRAMINEAE
**Origin :**
Europe, southern Canada, central Asia.

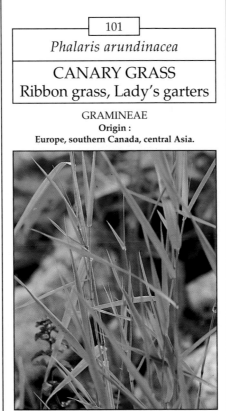

*Phalaris arundinacea*

This is a decorative grass commonly found in shallow areas at the edge of ponds. Its pointed, ribbon-like leaves, 1-2 cm (1 in) wide, are evergreen, and form spectacular clumps up to 2 m (7 ft) tall. The violet inflo-rescences which appear between July and November are appreciated by aquatic birds for their seeds.

• For the garden, choose *Phalaris arundinacea* var. *Picta* or 'Aureovariegata', a superb culti-var whose pale green foliage is striped with pinkish white, then pale yellow. A perfect hardy perennial with a creeping rhizome, it is best controlled by planting in a container. It is also useful for dry flower arrangements.

**Position :** sunny.

**Planting :** in groups (10-20 plants per sq.m)

---

*Phalaris arundinacea* var. *Picta*

in damp soil or submerged to 35 cm (14 in). Will also do quite well in dry ground.

**Height :** 80-150 cm (3-5 ft) .

**Decorative interest :** flowers June-July, foliage May-November.

**Propagation :** from seed, and division of crowns.

---

| 102 |
| --- |
| *Phragmites australis* Syn. *Arundo phragmites*, *Phragmites communis* |
| COMMON REED |

GRAMINEAE
**Origin :**
Subcosmopolitan, except Amazon

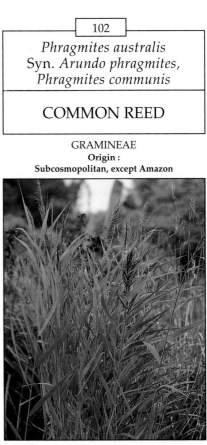

*Phragmites australis*

The common reed forms the greater part of pondside reedbeds. It is a vigorous, hardy perennial which can reach 2-4 m (7-13 ft) in height. Its flexible, evergreen round stalks and deciduous blue-green leaves form an

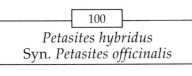

erect clump, with panicles of violet-brown flowers in August-November. The roots spread rapidly, and make the common reed a useful plant for stabilising pond margins.

• *Phragmites karka*, from Japan, has evergreen foliage. Height : 3.5-4.5 m (11-15 ft)

• *P. karka* 'Variegatus' (variegated reed) is a decorative cultivar with fine yellow stripes. A slow grower, well-suited to small gardens.

• *P. stolonifera* is a smaller species 60-120 cm (2-4 ft) with attractive purplish stems.All these reeds dry well and are excellent for flower arrangements.

**Position :** any.

**Planting :** any type of soil, even salty; dry to flooded, down to 50 cm (20 in) under water). Install a root barrier 60 cm (24 in) deep, or cultivate the plant in a container to keep the creeping rhizome under control. It may grow to a length of 10 m (33 ft) in a few years!

**Propagation :** from seed, or root cuttings with at least one eye.

---

## 103
### *Physostegia virginiana*
## OBEDIENT PLANT

**LABIATAE**
**Origin :**
**North America**

*Physostegia virginiana*

This hardy perennial border plant produces numerous pink flowers in summer, in long vertical spikes. It owes its name to the fact that the stems stay in the position in which one puts them.

• In addition to the pink and white varieties *speciosa* 'Bouquet Rose' and 'Alba' respectively, there is also a very decorative mauve-flowered variety with pinkish white variegations on the foliage, *Physostegia virginiana* 'Variegata'.

**Position :** sun and semi-shade.

**Planting :** in moist or damp soil.

**Height :** 60-80 cm (24-30 in).

**Decorative period :** flowers July-September.

---

**Propagation :** divide the clumps.

**Use :** excellent nectar plant, good flowers for cutting.

## 104
### *Pilea cadierei*
## PILEA
## Aluminium Plant

**URTICACEAE**
**Origin :**
**Tropical zones**

These perennials from tropical rain forest are cultivated in the hothouse for their foliage which is evergreen, slightly crimped, with creamish-white variegations. Place them at the side of the pool, out of direct sunlight, in damp to very wet soil.

## 105
### *Pistia stratiotes*
## WATER LETTUCE

**ARACEAE**
**Origin :**
**Tropical and subtropical regions**

*Pistia stratiotes*

This is a splendid floating perennial plant of tropical origin. Its rosettes of thick pale green leaves have a very characteristic velvety appearance. The water lettuce likes calm, shallow water which warms up quickly. It increases rapidly by throwing out lateral shoots, but is easily controlled by regular division. Its roots serve as a depository for fish spawn and provide shelter for the fry.

**Position :** hot and sunny.

**Planting :** allow to float freely in water 10-40 cm (4-16 in) deep.

**Height :** 5-10 cm (2-4 in) above the water.

---

**Position :** light, without direct sun.

**Planting :** in damp or very wet soil, with a good proportion of leaf mould.

**Height :** 20-40 cm (8-16 in).

**Care :** min. winter temperature 12 °C (53 °F).

**Propagation :** from cuttings, in spring.

*Pilea cadierei*

**Decorative period :** velvety green foliage, June till October.

**Care :** the water lettuce is frost tender. Bring some plants inside at the end of September, and winter over in an aquarium or in a tub of moist peat, in a light place and at a temperature of 16-18 °C (60-64 °F). Take out again in May.

**Propagation :** spontaneous, as soon as the temperature rises above 20 °C (68 °F). Separate the lateral shoots which have produced roots.The seeds, which form in autumn, can be conserved in water and set to germinate in spring, in water at a temperature of 30 °C (86 °F).

<table>
<tr><td>106</td></tr>
</table>

## *Polygonum and Persicaria* spp.

## KNOTWEED

POLYGONACEAE
**Origin :**
**Northern hemisphere**

*Persicaria amphibia* (aquatic habit)

These particularly vigorous hardy
perennials have sprawling evergreen foliage
which provides excellent ground cover
for shady areas. Numerous spikes of
pink or white flowers appear from June
till October.

**Position :** any.

**Planting :** prefers a rich, moist soil, but
tolerates poor, occasionally dry soil.

**Decorative period :** pink or white flowers,
June till October.

**Care :** cut flower stems back to ground level
towards the end of October.

**Propagation :** very easy, from cuttings.

*Persicaria amphibia* (terrestrial habit)

*Persicaria affinis* 'Superba'

**Species or varieties :**

• *P. affinis* 'Darjeeling Red' has darker red
flowers. Height : 30 cm (12 in).

• *P. affinis* 'Donald Lowndes', has very dense
spikes of salmon pink flowers.
Height : 30 cm (12 in).

• *P. affinis* 'Superba' forms a carpet of leaves
which are brown in winter, turning green in
spring. Numerous spikes of pink, then red
flowers, till the frosts. Height : 30 cm (12 in).

• *P. amphibia* is a native species suitable for
any situation, damp to moist, or submerged
to 50 cm (20 in). In the latter case the leaves
float and the pink or red floral spikes rise
above the water, from July till September.

• *P. amplexicaulis* has large deep green leaves
forming a clump from 1-1.5 m (3-5 ft) high.
Erect spikes of pale pink flowers. Moist soil.

• *P. amplexicaulis* 'Atrosanguinea' has brick
red flowers. Height : 40-60 cm (16-24 in).

• *P. bistorta* 'Superba' has compact, bright
pink flower spikes, much more decorative
than the species. Height : 60 cm (24 in).

• *P. tenuicaulis*, a white-flowered species
from Japan, prefers shade and is rather
tender. Height : 30-40 cm (12-16 ft).

• *P. vacciniifolia* is also a very good cover
plant. Drooping, pale pink flowers.
Height : 30 cm (12 in).

• *Polygonum cuspidatum* is a species
with rigid stalks up to 3 m (10 ft) tall.
Heart-shaped deciduous leaves turning
an attractive golden colour in autumn.

<table>
<tr><td>107</td></tr>
</table>

## *Pontederia cordata*

## PONTEDERIA

PONTEDERIACEAE
**Origin :**
**Central and Equatorial America**

*Pontederia cordata*

This is a perennial with very decorative
spear-shaped leaves and tight spikes of blue
to purple flowers rising above the water in
summer. Plant in small, isolated groups at
the end of the pool.

• *Pontederia cordata* 'Alba' is a handsome
white-flowered cultivar.

• *P. C.* var *lancifiola* is a taller species up to
1 m (40 in), whose leaves are also longer.

**Exposition :** sun or semi-shade.

**Planting :** 6 plants per sq.m. Rich soil,
submerged 15-40 cm (6-16 in).

**Height :** 40-65 cm (16-26 in).

**Decorative period :** blue flowers, June
till August.

**Care :** protect crown against frost.

**Propagation :** divide roots in April-May.

*Pontederia cordata* var. *lancifiola*

## 108

### *Potamogeton* spp.

### PONDWEED

POTAMOGETONACEAE
Origin :
Europe, Africa, Asia, Australia

*Potamogeton natans*

Pondweeds are hardy perennial plants with submerged or floating leaves. Their creeping rhizomes colonize the waters of ponds and slow-moving streams and serve as oxygenators.
They have unremarkable spikes of flowers which sink into the water after fertilization. All the pondweeds provide food and shelter for water snails and fish.

**Position :** sunny.

**Dimensions :** stems are from 0.5-5 m (20 in-16 ft) long, according to species.

**Propagation :** from cuttings.

**Species or varieties :**

• *Potamogeton crispus* (curly pondweed) is easily identified by its long, wavy, pale green submerged leaves, which sometimes have a reddish tint in a sunny position. It is found in nitrogen-rich, still or sluggish, even deep water in tropical and temperate zones. It is not particularly invasive, and is propagated by lateral offshoots (hibernacles). A small white inflorescence appears between June and August. Plant 1-5 per sq.m, in 20-300 cm (8 in-10 ft)of water.

• *P. densus* has oval opposed leaves, in pairs.

• *P. fluitans* has submerged or floating leaves longer in shape than those of *Potamogeton natans*.

• *P. lucens* (shining pondweed) has submerged leaves, oval or spear-shaped, up to 25 cm (10 in) long, pale green and translucent with visible veining.

• *Potamogeton natans* is the most common. Its submerged leaves are linear at first, then as they start to float they take the form of a long ellipse 12 cm (5 in). They vary in colour from green to brown. This pondweed likes still water, even if lacking in nutrients. It tolerates any climate. The greenish-yellow inflorescence appears between June and September. Plant at a depth of between 40-100 cm (16-40 in).

• *P. pectinatus* has linear leaves and branching stems.

• *P. perfoliatus* is a submerged perennial from temperate and hot zones. Its leaves are heart-shaped at the base, 6 cm (2 in) long. It likes deep, nutrient-rich running or still water.

*Potamogeton crispus*

P. crispus    P. densus    P. fluitans    P. lucens    P. natans    P. pectinatus    P. perfoliatus

## 109

### *Potentilla palustris*
### Syn. *Comarum palustre*
### *Potentilla comarum*

### MARSH POTENTILLA

ROSACEAE
Origin :
Europe, Asia

*Potentilla palustris*

This is an attractive perennial, once very common in marshes and beside ponds, but now becoming very rare. Its handsome pale green leaves with toothed leaflets arranged in a star shape turn a beautiful crimson, from August. Reddish-brown flowers appear in June. Height : 30-70 cm (12-28 in).

• *Potentilla anserina* (silverweed) is a creeping species whose leaves can have up to 25 dentate leaflets. They are richly-coloured, ranging from blue-green to silver-grey, through all the range of yellows and reds. The five-petalled yellow flower, 2-3 cm (1 in) in diameter, appears between May and September. It is also a medicinal plant, with anti-inflammatory properties.
Height : 15-50 cm (6-20 in), stems may be up to 1 m (40 in) long.

**Position :** sunny.
**Planting :** in rich soil, damp or submerged down to 15 cm (6 in).
**Decorative period :** June to November (foliage).
**Propagation :** from fragments of stem containing a node, or by division of the clump.

*Potentilla anserina*

110

## *Primula* spp.

## PRIMULAS

PRIMULACEAE
Origin :
Eurasia

*Primula denticulata*

Primulas, which originated in China, Tibet and the Himalayas, are hardy perennial plants which appreciate a rich, damp soil. Plant them in a sunny or semi-shaded position, in autumn or early spring. Apply a fertilizing mulch every two years, to smother weeds and prevent drying out. Propagation is carried out by dividing the clumps after flowering.

**Species or varieties :**

• *Primula beesiana* is a mauve-flowered species, May-June. It self-seeds.
Height : 50-70 cm (20-28 in).

• *P. bulleyana* is another candelabra species, with orange flowers.

• *P. denticulata* produces (April-May) large, spherical inflorescences, purple, red, white or mauve. Height : 30 cm (12 in).

• *P. florindae* (giant cowslip) is 60-90 cm (24-35 in) tall. Its bright yellow umbels of flowers appear at the beginning of summer. It likes semi-shade, and acid, very damp soil, with its root in the water.

• *P. prolifera*, 1 m (40 in) tall, has deep yellow flowers.

• *P. japonica* (Japanese primula) forms spectacular groups. Its tall stems carry whorls of flowers which come out in stages, from April to June. Exists in shades of pink to blue, deep pink (*P. j.* 'Rosea'), white (*P. j.* 'Fuji'), bright crimson (*P. j.* 'Miller's Crimson'). Sun or partial shade.
Height : 40 cm (16 in) leaves,
1 m (40 in) flowers.

• *P. rosea* is of Tibetan origin. Its umbels of reddish-pink flowers with a yellow eye appear early (March-April). Height : 15-20 cm (6-8 in).

• *P. vialii* has surprising, conical spikes of violet and purple flowers, from April to June. Height : 40-60 cm (16-24 in).

*Primula japonica*

*Primula* Inshriach hybrid

111

## *Ranunculus* spp.

## BUTTERCUP

RANUNCULACEAE
Origin :
Europe, Central Asia

*Ranunculus aquatilis*

Water buttercups form a vast family of native perennial plants providing decorative interest from May till September. They are perfectly hardy and can be used to good effect in informal gardens, but it is sometimes necessary to curb their growth, since they may crowd out less vigorous plants.

**Position :** sun or semi-shade.

**Planting :** in damp soil, or submerged to 80 cm (30 in)).

**Decorative period :** bright yellow flowers, May to September.

**Propagation :** in spring, from seed or division of crowns.

**Species or varieties :**

• *Ranunculus aquatilis* (water buttercup) has little white flowers, 1-2 cm (half an inch ) in diameter, with a yellow centre. They appear above the water between April and July. The submerged leaves are divided into sheaves of fine, flexible strands; the floating leaves are a rounded kidney-shape, with 3-5 slightly dentate lobes. If the water is sufficiently deep, more than 60 m (200 ft) for submerged leaves to develop, it makes a good oxygenating plant. It will grow in still or running water, and is appreciated by all the pond fauna. 1-5 plants per sq.m. 5-100 cm (2-40 in) deep.

• *R. flammula* (lesser spearwort) is an emerging plant, 20-30 cm (8-12 in) tall. Its shining yellow flower looks like that of the buttercup, and it grows vigorously all winter. Well suited to small pools. Plant in very wet ground or submerged to 20 cm (8 in).

*Ranunculus flammula*

• *R. fluitans* has small white flowers, 1-2 cm (half an inch) in diameter. It floats only in swift-running water and is identifiable by its drooping "bundles" of leaves, rather like locks of hair. For streams and cascades, where it provides shelter for aquatic animals. Depth : down to 1 m (40 in).

*Ranunculus lingua*

• *R. lingua* prefers calm water, where it will grow to a length of 1.3 m (4 ft 6 in). It owes its name to its long, tongue-shaped leaves. Its large, bright yellow flowers are 4-5 cm (1-2 in) in diameter, and appear between May and late September. Plant in a large pool or in a pond, under 10-80 cm (4-30 in) of water, 6-10 per sq.m.

---

112

### *Rheum palmatum*

# ORNAMENTAL RHUBARB

---

POLYGONACEAE
**Origin :**
**China, Mongolia**

This hardy perennial is always decorative beside a pool. It grows rapidly and its deeply-lobed leaves can reach 90 cm (35 in) in diameter. In summer it produces a

purplish stalk of flowers which can be as much as 3 m (10 ft) tall.

**Position :** sun or semi-shade.

**Planting :** from February-March, in moist, rich soil.

**Dimensions :** 1.8 m (6 ft) tall and 2 m (7 ft) wide.

**Decorative period :** flowers in June.

**Propagation :** divide crown in spring.

**Cultivars :**

• *Rheum palmatum* 'Atrosanguineum' is a cultivar whose young, finely-cut foliage is very red in spring. Inflorescence is a handsome violet-red.

• *R p.* 'Bowles' Crimson' has the same type of foliage, and a creamy white inflorescence.

*Rheum palmatum*

• *R. p. tanguticum* has large palmate leaves and a red inflorescence up to 2.5 m (8 ft) tall.

---

113

### *Rhododendron* spp.

# RHODODENDRON AND AZALEA

---

ERICACEAE
**Origin :**
**China, Japan**

*Rhododendron* sp.

Rhododendrons and azaleas are superb garden plants imported from China and Japan in the 19th century. A large number of horticultural varieties have been created by cross-breeding the botanical species, of which there are more than 1000. All prefer moist, acid soil and semi-shade. They are precious in small gardens, many being moderate in size, with handsome, often evergreen foliage and brilliant flowers. They are hardy.

**Position :** full to half shade, out of direct sun. (Some exceptions.)

**Planting :** after flowering, in rich, moist to damp soil. If your garden soil is alkaline, dig a hole about 60 cm (24 in) deep and line it with rot-proof, permeable horticultural fibre; fill the hole with a mixture of 1 third peat, 1 third leaf-mould and 1 third acid soil.

**Height :** 0.3-3 m (1-10 ft) according to variety.

**Decorative period :** April to July, according to variety.

**Propagation :** by layering, or cuttings, from August.

**Care :** apply a good mulch (pine bark or other) to retain moisture, protect from cold and keep weeds down.
Yellowing leaves may indicate chlorosis, a condition in which the plant is unable to assimilate iron. This may be due, for instance, to watering with limy water. Lightly cultivate into soil, being careful not to injure surface roots, sequestrene iron or granulated sulphur. Water with rain water.

*Rhododendron* sp.

## 114

### *Rodgersia* spp.

## RODGERSIA

SAXIFRAGACEAE
Origin :
China, Japan

*Rodgersia aesculifolia*

These superb ornamental perennials, originating in the Far East, have remarkable panicles of flowers and large composite leaves up to 50 cm (20 in) wide. They can be burned by strong sun, and prefer shade or semi-shade with good shelter. They grow rather slowly, but resist cold and produce fine groups of flowers.

**Position :** shade or semi-shade. Avoid prolonged exposure to sun.

**Planting :** in rich, moist or damp soil, from March-April.

**Dimensions :** up to 1.5 m (5 ft) tall and 80 cm (30 in) wide.

**Decorative period :** flowers in June-July.

**Propagation :** from seed, or division of crown in spring.

*Rodgersia podophylla*

*Rodgersia pinnata*

**Species or varieties :**

• *R. aesculifolia* has olive green crinkled leaves, deeply dentated, like the horse chestnuts. Its pyramidal creamy-white inflorescences appear in June. Height : 1-1.5 m (3-5 ft).

• *R. pinnata* is rather similar to *R. aesculifolia*, but smaller, up to 1 m (3 ft) high.

• *R. p.* 'Superba', has handsome bronze foliage and a purplish-pink flower in May. Height: 1.2 m (4 ft).

• *R. podophylla* has large palmate leaves of an attractive satiny bronze colour, which become progressively greener in summer. Pyramidal panicles of white flowers. Height : 1.5 m (5 ft).

• *R. podophylla* 'Rotlaub' is a cultivar with superb purplish bronze foliage. Height : 1.5 m (5 ft).

• *R. sambucifolia* has deeply-cut foliage ; narrow lobes. White flowers. Height : 1.2 m (4 ft).

• *R. tabularis*, see *Astilboïdes tabularis* page 115.

## 115

### *Sagina subulata*

## SAGINA

CARYOPHYLLACEAE
Origin :
Europe

*Sagina subulata*

This is an excellent evergreen ground cover plant whose use will save many hours of weeding. It forms an extensive, mossy green carpet, and can be used to good effect among rocks, in the Japanese manner. It is a hardy perennial, not very demanding, and will stand being walked on.

**Position :** shade and half-shade, or sunny, as long as the soil is kept moist.

**Planting :** in moist or damp soil.

**Hight :** 2-5 cm (1-2 in).

**Decorative period :** minute white flowers, May to July.

**Care :** if it is exposed to the sun, water twice a week during the hottest part of summer. Even when they are yellowed from a prolonged dry period, the tufts of *Sagina* become green again in autumn

**Propagation :** all the year, by dividing the crown.

## 116

### *Sagittaria sagittifolia*

## ARROWHEAD

ALISMATACEAE
Origin :
Europe, Asia, America

*Sagittaria sagittifolia*

This handsome, emerged perennial with a short, branching rhizome does well in calm and shallow water. During growth, the leaves are at first ribbon-like and totally submerged. Next there appear long-stemmed, oval, floating leaves, followed by elegant arrow-shaped leaves rising above the water. The stalks are triangular, and have groups of three large flowers with three white petals. The male flowers, slighly violet in the centre, are at the top of the inflorescence, above the female flowers. The arrowhead is hardy and likes a rich soil. Propagation is carried out by means of bulb-like stolons which separate at the end of autumn and form hibernacles. These are rich in starch and protein and can be consumed raw or cooked. They are a favourite source of food for aquatic birds and herbivorous fish.

**Position :** sun or semi-shade.

**Planting :** plant in a large container filled with good garden soil with 1/3 well-rotted manure, under 5-30 cm (2-12 in) of water. 10 plants per sq.m. Do not submerge too deeply, otherwise flowering will not be abundant.

**Height :** 30-80 cm (12-30 in).

**Decorative period :** white flowers, June to August.

**Propagation :** from seed and stolons.

### Other species or varieties :

• *Sagittaria sagittifolia* 'Flore Pleno' is a double-flowered horticultural variety.

• *Sagittaria latifolia* (*S. hastata*) is a North

American species, 40-60 cm (16-24 in) tall. Its leaves are less clearly arrow-shaped. It needs winter shelter.

• *Sagittaria montevidensis* is a South American species reaching a height of 1.3 m (4 ft). Cultivate in a heated greenhouse, where the red-marked white flowers will bloom without interruption from May to December, or use outdoors in summer only.

• *Sagittaria subulata* is another American species. Planted under 30-80 cm (12-30 in) of water, it forms a decorative oxygenating "carpet".

---

### 117
## *Salix* spp.
## WILLOW

SALICACEAE
**Origin :**
Temperate and cold zones, northern hemisphere

*Salix caprea* 'Pendula Kilmarnock'

The willow family includes numerous species or varieties. Most are bushes or shrubby trees, with fine, silvery foliage and attractive coloured catkins in spring. Whether erect or weeping, prostrate or twisted, willows are fast growers with a preference for damp soils. The best known is probably the majestic *Salix babylonica* (or weeping willow), celebrated by ancient and romantic poets, and often found at the waterside in parks and large gardens.

**Position :** sunny or semi-shade.

**Planting :** plant in moist or damp soil, even subject to occasional flooding.

**Propagation :** from cuttings, in spring.

### Prostrate species and varieties :

• *Salix integra* 'Albo-marginata' is a bush 1.5 m (5 ft) tall, with creamy-white variegated foliage.

• *S. i.* 'Hakura Nishiki', of Japanese origin, is an attractive cultivar with fine pale green foliage marked with white and pink in spring. Height : 1 m (3 ft).

• *S. irrorata* comes from the U.S.A. Its branches are green in spring, turning purple in summer, with astonishing white flowers in spring. Height : 80 cm (30 in).

• *S. lanata* (woolly willow) is a handsome shrub with downy white branches. Slow grower. Attractive bluish foliage. Height : 80 cm (30 in).

• *S. gracilistyla* 'Melanostachys' (black willow) has spear-shaped leaves and splendid black and yellow catkins. Height : 80 cm (30 in).

• *S. purpurea* 'Nana', or purple osier, is a dwarf shrub from Asia. Its red branches have fine grey foliage forming a spherical shape. Height : 80 cm (30 in).

• *S. p.* 'Nancy Saunders' is a rounded shrub with purple stems and silvery foliage. Height : 80 cm (30 in).

• *S. reticulata* (net-veined willow) is a low, sprawling species with large rounded leaves. Height : 80 cm (30 in).

• *S. serpillifolia* is a prostrate alpine species with twisted branches and fine, shining leaves. Height : 30 cm (12 in).

### Small species and varieties :

• *Salix alba vitellina* 'Britzensis' is a robust cultivar which must be cut back severely

every year to keep the bright red stems. Height : 2 m (7 ft).

• *S. alba vitellina* has superb scarlet branches.

• *S. a. sericea* has superb silvery foliage and is only 3 m (10 ft) tall.

• *S. caprea pendula* is a miniature weeping-willow about 2 m (7 ft) tall, perfectly happy in small gardens.

• *S. elaeagnos angustifolia* (syn. *S. rosmarinifolia*), the hoary willow, has dense, very fine foliage. No more than 2 m (7 ft) tall.

• *S. exigua* has long, downy leaves with a silvery-blue gleam. No more than 2 m (7 ft) tall.

• *S. gracilistyla*, with a rounded silhouette, is of Japanese origin. Its fine, silvery grey foliage grows on red stems. Height : 2 m (7 ft).

• *S. magnifica*, from China, is not more than 3 m (10 ft) tall. In spring, it has superb red-veined leaves and giant catkins.

• *S. udensis* 'Sekka', is rounded in shape with flattened twisted stems. It grows rapidly, but can be kept at a height of 3 m (10 ft) by annual pruning.

### Large species and varieties :

• *Salix alba* (white or silver willow) is the giant of the family, reaching a height of 25 m (80 ft). Its yellow or reddish shoots have magnificent grey-blue foliage.

• *S. a.* 'Aurea' is a cultivar with yellow-green branches and golden foliage. Height : 20 m (65 ft).

• *S. babylonica* (weeping willow), of Chinese origin, has become very common. 18 m (60 ft) high, it needs a lot of space.

• *S. sepulcralis chrysocoma* (golden weeping willow), a cross between *Salix alba* and *Salix babylonica*, rapidly grows to 15-20 m (50-65 ft).

• *S. matsudana* 'Tortuosa', the dragon's claw willow, is a slender tree with golden bark, from China and Korea. It grows rapidly, to a height of 6-8 m (20-26 ft). Needs hard pruning.

*Salix matsudana* 'Tortuosa'

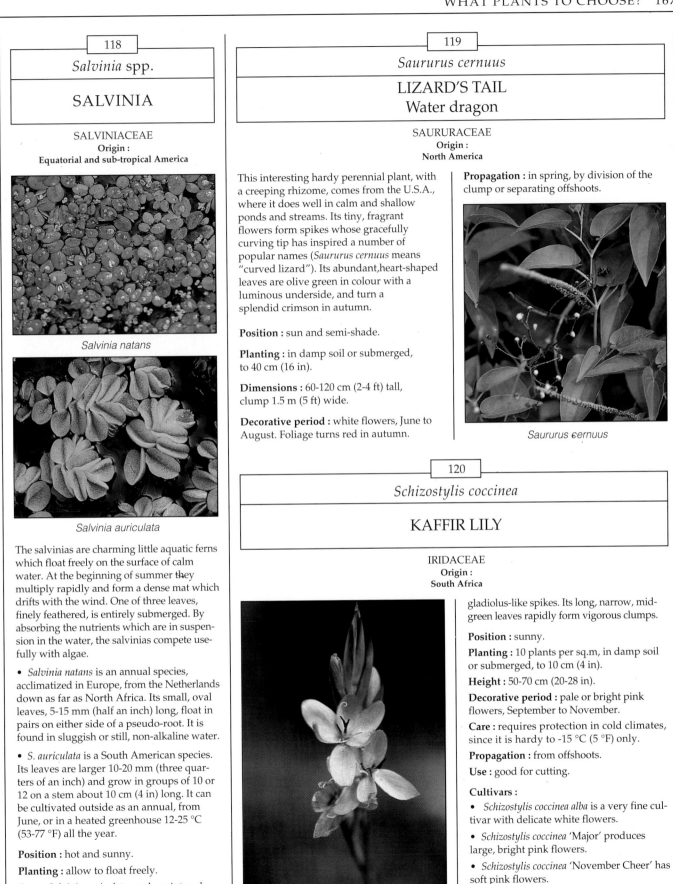

## 118
### *Salvinia* spp.
### SALVINIA

SALVINIACEAE
Origin :
Equatorial and sub-tropical America

*Salvinia natans*

*Salvinia auriculata*

The salvinias are charming little aquatic ferns which float freely on the surface of calm water. At the beginning of summer they multiply rapidly and form a dense mat which drifts with the wind. One of three leaves, finely feathered, is entirely submerged. By absorbing the nutrients which are in suspension in the water, the salvinias compete usefully with algae.

• *Salvinia natans* is an annual species, acclimatized in Europe, from the Netherlands down as far as North Africa. Its small, oval leaves, 5-15 mm (half an inch) long, float in pairs on either side of a pseudo-root. It is found in sluggish or still, non-alkaline water.

• *S. auriculata* is a South American species. Its leaves are larger 10-20 mm (three quarters of an inch) and grow in groups of 10 or 12 on a stem about 10 cm (4 in) long. It can be cultivated outside as an annual, from June, or in a heated greenhouse 12-25 °C (53-77 °F) all the year.

**Position :** hot and sunny.

**Planting :** allow to float freely.

**Care :** *Salvinia auriculata* can be wintered over in a tub of water in a light, frost-free position.

**Propagation :** separate young plants in summer.

## 119
### *Saururus cernuus*
### LIZARD'S TAIL
### Water dragon

SAURURACEAE
Origin :
North America

This interesting hardy perennial plant, with a creeping rhizome, comes from the U.S.A., where it does well in calm and shallow ponds and streams. Its tiny, fragrant flowers form spikes whose gracefully curving tip has inspired a number of popular names (*Saururus cernuus* means "curved lizard"). Its abundant, heart-shaped leaves are olive green in colour with a luminous underside, and turn a splendid crimson in autumn.

**Position :** sun and semi-shade.

**Planting :** in damp soil or submerged, to 40 cm (16 in).

**Dimensions :** 60-120 cm (2-4 ft) tall, clump 1.5 m (5 ft) wide.

**Decorative period :** white flowers, June to August. Foliage turns red in autumn.

**Propagation :** in spring, by division of the clump or separating offshoots.

*Saururus cernuus*

## 120
### *Schizostylis coccinea*
### KAFFIR LILY

IRIDACEAE
Origin :
South Africa

*Schizostylis coccinea*

This elegant perennial, on a rhizomatous rootstock, flowers late in the season, with magnificent pink star-shaped flowers in gladiolus-like spikes. Its long, narrow, mid-green leaves rapidly form vigorous clumps.

**Position :** sunny.

**Planting :** 10 plants per sq.m, in damp soil or submerged, to 10 cm (4 in).

**Height :** 50-70 cm (20-28 in).

**Decorative period :** pale or bright pink flowers, September to November.

**Care :** requires protection in cold climates, since it is hardy to -15 °C (5 °F) only.

**Propagation :** from offshoots.

**Use :** good for cutting.

**Cultivars :**

• *Schizostylis coccinea alba* is a very fine cultivar with delicate white flowers.

• *Schizostylis coccinea* 'Major' produces large, bright pink flowers.

• *Schizostylis coccinea* 'November Cheer' has soft pink flowers.

• *Schizostylis coccinea* 'Sunrise' has salmon pink flowers.

• *Schizostylis coccinea* 'Vicountess Byng' has flowers with narrow, pale pink petals.

121

*Scirpus* spp.

# CLUB RUSH

CYPERACEAE
**Origin :**
**Europe, Asia, Australia, North and Central America**

*Schoenoplectus lacustris*

These are hardy perennial plants often forming colonies beside ponds. Their long, fine, round stems, usually without aerial leaves, arch gracefully over the water. The very decorative reddish-brown inflorescences appear between June and September. Club rushes are robust and undemanding plants with a fairly slow rate of growth but it is best to cultivate them in containers to limit the spread of their creeping root systems. Once very common in wet zones, these plants are now under threat, as their natural habitat disappears.

*S. l. tabernaemontani* 'Albescens'

*S. l. tabernaemontani* 'Zebrinus'

**Position :** sun or semi-shade.
**Planting :** any soil, submerged to a depth of 5-300 cm (2 in-10 ft).
**Propagation :** divide the clumps in spring.

**Species or varieties :**

• *Scirpoides holoschœnus* (round-headed club rush) has rounded, leafless stalks, which bear, from June-September, lateral inflorescences formed of several globe-shaped heads. It is 0.6-1.3 m (2-4 ft) tall; well-suited to small pools. Plant at depth of 5-20 cm (2-8 in).

• *Schoenoplectus lacustris* (syn. *Scirpus lacustris*), is the true bulrush. It is also known as the cooper's rush or plaiting rush, since its fine submerged leaves were formerly used for seaming barrel staves, and for rush-bottomed chairs. It has a creeping rootstock and dark green, smooth, cylindrical stalks forming a clump 2-3 m (7-10 ft) tall and 1 m (3 ft) wide. It is best suited to large areas of water more than 30 sq. m (36 sq yd) where it serves as shelter for aquatic birds. Plant at a depth of 0.5-2 m (2-7 ft).

• *Schoenoplectus lacustris tabernaemontani* (glaucous bulrush) is a sub-species whose glaucous stems are only 1-1.5 m (3-5 ft) tall, forming a clump 60 cm (2 ft) wide.

• *S. l. t.* 'Albescens' is a decorative cultivar; stalks have vertical stripes of light green and cream. Height : 1.5-1.7 m (5-6 ft).

*Scirpus lacustris tabernaemontani*

*Scirpoides holoschœnus*

• *S. l. t.* 'Zebrinus' (zebra rush) whose stalks have yellow and white transverse stripes, is effective in tight clumps. Height : 1.5-1.8 m (5-6 ft). Plant at a depth of 5-40 cm (2-16 in).

• *Scirpus mucronatus* is an annual, with leafless stems 40-80 cm (16-30 in) tall.

• *Eleocharis palustris*, syn. *Scirpus palustris*, has slender stems with a solitary tapering spikelet. Wet soil, or submerged to 10 cm (4 in). Height : 80 cm (30 in).

• *Scirpus sylvaticus* (woodrush) is a shade plant 1-1.2 m (3-4 ft) tall. It has light green leaves 1 cm (half an inch) wide. Between May and July a large greenish inflorescence appears, taking the form of a compound panicle 30 cm (12 in) in diameter.

*Scirpus mucronatus*

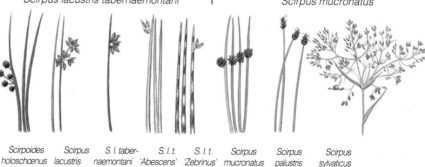

Scirpoides holoschœnus / Scirpus lacustris / S. l. tabernaemontani / S. l. t. 'Abescens' / S. l. t. 'Zebrinus' / Scirpus mucronatus / Scirpus palustris / Scirpus sylvaticus

## 122

### Senecio paludosus aquaticus

### SENECIO

ASTERACEAE COMPOSITAE
**Origin :**
**Europe**

*Senecio paludosus aquaticus*

The *Senecio* genus contains a number of species, mostly perennial and not very hardy, and of varied appearance. *Senecio aquaticus* is a biennial, 40-80 cm (16-30 in) tall, found near springs and in marshes and peatbogs. Its yellow flowers form large corymbs at the end of a long, erect stalk.

• *Senecio fuchsii*, with long, spear-shaped leaves, can be up to 1.5 m (5 ft) tall.

• *Sinacalia tanguticus* is a species with compound leaves, which can grow to 2 m (7 ft) in height, and become invasive.

**Position :** light, but sheltered from direct sun.

**Planting :** prefers lime-free soil, damp to very wet.

**Decorative period :** yellow flowers, June-September.

**Propagation :** cuttings in summer.

*Sinacalia tanguticus*

## 123

### Sidalcea malviflora

### SIDALCEA

MALVACEAE
**Origin :**
**Europe**

*Sidalcea malvaiflora*

This is an attractive hardy perennial for damp or wet ground, with small, rounded leaves with a toothed edge, and sprays of pink flowers at the end of erect stems. It does well in shade.

• *Sidalcea candida* is a related species with white flowers.

**Position :** any.

**Planting :** damp or very wet ground.

**Height :** 60-80 cm (24-30 in).

**Decorative period :** pink flowers, July till October.

## 124

### Sisyrinchium brachypus
### Sisyrinchium micranthum

### SISYRINCHIUM

IRIDACEAE
**Origin :**
**North America**

*Sisyrinchium brachypus*

• *Sisyrinchium brachypus* (golden-eyed grass) forms an evergreen tuft similar to that of a miniature iris, with characteristic buds. It is a hardy perennial of an unusual shape, rising up to 30 cm (12 in) above the water, with numerous small yellow star-shaped flowers from July till September.

• *Sisyrinchium micranthum* (syn. *S. iridifolium* ) is a taller species 60-70 cm (24-28 in) with evergreen foliage. It is a native of Central America, and is frost tender.

**Position :** hot and sunny.

**Planting :** damp soil or slightly submerged no more than to 5 cm (2 in).

**Decorative period :** canary yellow flowers, July-September.

## 125

### Sorghum halepense

### SORGHUM

GRAMINEAE
**Origin :**
**Tropical Africa and Asia**

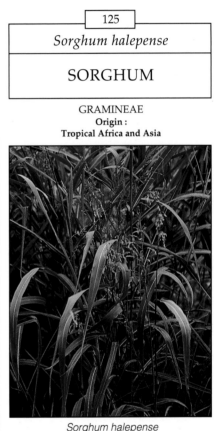

*Sorghum halepense*

This is a very handsome perennial with a creeping rootstock, and long, broad, blue-green leaves with a cream midrib, forming a majestic, arching clump. A violet-brown inflorescence appears between August and September. It is easily cultivated in a mild climate, and adds an exotic touch to an informal scene. The grain is used for food in many hot regions.

**Position :** sunny.

**Planting :** in dry sandy soil.

**Height :** 2 m (7 ft).

**Decorative period :** violet-brown inflorescence, August-September.

**Care :** hardy in a mild climate. Use the dry stalks to protect the crown over winter.

**Propagation :** from seed, or by division of the crown.

## 126
### *Sparganium erectum*
### Syn. *Sparganium ramosum*
## SPARGANIUM
## Bur reed

TYPHACEAE
**Origin :**
**Europe, North Africa, Asia, Japan**

*Sparganium erectum*

This is a hardy native perennial with floating or aerial foliage. It resists cold, and likes calm and still nutrient-rich water. The branching stalk has erect, ribbon-like leaves with a triangular base. The small, round, club-shaped male flowers are found at the top of the shoots, and the female flowers, noticeably larger, grow lower down. They produce a spherical, prickly green fruit. The *Sparganium* provides food and shelter for a variety of aquatic animals. Use it with reed-mace and bulrushes, in informal gardens.

**Position :** sun or semi-shade.

**Planting :** in rich soil, very wet or sub-merged to 40 cm (16 in). Plant in a container to keep it under control.

**Height :** 0.3-1.5 m (2-5 ft).

**Decorative period :** yellowish flowers, June-September, followed, at the end of summer, by prickly round fruit.

**Propagation :** from seed or stolons.

**Other species or varieties :**

• *Sparganium emersum* (syn. *Sparganium simplex*) has inflorescences forming a single spike.

• *Sparganium minimum*, or bur reed, is a smaller species found beside cool, swift mountain streams.

## 127
### *Spartina pectinata*
### Syn. *Spartina michauxiana*
## SPARTINA

GRAMINEAE
**Origin :**
**Western central United States**

*Spartina pectinata*

This very attractive ornamental grass with gracefully-arching ribboned leaves, deserves to be better known. It is a creeping, rhizomatous hardy perennial from the wet zones of the American Middle West.

• *Spartina pectinata* 'Aureomarginata' has soft green foliage with a fine, yellow edge, which gives the plant a splendid luminous quality.

**Position :** sunny.

**Planting :** damp or very wet soil.

**Dimensions :** clump grows 1.5-2 m (5-7 ft) tall, with a spread of 1 m (3 ft).

**Decorative period :** foliage June-November, brown inflorescence in September.

**Propagation :** from seed, and division of the rootstock.

**Use :** in large "wild" compositions. Can be used to stabilize pond margins or coastal sand dunes.

## 128
### *Spathiphyllum wallisii*
## SPATHIPHYLLUM

ARACEAE
**Origin :**
**South and Central America**

This is a plant for the heated greenhouse, a native of Colombia, with dark green, shining, spear-shaped leaves. The flowers are composed of a white spathe enclosing a yellow spadix. The *Spathiphyllum* requires year-round constant high humidity. Place it at the edge of the pool, on the margin or half-submerged, out of direct sunlight.

*Spathiphyllum wallisii*

**Position :** shaded.

**Planting :** in a mixture of 1/3 humus-rich soil and 2/3 peat and sand.

**Height :** 30-40 cm (12-16 in).

**Care :** keep the rootball damp in summer. Requires temperatures of 18-25 °C (64-77 °F) in summer; winter minimum of 16 °C (60 °F).

**Propagation :** from seed, and division in spring.

## 129
### *Stachys palustris*
## MARSH BETONY

LABIATAE
**Origin :**
**Europe**

*Stachys palustris*

This hardy perennial is to be found near ponds and marshes all over Europe. It produces runners from which spring relatively unbranching stalks about 1 m (3 ft) tall, carrying long, saw-toothed, opposite leaves. The pinkish-purple flowers grow in spikes at the top of the stalk. It is a medicinal plant with antiseptic and healing properties.

**Position :** shade or semi-shade.

**Planting :** in damp or very wet soil.

**Height :** 30-100 cm (1-3 ft).

**Decorative period :** purplish-pink flowers, June till September.

**Propagation :** from seed and runners.

## 130

### *Stipa gigantea*

## STIPA

GRAMINEAE
**Origin :**
Tropical and dry temperate zones

*Stipa gigantea*

*Stipa gigantea* (golden oats) is a superb hardy perennial ornamental grass, excellent in a "wild" environment. It forms a clump of very narrow, long, pointed, straw-yellow leaves, 1.8 m (6 ft) tall.
• *Stipa splendens* is a medium-sized species 70 cm (27 in) with brown spikes.
**Position :** sunny.
**Planting :** in dry, sandy, even calcareous soil.
**Decorative period :** all year round.
**Propagation :** by division of the clump.

## 131

### *Stratiotes aloides*

## WATER SOLDIER

HYDROCHARITACEAE
**Origin :**
Europe

The water soldier is a hardy native perennial which does well in still, shallow, nutrient-rich water. It has rosettes of long, thick, stalkless leaves with serrated edges. In spring, it frees itself from the bottom of the water and floats, half sub-merged, at the surface, where it rapidly forms dense colonies. It has large flowers with three green sepals and three white petals, which have stalks and are grouped on the male plants, and are stalk-less and isolated on the female plants. After fertilization, the plant takes root again till the following spring, forming a decorative, oxygenating carpet at the bottom of the pond throughout the winter. It is a very precious addition to a shallow pool, the more so since it is tending to disappear from its natural habitat.

*Stratiotes aloides*

**Position :** sunny.
**Planting :** allow it to float freely in relatively shallow water 30-100 cm (1-3 ft) where it will take root in autumn and spend the winter under water.
**Dimensions :** clump is 50 cm (20 in) in diameter and 30-40 cm (12-16 in) tall.
**Decorative period :** May-July, white flowers.
**Propagation :** separate runners in spring.

## 132

### *Symphytum officinale*

## COMFREY

BORAGINACEAE
**Origin :**
Europe, temperate Asia

*Symphytum officinale*

Comfrey is a vigorous, hardy native perennial, very common in wet zones near ponds and water-courses. From May till August it produces purple and cream tubular flowers in false umbels.

There are a number of cultivars with fine yellow-variegated foliage, such as S. 'Goldsmith' and S. x *uplandicum* 'Variegatum'.

• *S. asperum* has long-stemmed leaves and carmine flowers which take on a sky-blue tinge.
• *S.* 'Rubrum' has mat-forming, dark green foliage.

As its Latin name indicates, comfrey possesses medicinal properties which were already known in the Middle Ages and which are still recognized today.

**Position :** semi-shade.
**Planting :** 6 plants per sq.m. Wet ground, or submerged, to 20 cm (8 in).
**Height :** 20-120 cm (8 in-4 ft).
**Decorative period :** May-August, mauve or white flowers.

## 133

### *Taxodium distichum*

## BALD CYPRESS, SWAMP CYPRESS

TAXODIACEAE
**Origin :**
North and Central America, China

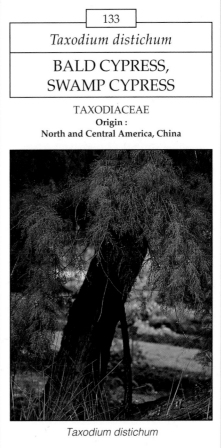

*Taxodium distichum*

*Taxodium distichum* is a tree of a quite regular, conical shape, with very fine, soft green leaves. It is called the bald cypress because it loses its leaves in winter after a period of brilliant autumn colour. It is native to both China and America, and is common in the southern part of the United States. It does well in wet ground beside rivers, and is remarkable for the strangely contorted roots, called "knees" or pneumatophores which rise above the water.

**Position :** sunny.
**Planting :** wet soil, or submerged.
**Height :** 12-20 m (40-65 ft).
**Decorative period :** May to November.
**Propagation :** from seed, or cuttings.
**Use :** beside large expanses of natural water.

## 134

### *Thalia dealbata*

## THALIA

MARANTACEAE
Origin :
**South-eastern United States**

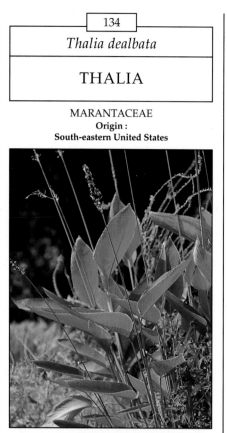

*Thalia dealbata*

This sub-tropical perennial has blue-green, solitary oval leaves borne horizontally on long, erect stems at the end of which is a spike of violet flowers. Its elegant architectural shape is a very useful addition to an exotic *décor*. It is a tender plant, so must be planted below frost level, or in a container which can be brought in under cover for the winter.

**Position :** hot and sunny.

**Planting :** in rich soil, under 20-60 cm (8-24 in) of water, according to local frost level. Cultivation in a container is essential in a continental climate, where winter shelter is required.

**Height :** 1-1.8 m (3-6 ft).

**Decorative period :** indigo flowers, June-September.

**Propagation :** separate suckers in spring.

## 135

### *Trapa natans*

## WATER CHESTNUT

TRAPACEAE
Origins :
**Europe, Asia, South Africa**

The water chestnut is an annual, floating plant, quite common throughout temperate Europe. It colonizes sunny, shallow,

calm or still water, forming a thick, coloured carpet throughout the summer. It has a long stem, one end of which is rooted in the water, whilst the other end carries rosettes of leaves which float on the surface, supported by their swollen stalks which serve as bladders.
The leaves appear in May, and are lozenge-shaped, with a toothed front edge. At this stage of development, the stem of the water chestnut decays, liberating the plant which then drifts. Between June and August, isolated white flowers spring from the leaf axils, rising above the water at the end of a long stalk. After pollinization, the flowers sink down and form a black, woody fruit with four hooked spikes. In autumn, the ripe fruit separates from the rosette and drops to the muddy bottom, where it attaches itself with its spikes.The water chestnut is a very ancient plant, as evidenced by the discovery of fossils dating from the Tertiary era. Ancient lake dwellers used it for food, raw, oiled or roasted, as it is indeed used still in parts of Europe and in the Far East.

*Trapa natans*

**Position :** sunny.

**Planting :** allow to float freely in calm, shallow water 20-80 cm (8-30 in) with a muddy bottom.

**Dimensions :** clump is 20-40 cm (8-16 in) in diameter. Stem up to 1.5 m (5 ft) long.

**Decorative period :** dark green, bronze-tinted foliage, May-October.

**Care :** remove some of runners to limit development. In cold climates, it is prudent to collect some ripe fruit in autumn and winter them over under cover. Keep them in water, cold but not freezing (an aquarium of cold water will do perfectly well). In spring, after the last frosts, put them back in the pool, and they will get off to a good start.

**Propagation :** separate side shoots in spring.

## 136

### *Trollius europaeus*

## GLOBEFLOWER

RANUNCULACEAE
Origin :
**Europe**

*Trollius europaeus*

The European globeflower is an attractive hardy perennial with divided foliage and erect stems bearing one to three bright yellow, globe-shaped flowers with numerous pistils and stamens. It is found in large colonies in damp hill or mountain meadows throughout Europe. It is a protected species in a number of countries, but several horticultural varieties are available, and these generally have larger flowers 4-5 cm (2 in) in diameter, in colours ranging from canary yellow (*Trollius* x *cultorum* 'Canary Bird', *Trollius* x *cultorum* 'Superbus') to golden yellow (*Trollius* x *cultorum* 'Goldquelle' with very divided leaves) or orange (*Trollius* x *cultorum* 'Etna' and *Trollius* x *cultorum* 'Orange Princess'). *Trollius chinensis* (*Trollius ledebourii*) comes originally from eastern Siberia. *Trollius yunnanensis* has flowers with more open corollas, yellowish-orange in colour. There are also two dwarf species, *Trollius patulus* and *Trollius pumilus* 10-15 cm (4-6 in) tall, which are useful for the edge of the pool.

**Position :** sun or semi-shade.

**Planting :** any soil, damp or very wet.

**Height :** 40-80 cm (16-30 in).

**Decorative period :** May-June.

**Propagation :** in spring or autumn, from seed or by division of clumps.

**Use :** beside a pool or watercourse, with other perennials, or isolated among rocks.

## 137

### *Typha* spp.

## CAT-TAIL, BULRUSH, MACE

TYPHACEAE
Origin :
Hot and temperate zones of the northern hemisphere, Australia, Polynesia, South America

*Typha latifolia*

These hardy perennial rhizomatous plants are common beside ponds. They are easily recognizable, with their long, ribbon-like leaves and velvety, dark brown, cigar-shaped spikes, called spadices, which are the female inflorescences, composed of numerous tiny, closely-packed flowers without corollas. The male flowers are situated above the females, and are composed of a great number of stamens in a loose tuft. Flowering, between June and August, is not simultaneous.

**Position :** hot and sunny.

**Planting :** from May to October, in rich soil. To restrain the invasive rhizome, all *Typha* are best cultivated in tubs.

**Propagation :** divide the rhizome in spring, keeping at least one bud per segment.

**Species or varieties :**
For large pools or ponds, choose the more vigorous species, planting 5 per sq.m at a depth of up to 80 cm (30 in).
• *Typha domingensis*, narrow leaves 3-4 m (10-13 ft) tall; spike up to 50 cm (20 in) long.

• *T. latifolia* (reed mace) has glaucous green leaves 2-3 m (7-10 ft) long. The female flower spike, about 15 cm (6 in) long, is dark brown and situated alongside the male spike.
• *T. latifolia* 'Variegata' has superb foliage with a pale yellow variegation.
• *T. shuttleworthii* is a species whose male spike is much shorter than the female. The following species, which are smaller, are better adapted to small pools.

*Typha stenophylla*

Plant 10 per sq.m, 5-40 cm (2-16 in) deep.
• *Typha angustifolia* (narrow-leaved mace) has light green leaves, 5-10 mm (half an inch) wide and 1.5-2 m (5-7 ft) in length. The female flowerhead, which is reddish brown, is 12-25 cm (5-10 in) in length, and is clearly separated from the male spike.
• *Typha laxmanii* has narrow, greenish-yellow leaves, 0.8-1.2 m (3-4 ft) long. The female flower head is globe-shaped and measures about 5 cm (2 in).
• *T. minima* has narrow leaves which are 2 mm (fourteenth of an inch) wide and 50-75 cm (20-30 in) long, and little spherical flower heads, 2-4 cm (1-2 in) long.

Typha domingensis | Typha latifolia | Typha l. Variegata | Typha shuttleworthii | Typha angustifolia | Typha laxmanii | Typha minima | Typha laxmanii

## 138

### *Utricularia vulgaris*

## UTRICULARIA
## Bladderwort

LENTIBULARIACEAE
Origin :
Northern hemisphere

*Utricularia vulgaris*

This is a hardy perennial, insectivorous aquatic plant which floats half-submerged in calm water and marshes. Its stems are reddish brown and carry leaves composed of several deeply laciniated leaflets. The plant has no roots, and survives in an environment poor in nutrients by "digesting" small invertebrates which it captures with its pear-shaped bladders. These are about 4 mm (a fifth of an inch) in diameter, and closed by a fine membrane opening towards the interior and surrounded by tactile filaments. When an animal touches these filaments, it is instantly drawn inside the bladder, while the membrane closes behind it. The prey is then slowly decomposed by enzymes, and the plant can absorb the nitrogen which it needs. Small golden-yellow flowers appear above the water between June and August. Reproduction takes place when fragments of stem and fruit (hibernacles) settle at the bottom of the water in autumn.

The *Utricularia* is a good oxygenating plant which absorbs the carbon dioxide in the water in order to keep afloat. It is found naturally throughout the temperate zones of Europe, but is becoming rarer because of the destruction of its natural habitat.

**Position :** sun or half-shade.

**Planting :** allow to float freely in calm water, preferably warm and not calcareous, and rich in microscopic animal life.

**Dimensions :** submerged stems 15-70 cm (6-27 in) long, emerged section 10-20 cm (4-8 in).

**Decorative period :** bright yellow flowers, June to August.

**Propagation :** in spring, by division of the clump or separation of suckers.

## 139

### *Veronica beccabunga*

### VERONICA BECCABUNGA
### Brooklime

SCROPHULARIACEAE
Origin :
**Europe, western Asia,
North Africa**

*Veronica beccabunga*

Brooklime is found beside shallow streams of swift, well-oxygenated water. It is recognized by its brilliant, oval, crenelled opposite leaves and small blue flowers growing in clusters from the leaf axils. It is a hardy perennial with a creep-ing rhizome, and grows rapidly. It does equally well in still water with a nutrient-rich soil, and can form large colonies when it does not have any competition.

Use it at the pond margin or beside a cascade, since its foliage is evergreen when totally or partially submerged.

**Position :** sun or half shade.

**Planting :** use 10 plants per sq.m in wet soil, or submerged down to 20 cm (8 in).

**Dimensions :** stems are prostrate, then erect, 20-60 cm (8-24 in) long.

**Decorative period :** blue flowers, May-September.

**Propagation :** from seed, or separation of suckers. The fruit is a rounded capsule enclosed in persistent sepals.

**Use :** ponds and watercourses.
The young shoots are edible, and the plant has antiscorbutic, sedative and expectorant properties.

**Other species :**
• *Veronica anagallis-aquatica* (water pimpernel) is more rare. It has a distinctive quadrangular stalk and pointed leaves.

## 140

### *Zantedeschia aethiopica*
### Syn. *Richardia africana,*
### *Calla aethiopica*

### ARUM LILY

ARACEAE
Origin :
**South Africa**

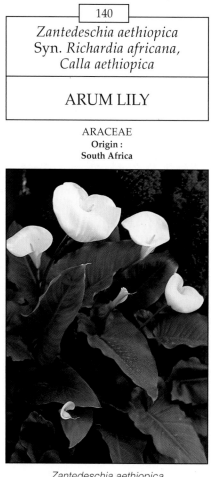

*Zantedeschia aethiopica*

The characteristic large, open horn-shaped flowers of the arum are composed of a fragrant yellow spadix surrounded by a decorative white spathe. It has remarkable dark green foliage and can be used to good effect either on its own or in groups.
Plant in deep, very moist soil, or in a large, slightly submerged container. It is easy to cultivate, and can be safely overwintered in all but the coldest regions by growing it submerged under 23 cm (9 in) of water.

**Position :** full sun or semi-shade.

**Planting :** in very damp soil, or submerged to 30 cm (12 in).

**Decorative period :** white flowers, spring and summer.

**Care :** in winter, protect the crown with peat or straw, because it is frost-tender. In more extreme climates, it is prudent to winter it in a cool place.

**Propagation :** in September, by division of rhizome or removal of suckers.

**Use :** attractive for cutting.

**Other species or varieties :**
• *Zantedeschia elliottiana* is a natural hybrid with heart-shaped, dark green leaves and bright yellow flowers.
• *Z. angustiloba* has spear-shaped leaves. Flowers are white at first, turning bright red.

## 141

### *Zizania latifolia*
### Syn. *Hydropyrum latifolium*

### ZIZANIA
### Wild rice

GRASSES
Origin :
**Asia**

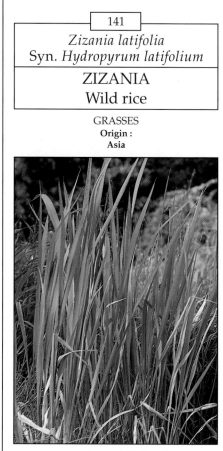

*Zizania latifolia*

This magnificent grass will add a wild, exotic touch to your garden. Its long, slender leaves with slightly arching tips form an elegant and graceful clump. The decorative effect is enhanced in autumn by the colour of the stalks.
The seeds are eaten by fish and by aquatic birds, which use its strong leaves for their nests.
• Slightly less decorative, *Zizania aquatica* is a North American species which reaches a height of 3 m (10 ft).

**Position :** sunny.

**Planting :** in rich soil, submerged to 5-80 cm (2-30 in). Plant below frost-level to ensure winter protection.

**Height :** 1.5-2 m (5-7 ft).

**Decorative period :** foliage, May-December.

**Care :** cut back the stalks in spring after the last frosts.

**Propagation :** from seed, or by division of the rhizome, in spring.

**Use :** large pools and ponds.

*Chapter*
**5**

# Aquatic Fauna

# CREATING AN IDEAL BIOTOPE

If you wish to make your watergarden a welcoming place for animals living in or near the water, the best solution is to take their requirements into account right from the planning stage. But there are also ways of improving those pools which have not been designed originally to accommodate aquatic fauna.

NFORMAL PONDS PROVIDE the most favourable environment for aquatic fauna. Their irregular shape, together with an abundant and varied vegetation, provide conditions close to those of the natural habitat, offering a wide range of hiding-places and ecosystems both in the water and on the banks. Ornamental pools with rigid geometrical shapes and straight sides, on the other hand, are not well-adapted to the life of wild animals. They are usually too shallow and too small, and are most often surrounded by unhospitable lawns or set in the middle of a patio or terrace which becomes overheated in summer. But with a little imagination and by following a few simple principles, it is possible to build a pool which is aesthetically satisfying and biologically viable and welcoming for wild animals.

## A spacious pool

A large area of water is almost always preferable to a small pool. Ideally, its area should be between 25-35 m² (270-370 ft²), but it should not be less than 15 m² (160 ft²). A large surface provides better conditions for gas exchanges between the water and the atmosphere, improving the oxygenation of the pool. It also allows for better light penetration, which is indispensable for the submerged plants whose cleansing and oxygenating action is vital for the biological balance of the pool.

▼ *The common frog* (Rana temporaria), *most active at night, is to be found in pools in spring and autumn.*

## A stepped profile

A pool which becomes progressively deeper, 20 cm (8 in) at a time by a series of steps, is always preferable to a pool with gently sloping or steep sides. The stepped profile is more suitable for cultivating aquatic plants, and makes pool maintenance easier. It also has a beneficial effect on the temperature of the water, which is of vital importance for the metabolism of cold-blooded animals (fish, amphibians) : the shallow zones warm up rapidly in the sun, whilst in the deeper zones, 60 cm (2 ft) and more, the temperature remains practically constant. This gradation of water temperature ensures that animals can always find a zone meeting their particular requirement.

## A deeper zone in the centre

The water should be 60-120 cm (2-4 ft) in at least one part of the pool (preferably well away from the edge, for reasons of safety). This increases the total volume of water (which ensures a better biological balance), and creates a constant temperature zone which will serve as a refuge for the fauna when atmospheric conditions change abruptly. Aquatic animals are extremely sensitive to sudden temperature variations. The considerable stress which results causes the animal to weaken; its growth may be retarded, it is less resistant to infection, and may die prematurely. Finally, this deep zone provides a place where animals can hibernate safely under water below freezing level.

## Shape of the pool

The shape of the pool is of little importance and you can give free rein to your imagination, limited only by considerations of style, and the physical conditions of the site. But the outline should be kept simple and natural, without exaggerated curves. This will simplify construction, and allow the water to circulate more freely. If the area of water is large, the shape can be more complex, with small bays or peninsulas and even islets. See that part of the bank slopes gently down so that small animals can enter the water and leave it in perfect safety. By doing this you will save from drowning a number of birds and small mammals (hedge-hogs, for example) which come to drink at night. This beach area should be on the sunniest side of the pool, and the immediate surroundings will be kept clear, to limit as far as possible the risk of attack by predators (beware of cats!).

### Varied and abundant flora

Aquatic plants are indispensable to the well-being of the wild-life, providing food, shelter and spawning grounds. Prefer the wilder species such as *Callitriche, Phalaris, Glyceria, Phragmites, Polygonum, Elodea, Myriophyllum* and *Ceratophyllum*. Submerged and emerg-ing plants can cover between one half and two thirds of the surface of the water, according to the length of exposure to sunlight, which must be at least 6 hours per day, in summer. Vegetation will cover about two thirds of the surface of the banks, providing the plant cover which is vital for most species of animal.

### Unexpected visitors...

It may happen that amphibians from a nearby pond decide to settle in your pool. In rural areas, in zones of inten-sive cultivation, these animals fall vic-tim to ploughs, harvesters and insecti-cides and your garden pool can be a veritable Noah's Ark for them. If the area of water is calm and spacious, aquatic birds may come to the water in the early morning, leaving behind them some spawn of fish or amphibians which had adhered to their feathers. Even if they were not included in your original plans, you can improve the lot of these uninvited guests by installing some suitable aquatic plants, distribut-ing a little food in spring and autumn, or simply by remaining vigilant during freezing weather. You can also provide suitable shelters near the pool, to encourage hibernation.

▲ *After spending several years at the bottom of the pond, the nymph of the* Aeschna cyanea *comes up to the surface to emerge from its carapace.*

### What animals can be introduced?

If you live in an urban or suburban area, do resist the temptation of intro-ducing amphibians, unless conditions are particularly favorable. This may be the case if your garden is at least 700 m² (7500 ft²) and very sunny, with vegeta-tion which is sufficiently rich and var-ied. Before making a decision, be sure to find out exactly what the requirements are for the species you wish to intro-duce. Remember that most amphibians will naturally be drawn to emigrate sooner or later towards another pool, which will condemn them to a sad end in a highly urban environment.

▲ *The goldfish* (Carassius auratus auratus) *is a very sturdy cold-water fish.*

If your garden is in the country, in a relatively untouched area, you can introduce whatever animals you wish, according to the possibilities offered by your garden, and in conformity with relevant regulations. The animals you introduce must be drawn from the species habitually found in your region. If this is not the case, and any of them return to the wild and become established, to the detriment of local species, as often happens, you may be responsible for upsetting the ecological balance. Contact wild-life and environ-mental protection organisations for fuller information on this subject.

### Avoid imported species

Some species from foreign countries can also represent a considerable danger for local fauna. Remember that even if your garden is completely enclosed, it will be quite impossible for you to prevent all migration of these animals into the wild. You should therefore pay great attention to the origin of the species you find in shops and garden-centres. Exotic animals, such as the Florida turtle (*Chrysemys scripta elegans*) are intended principally for collectors who raise them in inside terrariums. If you introduce them into your garden, it is on your own responsi-bility. You must take all the precautions necessary to prevent them from spreading into the countryside, where conditions are unsuitable.

### Ornamental fish

This restriction concerning species of foreign origin applies equally to ornamental fish. But unless your pool is sufficiently large and isolated to attract wild birds there is little chance that the fish spawn will be disseminated. However, if there is a risk that this may happen, choose native species, or else exotic fish which do not reproduce in your local climate : this is the case, for example, with the white amur and the silver amur.

# INVERTEBRATES

As soon as the first aquatic plants are introduced, the water of the pool is rapidly colonised by numerous species of invertebrates which play an important role in establishing a biological equilibrium. Their presence is a sign that your pool is ready to receive more evolved species : amphibians, fish and water birds.

FOR THE MOST PART, invertebrates will come spontaneously into your pool. Dragonflies and aquatic coleoptera are capable of travelling considerable distances from one pool to another. The more sedentary species, such as water snails, live on the leaves or roots of immersed plants, and are generally introduced "accidentally", at the same time as the aquatic plants, most often in the form of eggs or larvae.

### A wide range of species

The small animals living on the bottom of the pond constitute the benthos, whilst species living in suspension in the water form the plancton. This comprises unicellular algae, or phytoplancton, and a huge number of prolific, microscopic animals, the zooplancton, including the rotifers and protozoa, no larger than 0.1 mm, and various crustaceans (daphnia, copepods) which can reach 2 mm (14th of an inch). Most of these microscopic animals are phytophagous, and consume unicellular algae. Some are carnivorous and feed on smaller animals, while others again are

detritivores, and consume the organic waste material produced by the flora and fauna of the pond. The plancton and the benthos together play a very useful role, providing natural filtration of the water, which is completed by the action of the molluscs (freshwater mussels) and gastropods (various types of freshwater snails).

Insects are well represented, at both the larval and the adult stage. They constitute a source of food which is indispensable for the amphibians and the fish. To accelerate the biological development of the pond, you can introduce water snails (five specimens of each species are generally sufficient). The equivalent of a jar of water and mud (for the plancton and the benthos) taken from a healthy pond is enough to seed a pool of 5-10 m³ (175-350 ft³) which already contains plants. Wait 3 to 6 weeks before introducing the fish, to give the microscopic fauna time to colonize the whole of the pool.

▼ *Young adult* Anax imperator *shortly after its last moult.*

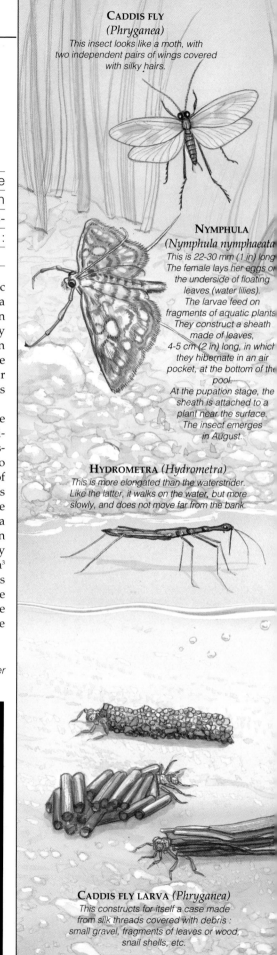

**CADDIS FLY**
(*Phryganea*)
This insect looks like a moth, with two independent pairs of wings covered with silky hairs.

**NYMPHULA**
(*Nymphula nymphaeata*)
This is 22-30 mm (1 in) long The female lays her eggs on the underside of floating leaves (water lilies).
The larvae feed on fragments of aquatic plants They construct a sheath made of leaves, 4-5 cm (2 in) long, in which they hibernate in an air pocket, at the bottom of the pool.
At the pupation stage, the sheath is attached to a plant near the surface. The insect emerges in August.

**HYDROMETRA** (*Hydrometra*)
This is more elongated than the waterstrider. Like the latter, it walks on the water, but more slowly, and does not move far from the bank.

**CADDIS FLY LARVA** (*Phryganea*)
This constructs for itself a case made from silk threads covered with debris : small gravel, fragments of leaves or wood, snail shells, etc.

## MAYFLY
*(Ephemera vulgata)*
Lives for only a few days at the adult stage.

## DRAGONFLY OR ANISOPTERA
*(Libellula depressa )*
This species, 45 mm (2 in) long, is recognizable by its flattened abdomen, light blue in the male and light brown in the female. It can hover, and fly backwards, and feeds on flies caught in flight.

## DAMSEL FLY, ZYGOPTERA
*(Ischnura elegans)*
Its slender abdomen, black with light blue segments, is turquoise or violet coloured in the female. The larvae develop in the water for a year.

## AESCHNA *(Aeschna grandis)*
This is a large dragonfly, with a wingspread of up to 10 cm (4 in). It flies with great speed and agility, and can carry out the most complicated manoeuvres in flight.

## MOSQUITO *(Culex piplens)*
Only the female requires blood, for the maturation of her eggs. In summer, after mating, the female deposits on the water up to six cigar-shaped clutches of eggs about 7.5 mm (5th of an inch) long, each clutch containing 200-300 eggs.

## WATERSTRIDER
*(Gerris lacustris)*
8-10 mm (half an inch) long, this insect has specialized, waterproof hairs on its legs, enabling it to move over the water with a rapid, jerky action. It feeds on insects which fall into the water, sucking out the interior through its piercing mouth parts. It hibernates among stones on the bank, or in the reedbeds.

## EGGS OF THE MOSQUITO
*(Culex piplens)*

## WHIRLIGIG BEETLE
*(Gyrinus substriatus)*
5-7 mm (5th of an inch) long, this insect lives in groups, whirling about on the surface of the water. It is a good diver and very mobile, catching mosquito larvae, and insects which fall in the water. Its eyes are divided horizontally, so that it can see simultaneously above and below the water.

## MOSQUITO LARVAE *(Culex piplens)*
They hang suspended from the smooth surface film of quiet water, breathing through an abdominal siphon and feeding on micro-organisms and algae. At the first sign of danger, they submerge. Mosquito larvae are a favourite source of food for waterstriders, whirligigs, amphibians and fish, so that mosquitos will not be a problem if your pool contains a variety of aquatic fauna. The same cannot be said of puddles and polluted water holes.

**MAYFLY LARVAE** *(Ephemera vulgata)*
They feed on animal and vegetable matter.

## DRAGONFLY LARVA
*(Libellula depressa)*
45 mm (2 in) long, it lives at the bottom of the pool for 2 years, moulting about 10 times.

## AESCHNA LARVA *(Aeschna grandis)*
Its mouth parts form a prehensile "mask" which it projects forward to seize its prey.

**DAMSELFLY LARVAE** *(Ischnura elegans)*
30 mm (1 in) long, these live for a year at the bottom of the water among the aquatic plants, lying in wait for their prey which they seize with their prehensile lower lip (labium).

**BITHYNIA** (*Bithynia tentacula*)
*Its elongated shell 12 mm long (half an inch) is closed by an operculum. This animal breathes through gills and so can survive even in slightly polluted biotopes. It feeds on particles of animal and plant matter.*

**VIVIPARUS**
(*Viviparus contectus*)
*This gastropod has a shell 5-15 mm (5th-3 5ths in) broad, which can be closed by a watertight operculum; breathes through gills; feeds on algae and plancton.*

*Lymnaea (Radix) peregra*

*Physa acuta*

**WATER SCORPION** (*Nepa rubra* )
*This insect is 20 mm (1 in) long, and has a breathing tube at the end of the abdomen, so that it can breathe at the surface of the water. It is an indifferent swimmer, and prefers to lie in wait for its prey, hidden in the plants. It seizes small aquatic insects with its prehensile feet, and feeds on them through its sucking mouth parts. (Its bite is painful).*

**FRESHWATER PLANARIAN** (*Dugesia*)
*This flatworm is 15-20 mm (up to1 in) long, and either crawls along the bottom of the pool or swims on the surface. It feeds on protists, small crustaceans, particles of rotting matter, drawn in through an extensible pharynx on the underside of the abdomen.*

*Lymnaea (Radix) auricularia*

**POND SNAIL**
(*Lymnaea stagnalis*)
*This pond snail, 40-60 mm (2 in) long, feeds on algae and rotting material. It often comes to the surface for air, but can also breathe under water through its gills. Its eggs (about 200) form gelatinous bands 30-50 mm (1-2 in) long, stuck to the underside of floating leaves.*

**POND SNAIL**
(*Planorbis planorbis*)
*Its shell is 15 mm (3 5ths of an inch) in diameter, with 5-6 spires. It has both lungs and gills, so that it can survive frost or drying out of the pond. It browses on algae growing on plants and stones.*

**POND SNAIL**
(*Planorbis carinatus*)
*The shell of this planorb has 4-5 spires. It prefers clear, even deep water, rich in plant life.*

**POND SNAIL** (*Planorbis corneus*)
*This measures up to 35 mm (1 and a half in). It has gills and lungs, and can survive in poorly oxygenated water, since its blood is rich in hemoglobin. It lays "cakes" of 20-30 eggs on aquatic plants.*

**WATER SLATER**
(*Asellus aquaticus*)
*4-8 mm (5th of an inch) long, it feeds on decomposing plant matter.*

**FRESHWATER SHRIMP**
(*Gammarus roeselii*)
*This animal, 10 mm (half an inch) long, lives among the aquatic plants and feeds on animal and plant debris. It requires water rich in oxygen and in lime, for the construction of its carapace.*

*Chironomidae*

**TUBIFEX WORMS** (*Tubifex tubifex* )
*These are thin worms, 80 mm (3 in) long. They shelter in vertical tubes construted from mucous secretions and mud. The rear part of the body protrudes from the tube and undulates, drawing in water. Tubifex worms are a favourite food for fish, and also play an important part in transforming the silt (mineralization).*

**FRESHWATER MUSSEL** (*Anodonte cygnea*)
*This large bi-valve lives on the bottom, moving slowly by means of its strong "foot". It draws in and expels large quantities of water from which it extracts the organic matter in suspension, thus helping to keep the water pure and transparent. The eggs are incubated in the gills of the females. When they hatch, the larvae complete this stage of development by attaching themselves to the gills of fish for several weeks, after which they drop to the bottom. This mussel plays an important part in the reproductive cycle of the bitterling.*

### ACILIUS (*Acilius sulcatus*)
This water beetle, 16-18 mm (3-4 5ths of an inch) long, is an agile swimmer, and feeds on tadpoles, insect larvae and water fleas. The female lays about 500 eggs in a damp place on the bank. The larvae crawl to the water, but return to land to pupate.

### WATER BUG (*Naucoris cimicoides*)
This insect is oval in shape and swims on its belly, unlike the backswimmer. It dives deep under water to catch small aquatic animals.

### GREEN HYDRA (*Chlorohydra viridissima*)
This is a very primitive animal with an elongated, vase-shaped body, 1-2 cm (2-4 5ths of an inch) long. It clings to aquatic plants and feeds on microscopic animals and fry which it captures by means of the eight tentacles (equipped with adhesive pads and paralysing cells) around its mouth parts. It moves in a series of somersaults and reproduction is asexual, by budding.

### DIVING BEETLE
(*Dytiscus marginalis*)
This water beetle, 30-40 mm (1-2 in) long, can stay under water for 15 mn. To breathe, it raises the end of its abdomen above the surface and imprisons air in its stigmas. It is a voracious predator, and immobilizes its prey (tadpoles, fry) in its mandibles and sucks out the interior. Its "bite" is quite painful. In spring, the female inserts her eggs into the stem of aquatic plants.

### DIVING BEETLE LARVA
(*Dytiscus marginalis*)
This rapidly grows to a length of 80 mm (3 in). It is a voracious feeder, preying on tadpoles small fish and fry. In summer, it leaves the water to pupate in the ground. The young beetle emerges 2 weeks later.

### WATER MITES
(*Hydrachnellae*)
1.5 mm (16th of an inch) long, these animals breathe through their skin. They are in constant movement, never come up to the surface, and suck the blood of small crustaceans or annelids; larvae are parasitic on water insects.

### WATER BOATMAN (*Notonecta glauca*)
This is 16 mm (3 5ths of an inch) long, flies well and swims fast head downwards near the surface. It catches mosquito larvae, tadpoles and small fry, which it pierces with its proboscis and sucks dry. It can inflict a painful "bite".

*Piscicola geometra*

### WATER SCORPION (*Ranatra linearis*)
This is about 30 mm (1 in) long, and breathes through a tube which is an extension of its abdomen. It lies in wait for its prey, hidden in the immersed plants. It seizes the animals with its prehensile front legs then devours them with the help of its rostrum.

### AQUATIC SPIDER (*Argyroneta aquatica*)
This is a water spider whose body measures 8-15 mm (up to half an inch). Under the water, between the aquatic plants, it weaves a thimble-size bell-shaped web, which it fills with air by means of the hairs on its abdomen, where it hides, feeding on insect and crustacean larvae.

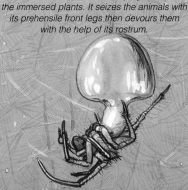

### CRAYFISH (*Astacus astacus*)
The crayfish is an omnivorous, occasionally necrophagous scavenger. The female carries her eggs in a mass under her abdomen. The young undergo a series of moults.

# AMPHIBIANS AND REPTILES

Opportunities of observing amphibians in their natural habitat have become quite rare, because of the gradual disappearance of wetlands. By creating a pool in your garden and encouraging them to adopt it you will have a chance to study the habits of these misunderstood and sometimes maligned animals.

F YOUR POOL OFFERS A favourable environment, you may be lucky enough to find that frogs, toads or newts will spontaneously make it their home. You can also introduce these animals yourself : you will be surprised to discover that these usually timid animals soon become used to the presence of humans, and are most interesting to observe.

## AMPHIBIANS

### Anoura and urodeles

Amphibians (or batrachians) are divided into two genera : the **urodeles**, which have a tail (salamanders, newts) and the **anoura**, which have no tail at the adult stage (frogs and toads). Their skin is smooth or warty, without scales or shell. It is very thin and must be kept constantly moist. It is a respiratory organ, providing them with sufficient oxygen both in the water and out, in a damp environment. This cutaneous breathing allows the animals to hibernate under water for several months without coming to the surface. Juveniles, especially tritons, also have gills, which are progressively replaced by a very primitive form of lung.

### A favourable biotope

Amphibians can be happy in pools of any size, although 4 m² (43 ft²)is a minimum, provided there is sufficient depth in the centre for them to hibernate safely (60-100 cm [24-40 in], according to the climate). They need shallow marginal water, 5-30 cm (2-12 in), sun (at least 6 hours per day) and thick, submerged or floating vegetation (*Potamogeton natans, Callitriche,*

*Elodea, Nymphoides*) for shelter and spawning, and to serve as a springboard for reaching the shore.
Waterlily leaves and fallen branches will also serve. A bog area on the sunniest side of the pool provides the most favorable conditions for reproduction. It should be a few metres wide, with plenty of low herbaceous plants (*Carex, Juncus, Caltha*), and inaccessible to fish and swimming birds, if these are also present, which might devour all the spawn and larvae.

### Pool surroundings

The garden surrounding the pool must be large enough to provide a hunting territory for all the inhabitants. Amphibians quite often travel up to 20-30 m (8-12 in) from the pool, during the night. Tree-stumps and small heaps of stones or wood placed near the pool will provide shelter during the day. And of course your pool should not be too close to houses, since the croaking of frogs and toads may prove to be a nuisance, especially at night during the mating season.

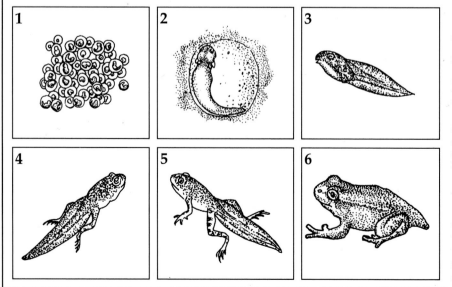

METAMORPHOSIS OF THE FROG

1 The embryos are easily distinguished in their gelatinous envelope which protects them from microbial infections.

2 From the fourth day, the larvae start to move in the egg. Their external gills are clearly visible.

3 After about 10 days the larvae hatch. They are able to swim, thanks to their long tail, and the external gills become internal. The tadpoles have a horny beak with which they browse on the layer of algae which covers aquatic plants.

4 The hind legs appear, though the tadpoles continue to swim by means of their powerful tail.

5 The forelegs appear and the tail starts to atrophy. Gills are replaced by lungs. The tadpole becomes carnivorous.

6 At the end of about four months the metamorphosis is complete and the young frog emerges from the water.

# FROGS

Frogs live in colonies in open water, and like to bask on waterlily leaves. They are generally active day and night. They feed on insects, which they snap up as they fly past, worms, spiders, snails and small vertebrates. Spawning takes place between April and June in sunny, shallow water, 5-30 cm (2-12 in). Gelatinous masses containing more than 10 000 eggs each are deposited on submerged aquatic plants. Frogs spend the winter buried in soft ground in the side of the pond.

**LAUGHING FROG** *(Rana ridibunda)*
Length : 12-17 cm (4-6 in) Ranidae.
*This is the largest European frog.*
*The males have two external vocal sacs which act as resonators, and emit loud cries in rapid succession, day and night, which are taken up in a chorus. The tadpoles are light green in colour and measure up to 9 cm (4 in) in length.*

**LESSON FROG**
*(Rana lessonae)*
Length : 6-9 cm (2-4 in)
Ranidae. *Lives from March till October in the zone of reproduction, preferring shallower water and marginal vegetation. Day and night during the mating season, the males produce a continous loud bleating sound which is amplified by two external vocal sacs.*

**MEADOW FROG**
*(Rana arvalis)*
Length : 6-8 cm (2-3 in) Ranidae.
*The frog is found in damp meadows and peat bogs up to the Arctic circle. It has a more pointed snout than the common frog, Rana temporaria. In the mating season the males make a quavering croaking sound, and their skin takes on a characteristic blue colour.*

**COMMON FROG**
*Rana temporaria*
Length : 6-10 cm (2-4 in) Ranidae.
*This frog has a broad, round snout. It lives in damp, wooded meadowland up to an altitude of 3000 m (9850 ft). It is active day and night, and goes to the water only in March-April, for spawning, and in autumn, to hibernate at the bottom of the pool. It is best to introduce it only if you have a large amount of ground around the pond. The males have no vocal sacs, and their quiet croaking is rarely heard at night.*

**GREEN TREE FROG** *(Hyla arborea)*
Length : 3-5 cm (1-2 in)
Hylidae. *This is a mainly nocturnal frog, found at the edge of the water, where it clings to tall grasses by means of the suction pads at the ends of its fingers. The male has a single vocal sac and produces a chirping call which is gradually amplified and taken up in chorus by all the group. Eggs are deposited at the bottom of the water in walnut-sized spherical heaps. This frog hibernates on dry land.*

**AGILE FROG** *(Rana dalmatina)*
Length : 5-9 cm (2-4 in). Ranidae.
*Found near tall grass, it takes shelter at the least sign of danger, leaping up to 2 m (7 ft). It stays in the water between March and April, for spawning, and to hibernate. For this reason it is better to wait for it to come into the pool naturally, rather than try to introduce it. The male has no vocal sacs, and produces a rapid, muted cry.*

**GREEN EDIBLE FROG** *(Rana esculenta)*
Length : 9-12 cm (3-5 in) Ranidae.
*This frog lives in colonies in ponds and water-holes, and is active day and night, hunting in water or on dry land. It quite happily migrates from one pool to another (up to 2 km [1 m] away) if there is over-crowding. Males produce a noisy croaking, amplified by two spherical vocal sacs.*

### Stocking the pool

The best way to obtain spawn, larvae or aquatic tortoises is to contact a professional or amateur who supplies animals bred in captivity. Wild-life protection associations will be able to supply addresses. Spawn and larvae can be transported in glass containers with watertight lids, containing one-third pond water and two-thirds air, to supply oxygen to the water. A carpet of moss or weed will help to prevent the animals from being too shaken about during transport.

Before releasing the new tenants, place the opened jar in the pool for about 10 minutes, so that the water temperature in the container and the pool temperature match.

The number of eggs or tadpoles that can be introduced into a pool depends on the total volume of water, and on the number of predators present (fish, aquatic birds, tritons, dragonfly larvae, water beetles, etc.). At best, 5% of the eggs will survive to produce a mature adult. But it is quite likely that all the spawn or larvae will be destroyed by predators or die for reasons connected with the environment (too low temperatures, lack of food, pollution).

So for the first year it is wise to keep the eggs, until they hatch, in an aquarium or in a separate small pool.

The tadpoles must be able to find food and shelter, so their area should be densely planted. If the eggs are hatched in an aquarium, release the tadpoles into the pool as soon as possible, otherwise the biggest ones will eat the others. The tadpoles of tritons are particularly voracious and will not hesitate to eat one another if food is short.

---

The Salamandridae include salamanders (whose tails are rounded) and newts (with flattened tails). For the first months of their life they are aquatic, after which they become mostly terrestrial except in spring during the mating period. Unlike toads and frogs, the Salamandridae make no calls, for they have no vocal organs.

**BLACK OR ALPINE SALAMANDER**
*(Salamandra atra)*
Length : 11-16 cm (4-6 in).
*This variety is found under stones in zones of stunted scrub and scree, at altitudes of 800-3000 m (875-3280 yd). The black salamander is viviparous, the embryos developing inside the female for 1-3 years during which time the larvae feed by means of suckers which disappear at birth.*

## SALAMANDERS

Salamanders live near water in hills and wooded valleys, up to 2500 m (2730 yd) in altitude. They are cautious, nocturnal animals, hiding during the day under stones or among vegetation. They are generally inactive in summer, except in cool, damp weather. Their diet is composed of insects, worms and slugs. In spring, the females lay their eggs in the water of ponds and slow-moving streams. The young salamanders leave the water after the metamorphosis and go into the neighbouring woodland. To discourage predators, salamanders have venom-secreting parotid glands. Contact may cause skin irritation but is not dangerous to humans. It is difficult to introduce salamanders artificially into a garden, but they may come of their own accord if there is a place where they can hibernate in safety, with old tree stumps, piles of stones or wood, and moist, soft soil.

**FIRE SALAMANDER**
*(Salamandra salamandra)*
Length : 15-20 cm
*Its bright colours are a warning to imprudent predators. Mating takes place on dry land in April-May. The female is ovoviviparous, and deposits her eggs in the water, stuck on stones. The membrane ruptures almost immediately, releasing larvae which are already well-developed.*

### Preservation of natural equilibrium

• All European amphibians and reptiles, and their spawn, are protected. It is illegal to remove them from their natural habitat and transport them without official permission, for whatever purpose, private or scientific, unless they come from a private pool or have been raised in captivity.

• Do not introduce species from other regions or foreign countries unless they are naturally present in your vicinity.

• Do not transplant young or adult amphibians, because their natural instinct is to return to their place of birth, even though they have no chance of success.

**CRESTED NEWT** (*Triturus cristatus*)
Length : 14-16 cm (5-6 in).
This is the biggest European newt, and is found up to
an altitude of 2000 m (6,500 ft) all over the continent (except in
Ireland and Scandinavia). Both sexes are blackish-brown
with darker markings, with a bright orange-yellow belly with black markings. During the
nuptial display the male has a deeply indented dorsal crest, quite separate from the
tail crest. This newt prefers large, sunny ponds with plenty of vegetation and
can emigrate from one pool to another over a distance of up to 3 km (2 miles).

## NEWTS

Newts enjoy cool lowland,
and sunny places in the
mountains, where they are
found up to an altitude of 2500 m (8200 ft).
Very early in spring they go to their
spawning grounds in clear, slow-running
streams or shallow pools rich in vegetation.
During the mating season the male assumes bright
colours and a dorsal crest, which is absent in the
female. He deposits on the water plants and on stones
at the bottom of the pool a number of spermatophores
which the female collects in her cloaca. During the
days following the fertilization, the female fixes more than
250 large eggs, one by one, to aquatic plants close
to the water's edge. The larvae appear 7-10 days later.
After metamorphosis, towards the fourth month,
the juveniles hoist themselves out of the water.
Newts are active day and night in the water,
feeding on insects and larvae, small crustaceans,
water-fleas and worms. On land,
they are nocturnal, feeding on insects,
spiders, worms and snails. In June-July
they shelter near the water under
dead leaves, rotting stumps,
stones or moss. From September to October,
newts burrow deeply into the ground
to hibernate away from frost. Some
choose to hibernate in the mud
at the bottom of a pool.

**MARBLED NEWT**
(*Triturus marmoratus*)
Length : 13-14 cm (5 in).
This newt is found in
low-lying areas of
south-western Europe.
It spends most of
the time in dry,
wooded areas, but
seeks out springs and
small pools in spring. With its dark green
marbled back it is easily recognizable. During the mating season,
the crest of the male has contrasting transverse stripes.
Females have a red or orange dorsal line.

**COMMON TRITON**
(*Triturus vulgaris*)
Length : 8-11 cm (3-4 in).
This newt is found throughout Europe,
in plains and hills, up to 2000 m (6500 ft).
Its back is yellowish-brown with black markings,
while the throat and belly are reddish-orange with black
markings. The underside of the tail takes on a blue
and orange coloration. During the
mating period, from April to June,
the male has a high, wavy dorsal crest
which continues right to the end
of the tail.

**WEB-TOED NEWT**
(*Triturus helveticus*)
Length : 7-9 cm (3-4 in).
This newt is found throughout western
Europe in hilly regions of deciduous forest, up to an
altitude of 1000 m (3300 ft). Its back is olive-brown/yellow-brown
heavily marked in black. The belly is yellow with black spots
and the throat is pink. During the mating period, the male has
a low dorsal crest prolonged by a black caudal filament to the
end of its broad, natatory tail. Its back toes have a large
black web. The female is slightly bigger, and her rear toes
are not webbed, since her tail is not truncated. This newt never
moves from its usual spawning grounds and habitat,
and requires cool temperatures.

**ALPINE NEWT**
(*Triturus alpestris*)
Length : 8-12 cm (3-5 in).
This newt is found in central Europe, in the Alps
up to 2500 m (8200 ft), in the north of Spain, and has been
acclimatized in Great Britain. It likes a cool climate, and will
not tolerate temperatures more than 22 °C (71 °F) for very long,
whether in the water or on land. It prefers small, shady pools,
and does not go far away. During the mating period, from
February to May, the male has a bright blue coloration on the
flanks, and a continuous low crest from back to tail. From
June onwards, the newt usually stays within a few
metres of the water, hidden under a stone,
thick moss or a rotting stump.

These two species of newts need water which is partly in sunlight, at altitudes greater than 500 m (1640 ft). In low country, they need
cooler, shady water, at a temperature no higher than 18 °C (64 °F).

## TOADS

Toads are mainly
terrestrial animals,
except during the mating season.
They prefer to hunt at night, and feed
on insects, worms, snails and slugs. During the day,
they shelter in cool places, under stones or in a burrow.
During the mating period, which extends from February to
May and even into summer, toads seek stretches of water
offering both sun and shade. Several thousands of eggs
are deposited in strings or gelatinous clusters in sunny
places, in water 5-30 cm (2-12 in) deep, attached to aquatic
plants or to roots overhanging the water. The tadpoles
rapidly grow to a length of 5 cm (2 in). Toads hibernate
on land, in a deep hole under roots or stones.

**COMMON TOAD** *(Bufo bufo)*
Length : 8-15 cm (3-6 in). Bufonidae.
This animal is found all over Europe,
up to an altitude of 2000 m (6500 ft). During the mating
season the males produce a kind of melodious cooing
noise which is not unpleasant. The females
wind their strings of 2 to 4 rows of black eggs
around water plants. To hunt, they may
go as far as 1500 m (4900 ft) from
the spawning grounds.

**GREEN TOAD**
*(Bufo viridis)*
Length 8-14 cm (3-6 in)
Bufonidae.
Often seen during the
day, the green toad likes
warm, dry, sandy or stony
flat ground, up to an
altitude of 500 m (1600 ft) and sometimes
more, if conditions are favourable. Spawning
takes place in shallow, even brackish water, between April and
June. The call of the male resembles that of the cricket.
This toad needs a sunny hunting ground and soft soil
into which he can burrow.

**MIDWIFE TOAD** *(Alytes obstetricans)*
Length : 4-5 cm (2 in). Discoglossidae.
Found in western Europe, in dry, stony regions up to 2000 m (6500 ft).
Hunts only at night, without going more than 10 m (35 ft) from its hiding
place The male emits a soft, melodious call at the rate of once a second.
The mating period lasts several months, during which time the
female produces, on land, strings of 40-60 quite large yellow eggs.
The male winds the strings of eggs around his hind legs and carries
them about for 3 to 6 weeks, keeping them moist in the water of the
spawning ground, where they will hatch.

**SPOTTED SPADEFOOT TOAD**
*(Pelodytes punctatus)*
Length : 4-5 cm (2 in).
Pelobatidae.
This member of the spadefoot toad family,
which looks rather like a small frog, is found
in the west of Europe, from Spain to Belgium.
Its pupils contract vertically.
It approaches water only for spawning.
In the mating season the male produces
a deep call, repeated incessantly.

**YELLOW-BELLED TOAD**
*(Bombina variegata)*
Length : 5 cm (2 in).
Discoglossidae.
This toad is found near very small areas of water
(holes, puddles, ruts) which receive sun all day
and are surrounded by low foliage to provide cover.
It is active day and night, and lives in the spawning ground
from April till October. Its skin secretes a poison, and it
warns predators by turning on its back
and exposing its brightly-coloured
belly. During the mating season
the males, which have no
vocal sacs, emit a soft,
fluting call to mark their
territory, about
1 m² (10 ft²). This prevents
overcrowding of
the puddles.

**NATTERJACK OR**
**RUNNING TOAD** *(Bufo calamita)*
Length : 7-10 cm (3-4 in). Bufonidae.
The natterjack is found on plains, on dry,
sunny ground with sparse vegetation and a mild climate,
though it has been reported up to 2000 m (6500 ft). It tolerates
brackish water and drought, and appreciates light, sandy soil into which
it can easily burrow. Its pupils contract horizontally.
It has short legs and moves at a kind of run, since,
unlike other species, it is unable to leap. Its loud,
raucous cries are amplified by an enormous
internal vocal sac.

## EUROPEAN TURTLE
*(Emys orbicularis)*
Length : 20-25 cm (8-10 ft). Emydidae.
*In May-June, the female digs a hole in sand or dry soil, sometimes far from the water, and deposits about 15 eggs with thick, calcareous shells. The little turtles emerge in August-September (when the summer is hot) or in the following spring. The turtle hibernates in the mud at the bottom of the water. Formerly found throughout Europe as far north as Scandinavia, these turtles are now to be found only in a few regions in the south of Europe.*

## REPTILES

Certain snakes like to live near water, where they find abundant food. Many of these water snakes are timid and completely harmless, and rarely observed in their natural habitat. Freshwater turtles, of the Emydidae family, which have a flattened shell, a long tail and webbed feet, are just as timid. They breathe through lungs, but have a complementary respiratory device (an anal bladder which acts like gills) which enables them to hibernate under water from October to April. In summer they live in streams (in the mountains) or boggy areas in the plain, where they like to bask in the sun, but dive into the water at the slightest alert. They feed on worms, aquatic molluscs, small fish and frogs, and prefer to attack animals which are weak or ill. Young animals enjoy vegetation, so allow plants time to become well-established and luxuriant before introducing turtles. For basking, provide a flat surface at water level (fallen tree trunk, raft or flat stone) in a calm, sheltered position. Freshwater turtles can be fed with cat food (pellets), and pieces of finely chopped meat or fish placed on their raft.

## CHRYSEMYS, OR FLORIDA TURTLE
*(Chrysemys scripta elegans )*
Length : 20-25 cm (8-10 in). Emydidae.
*This animal is suitable only for an indoor pool, provided it is spacious and well-lit. The turtles must have a sunny platform all year round, or else a sun lamp providing the heat and UV radiation necessary for their metabolism.*

### European turtle under threat from the Florida turtle

Each year, several million *chrysemys* (Florida turtles) are sold in Europe when only a few days old. They are produced on farms, where they are hatched in incubators, or gathered from their native habitat. Very little information is supplied to the prospective owner and most of these turtles die very rapidly for lack of adequate care (90% death rate in the first year). Some do survive to adulthood, when they weigh 2 kg (4 lb). It is then difficult to keep them in an apartment, and they are often handed over to a zoo, or simply released in the wild, where they become established, or perish.

Unfortunately the *chrysemys*, which is more aggressive and hardier than the European turtle, also breeds more rapidly, with the result that the native species, subjected to intense competition in its own biotope, finally disappears wherever the two species co-habit.

• Do not raise *chrysemys* in your garden. Choose a European turtle purchased from a reputable breeder, who sells only animals bred in captivity.

• Under no circumstances must Florida turtles be released into the wild.

• If you wish to raise a turtle in an indoor pool or aqua-terrarium, do not buy a *chrysemys*, but adopt one of those which are disposed of each day to zoos and aquariums in your region.

## GRASS SNAKE *(Natrix natrix)*
Length : 80-200 cm (2-7 ft).
Colubridae.
*The common grass snake hides in natural cavities under tree trunks or large stones, not far from pools and slow-flowing rivers. It is active during the day and hunts near to and in the water. It feeds on young rodents, amphibians and fish. At the beginning of spring the female lays from 30 to 50 eggs in a nest in a warm place, sometimes in a compost heap. The young hatch after about two months, and measure 15-19 cm (6-8 in). Like all the other grass snakes found in wet zones, this is an inoffensive animal which never bites man. If seized, it defends itself by expelling the contents of its anal glands, or simulates death by lying on its back. It hibernates in a burrow or under rocks, sometimes far from the water.*

# POND FISH

As well as bringing colour and animation to your pond, fish play an important part in the biological cycle. To preserve the equilibrium, you must avoid overcrowding, and distribute food in measured amounts. Otherwise a filter system will be necessary to prevent rapid pollution of the water.

IN THE ABSENCE OF NATURAL predators, pond fish grow and multiply rapidly. The rate of growth of each species, the volume of water available and the natural resources of the pond must all be taken into account when deciding how many fish to introduce.

## Ideal conditions

Choice of species is determined by the size of pond. Japanese carp (Koï) can grow to 80 cm (30 in) in a few years, and really need a volume of water greater than 10 000 litres (2640 gallons) and a minimum area of 20 m² (215 ft²), ideally between 40-60 m² (430 -645 ft²). With ponds of a partial depth of 1 m (3 ft) or more, filtration is advisable.

Smaller species (gold-fish, bitterling) are happy in a smaller pool, 10-15 m² (100-160 ft²) with a capacity of about 3000 litres (800 gallons). Smaller pools may also be equipped with a filtration and oxygenation system. In any case, the depth in the centre of the pool should be at least 45 cm (18 in). This area must contain appropriate quantities of oxygenating and purifying vegetation: *Myriophyllum*, *Ceratophyllum*, *Elodea*, *Callitriche*, *Potamogeton*.

The peripheral zone can be less thickly planted, for a better view of the fish as they swim over the bottom.

Finally, it should not be forgotten that fish eat the eggs and larvae of amphibians, which makes co-habitation for any length of time somewhat difficult. If possible, set aside a special zone for amphibians by creating one or more additional pools, in a water-course, for example.

## Well-balanced water...

Whether the water comes from a tap, a spring or a well, check that it has a pH of between 6 and 8.5. The chlorine present in tap water is partly eliminated when the pool is filled, if you use a spray jet, and will disappear completely by evaporation in the course of a few days. If the pool is a new one (and especially if it is made of concrete) it should be rinsed several times with clean water before the final filling. Avoid using rainwater collected from the roof, because the zinc from the guttering and the carbon dioxide from the atmosphere could pollute the pool. Moreover, rainwater, which contains no minerals, is of poor quality. Always use as little fertilizer and pesticide as possible in the immediate proximity, since the water can be polluted by stormwater run-off.

## PRINCIPAL CHARACTERISTICS OF POND FISH

The choice of species will be determined by certain parameters, such as : size of adult fish, surface and total volume of the pool, depth, the range of temperature, on which depends the oxygen content, the nature of the bottom. Do not forget that fish grow rapidly when conditions are favourable. Their weight can double by the third year, and this can sometimes upset the biological balance. In the first year, count an average of 50-100 g (2-4 oz) of fish per 1000 litres of water.

| Species | Size average adult | Number of fish per 1000 litres of water unfiltered | filtered | Minimum area of pond | Type of bottom | Temperatures Minimum | Maximum | Reproduction Period | Optimum temperature |
|---|---|---|---|---|---|---|---|---|---|
| Bleak | 5 - 9 cm | 8 | 20 | 15 m² | mud, plants | 4 °C | 28 °C | April/June | 18 °C |
| Bleak (ablet) | 15 - 17 cm | 3 | 15 | 20 m² | gravel, sand, rocks | 4 °C | 18 °C | April/July | 16 °C |
| Amurs | 40-120 cm | 0,1 | 0,2 | 25 m² | mud, plants | 4 °C | 36 °C | April/August | 22 °C |
| Bitterling | 6 - 8 cm | 7 | 16 | 10 m² | mud, plants | 4 °C | 28 °C | April/August | 16 °C |
| Goldfish (crucian carp) | 15 - 35 cm | 2 | 10 | 5 m² | mud, plants | 0 °C | 36 °C | May/June | 16 °C |
| Koï carp | 30-120 cm | 0,3 | 1 | 25 m² | mud, sand, pebbles | 4 °C | 36 °C | May/July | 18 °C |
| Sticklebacks | 6 - 10 cm | 4 | 4 | 15 m² | mud, sand, pebbles | 4 °C | 28 °C | March/June | 16 °C |
| Golden ide or orfe | 35 - 50 cm | 2 | 4 | 25 m² | mud, pebbles, plants | 4 °C | 28 °C | April/June | 16 °C |
| Japanese (sarasa, oranda) | 6 - 15 cm | 5 | 15 | 5 m² | sand, gravel, plants | 12 °C | 33 °C | May/July | 26 °C |
| Sunfish | 15 - 20 cm | 3 | 6 | 20 m² | mud, pebbles, plants | 3 °C | 32 °C | April/June | 16 °C |
| Mongolian tench | 30 - 60 cm | 1 | 3 | 25 m² | mud, plants | 2 °C | 36 °C | May/July | 18 °C |
| Minnow | 6 - 10 cm | 5 | 20 | 15 m² | mud, plants | 4 °C | 18 °C | May/June | 15 °C |

## NATIVE FISH

Among our native pond and river fish, some species adapt themselves readily to life in a pool. These are mostly omnivores, feeding on unicellular algae or aquatic plants, zooplancton, crustaceans, larvae and insects. Procure your fish from fish-farms (all these species are available) or specialist suppliers, to help preserve the natural habitat. The species indicated below have been selected for their colouring or the interest of their mating habits.

### BITTERLING *(Rhodeus sericeus arnarus)*

This little fish, 6-8 cm (2-3 in) long, lives on the muddy bottom of shallow water rich in plant life, where it feeds on benthic organisms. Its reproduction requires the presence of freshwater mussels (Anodonte, Unio) : guided by the male in his nuptial finery, the female deposits her eggs between the two valves of the mussel, by means of a long ovipositor. The male releases his milt above the orifice through which the mussel absorbs water, and fertilization takes place inside the mollusc. The eggs hatch after an incubation period of 20 days, and the larvae develop among the gills of the mussel for 3 days. The life expectancy of the bitterling is not more than 5 years. Introduce more freshwater mussels than you have male bitterlings.

### BLEAK *(Leucaspius delineatus)*

This is a surface dweller no longer than 8 cm,(3 in) which feeds on zooplancton and phytoplancton, and rarely lives longer than 3 years. In a confined space it is prolific, but tends to become smaller, 3 cm (1 in).

### MINNOW *(Phoxinus phoxinus)*

8-14 cm (3-6 in) long, the minnow lives in schools in clear, shallow, well-oxygenated water with a sandy bottom. During the mating period, the breast of the male turns red. The female deposits her eggs in the shallows, on clean gravel or sand.

### GOLDEN ORFE *(Leuciscus idus orfus)*

This is a surface dweller with a very decorative bright orange back. It likes deep, well-oxygenated water and feeds on zooplancton and fish. It can grow to 30-50 cm (12-20 in), and lives about 15 years.

### SUNFISH, OR PUMPKIN-SEED SUNFISH *(Lepomis gibbosus)*

This feeds on insects, small fish, tadpoles and frogs. Its small size and iridescent colours make it an attraction throughout the year. During the spawning period, the male jealously guards the eggs gathered together in a nest which he protects against intruders, until hatching. Introduce 1 male for 2 or 3 females. The sunfish will live about 15 years.

### THREE-SPINED STICKLEBACK *(Gasterosteus aculeatus)*

The stickleback is 7-8 cm (2-3 in) long, and prefers shallow water. During the nuptial period the male, in splendid scarlet, builds a conical nest out of debris of various kinds, with the entrance at the summit. Several females lay their eggs in turn, while the male guards the nest from intruders. When the young fish hatch, and start to stray too far from the nest, the male gathers them in his mouth and brings them back to safety. The stickleback lives for about 4 years. It is preferable not to have more than two couples at a time

### BLEAK, OR ABLET *(Alburnus alburnus)*

This is a surface fish which prefers roomy pools without too much vegetation. It needs clear, well-oxygenated gently-moving water. It rarely lives longer than 6 years.

## Temperature and oxygenation

Fish are very sensitive to thermal shocks : a drop in water temperature of 4 °C (39 °F) in one hour is sufficient to destroy spawn and fry. For this reason it is never advisable to add large quantities of cold water to a pool : do it gradually. Shallow pools warm up rapidly in summer and oxygenation will be improved if the water is kept moving by means of a fountain or a cascade. Our native species will tolerate water temperatures ranging from 4 °C (39 °F) in winter to 28 °C (82 °F) in summer. Koï carp and crucian carp, which are very hardy, will accept higher temperatures and a lower oxygen content. Certain species, though, such as bleaks and minnows become weak if the water is not cool and/or well oxygenated, then die rapidly. Remember this when choosing species for your pool.

## Nutritive quality of the water

When the pool is filled, the water is transparent and seemingly sterile (and chlorinated if it comes from the tap). This is why it is necessary to wait from 4 to 6 weeks before introducing fish into a newly-filled pool, so that the water can achieve biological equilibrium. During the first week, it warms up gradually and takes on a green colour, evidence of the presence of phytoplancton. At this stage, submerged and surface aquatic plants should be installed.

During about the second week, the water becomes cloudy, and zooplancton develop. From the third week, the waste produced by the zooplancton gives the water a brownish colour, disappearing progressively, between the fourth and the sixth week, thanks to the action of the aquatic plants which absorb the elements in suspension and produce oxygen. The water becomes clear again, and biological balance has been attained. It is time to introduce the fish.

## Feeding the fish

Fish find food easily in a natural-style pond. Supplementary feeding may be necessary in spring, and especially in autumn to help the fish to build up reserves for the winter. If the pool is heavily stocked, it is preferable to feed the fish throughout the summer. The following may be used : mud worms, small crustaceans (daphnia), finely chopped fish, ox-heart, boiled potatoes, cooked haricot beans, kibbled wheat, or proprietary blends.

If the pool is small, it is preferable to use commercially-prepared food (flakes or pellets), which is more expensive, certainly, but is well-balanced and will create less of a pollution problem. Distribute very small quantities at a time, since the excess food which is not taken up by the fish can pollute the water and favour the development of certain diseases. A correct quantity should always be eaten within a few minutes.

If you should be absent for a week or two, the fish will not suffer from lack of feeding. If your absence is longer, you should arrange for a neighbour to distribute the daily ration which you will have prepared in advance. As the season advances, stop feeding the fish as soon as the water temperature falls below 8 °C (46 °F). At this point, the fish go into a semi-lethargic state and consume practically nothing.

---

### OTHER NATIVE SPECIES SUITABLE FOR GARDEN PONDS

Other native species can easily adapt to life in the pond, but have less decorative interest :

- THE BLENNY (Blennius fluviatilis), 8-12 cm (3-5 in) long, likes clear, running water, shallow, with rocky, stony or sandy bottom.

- THE CRUCIAN CARP (Carassius carassius), 15-30 cm (6-12 in) long, can adapt to environments unsuitable for other species. Use it even in very small pools, and those which are too shallow and invaded by luxuriant vegetation. It stand up remarkably well to a lack of oxygen in summer and to frost in winter.

- THE CARP (Cyprinius carpio), 40-80 cm (16-30 in) long, likes nutrient-rich, even somewhat oxygen-starved water. It eats a large quantity of zooplancton and phytoplancton, aquatic grasses and gastropods which it finds on the bottom or on the plants. It is very prolific, grows quickly, and can reach 1.5 kg (3 lb) in two or three summers.

- THE ROACH (Rutilus rutilus) reaches 30-35 cm (12-14 in). It feeds on animal or vegetable plancton, aquatic plants, gasteropods and insects. It also tends to eat newly laid carp eggs.

- THE GUDGEON (Gobio gobio), 10-15 cm (4-6 in) long, prefers clear water, not too cold, with a sandy bottom. It stays close to the bottom, where it pokes about in search of food (worms, gastropods, larvae). It is sensitive to pollution and silting-up, and needs clear water, deep in places, 100-150 cm (40-60 in).

- THE RED-EYE OR RUDD (Scardinius erythroptalmus), 20-35 cm (8-14 in) long, is a surface fish sharing the same habitat as the roach, with which it easily interbreeds. Its fins are differently coloured (bright red in the rudd, pale orange in the roach) and it is more rounded in shape than the roach.

- THE TENCH (Tinca tinca) grows to 40-60 cm (16-24 in). It is a very hardy fish, and feeds mainly on vegetable and animal matter on the muddy bottom. It is not much affected by a reduction in the oxygen content of the water.

## JAPANESE FISH

The goldfish (*Carassius auratus auratus*) is undoubtedly the most popular and the hardiest ornamental fish. It is of Chinese origin, from a variety of crucian (*Carassius auratus gibelio*) very similar to the European crucian, of the Cyprinidae family. The Chinese were already raising it in the early part of our era (260-400 A.D.), and improving its colours by patient selection. It gradually became a pet, and was extraordinarily popular during the Ming dynasty (1368-1644), and in Japan, where it was bred from about the year 1500. Introduced into Europe at the end of the 17th century, it rapidly became widely popular. Certain successive mutations and crosses have produced a number of different varieties in a range of colours, with a more rounded shape and atrophied or hypertrophied fins. These are mostly known today by Japanese names : shubunkins, orandas, sarasas, etc. The so-called "monsters" or "Japanese" varieties are less hardy than the classic goldfish, but in summer, they will accept a lower temperature in a large, outside pool than in a household aquarium. In autumn, as soon as the water temperature falls below 15 °C (59 °F), it is vital to place them in a roomy, unheated, indoor aquarium until the spring. But the ordinary goldfish, the comet and the shubunkin can spend the winter in the pool provided it is at least 80 cm (30 in) deep, 120 cm (48 in) in a continental climate. All these fish are omnivorous, and feed on aquatic plants, water snails, insects and larvae.

**COMET**
*This is the result of selections carried out by American breeders. Comets are robust fish, generally similar in shape to goldfish, but with noticeably longer fins. They also have a distinctive range of markings and colours, from white to black and from gold to vermillion, and various combinations of these colours. They will stand up to winter temperatures in a pool deeper than 80 cm (30 in).*

**GOLDFISH**
*12-30 cm (5-12 in) long, this crucian likes stagnant, shallow water, heavily planted. It can be introduced safely into shallower pools, where it will stand up to the most severe conditions: it accepts cold water in winter, and warm, poorly-oxygenated water in summer. It lives 6-8 years. Goldfish fry are transparent, then brown, and take on a golden colour only at about 6 months.*

**SHUBUNKIN**
*Similar to the comet, with a variety of colours, it can remain in the pool over winter if the water is more than 80 cm (30 in) deep.*

**VEILTAIL GOLDFISH**
*This is more delicate than the comet and the crucian, and requires water with a winter minimum temperature of 10 °C (50 °F) and a summer maximum of 25 °C (77 °F). It is a stocky shaped fish with well-developed fins (the tail has three or four lobes) and requires a lot of space to do well.*

**ORANDA**
*Very similar to the lionhead, but has a dorsal fin.*

**TELESCOPE**
*So named because of its protuberant eyes. There are several varieties with varying colours, with or without a dorsal fin.*

**LIONHEAD**
*Adults have swollen excrescences on the top and sides of the head, forming a kind of brightly-coloured cap.*

### Winter care

If your fish have been able to build up good reserves at the end of the summer, they will have no trouble in surviving the winter. In the deepest part of the pool, below 60 cm (24 in), the water temperature remains constant at about 4 °C (39 °F), whatever the atmospheric conditions. For this reason, and to keep sediment from releasing excess gaseous waste, it is important not to stir up the bottom water to avoid mixing it with the colder surface water. Even in a mild climate there may be several days of hard frost, with more or less disastrous results, depending on how shallow the pool is. If there is any risk, you can cover the pool in autumn with the sort of protective cover usually used for swimming pools, withdrawing it progressively as the weather improves. In very small pools, a specially designed pool heating cable will be sufficient to prevent the surface freezing over.

## CHINESE CARP

These originate in the temperate, calm waters of the Amur river, which forms the natural frontier between Manchuria and Siberia. They grow rapidly (two or three times more quickly than ordinary carp) and need a pool with an area of at least 25 m² (270 ft²) and a depth of 80-100 cm (30-40 in). Because they keep aquatic plants down and filter the water, Chinese carp play an important part in the control of eutrophication in waters which are rich in organic matter or polluted by excess nitrates and phosphates. It is forbidden to introduce them into open water, to prevent native species from competing with them. Chinese carp do not reproduce naturally in a northern climate since the eggs must be incubated at a temperature of 20-25 °C (68-77 °F).

**TENCH** (Tinca tinca)
This common tench is attractively coloured, from pale yellow to bright orange. Its back often has ivory coloured markings. It resists cold and does equally well in acid, peaty water or warm, oxygen-starved water. It feeds on molluscs, worms, insect larvae which it finds on the vegetation and in the muddy bottom.

**WHITE AMUR, HERBIVOROUS CARP, OR GRASS CARP**
(Ctenopharyngodon idella)
The white amur feeds on filamentous algae and soft aquatic plants (Elodea, Myriophyllum, Potamogeton, water lilies, duckweed, etc.). In summer, as soon as the temperature reaches 18 °C (64 °F), it eats the equivalent of 150 % of its body weight. Its annual growth rate is 1 kg (2 lb) for 40 kg (90 lb) of vegetable matter consumed. It is possible to satisfy the appetite of large individuals by providing extra food in the form of breadcrumbs, cooked maize, lettuce hearts, lawnclippings (untreated), potatoes, broad beans and peas which they particularly appreciate. The natural mowing action of the amur helps limit the development of oxygenating plants and water lilies in large ponds or pools. It is rarely available, except under certain permits, because of its incredible appetite for all sorts of vegetation.

**MARBLED AMUR**
(Aristichthys nobilis)
This fish consumes a great deal of algae and zooplancton, and thus provides a natural solution to the problem of green or brown water.

**SILVER AMUR**
(Hypothalmichthys molitrix).
This carp feeds exclusively on vegetable matter and unicellular algae which it filters through its gills. A fish weighing 1 kg (2 lb) can filter 100 litres (25 gallons) of water per hour, and consume 6-12 g (half oz) of phytoplancton. It can reach 5 kilos (10 lb) in the fourth year, and old specimens can weigh as much as 40 kilos (90 lb). The combined action of the silver amur and the white amur clears the water and prevents the formation of slime.

**ROYAL AMUR**
This is a hybrid between the marbled amur and the silver amur. Like the latter, it feeds on phytoplancton and vegetable debris.

## JAPANESE "KOÏ" CARP

The ballet of Koï carp moving slowly beneath the surface of the water is a fascinating sight even for a non-specialist. The diversity of pattern and their magnificent colours, often with a metallic gleam, are the result of rigorous selection and repeated crossings carried out over a number of centuries in Japan. Like the common carp (*Cyprinus carpio*) from which they are derived, the Koï have two barbels on either side of the mouth, but their body is longer, and can measure up to 120 cm (50 in). During spawning, the females deposit their eggs (more than 300 000 per kilo of live weight) on aquatic plants. They are peaceable animals, easy to tame, and will take food from the hand. Although their colours appear to best advantage in clear water, Koï are quite happy in rather murky water rich in nutrients and minerals. You can introduce them into your pond, even if there is no filtration, provided they have plenty of room. Simply make sure that they do not suffer any thermal shock, and that the water is not polluted by waste food. In favourable conditions, Koï can live up to 70 years ! There are a great number of patterns and colours, single or multiple, which are carefully catalogued. Here are some of the finest.

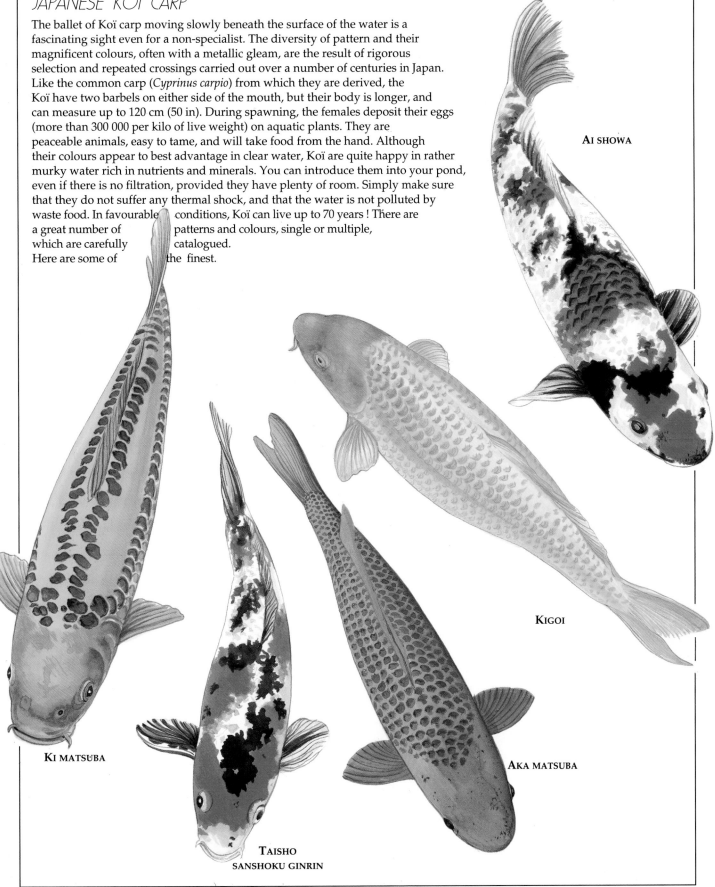

AI SHOWA

KIGOI

KI MATSUBA

TAISHO
SANSHOKU GINRIN

AKA MATSUBA

# WATER BIRDS

The resonant calls and the activity of water birds dabbling and diving bring additional animation to the garden pool and provide a touch of authenticity. Preference should be given to species like teal and mandarin ducks which do not severely damage planted areas, and are small enough for the limited area usually available.

SWIMMING BIRDS LIKE CALM and shallow water, rich in aquatic vegetation. If they are to find their food on the bottom, a good part of the pool must not be more than 20-30 cm (8-12 in) deep.

## The ideal biotope

A considerable part of the margin must be covered with dense vegetation (*Phalaris, Glyceria, Carex, Juncus, Scirpus, Typha,* ferns), to provide shelter and nesting places for the birds. A gently-sloping, unplanted section of the bank will give access to a grassy zone of about 100 m² (1075 ft²), providing a dry resting place. For the nestlings, which are equally sensitive to cold and to heat, provide a raised shelter on the bank or on an islet in the centre of the pond. This may be a wicker nesting-basket or a small hut made of branches. In some cases it may be preferable to fence off the part of the garden which is reserved for the birds. This will keep predators at a distance and help to prevent the birds from plundering your flowerbeds.

## Choice of species

The size of the pool must be adapted to the choice of birds : an area of 25 m² (270 ft²) is sufficient for a pair of teal or garganey. Ducks and geese need 40-50 m² (430-540 ft²), while a pair of swans will do well only on a pond of at least 80 m² (860 ft²). But it should be remembered that these birds tend to damage planted areas, since they eat the young shoots and tender leaves. Some anatidae (teal, mandarin duck,) do little damage to vegetation, especially if they are fed regularly. Their small size and attractively coloured plumage make them a good choice for small garden ponds. Avoid having too many birds, however, because their excrement will eventually create a water pollution problem. Make sure that the selected species will live happily with the other garden inhabitants : beware of geese, which hunt frogs mercilessly, and have a tendency to peck at any person or animal invading their territory.

▼ *For nesting, water birds like the security of an islet or a raft.*

## Trimming or clipping of wings

To prevent birds from migrating, their living conditions must be well-suited to their requirements. A couple will settle in quite happily to its new territory if provided with a relative degree of comfort : an appropriate shelter (nesting box or hut), abundant vegetation and regular supply of food. In some cases it may be necessary to trim the wings (shortening the feathers to prevent flight). The first time, this operation should be carried out by an experienced person (vet or breeder), who will show you how to do it. It must be renewed after each moult (once or twice a year, according to the species). Alternatively, clipping consists of amputating the wing at the last articulation. This is a permanent operation, which must be carried out by a vet within hours of hatching or at most within the first week.

## Feeding water birds

Swimming birds find varied food in a natural-style pond by filtering the particles in suspension in the water through the horny lamellae in their beaks. They remove algae and duck-weed, and many insect larvae. But this diet is dangerous for the eggs of frogs and newts and certain fish, and for the young shoots of aquatic plants. For this reason it is preferable to supply food in the form of pellets, or a mixture of wheat, kibbled maize, and barley, salad greens, fruit and vegetable peelings. Work on the basis of 100 g (4 oz) of food per day, per adult bird. For nestlings, the daily allowance is 10 g (3rd oz), for the first week, increasing progressively to 80 g (3 oz) in the fifth week.

Food must be distributed at regular times, and always in the same place. Throw it into the water, where the depth is no more than 20 cm (8 in). You will thus avoid soiling the bank, and attracting unwelcome guests. To help the teal and mandarin ducks to grind the grain in their gizzard, place a little flinty gravel on the shore.

# WATER BIRDS

Thanks to their broad, webbed feet, teal, ducks and swans are excellent swimmers, protected by their thick, completely waterproof plumage. Most swimming birds migrate each year to warmer climates in Africa and Asia. They leave about the middle of summer, as soon as the young birds can fly, and start their return flights from mid-January. The nesting season is from mid-April till the end of May, and the nests are hidden in the thick vegetation by the waterside. They are made from dry grass, and the entrance is always south-facing. Incubation lasts 2-3 weeks. Young ducks and teal are raised by the mother bird alone, but the male swan helps his mate to feed and raise the young. Juveniles start to fly after 35-40 days.

**GARGANEY**
(*Querquedula querquedula*)
*Feeds on plants and minute aquatic animals as it swims with its head under water.*

**NORTH AMERICAN WOOD DUCK**
(*Aix sponsa*)
*A native of North America, it likes tree-edged pools. Incubation period April-June.*

**MANDARIN DUCK**
(*Dendronessa galericulata*)
*Originally from eastern Asia, also present in northern Europe. Incubation period April-May.*

**TEAL**
(*Anas nettion crecca*)
*This is the smallest of the European Anatidae. Either sedentary or migratory, it lives in couples or in little flocks on small ponds with shallow edges and dense marginal vegetation. It is an eclectic feeder : seeds and shoots of grasses, Juncus, Polygonum, duckweed,as well as various invertebrates (molluscs, gastropods, insect larvae). Incubation period May-June.*

**MALLARD**
(*Anas platyrhynchos*)
*Very widespread through the northern hemisphere, this is the biggest European duck.*

## NESTING BASKETS AND SHELTERS FOR WATER BIRDS

*Reasonably priced and easy to instal, wicker nesting baskets blend well into the environment of the water garden. They provide shelter and comfort for sitting ducks and provide favorable conditions for laying when there are several pairs of birds on the same pond. Place the basket with the opening facing south, and put dry grass inside. The clutch will be better protected against predators (cats, dogs, rodents, etc.) if the basket is raised above the water on posts, or on an islet in the middle of the pond. It can also be placed on a raft made from planks or bundles of branches tied together.*

*The nesting basket is supported about 20 cm (8 in) above the water by four poles arranged in an x-shape.*

*Placed on a raft, the nesting basket follows the movement of the water.*

# MAMMALS

Mammals living near the water's edge are mostly rodents. Some once-common species such as beaver and otter have practically disappeared from many regions because they were extensively hunted for their fur. Efforts are now being made to re-introduce them, and care should be taken not to confuse them with harmful species.

MAMMALS LIVING BY THE side of the pool find in the water and the vegetation an abundant source of food, and shelter from predators. Quite recently, beavers, otters and raccoons have been introduced or re-introduced with some success, in spite of the disappearance of part of their natural habitat. These species have a part to play in maintaining natural equilibrium, and co-habitation with humans does not create any problems. It is unlikely that these timid animals will venture into your garden. But man has unfortunately introduced into Europe other species of rodents, some of which are undesirable and sometimes harmful.

## Harmful or undesirable species

By destroying large numbers of foxes and birds of prey, man has undoubtedly favoured the proliferation of certain rodents. In the absence of natural predators, these rodents multiply rapidly. Their mere presence beside the water perturbs the balance of the natural food chain and causes severe damage to flora; radical measures must then be taken to eliminate the vermin.

• The best known of these rodents is certainly the brown rat, also known as the water rat or sewer rat (*Rattus norvegicus*), introduced into Europe in the 18th century. Its voracious appetite (destruction of nests and broods) and its prolific breeding habits make it necessary to apply radical methods of elimination.

• The coypu (*Myocastor coypus*) and the muskrat (*Ondatra zibethica*) were introduced into Europe at the beginning of the 20th century. Like mink, they were farmed in large numbers for their fur, and some individuals escaped and became acclimatized in the wild. This process was made easier by the increasing rarity of predators capable of providing natural methods of control (otters, foxes and birds of prey). The coypu and the muskrat dig extensive burrows which damage plants and cause banks to collapse. They also eat the roots of many aquatic plants. Like the brown rat, the muskrat attacks the broods of water birds.

• The water-vole (*Arvicola amphibius*) lives by the water, in competition with the brown rat and the musk-rat. Like them, it digs numerous galleries in the banks, and feeds on plants, roots and tree-bark. It also attacks amphibians, crayfish and fish. Its cousin the field-vole has similar habits.

The presence of these species is therefore undesirable near any area of water, and most particularly in the water garden, where there are no natural predators to keep their numbers down. The appearance of burrows or mud-flows at the edge of the pool is a sign of the presence of this vermin (mostly nocturnal), and it will be necessary to lay traps.

## Trapping

To avoid any danger to other garden animals, or to children, use poisoned bait, not mechanical traps. Check with local governing bodies about legislation affecting the trapping, baiting, or poisoning of wild vermin. Poisoned bait usually takes the form of grains of wheat or barley treated with an anti-coagulant. The baits are placed near the entrance to the galleries, in a PVC or fibro-cement tube about 40 cm (16 in) long and of the same diameter as the burrow. Thus, the poison will be accessible only to the animals for which it is intended. The use of cage-type traps makes it possible to see what is caught. Bait them with pieces of apple, celery, beet, or carrot, and place near the entrance to the burrow. The success rate is higher in winter or spring when food is scarcer.

---

### HOW TO ELIMINATE VERMIN

*Certain systems for trapping vermin which are available on the market are not suitable for use in a garden, where they present a danger for humans and for all the fauna (ducks, etc). The easiest method to use is poisoned bait, placed inside a PVC tube about 40 cm (16 in) long, and of a diameter corresponding to the size of the animals to be eliminated.*

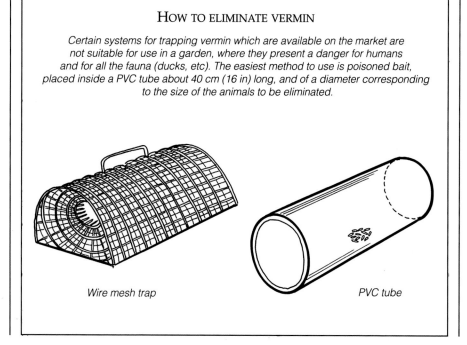

Wire mesh trap                    PVC tube

# MAMMALS

Mammals living at the water's edge are usually nocturnal in habit and difficult to observe.

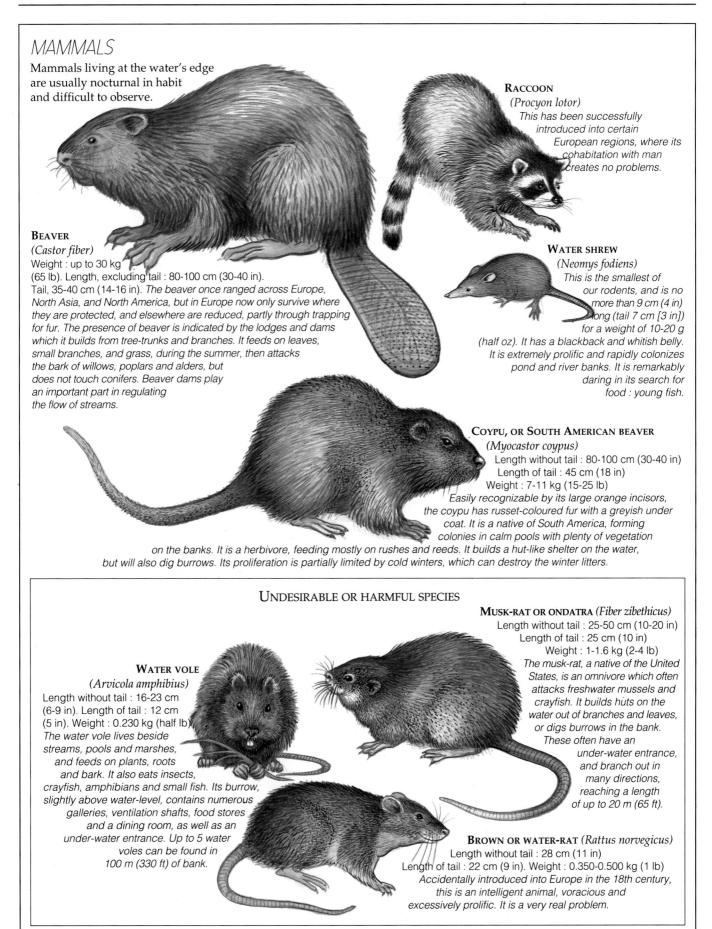

## RACCOON
### (*Procyon lotor*)
*This has been successfully introduced into certain European regions, where its cohabitation with man creates no problems.*

## BEAVER
### (*Castor fiber*)
Weight : up to 30 kg (65 lb). Length, excluding tail : 80-100 cm (30-40 in). Tail, 35-40 cm (14-16 in). *The beaver once ranged across Europe, North Asia, and North America, but in Europe now only survive where they are protected, and elsewhere are reduced, partly through trapping for fur. The presence of beaver is indicated by the lodges and dams which it builds from tree-trunks and branches. It feeds on leaves, small branches, and grass, during the summer, then attacks the bark of willows, poplars and alders, but does not touch conifers. Beaver dams play an important part in regulating the flow of streams.*

## WATER SHREW
### (*Neomys fodiens*)
*This is the smallest of our rodents, and is no more than 9 cm (4 in) long (tail 7 cm [3 in]) for a weight of 10-20 g (half oz). It has a blackback and whitish belly. It is extremely prolific and rapidly colonizes pond and river banks. It is remarkably daring in its search for food : young fish.*

## COYPU, OR SOUTH AMERICAN BEAVER
### (*Myocastor coypus*)
Length without tail : 80-100 cm (30-40 in)
Length of tail : 45 cm (18 in)
Weight : 7-11 kg (15-25 lb)
*Easily recognizable by its large orange incisors, the coypu has russet-coloured fur with a greyish under coat. It is a native of South America, forming colonies in calm pools with plenty of vegetation on the banks. It is a herbivore, feeding mostly on rushes and reeds. It builds a hut-like shelter on the water, but will also dig burrows. Its proliferation is partially limited by cold winters, which can destroy the winter litters.*

## UNDESIRABLE OR HARMFUL SPECIES

### MUSK-RAT OR ONDATRA (*Fiber zibethicus*)
Length without tail : 25-50 cm (10-20 in)
Length of tail : 25 cm (10 in)
Weight : 1-1.6 kg (2-4 lb)
*The musk-rat, a native of the United States, is an omnivore which often attacks freshwater mussels and crayfish. It builds huts on the water out of branches and leaves, or digs burrows in the bank. These often have an under-water entrance, and branch out in many directions, reaching a length of up to 20 m (65 ft).*

### WATER VOLE
#### (*Arvicola amphibius*)
Length without tail : 16-23 cm (6-9 in). Length of tail : 12 cm (5 in). Weight : 0.230 kg (half lb). *The water vole lives beside streams, pools and marshes, and feeds on plants, roots and bark. It also eats insects, crayfish, amphibians and small fish. Its burrow, slightly above water-level, contains numerous galleries, ventilation shafts, food stores and a dining room, as well as an under-water entrance. Up to 5 water voles can be found in 100 m (330 ft) of bank.*

### BROWN OR WATER-RAT (*Rattus norvegicus*)
Length without tail : 28 cm (11 in)
Length of tail : 22 cm (9 in). Weight : 0.350-0.500 kg (1 lb)
*Accidentally introduced into Europe in the 18th century, this is an intelligent animal, voracious and excessively prolific. It is a very real problem.*

# CARING FOR ANIMALS

If their environment provides living conditions adapted to their needs, pond animals are not often subject to disease or infestation by parasites. In most cases, these problems arise as a result of biological imbalance in the pool, which must be corrected. The following indications will be of assistance in establishing an early diagnosis

REGULAR OBSERVATION OF the animals in your pond will soon make you familiar with their usual appearance and behaviour. Any animal whose appearance or attitude seems abnormal should be removed from the pool and placed for a time in an aquarium equipped with a water circulator and filter, and containing plants.

This will make it easier to try to find out what is wrong : the animal may be ill, or injured, or have some form of parasite. The various symptoms described below may help you to identify the most common problems. The animal will be cared for until it is completely recovered, and then kept in quarantine for 2 or 3 weeks to avoid the risk of spreading the disease. In some cases it may also be necessary to carry out a check of the general state of the pool, to locate any possible sources of infection.

## CARING FOR FISH

In an ill-adapted or unbalanced environment, fish may suffer from stress and general weakness which makes them vulnerable to disease or poison-ing. Although the causes of biological imbalance are sometimes external or accidental (high tempera-tures, pollution from fertilizers and pesticides, failure of the filtration system), they are more often due to unsatisfactory design or improper use. Some of the most common factors are : insufficient volume of water, thermal shock due to lack of depth, overcrowding, which can cause a food shortage and excess organic waste, competition between rival species, lack of hiding places, accumulation of toxins, lack of oxygen, poor quality water or food, etc. The influence of the environment is evident when numbers of fish die in spring, at a time when the water

temperature is rising and the pond is coming back to life. Weakened during the winter by poor water-quality, the fish are unable to resist infection. After immediate "first-aid" has been applied, the root causes of the imbalance must be treated to provide lasting improvement.

### DETERIORATION OF THE HABITAT

**Chemical causes :**

**Changed pH** : the acidity of the water decreases the thickness of the layer of mucus which protects the skin of the fish, and makes them more vulnerable to injury and parasites. Most fish die suddenly when the pH goes lower than 5.5 or higher than 9.

• pH can drop if conifers are planted on the pond margin : the water can become very acidic through run-off from rain, and from the needles which fall into the pool.

• Conversely, the presence in the water of calcareous rocks and pebbles may cause the pH to increase.

*Treatment consists in removing the cause, then changing the water gradually.*
*Acid water can be treated by the addition of lime.*

**The appearance of putrid, foul-smelling black sludge** is the sign of excess organic matter in the process of decomposition. This generates ammonia and nitrites, which are highly toxic to fish. The condition may be caused by :

• overabundant food supplies (food is wasted or incompletely digested),

• accumulation of excrement when the pool is over-populated or has insuffient plant life.

• accumulation of dead vegetable material in autumn : this is a real time-bomb, since decomposition accelerates abruptly at the beginning

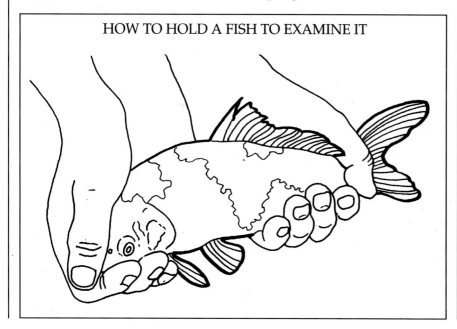
HOW TO HOLD A FISH TO EXAMINE IT

of spring, when temperatures begin to rise, causing the oxygen content to drop dangerously and producing toxins.

*Treatment consists in removing the cause, then changing the water gradually.*

*It may be helpful to remove the silt from about a third of the pond area.*

• excessive doses of medicinal products, zinc from guttering, nicotine, copper, solvents, herbicides, insecticides, etc.

• the leaves of certain trees release substances which are toxic to aquatic fauna : all the conifers, laburnums, weeping willows.

*Remove the cause, if known. Check the origin of and the path followed by ground water which may flow into the pool.*

*If possible, change the water completely after removing all the fish. If pollution is serious, it may be necessary to clean the pool thoroughly.*

**Water temperature :**

**A rapid drop in temperature** may bring about the simultaneous death of a number of fish and all or part of the spawn and fry. This may occur:

• when a large quantity of the water in the pool is changed too rapidly ;

• if the air temperature drops rapidly ;

• as a result of heavy rain or hail storms.

*The only real protection here is to have a pond that is deep enough to ensure a sufficient degree of thermal inertia.*

*However, if the pond is too shallow, all or part of it can be protected during the worst weather with a special cover of the type used for swimming pools.*

**An excessive rise in temperature** will cause a drop in the oxygen content of the water, and may kill the weaker fish.

*Without delay, start up the oxygenation and filtration equipment, the fountains and cascades. If you do not have these elements, change the water gradually and provide shade to lower the temperature.*

**The oxygen content :**

If you see fish coming to the surface to breathe, there is not enough dissolved oxygen in the water.

• A fall in the oxygen content may be caused by the decomposition of organic matter, which consumes a large part of the oxygen.

• At night, water plants absorb dissolved oxygen and release carbon dioxide into the water : if there is too much vegetation, this natural process may cause asphyxiation of the fish.

• An abrupt drop in atmospheric pressure (as happens before a storm) may cause the oxygen content to fall.

• Fish that are too well fed use more than the normal quantity of oxygen.

*In all these cases, start up filter, pumps, oxygenators, fountains and cascades, to get the water moving.*

*Or gradually change part of the water. Eliminate the cause where possible.*

**An excessive supply of oxygen** may cause cardiac embolism. This occasionally occurs in small pools if oxygenating equipment is operating incorrectly, or when oxygenating plants are too numerous. The phenomenon is identifiable by the small bubbles of gas which form under the skin of the fish or in the fins.

*Set the oxygenating equipment correctly, or reduce the number of oxygenating plants.*

---

**SOME PHYSIOLOGICAL CHARACTERISTICS OF FISH**

• Fish are vertebrates whose body temperature remains at the same temperature as the water, whatever the variations in ambient temperature. Consequently they expend little energy, so that all the food they absorb is used for growth. In addition, they expend little energy on movement because of the buoyancy of the water.

• Common fish have four pairs of gills at each side of the head, protected by gill-covers. Oxygen-laden water is taken in through the mouth and discharged under the gill-covers, the oxygen having been replaced by carbon dioxide. The gills may become obstructed by particles of mud, silt or iron hydroxide, making breathing difficult and causing asphyxia.

• The Cyprinidae, which have no clearly-defined stomach sac, do not stop eating when they find something that pleases them (e.g. wheat, maize or pellets). Digestion will then be incomplete and much of the food will be wasted if too great a quantity is distributed.

• The mouth-parts of fish are adapted to their methods of feeding : the bleak, which feeds on flies, opens its mouth upwards, while in the bream, which forages in the mud, the mouth opens downwards.

• Appetite increases with temperature, the optimum being different according to species.

• The senses of taste and smell are highly developed in fish (200 times greater than in man) and they detect certain pollutants very efficiently.

• Fish "hear" through shock waves.

• They do not have three-dimensional vision. Some have good colour perception, but can not distinguish shapes very well.

• Water temperature is of prime importance for successful reproduction, and each species has an optimum requirement. While eggs are being incubated, abrupt changes of temperature can kill the embryos. Some species lay on gravel, and others on submerged foliage.

## A change of habitat :

Any modification of the habitat creates a problem for the fish, depriving it of its usual points of reference (quality of water and food, cohabitation with other species whether friends or rivals, sleeping places). This causes considerable stress, expressed by lethargy and refusal to feed; normal behaviour gradually returns, after a few days' adaptation.

## INJURIES

Any injury must be closely examined, to determine the cause.

*Avoid introducing into the pond any sharp-pointed stones or other objects.*

*When the water is clean, and the fish healthy, injuries usually heal spontaneously. Only serious wounds require attention to prevent infection.*

*Apply a product such as methylene blue to any wound.*

## ALIMENTARY PROBLEMS

See that your fish receive a varied and balanced diet in appropriate quantities. Feeding problems produce a number of symptoms, such as swelling, bristling of scales, mucous excreta and retarded growth. They can be caused by :

• insufficient food, ill-adapted, monotonous or of poor quality, which can provoke vitamin deficiency or digestive troubles;

• prolonged fasting (more than three weeks) which weakens fish and makes them more vulnerable to disease and parasites;

• over-abundant food, which pollutes the water, or poorly-digested food which encourages the development of germs in the water and fishes' guts.

*The total quantity of the ration of food distributed must be consumed within three minutes.*

## VIRAL AND BACTERIAL INFECTIONS

**Viruses** are distinctive in that they infect a certain type of cell in a particular species of animal, but cannot spread to another species. A viral infection can be suspected when all the animals of a given species are affected, but no others.

**Bacteria** multiply more slowly than viruses, only by division. They can infect different, unrelated species. A healthy fish will resist attack by bacteria : its white blood cells will destroy them and antibodies will provide protection against renewed infection.

**Infectious dropsy** is a well-known disease caused by bacteria of the *Pseudomonas* genus. In the acute form fish die rapidly, either individuals, or large groups, for no apparent reason. Latent dropsy produces very recognizable symptoms : lethargy, swollen belly, bristling scales, sunken or staring eyes. The animal takes days or even several weeks to die.

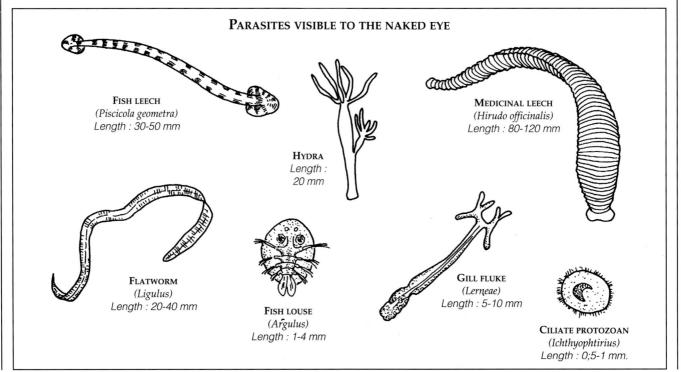

### PARASITES VISIBLE TO THE NAKED EYE

**FISH LEECH**
(*Piscicola geometra*)
*Length : 30-50 mm*

**HYDRA**
*Length : 20 mm*

**MEDICINAL LEECH**
(*Hirudo officinalis*)
*Length : 80-120 mm*

**FLATWORM**
(*Ligulus*)
*Length : 20-40 mm*

**FISH LOUSE**
(*Argulus*)
*Length : 1-4 mm*

**GILL FLUKE**
(*Lerneae*)
*Length : 5-10 mm*

**CILIATE PROTOZOAN**
(*Ichthyophtirius*)
*Length : 0;5-1 mm.*

## HOW TO ADMINISTER MEDICATION

- Before starting any treatment, take the fish out of the pool with a net and put it in a container with an air circulator.
- The filtration system must be taken into account when dosage is estimated according to total water volume to be treated.
- When treatment is completed, change half the water.

**Important :** if two or more treatment products are to be used together, be absolutely certain that they are compatible, or you may kill yourself.

- These bacteria are present in a latent state in all expanses of water. Healthy fish produce antibodies and resist familiar strains of microbe .

- If the fish loses condition or undergoes a change of habitat, or if a new strain of microbe is introduced, the fish may contract the disease.

*The fish should be placed in isolation and treated appropriately. Instructions must be followed scrupulously. Seek advice from a fish specialist*

### FUNGI OR MOULDS

Fungi grow on the damaged skin of weak fish, and on living or dead spawn, which they destroy. If no treatment is given, the organism is invaded by toxins and the fish dies.

**Saprolegniasis or fungus** is a mycosis caused by a parasitic fungus (*Saprolegnia ferax*). It takes the form of white, cotton-like patches.

**Bacterial fin rot** is caused by the *Achlya* fungus, which destroys the fins. This makes normal swimming, and consequently feeding, impossible.

**Mouth fungus**, a bacteria, *Columnaris* is treated in the same way as above.

These infections have a number of causes :

- stress, sometimes of known origin : chilling, overcrowding, reproductive period in spring, recent handling of the fish, etc.,

- earlier infection,

- damage to the mucus, loss of scales or a skin wound.

All these ailments can be treated with malachite green, methylene blue, or a proprietary treatment administered by prolonged bathing, or in food. A spontaneous cure may be observed if environmental conditions are satisfactory : warmer water, elimination of causes of stress.

*If the case is serious, proprietary products may be used, or a solution of sodium chloride (sea salt) :*
*- Place the sick fish in a container without any vegetation.*

*- Every two hours, add a small quantity of sea salt to the water, until the proportion of 10 g per litre (half oz per gallon) is obtained.*

*- When the condition is cured, start replacing the salt water by fresh, at two-hourly intervals, starting with one third, then half, then another half. Use water which has been kept at room temperature, in jerricans, for example.*

*The use of methylene blue should be carried out with care, as it is a product which permanently stains many materials.*

*It is also possible to use a combination of acriflavine, sea salt and methylene blue by prolonged immersion.*

If the treatment is not a complete success, it is preferable to eliminate the affected fish to avoid contaminating healthy animals.

### PARASITISM

These infections are caused principally by metazoa and metaphyta, protozoa and protophyta, protista. These develop in fish and also in plancton, but snails, tubifex and mud worms are also infested. The largest, such as leeches and fish lice, are visible to the naked eye or with a hand lens. They are worms or crustaceans which attach themselves to the skin or gills of the fish by means of hooks or suckers. Their mouth-parts pierce the skin and open the way to secondary bacterial or fungal infections. Symptoms of parasitism are :

- excitation, lethargy, partial or total loss of appetite, loss of weight, rubbing against the bottom of the pool;

- appearance, on the surface of the body and the fins, of fine, brownish spots visible under a certain angle of lighting or by transparency (on the fins). The back can take on a velvety appearance. The fins fray;

- the fish reacts by hypersecretion of mucus;

- this additional mucus perturbs the respiratory functions and exchanges which take place through the skin;

- progressive destruction of the fins, with haemorrhaging and ulceration.

**The fraying of the fins,** lethargy and erratic swimming, atypical movements and respiratory troubles, rubbing against different objects, are all indications of the presence of flukes of the *Dactylogyrus* genus which infest the gills, and *Gyrodactylus*, which attack the skin.

*Best results are obtained by treating the entire pond environment which is contaminated with the parasites with poprietary products used according to label.*

*Results are obtained with potassium permanganate : dissolve 1 g of permanganate in 250 cm³ (15 in³) of water. Then mix 40 g (1 oz) of this solution with 10 litres (3 gallons) of water. Bathe the fish in this*

---

### QUARANTINE : A NECESSARY PRECAUTION

• The appearance of a viral or parasitic infestation is often due to the introduction of animals, food items (zooplancton) or plants from a natural pond or contaminated pool.

• Before being introduced into your pool, fish should be placed for 3-6 weeks in an isolation tank equipped with aerator and filter. This is generally long enough to detect odd behaviour or the presence of parasites, and to eliminate to a large extent the risk of spreading a virulent disease. Each time you change the water of the holding tank, add a proportion of water from your pool, until a complete exchange has been made.

• If nothing abnormal has been observed, you can safely introduce the fish into your pool. Purchase of fish from a reputable supplier with their own quarantine facilities can save you the trouble of quarantining the fish yourself.

• In spite of these precautions, it is possible for an apparently healthy fish to be a carrier of some disease in latent form, which could declare itself in case of stress or environmental imbalance. It is impossible to eliminate all element of risk.

• If you collect live food in other wet zones, this zooplancton can also propagate certain diseases or parasites. Do not risk contaminating the pool you have created : the environment it offers is healthy but fragile, because of its confined nature.

---

*solution for 20 minutes, and repeat 48 hours later, if necessary. The more resistant fish (carp, tench) will stand being immersed for 30 minutes.*

*Another treatment consists in bathing the fish for short or long periods in a solution of neutral water (pH 7.0) and copper sulphate CuSO⁴, made up strictly according to the manufacturer's instructions.*

*Immersion of 30 to 60 minutes in a solution of formaldehyde (formol) at 40% concentration, in the proportion of 1 ml to 5 litres (1 gallon) of water also gives good results.*

**N.B : Always seek professional guidance with proprietary products.**

**Ichthyophthyriosis**, commonly known as **"white spot"** (or **"ich"**) is caused by the ichthyopthtirius, a ciliated protozoan 0.5 mm (50th in)long. This appears as a result of stress or chilling, and takes the form of 4 or 5 clearly-marked white spots, most often on the caudal or dorsal fin. In the more serious forms of white spot, the spots are less regular in shape and appear on the body.

*There are products available on the market which give excellent results. It is prudent to have them on hand, since the*

*sooner you treat the disease, the better the results will be. Be sure to check label dates for freshness*

*It is also possible to use a solution of 40% formaldehyde in the proportion of 1 ml for 5 litres (1 gallon) of water or a solution of malachite green made up strictly in accordance with instructions. Treatment is extended in cooler water.*

**Oodinium** (velvet) is a serious illness caused by a phytoflagellate parasite of the *Amyloodinium* type. Like ichthyophthiriosis, with which it can easily be confused, oodinium shows as a complete dusting of white powder.

*Treat as soon as possible. A number of products are available, some of which treat all forms of white spot disease.*

The appearance on the back of the fish of a **blue-grey film** and reddish haematoma is a sign of the presence of a flagellate : *Ichthyobodo necatrix.*

*Treat with a solution of 40 % formaldehyde as indicated above.*

**Argulosis** is caused by the fish louse (*Argulus*), a parasitic crustacean which attaches itself with suckers to the scales or gills. It measures 1-4 mm (5th of an inch) in diameter and is easily visible.

*The fish louse can be removed with tweezers.*

*Potassium permanganate can also be used. Prepare a solution of 1 g (0.03 oz) permangate for 10 litres (3 gallons) of neutral water, mixing well with an aerator, and plunge the fish into the solution, in a net, for 5-10 mm (up to half an in). The permanganate will cover the gills of the louse and it will drop off. But if the fish is too weak it may die.*

*Your aquatic supplier can also recommend appropriate products, which are to be used according to the instructions.*

**Lerneosis** (anchor worm) is caused by a worm-like crustacean (*Lerneae*) 5-10 mm (5th-2 5th in) long, which hooks itself on to the fish, causing the scales to lift and bleed. It is usually attached at the back of the dorsal fin.

*These parasites can be removed with tweezers. Disinfect the wound with a suitable antiseptic.*

*If the infestation is serious, use a proprietary product. Follow the instructions carefully, since these products can be toxic.*

The **fish leech** (*Piscicola* or *Hirudo medicinalis*) is a round worm-shaped parasite, 3-5 cm (1-2 in) long, which attaches itself to the side of the fish.

*Leeches can be removed with tweezers. They can be caught with mutton or chicken bones put in a large-meshed net at the bottom of the pool for two or three hours. The leeches attach themselves to the bones and can be easily disposed of.*

## NECESSARY PRECAUTIONS

• Medicinal products are sometimes highly toxic. Keep them in a safe place out of reach of children. Respect proportions scrupulously.

• Wash your hands carefully after handling plants, animals or the water of the pool. Like garden soil or any other living biological *milieu*, your pool may contain pathogenic germs which can be transmitted to man. For example, in tropical or Mediterranean countries, water snails can be the intermediate host of the liver fluke. Although this would be an extreme case, it makes good sense to respect simple rules of hygiene, especially for children playing near the water.

• It is very important not to give antibiotics (especially as "preventive" treatments) when their use is not essential, since this helps to develop resistant strains of microbes, which can then proliferate in your pool and outside it, and become impossible to combat.

## CONCLUSION

It is true that prevention is better than cure. The golden rule for pool hygiene is that animals must have an environment that is adapted to their specific requirements, clean water, and a varied and balanced diet in sufficient quantities. All animals which are introduced, whether they come from another pond, a specialized supplier or an apparently healthy pool, should be isolated for a period, to ensure that they are not carrying germs or parasites.

### NATURAL PREDATORS

Animals in outside pools attract cats, which attack ducklings and carp, especially at night. Cover the pool with netting if this occurs. Dragonfly larvae, water beetles, water scorpions and water boatmen attack small fish and fry. The presence of fish will help to limit their proliferation. But if an adult water beetle is observed in a pool containing small fish or amphibians, remove it with a net (its bite is painful). Do not forget that water turtles may bite fish. Herons, protected by law, may also harvest choice pond fish and can be excluded by netting.

## CARING FOR BIRDS

• Before the reproductive period (February), a general preventive treatment may be given, mixed with food.

• At the same period, administer a treatment against viral hepatitis.

• Once a year, administer capsules of a preventive wormer.

• To get them away to a good start, give two-day-old ducklings a course of vitamins (dissolved in their drinking water).

**PREDATORY INSECTS**

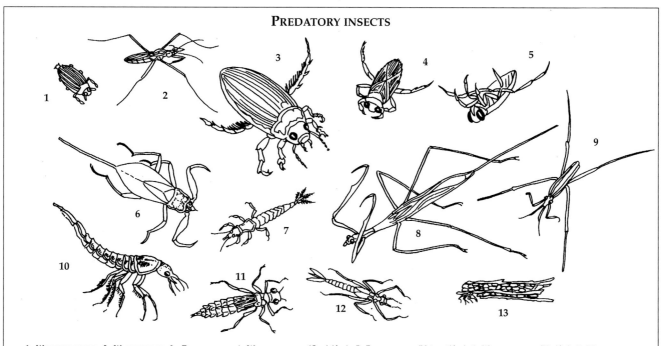

1 - WHIRLIGIG BEETLE  2 - WATER STRIDER  3 - DIVING BEETLE  4 - WATER-BOATMAN (*Corrixidae*)  5 - BACK-SWIMMER (*Notonectidae*)  6 - WATER SCORPION (*Nepidae*)  7 - MAY-FLY LARVA  8 - WATER SCORPION (*Ranatra*)  9 - WATER STRIDER (*Gerridae*)  10 - DIVING BEETLE LARVAE  11 - DRAGONFLY  12 - DRAGONFLY LARVA  13 - CADDIS FLY LARVA.

# POND HYGIENE

A garden pool is a confined space. Its biological equilibrium can be established on a scientific basis, but it will always be very much influenced by environmental conditions. For this reason, a regular check of a number of parameters is essential for preventing accidental imbalance, and correcting it if the need arises.

## THE WATER

### Sun

About 1/3-1/2 of the surface of the pool must be exposed to sunlight (1/3 is sufficient in very sunny climates).

When there is insufficient sunlight, the water does not heat up sufficiently, the fishes' metabolism is slowed down, and oxygenating plants cannot develop properly.

• Keep surfacing and floating plants under control by cutting back or removing parts of the most invasive species (*Azolla, Callitriche, Nymphoides, Potamogeton, Nymphaea, Lemna*, etc.)

• Prune (or move) plants on the banks which cast too much shadow over the water.

• If there is too much organic matter in suspension, the water will become cloudy. Water lilies, oxygenating plants, and fresh-water mussels will help to solve this problem.

Excessive sunlight encourages the development of filamentous algae and animals will suffer in over-heated and poorly-oxygenated water.

• Introduce plants with floating foliage : water lilies, potamogeton, azolla, lemna, etc.

• Plant trees and shrubs on the banks, but not too near the pool.

### Water level

There may be considerable loss from evaporation, especially in summer, depending on climatic conditions. Although rainfall will compensate to a certain extent, the best means of avoiding too great fluctuations in level is a level control device with a float.

• Failing that, add water regularly, in small quantities, to avoid a sudden drop in the water temperature.

A sudden fall in the water level may be caused by :

• the roots of plants on the banks (shrubs, grass);

• the collapse of the pond margin, if a flexible liner has been used (people walking over an area which has been incorrectly laid);

• a leak in the liner, which may be perforated by tools or damaged by burrowing animals. In this case, allow the water level to stabilize, then locate and repair the damage.

### Temperature

Water temperature could be regularly measured and recorded (once a week) during the first year. After that, special attention might be needed only during extremely hot or cold weather, although regular measurements would be necessary if the pool is particularly sensitive to weather conditions because it is shallow, less than 60 cm (24 in), or small in volume, less than 3.5 m³ (125 ft³). Measurements should be made in the morning and late afternoon, on the surface and at the deepest point. Use a maximum and minimum thermometer.

• In autumn, when the temperature drops towards 10 °C (50 °F), start protecting the pool against frost. In winter, check that the temperature in the deepest area does not fall below 3-4 °C (37-39 °F).

• In summer, when the temperature rises above 25 °C (77 °F), oxygenate the water by means of pumps, fountains, etc. If the pool is small, a gradual regular addition of fresh water, in the middle of the day, will help prevent the temperature from rising too high. The temperature of the water has a direct influence on oxygen content.

### Oxygen content

It may be necessary to measure the oxygen content of the water in order to determine what species of fish can be introduced. This content varies from 50 to 100%, according to season, time of day and pool position, and diminishes as water temperature rises. Observe the behaviour of the fish after a period of several days of hot weather, when the water temperature has risen to 25 °C (77 °F) or more. If they come to the surface gulping for air and leaving a trail of frothy bubbles, the oxygen content is insufficient. Breathing is laboured and rapid.

This lack of oxygen may be due to a number of factors :

• heating up of the water, caused by : excessive sun, insufficient depth, transparent water, absence of floating plants or shade from plants on the banks;

• pollution of the water (silting up, decomposition). A large quantity of oxygen is used by the decomposition of organic material;

• over-population of oxygen-consuming animals (fish);

• excessive planting of oxygenating pond plants, which causes excessive production of carbon dioxide on a hot summer night; the proliferation of thread algae (which consume quantities of oxygen at night);

| DISSOLVED OXYGEN CONTENT IN RELATION TO WATER TEMPERATURE | |
|---|---|
| TEMPERATURE | DISSOLVED OXYGEN |
| 5 °C (41 °F) | 12.74 mg/l |
| 10 °C (50 °F) | 11.26 mg/l |
| 15 °C (59 °F) | 10.08 mg/l |
| 20 °C (68 °F) | 9.08 mg/l |
| 25 °C (77 °F) | 8.25 mg/l |
| 30 °C (86 °F) | 7.52 mg/l |

The immediate remedy is to oxygenate the water by getting it moving by means of pumps, fountains, etc. Then examine other factors, and correct if required.

### Acidity of the water

Acidity (or alkalinity) is measured with a pH-meter, on samples from the surface and from the bottom. Daytime pH can be 1-3 points higher than that measured at night, because of photosynthetic activity.

• Acid water (pH 4-5.5) is aggressive to fish (the mucus layer on their skins becomes thinner).

• Neutral or slightly alkaline water (pH 7-8.5), on the other hand, stimulates the development of fish and plancton.

• To maintain a normal pH, prevent leaves and pine-needles from falling into the water and accumulating. In autumn, cover the pool with a fine-meshed net to make removal easier. This will prevent the formation at the bottom of the pool of sludge. As soon as the temperature rises, this organic matter ferments, consuming quantities of oxygen and producing toxins.

### Hard water

The presence of calcium salts in the water is essential for the formation of the skeleton or the shell of certain animals. Consult your local water authorities for an analysis of the calcium content.

For a favourable environment for aquatic life, the pond water should contain 15-120 mg of calcium salts per litre.

## MATERIAL AND EQUIPMENT

### Preparing for winter

• Cascades and fountains should be turned off at the approach of the first frosts (October-November). Remove equipment such as submersible pumps, clean thoroughly, and store in a dry place.

• Filtration equipment (biological filter, pumps) and water supply pipes outside the pool should be designed for winter use and protected from freezing. Otherwise clean them and make them ready for installation in spring.

## INVASIVE PLANTS

In combating the spread of certain aquatic plants, the use of chemicals provides only a partial and temporary solution. The usual method is to use copper sulphate solution, 0.5 g per m³ in acid water, and 1 g per m³ in hard water. However, this does not attack the real cause of the problem, which will reappear once the effects of the treatment have worn off. Furthermore, it destroys unicellular algae, daphnia and midge larvae, which are the basis of the food chain. The natural balance of the pool may be even more seriously perturbed. Therefore, it is preferable to attack the cause of the imbalance.

### Filamentous algae (Blanket weed)

These tend to proliferate when the pool is too exposed to sunlight, or when the phosphate content of the water is too high. There are a number of means of keeping numbers down.

• At the beginning of spring, remove the masses of filamentous algae which sometimes form over the planted areas of the pool. The algae will have no competition from the submerged plants which develop more slowly.

• In summer, the exposure to sunlight should not be too great. If necessary, increase the number of floating plants and aquatic plants whose leaves cover the water surface (*Azollea, Potamogeton, Nymphea, Trapa natans,* etc.).

• Do not overfeed the fish as excess food, or fish excrement, is a nutrient source for algae.

• Make sure that the population of pond snails (*Limnacidae, Planorbidae,* etc.) is sufficiently large. Check that their gelatinous spawn is present on the aquatic plants.

• If there is little chance that the natural balance of the pool will be achieved normally (for example if the fish population is too high, resulting in excessive production of organic waste), excess nutrient dissolved in the water, which feeds the algae, can be removed with a biological filter. An ultra violet light, sterilizing unit may also be installed.

• In small pools, some of the algae can be eliminated by using a charcoal or foam filter over the strainer of the pump used for fountains or water-courses, but the filter must be regularly cleaned or the pump will burn out.

### Duckweed

The proliferation of duckweed (genus *Lemna*) can occur when the water is too rich in nutrients (organic matter or nitrates). There are several ways of dealing with it :

• using a garden fork covered with fine-meshed netting, remove the excess duckweed;

• introduce goldfish or Koi carp, which are very fond of duckweed, if the pool is sufficiently large;

• clean the pond in autumn, removing all dead stems and leaves. Certain dry leaves can be left in place for winter decoration (e.g. some semi-evergreeen grasses, such as *Miscanthus, Spartina, Phalaris, Glyceria, Zizania latifolia,* etc.). They will provide shelter and food for a number of animals over winter, and can be cut back in spring.

# GLOSSARY

## A

**Acid** (of soil or water) : with a *pH value* of less than 7.

**Adventitious** : arising from places where growths do not usually occur; adventitious roots may arise from stems.

**Aerobic** : said of an organism which requires oxygen to survive.

**Algae** : unicellular organisms whose development is more rapid in warm, well-lit water.

**Alkaline** (of soil or water) : with a *pH value* of more than 7.

**Alternate** : said of leaves occurring successively at different levels on opposite sides of a stem. (cf *opposite* ).

**Anaerobic** : said of an organism which can develop in the absence of oxygen.

**Annual** : said of a plant that completes its life cycle in one growing season.

**Anther** : the part of the *stamen* that carries the pollen.

**Aquatic** : said of a plant that grows in water, either bottom-rooting or not, partly or completely submerged.

**Axil** : upper angle between a leaf and a stem, a main stem and a branch, etc.

## B

**Barbels** : soft, thread-like appendages situated near the mouth of certain fish. Their number, shape and position serve to identify the species.

**Benthos** : the flora and fauna living at the bottom of a body of water. (cf *plancton* ).

**Benthic** : said of the animals forming the benthos.

**Biennial** : A plant that flowers and dies in the second growing season after germination.

**Biocoenosis** : association of living organisms in a particular *biotope*.

**Biodegradable** : capable of being decomposed naturally by bacteria or other living organisms.

**Biomass** : the total quantity or weight of living organisms or of a particular group of organisms in a given area or habitat.

**Biotope** : an area of uniform and stable environmental conditions characterized by a relatively stable population of certain living species.

**Bract** : a modified, sometimes brightly coloured leaf at the base of a flower or *inflorescence*.

**Butyl** : Synthetic rubber. Used for waterproof pond liners.

## C

**Calcareous** : said of a soil rich in calcium carbonate; chalky.

**Calyx** : collective name for the outer, usually green segments that enclose the flower in bud.

**Chlorinated** : said of water to which chlorine has been added in order to sterilize it.

**Chlorophyll** : green plant pigment playing a part in *photosynthesis*.

**Chlorosis** : reduction or loss of green colouring in leaves often due to iron deficiency.

**Clay** : a common earth, malleable and impermeable, composed principally of fine sand and aluminium silicate. Some types of clay (e.g. bentonite) have an exceptional capacity for retaining water.

**Compacting** : packing down a material (soil, sand) to stabilize it and sometimes (in clay ponds) to make the bottom water-resistant.

**Compost** : material formed by natural decomposition of vegetable matter, used as a soil improver.

**Corolla** : inflorescences composed of several diverging *pedicels* of unequal length.

**Corymb** : a flat-topped or convex flower cluster.

**Cultivar** : (*Cultivated variety*). A cultivated plant variety created by selection and/or cross-fertilization.

## D

**Deciduous** : said of plants that shed their leaves in autumn.

**Dentate** : said of leaves that have a notched edge resembling teeth.

**Denticulate** : finely dentate or toothed.

**Detritivores** : organisms that live on the refuse or detritus of a community.

**Diatoms** : microscopic unicellular *algae* with a siliceous cell-wall.

**Dioecious** : bearing male and female reproductive organs on separate plants.

## E

**Ecology** : the study of the interactions of organisms with their physical environment and with each other.

**Ecosystem** : a biological community of interacting organisms and their physical environment.

**Eutrophic** : (of a lake, pond, etc) rich in nutrients and therefore supporting a large plant population, which kills animal life by depriving it of oxygen. The process is called **eutrophication**.

**Exotic** : said of a plant which is not native to the country in which it is cultivated.

## F

**Fertilizers, inorganic** : products containing nitrates, phosphates, sulphates, calcium, etc, used to improve soil fertility.

**Fertilizers, organic** : substances derived from decomposed plant or animal material, farmyard manure of all kinds, used to improve soil fertility.

**Foliole** : a division of a compound leaf; a leaflet.

**Friable** : (of soil) having a good, crumbly texture, due to the presence of a good proportion of sand or organic material.

**Fry** : young or newly-hatched fishes.

**Fungicide** : a chemical product (often based on copper or sulphur) that kills fungi, especially those responsible for various plant diseases.

## G

**Genotype** : the genetic constitution of an organism; the most typical *species* of a *genus*.

**Genus** (pl.Genera) : a category in plant classification above the *species*; a group of closely-related species.

**Glaucous** : greenish-blue.

**Ground-cover** : low-growing plants which spread out horizontally and form a dense mat of vegetation covering the ground.

## H

**Helophyte** : a plant growing in marshes and adapted to an amphibious life.

**Hermaphrodite** : an organism possessing both male and female reproductive organs functioning either simultaneously (molluscs) or in succession.

**Herbaceous** : said of non-woody plants in which the upper parts wither at the end of the growing season.

**Humus** : the organic matter of the soil, the residue of natural decomposition of leaves (leaf mould) and other vegetable matter. Enriches and improves garden soil.

**Hybrid** : plant resulting from the natural or artificial cross-fertilization of two different species or varieties.

**Hydrophyte** : a plant developing entirely in or on water.

## I J K

**Imparipinnate** : see *pinnate*

**Indigenous** : said of a plant or animal native to a given region.

**Inert** : without active chemical or other properties.

**Inflorescence** : a group of flowers borne on a single stem or axis.

**Inorganic** : said of *inert*, water-soluble material

## L

**Laciniate** : (of foliage) deeply slashed or fringed.

**Larva** (pl. **Larvae**) : an intermediate stage in the development of certain animals, between the egg and the adult (e.g. insects, batrachians, fish).

**Limb** : the broadest part of a leaf or petal.

**Linear** : (of leaves) narrow, with parallel edges.

## M

**Marginate** : having a margin or border, especially one of a distinct character, appearance or colour.

**Marsh** : very wet zone, totally or partially flooded, rich in plant life.

**Melliferous** : yielding or producing honey.

## N

**Naturalized** : said of a plant which grows and reproduces itself normally in a region of which it is not a native.

**Necrophagous** : feeding on carrion.

**Niche, ecological** : the position occupied by a species within an *ecosystem*. Characteristics of the ecological niche include habitat, the position of the species in the alimentary chain and the ecological requirements of the species.

**Nutrients** : water soluble organic and inorganic salts which are at the base of the alimentary chain.

## O

**Oligotrophic** : poor in organic matter (cf *eutrophic*).

**Opposite** : said of two leaves or other plant organs, at the same level on opposite sides of a stem. (cf *alternate*).

**Organic** (matter) : said of materials derived from dead or decaying plant or animal matter.

**Oviparous** : said of a species that lays fertilized eggs (after internal fertilization).

**Ovoviviparous** : producing young by means of eggs hatched within the body of the parent. When they emerge the young are capable of independent movement. The embryo feed exclusively on the reserves contained within the egg.

**Ovuliparous** : producing ovules (unfertilized eggs) which are fertilized externally.

**Oxygenating** : said of plants which release into the water large quantities of oxygen produced by *photosynthesis* (*Elodea, Myriophyllum, Ceratophyllum,* etc.).

## P Q

**Palmate** : said of a leaf which has lobes diverging from a single point.

**Paludal** : of or pertaining to a marsh. The roots of paludal plants develop in waterlogged ground or in shallow water.

**Panicle** : a loose, branching *inflorescence* composed of a number of *spikelets*.

**Peat** : vegetable matter, partially decomposed, which forms on the surface of waterlogged soils. Can be used to improve texture of garden soil.

**Pedicel** : the stalk supporting a single flower in an *inflorescence*.

**Peltate** : said of leaves whose stem is attached centrally underneath the limb (e.g. nasturtiums).

**Perennial** : a plant that persists in whole or in part for more than three years.

**Petiole** : the stalk of a leaf.

**pH** : a measure of alkalinity or acidity, as of soil or water.

**Photosynthesis** : process by which green plants absorb carbon dioxide and produce carbohydrates and oxygen.

**Phytophagous** : feeding on plants; herbivorous.

**Phytoplancton** : vegetable *plancton* (microscopic algae, etc.).

**Pinch (out)** : remove growing tips or buds of a plant.

**Pinnate** : said of leaves or leaflets arranged on either side of a common axis, in a feather shape. **Imparipinnate** or **odd-pinnate** leaves terminate with a single leaflet.

**Pistil** : the female organs of the flower.

**Plancton** : microscopic living organisms (animal and vegetable) floating freely in the upper levels of the water (cf *benthos*, living on the bottom).

**Protozoans** : microscopic unicellular organisms. Protozoans feed on bacteria.

## R

**Raceme** : a flower cluster with the separate flowers attached by short, equal stalks at equal distances along a central stem.

**Radical** : said of leaves that spring directly from the root of the plant.

**Rhizome** : a usually horizontal, underground stem. May be enlarged to act as a storage organ, and have a reproductive function, producing aerial shoots at the apex and along its length.

**Rosette** : circular cluster of leaves at ground level, around the rootstock.

## S

**Sepal** : one of the leaves of the *calyx* of a flower.

**Sessile** : of a leaf, flower, etc, attached directly by its base, without a stalk.

**Spadix** : a spike or head of flowers usually enclosed in a *spathe*.

**Spathe** : a *bract* or pair of bracts forming a conical envelope around a *spadix*.

**Spawning** : reproductive period and activity in fish.

**Species** : a category in plant classification containing closely related, similar individuals that can crossbreed spontaneously.

**Spikelet** : a small spike, forming part of a compound *inflorescence*.

**Stamen** : the male reproductive organ of a flower. Usually consists of a stalk or filament with a pollen-bearing *anther* at its tip.

**Sucker** : an aerial shoot that rises from the root of a plant and forms *adventitious* roots.

## T

**Tuber** : a swollen, usually underground organ derived from a stem or root, used for food storage.

**Tuberous** : said of a plant whose stem or root bears tubers.

**Turbid** : said of water which is cloudy because of the presence of particles of solid matter in suspension.

## U

**Umbel** : a flower-cluster in which stalks nearly equal in length spring from a common centre and form a flat or curved surface.

**UV** : ultra-violet. Rays of light having a wavelength between those of the violet end of the visible spectrum and X-rays.

## V W

**Variety** : sub-group of a *species* comprising individuals which have slightly different characteristics from those of the species to which they belong.

**Viviparous** : producing living young, not hatching them from eggs.

**Water table** : underground layer of water, whose level may be subject to seasonal and other fluctuations (infiltrations, etc).

**Whorl** : a ring of leaves or other organs growing at the same level around the stem of a plant.

## X Y Z

**Zooplancton** : animal *plancton* living in suspension in the water (protozoans, crustaceans, *larvae*).

# FAUNA INDEX

All photographs by Jean-Claude Arnoux with the exception of the following which were taken by :
**Bernard Vreicig** : 125 T, 147 T. L., 152 B, 158 T. R., 176, 178,
**Richard Cayeux** : 138T.L., 138C,
**MAP, N. et P. Mioulane** : 10 L,
**Guy Lainé** : 20 L, 20-21, 21 L, 21 R, 26, 32 L, 33 B, L,
**MAP, Yann Monel** : 171 T. L.,
Abbreviations used :
T = top, B = bottom, C = centre, L = left, R = right.

Garden designers are :
Jacques Gaillet, le Poisson d'Argent, 28 L,
Gilbert Galoché, 86, 101,
Guy Lainé, 20 L, 20-21, 21 C, 21 R, 26, 32 L, 33 B, L,
Camille Muller, 22 L, 22-23, 23, Jean Mus, 24-25, 24 B, R, 25 B, 27 B, 30-31, 33 B, R,
Albert Roguenant, 28-29,
Colette Sainte-Beuve-Plantbessin, 102,
La Bambouseraie de Prafrance, Anduze, 40 B, 34,
Parc Floral, Vincennes, Paris, 38-39,
Papiliorama de Marin/Neuchâtel, Suisse, 36-37,
Jardin botanique de Nancy, p. 36 L,
Kasteltuineen Arceen, Pays-Bas, 18 L, 35 T,
Villa Ephrussi de Rothschild, Saint-Jean Cap-Ferrat, 18-19, 19 B. L., 19 B. R.,